A GUIDE TO WELSH LITERATURE

A GUIDE TO
WELSH LITERATURE
c. 1700–1800
VOLUME IV

Edited by
BRANWEN JARVIS

UNIVERSITY OF WALES PRESS
CARDIFF
2000

British Library Cataloguing in Publication Data

A catalogue record for this book is available from the British Library

ISBN 0-7083-1482-1

Published with the financial support of the Arts Council of Wales

Cover illustration: *Aberystwyth Market* by Augustus Clissold, 1796. Reproduced by permission of the National Museums and Galleries of Wales

Cover design by Olwen Fowler
Typeset at the University of Wales Press
Printed in Wales by Dinefwr Press, Llandybïe

I Gwynn a Dafydd

CONTENTS

PREFACE

This guide introduces the reader to the most important aspects of literature in the Welsh language from about 1700 to the opening years of the nineteenth century. It is the aim of the book as a whole to place literature in its social and historical context. The period is complex, and pivotal in the history of Welsh literature. Old systems of patronage had disappeared; Wales had no national institutions, no university. Against such a background, Welsh literature could have moved further and further into decline. Readers of this guide will see that no such thing happened, and that, side by side with the continuing tradition of popular poetry, new forms and ideas emerged which laid the foundations of modern Wales. The old classical past was embraced and explored in a scholarly way; Iolo Morganwg's romantic vision created for Wales a new self-image, and religious traditions, both Anglican and Dissenting, were infused with new enthusiasms, largely Methodist, which produced an influential corpus of literary work.

Thirteen scholars have contributed to this guide, and I wish to record my gratitude to them both for their lucid essays and for their patience during the book's long gestation. It is inevitable that with so many authors there will be some differences of approach and occasionally some repetition, albeit slight. However, it is hoped that the variety and vigour of a multi-authored work and the specialized knowledge of each contributor will outweigh such deficiencies.

Ruth Dennis-Jones and Susan Jenkins of the University of Wales Press have been meticulous in their care for this book. I am deeply indebted to them for their professionalism and sound judgement. Any faults that remain are, of course, my responsibility.

Branwen Jarvis

A NOTE ON CONTRIBUTORS

Dr Glyn Tegai Hughes is a former lecturer in Comparative Literary Studies at the University of Manchester and a former Warden of Gregynog.

Professor Geraint H. Jenkins is Director of the University of Wales Centre for Advanced Welsh and Celtic Studies.

Professor Gwyn Thomas holds the Chair of Welsh at the University of Wales, Bangor.

Gerald Morgan was formerly Headmaster of Ysgol Gyfun Penweddig and is a lecturer and writer on literature and history.

Dr Branwen Jarvis is Head of the Department of Welsh at the University of Wales, Bangor.

Ffion Llywelyn Jenkins was formerly Director of Policy and Planning at Arts & Business, and is now a Director of Leonard Hull International.

Professor Ceri W. Lewis formerly held the Chair of Welsh at the University of Wales, Cardiff.

Glenda Carr is Academic Translator and Head of the Translation Unit at the University of Wales, Bangor.

Dr Rhiannon Ifans is a Research Fellow at the University of Wales Centre for Advanced Welsh and Celtic Studies.

Dafydd Glyn Jones is Reader in Welsh Language and Literature at the University of Wales, Bangor.

Dr Kathryn Jenkins was formerly a lecturer in the Department of Welsh at the University of Wales, Lampeter, and now works at the National Assembly of Wales.

Professor Brynley F. Roberts is a former Librarian of the National Library of Wales and formerly held the Chair of Welsh at Swansea.

Professor R. M. Jones formerly held the Chair of Welsh at the University of Wales, Aberystwyth.

CHAPTER 1

LIFE AND THOUGHT

GLYN TEGAI HUGHES

It was once possible to see eighteenth-century Wales as a quiescent enclave, with no major civil unrest and little intellectual ferment and with any, relatively minor, turbulence confined to religion. The tendency these days is to sense the coiled spring, to detect the harbingers of major social and economic changes, to uncover tensions between cultural isolation and mercantilist integration or exploitation. In the realm of ideas one might well at first sight believe that the rays of the Enlightenment reached Wales much attenuated, if they reached the Welsh-speaking population at all; but, in fact, partial acceptance of a new cultural climate—or reaction against it—is never far beneath the surface. Newton and Locke shimmer in unexpected places.

It seems that some 90 per cent of the population of a little under 400,000 spoke Welsh in 1700 and they lived, except for the substantial London diaspora, in small, and often dilapidated, towns and villages. Alone of western European nations, Wales had no town of any real size until some way into the nineteenth century; no centre, either in Wales or on the borders, could remotely compete with London.

Some town life and culture there was. Wrexham and Carmarthen maintained a reasonably well-developed social and economic structure throughout the century, though by the end Merthyr and Swansea had overtaken them. The Wrexham parish registers for the years 1703 to 1730 list very many different trades: weavers, tailors, drapers, wig-makers, butchers, bakers, fishmongers, a tobacconist, an ironmonger; bricklayers, glaziers, carpenters, plasterers; clock- and watchmakers, a spectacle-maker, dancing-masters and many others. Professional men included doctors, apothecaries, attorneys, excisemen, parish clerks, schoolmasters. Yet even in Wrexham and Carmarthen, 'one of the most wealthy and polite towns in Wales', the solid base of a prosperous merchant class, usually associated with larger towns, was lacking, with dispiriting consequences for intellectual and artistic development. Carmarthen had a dissenting academy, a grammar school, a non-classical school, a lending library and a lively book-trade; but nowhere were there major institutions to serve as growth points. Weimar, with a population rather similar to that of Wrexham, could sustain a rich theatrical and literary life centred around Goethe towards the end of the century and a musical culture enriched by Bach at its beginning, but this was a function of the existence of a princely court, however minor. The extraordinary burgeoning of philosophy and criticism in neighbouring Jena at the end of the century was chiefly an outgrowth from its ancient university allied to a vigorous publishing and periodical activity. Welsh towns had, at best, strolling players from England and, late in the century, occasional dramatic and musical entertainments usually aimed at the gentry: a rarity, Beaumarchais's *Marriage of Figaro* performed at Wrexham in March 1785 less than a year after its first presentation in Paris, was at the behest of the Wynnes of Garthewin, Denbighshire. A very few towns did, it is true, have musical, literary or reading clubs but they were unrepresentative and largely irrelevant to the Welsh-speaking population.

Carmarthen's architecture was praised by travellers; the German Karl Gottlieb Küttner in 1791 particularly noted the Doric columns of the town hall, but other Welsh towns made a less favourable impression on him and on some of his fellow countrymen. The approach from the fertile areas of the English border forced unflattering comparisons: 'no factories, no trade to speak of, no industry, none of the things that enliven even the smallest town in England'. Twelve years later, Christian August Gottlieb Göde made very similar observations:

> The broad, clean streets, the neat buildings so variously constructed, the splendid shops, the well-dressed people, the bustling activity, that take the stranger's eye in almost all parts of England, and not just in the towns but also in the villages, all these pleasing elements vanish when he enters North Wales.

A want of elegance there clearly was and, Beaumarchais apart, the towns provided scant basis for the production or reception of the kind of polite society literature one might have found in England

and on the Continent; there were no salons, no Fanny Burney novels, no bourgeois tragedies or tearful comedies. Still less was there a cosmopolitan society to produce a Mme Germaine de Staël. Most small towns had grown up around their fairs and markets; there were twenty-four market towns in north Wales in 1724, some, no doubt, miserable enough and not easy of access. Although craftsmen and itinerant traders moved around a good deal more than was once thought, and Methodist preachers covered vast tracts of the country on horseback, communications remained difficult until the coming of the railways. Only the drovers provided an extended link, often for instance supplementing the imports of the strolling players by bringing back songs from the London stage, a number of which became hymn-tunes. Life for the great majority of people was lived within the parish boundaries, with the market town as the focus for a group of parishes. The dirt roads, which it was the responsibility of the parishes to maintain, tended to keep even many of the gentry and the better-off yeomen farmers at home. It was perhaps pardonable exaggeration on the part of one traveller to complain that the pot-holes were as big as the horses. The positive side of restricted movement was the strong sense of inherited values and mutual dependence that existed within parishes, though this was to a great degree contingent on the attitude of the local squire. When it started to break down, unrest and social upheaval frequently followed. Isolation and remoteness had, in any case, been somewhat counteracted by the development of turnpike roads to meet the needs of industry, particularly at first the woollen industry, so that by the early 1780s a coach service ran between London and Holyhead and later in that decade from London to Swansea; but not until 1808 was there even a sketchy service between Shrewsbury and Aberystwyth.

For much of the century the prevailing political and social pattern was little challenged: the two overriding considerations were the maintenance of Protestant order and of property rights. Sectarian considerations were never far from the minds of legislators. The Protestant nature of the state had been established with the exile of James II in 1688 and was confirmed by the Act of Settlement of 1701, which brought the Hanoverians to the throne after Anne's death in 1714. Suspicion of France, first on religious grounds and later for commercial and colonial reasons, was the dominant feature of foreign policy and the prejudices engendered

were as rampant in Wales as anywhere. William Williams, Pantycelyn, exemplifies them very clearly in reporting to the *Sasiwn*
(Association) on the *seiat* (society) at Llanpennal on 7 January
1745–6: '—here is much hatred to the Pope, the Devil, Lukewarm-
ness, and [the] Pretender; they do pray much for the king and are
willing to go out against the Pretender'. There were indeed prominent Jacobite sympathizers grouped around the Cycle of the
White Rose in the north and the Sea Serjeants in the south, but
they did little but talk, and leading Welsh Jacobite figures like Sir
Watkin Williams Wynn kept prudently aloof from any overt
action. The growth of Cabinet government under Walpole and Pitt
provided some of the basis of a modern state, but government's
writ extended only spasmodically to the kingdom at large, and
Wales, on the periphery and contributing little in military or
economic terms, was generally allowed to go its own way.
Magistrates, mainly Tory landlords, constituted administration
and judiciary in the counties and exercised or neglected their
powers—controlling vagrants, maintaining roads and bridges,
licensing fairs and drovers, prosecuting criminals—according to
their own judgement and, even more readily, their own interests.

Landed families, great and small, had to adapt to changing
circumstances, one curious feature being the widespread failure to
produce male heirs and the consequent alienation of many of the
estates, with a good number passing by marriage to new owners
who also had property in England or Scotland. Arthur Blayney
(1716–95) of Gregynog in Montgomeryshire had been a bene-
volent squire, and incidentally an agrarian improver, during most
of the eighteenth century; his family had lived there for several
hundred years. He was, however, unmarried and on his death the
estate passed to Viscount Tracy, his English relative by marriage.

Arthur Blayney, one may guess, would have understood some
Welsh but not spoken it. The family had never been important
enough to support its own household bard, but had been hailed—
obviously for a consideration—by poets in the strict metres from
the fifteenth to the seventeenth centuries. Such patronage, which
had supported bards wandering over great stretches of Wales, had
very largely died out by the beginning of the eighteenth century.
Owen Gruffudd of Llanystumdwy, who died in 1730, was perhaps
the last of his kind but, although he produced large numbers of
cywyddau in praise of the gentry of Llŷn and Eifionydd, any

income from these only supplemented his earnings as a weaver. A deteriorating bardic tradition was still transmitted, largely orally, but it was close to being displaced by free-verse balladry, religious doggerel, stanzas for harp accompaniment (*penillion telyn*), and fairly sophisticated carols heavily dependent on matching music.

The gentry's loss of Welsh, part deliberate part creeping, varied according to locality and, to some extent, status and cross-border marriage. English was, of course, already well-established near the border, along the valleys of the greater eastern rivers and in the Vale of Glamorgan, south Gower and south Pembrokeshire. Elsewhere, too, there were some who were bilingual and travellers could find someone with a few words of English in the remotest areas of the west, even if they were, as Küttner recorded: 'Give, God bless you, Sir, a poor girl a half penny.' By the end of the eighteenth century even the minor gentry, even in the west, had retreated from Welsh (although some continued to subscribe to Welsh books), and had by doing so exacerbated the sharp division already inherent in the social structure. To a considerable extent, too, they dragged the Church, not wholly unwillingly, with them, with profound consequences for the religious life of Wales; although one must be careful to recognize that, in the middle of the century, parish church services were still being conducted in Welsh in over three-quarters of the country. Nevertheless, from being, even if unwittingly, protected by patrons, the language found itself on the open prairie of the common people, having to be argued for against its detractors by a relatively few enlightened scholars and clerics, among them the churchman and educator, Griffith Jones, Llanddowror, though it will be seen that his advocacy is solely in the service of theocratic purity:

> There are some advantages to the Welsh tongue favourable to religion, as being perhaps the chastest in all Europe. Its books and writings are free from the infection and deadly venom of Atheism, Deism, Infidelity, Arianism, Popery, lewd plays, immodest romances and love intrigues . . . 'Tis therefore no inconsiderable advantage, that our language is so great a protection and defence to our common people against the growing corruption of the times in the English tongue.

As the century progressed, the minor gentry were in many areas squeezed by the great landowners, but there was still enough of a gulf between them and the small tenant-farmer or the labourer. The yeoman farmer was a good deal less in evidence than in England and thus one tier that could bridge the gap was largely absent. The rural economy required craftsmen, tradesmen and casual labourers, and those engaged in subsistence farming usually had to turn their hand to some additional occupation. The large estates needed masons, glaziers, thatchers, carpenters, cobblers, saddlers, shearers, slaughterers and hedge-layers, not forgetting washerwomen, buttermakers and seamstresses. The woollen industry, particularly in mid-Wales, supported a rather more independent group of workers; most were part time, but by the middle of the century there were full-time cloth and flannel weavers and stocking knitters, and what had been an industry catering just for the local market began to export on a substantial scale. Family units predominated and the nature of the work and social interplay has intriguing poetic connections: Owen Gruffudd has already been mentioned, and among many others one might cite the poet and antiquarian Dafydd Ddu Eryri, the son of a weaver who followed his father's trade until he took up schoolmastering.

Living conditions were modest even for tenant farmers, and most labourers and their families had to make do with miserable hovels. By the end of the century, as less-demanding sheep had taken over from cattle and herdsmen no longer brought up livestock from the lowlands for the warmer months, smallholdings spread well up into the hills as the summer farmsteads (the *hafodydd*) became permanent homes. Even with a little land, however, the stock that could be kept was very limited, as growing grain for winter feed was difficult and transport costs made buying-in prohibitively expensive. Meat featured only rarely in the diet, and animals slaughtered in the autumn and salted might well not be for the family's own consumption. They, and *a fortiori* the very poor, fed mainly on barley- or oat-bread, cheese, milk or buttermilk, and flummery made of coarse oatmeal; vegetables were relatively uncommon and even potatoes were not widely cultivated in some counties until the last quarter of the century. It is scarcely surprising, given the deficiencies of accommodation and diet, that sickness was rife. This was especially the case when the harvests failed as they did in 1740 and 1741 and again in 1757 and 1758, with corn prices soaring out of the reach of ordinary people.

The old system whereby corn was sold only within the local community was breaking down, and the gentry in many places were less willing to help out. Small-scale riots broke out in parts of north Wales and Pembrokeshire, involving not merely agricultural labourers but craftsmen and industrial workers for, although Wales was still predominantly an agricultural and craft society, industries were beginning to grow and to change the pattern of life of many areas. Even so, it is important to realize that only relatively small areas, even of south Wales, were affected. Most of the country remained agrarian. The Industrial Revolution was a slow process, not a cut-off point.

Copper was, for many decades, the most significant industrial product. By the 1780s, Parys mountain in Anglesey employed 1,200 miners and Swansea was smelting by far the greatest proportion of Britain's needs. In both cases access to the sea was crucial, as ore was shipped from Anglesey (and in even greater quantities from Cornwall) to Swansea. Elsewhere, as in the lead-mining centres of Flintshire and Carmarthenshire, transport difficulties severely restricted growth but in the quarrying districts of Caernarfonshire, also employing about 1,200 men by the end of the century, some progress had been made in improving communications by constructing new roads including, in 1800, a horse-tramway between Penrhyn Quarry, Bethesda, and Port Dinorwic. Until the end of the century coal was firmly linked to the metal industries, particularly iron. There had been a long tradition of ironmaking in south Wales but major development came with new coke-fired furnaces centred around Merthyr, on the north-eastern rim of the coalfields, and by 1800 south Wales produced one-third of all British pig-iron. The tinplate industry made equally lush growth in the south-west, again allied to the easy availability of coal, but the spectacular growth of what one might call an independent coal industry came in the nineteenth century.

Much of the industrial activity here described was stimulated by the demands of successive wars, which greatly exceeded anything the Welsh domestic market would ever have sustained. There was, however, little domestic risk capital and the great majority of the new entrepreneurs were English—sometimes in alliance with the local landowner. Historians vigorously debate whether this was an aspect of colonialism or whether Wales, as a region, was as much part of core British development as relevant areas of England.

What is clear is that the new money did little for the language and not a great deal for cultural life generally. In the long run there were profound effects from the movement of Welsh speakers into new urban communities, often with a strong sense of identity, counterbalanced to some extent by the influx of workers from England and Ireland; but these developments were only just beginning by the end of the eighteenth century, though there were minor riots in the Wrexham area as early as 1776 in protest against the employment of English colliers. In general, however, indigenous society was still homogeneous enough to assimilate the immigrants. The nineteenth-century poet John Blackwell (Alun), for instance, was the son of a Derbyshire collier who had married a Welsh Calvinistic Methodist girl from Llangwm.

It is true that immigrants were often blamed for drunkenness and immorality, but there was no shortage of the home-grown variety. Popular pleasures were not of a refined nature: bear- and bull-baiting were not uncommon—Swansea had a corporation bull-ring between 1723 and 1769—but cock-fighting was the leading diversion. One of Howel Harris's correspondents in 1738 testified that a convert, after listening to one of Harris's sermons, had cut off the heads of his cocks. Methodist writers during the century and after it warmed to a lurid account of the wickedness of the pre-Revival days; but entertainment, on the edge of a harsh working-life, not unnaturally tended to be coarse and raw. Evenings offered little but playing cards, drinking, singing and dancing, but Saturday nights could extend into Sunday and parish revelry occurred on that non-working day. Before his conversion it is said that Daniel Rowland, then a curate, would spend Sunday after the morning service in frivolous games and sports—at which he excelled—and in carousing. A minor poet, Jenkin Thomas (1690–1762), includes among the follies of his youth pitching bar and stone, weight-lifting, wrestling, running, jumping, swimming and target shooting. Large crowds assembled particularly on the parish patron day (*gwylmabsant*) when an all-night vigil would be followed by a day's merrymaking, with feasting, singing, dancing and sports, frequently culminating in widespread fighting. (A mid-century poet, Dai Siôn, has a poem 'Counsel against dancing, particularly on a Sunday'.) Here and at the fairs there would be itinerant musicians, storytellers, quack doctors, and players presenting interludes—short plays of a farcical or satirical nature, often with robust if stereotyped attacks on some perceived social injustice, and not uncommonly crude in language and gesture. 'The Sabbath', reported the incumbent of Llandderfel in the 1730s, 'is not so well kept as I could wish. It is prophaned by plays, fiddling, and dancing. We could wish a stop was put to it, we do our endeavours to prevent it.'

Commentators, at the time and later, have seen the Methodist Revival as the movement that killed off many of these old traditions, and with them much of the folk-tale and folk-song wealth of Wales. There is certainly some truth in this: Edward Jones (1752–1824 and known as 'Bardd y Brenin', the King's Bard), writing in 1802, had no doubt who the culprits were:

> The sudden decline of the national Minstrelsy, and Customs of Wales, is in a great degree to be attributed to the fanatick impostors, or illiterate plebeian preachers, who have too often been suffered to over-run the country, misleading the greater part of the common people from their lawful Church; and dissuading them from their innocent amusements, such as Singing, Dancing, and other rural Sports, and Games . . .

Some of the old traditions were adapted—converted perhaps: the old folkstory-teller (*y cyfarwydd*) into the preacher and the interlude into the dramatic sermon; songs into hymns; dances into ecstatic 'jumping'; and revelry eventually into eisteddfodau. As we have seen, the Established Church itself was widely, though not widely enough, engaged in attempting to purify manners and Griffith Jones's overriding purpose, both in his preaching and through his schools, was to save souls by driving out sin. In many ways what happened was that the Puritan legacy of sobriety, good order and high seriousness came late to Wales, and in fact very similar movements, and effects on folk customs, can be seen in Continental societies.

The Newtonian enlightenment had established a sense of cosmic order and design that was a model for a providentially guided Christian polity, which allowed for some diversity of belief provided that basic stability was not imperilled. Countering the perceived threat of Catholicism and of assorted heresies came to appear a good deal more important than nurturing spiritual life or delivering social reform. So important was it that, in the interests of uniting all Protestants, concessions were reluctantly made to Dissenters, though in general they remained in a position of civic inferiority and intermittent petty persecution for the rest of the century. In the early decades, their spiritual state was not much more lively than that of the Established Church, as they too struggled with the ethos that was sliding away from a revealed personal religion to one that saw God as a presiding creator over-seeing a moral order, where respectability and benevolence were the Christian's chief duties. In Wales, Dissent was still relatively weak; some seventy meeting-houses appear to have existed by 1715, and about 25,000 individuals, concentrated in the counties of Carmarthen, Glamorgan and Monmouth, may have considered themselves to be Dissenters. They were generally serious-minded people who had, in many instances, made a conscious religious decision at some considerable disadvantage to themselves, and they formed a reasonable cross-section of the educated, the relat-ively prosperous and the generally disadvantaged. They also, both because of their isolated position within the state and their belief in local authority within the Church, tended to form rigorous closed communities, though it is a mistake to believe that this prevented missionary activity on their part. Relatively quiescent many pre-Revival Dissenters may have been, but it is still true, particularly of the Baptists, that men like Enoch Francis (1689–1740) were tireless preachers over a wide area and in chapels of different persuasions.

Dissenters were the old Presbyterians, far less successful in Wales than in Scotland, Independents or Congregationalists, and Baptists (Quakers were in a decline that led almost to extinction by mid-century), often co-operating in the face of external threat and separated less by doctrinal differences, except infant baptism, than by disagreements on church order; indeed the three co-existed in some chapels, often for decades. Theological argument was as likely to occur within sects as between them; in general it followed much the same pattern as in England. The main battleground was between Calvinism and Arminianism and the points at issue are all too easy to oversimplify. Proclaiming above all the sovereignty of God, stressing the authority of Scripture and the sinfulness of humankind, High Calvinism taught that God has predetermined that some (usually some few) will be saved through Christ's mediation. When God calls to salvation and belief, he guarantees that man will not fall out of His grace. The appeal of such a doctrine to small, unregarded groups was powerful, but intellectual difficulties led others to seek forms of modified Calvinism. For them, the experience of conversion gave a hope that one had been chosen by God. For some, the commitment to Christ, and the conviction that one was within God's covenant, of itself ensured that one was included; Howel Harris was considerably influenced by arguments of this nature by John Cotton on the Covenant of Grace. Opponents of High Calvinism claimed that the doctrine led to Antinomianism, or the belief that the moral law is not binding on Christians: if election is arbitrary, then what is the point of good works? Arminians denied that God had predestined some few souls arbitrarily, without regard to merit, and insisted that Christ died for all, and that free will enabled all to accept or reject God's free grace. Opponents of Arminianism claimed that it detracted from the majesty of God and that it led all too easily to a belief in justification by works.

There were subtler doctrinal variations within these main opposing camps and skirmishes of varying intensity took place within local societies, generally weakening the witness of Dissent, and notably giving rise to Williams Pantycelyn's later condemnation in his epic *Bywyd a Marwolaeth Theomemphus* of the kind of sterile dogmatizing that had split the congregation at the Independent chapel of Cefnarthen, which he had attended as a boy. ('The people's minds were thrown into confusion, with divisions on all sides—two opinions in one church, sometimes even eight or nine, and a zeal for the least important matters active in the blind.') What is, however, significant about many of these theological arguments is that they were the main way in which the workings of the mind can be seen to operate among the Welsh-speaking community, at least outside London. That community was, it must be remembered, predominantly Anglican throughout the century, even if replies to questions in episcopal visitations show Easter communicants varying between three-quarters and as few as a fifth of parishioners. Most church-goers were no doubt relatively unreflective, with their traditional superstitions only partly transmuted into Christian beliefs and observances. Some clergy, notably the satirist Ellis Wynne, were greatly exercised by the enfeeblement of the Church, others were not much perturbed by ignorance—a few were scarcely more enlightened themselves—and

earlier Methodist historians seized with some relish on the
deficiencies of the Established Church before the Revival.
Pantycelyn himself, ordained Anglican though he was, had set the
tone by his reference to the 'pitch-black night' of the period:

> Pan 'r oedd Cymru gynt yn gorwedd
> Mewn rhyw dywyll farwol hun,
> Heb na phresbyter na 'ffeiriad,
> Nac un esgob yn ddi-hun; . . .

[When Wales formerly lay in some dark deathly sleep, with no
presbyter or priest or bishop awake . . .]

It would be idle to deny that there was a great deal wrong with
Anglicanism in early eighteenth-century Wales: resident clergy
were frequently badly educated and poorly paid, in many cases
because the livings were in the gift of laymen or corporations who
took the tithes and paid the incumbent a fraction of the receipts.
Many wholly poverty-stricken parishes suffered crumbling buildings, services rushed by pluralists hastening to some distant en-
gagement, infrequent or non-existent communion services, feeble
and scarcely literate sermons. Clerical morals were often little, if
any, better than those of their parishioners, and allegations of
drunkenness and sexual impropriety were commonplace. Even
where the living was a reasonably comfortable one, and perhaps a
quarter of livings throughout Wales were at a level that enabled
the parson to hold his own with the squire, there was no guarantee
that the moral climate would be any purer: Robert Edwards,
Rector of Llandderfel, with an income of £100 a year, was accused
in the deanery report of 1731 of neglecting church services and
failing to visit the sick, and in addition he was suspected of
insobriety, lustful behaviour, arson and attempted murder.

Bishops varied greatly in their concern for the diocese, its
buildings, its clergy and its people; language and remoteness from
London were great barriers and the Welsh sees were not the most
desirable of appointments. Three bishops only were Welsh-
speaking, Humphrey Humphreys and John Evans of Bangor and
John Wynne of St Asaph, and after the latter's translation to Bath
and Wells in 1727 no others were appointed until 1870. Many
clergy and bishops were, perhaps needed to be, pluralists:

Benjamin Hoadly, whose sermon arguing that the true Church was invisible in its nature sparked off the Bangorian controversy, occupied the see from 1715 to 1721 but lived in London, retaining his two livings there. Lame and unable to ride a horse, he never visited his diocese; but most bishops spent some summer weeks or months—when Parliament was not sitting—in their diocese, and a very few actually lived there.

By no means all was gloom or corruption. Some bishops were scholarly, some conscientious, some supportive of educational work, one or two—notably George Bull of St David's— saintly. The same could be said of many of the clergy, often working diligently and with scant reward, conducting seemly and enriching devotions, or working away at translating theological texts, many, of course, polemical. Griffith Jones depended on co-operation within parishes for his circulating schools, and over the years more than 300 incumbents seem to have supported him. Particularly in south Wales, educational and charitable enterprises benefited greatly from the interest of Anglican laymen like Sir John Philipps or John Vaughan, Derllys. The Church also had stout defenders, like Theophilus Evans, whose *Drych y Prif Oesoedd* (A Mirror of the First Ages, 1716 and 1740) sought to link the present-day Church with his vision of a pure, Protestant, seventh- and eighth-century Welsh church: 'In those happy former days . . . no one was permitted to withdraw from the Church, and to hold separate meetings or to preach in houses. And if some fanatic dared to do so, he would be condemned out of hand.' Thus he linked a fierce patriotism with staunch Tory Anglicanism, and a boundless contempt for 'enthusiasm'.

Enthusiasm, in the form of the Methodist Revival, was however the source of much of the most significant literature of the second half of the eighteenth century—and of much of the worst of the next. Through it sensibility entered Welsh literature, though as Calvinist virtue rather than well-bred vapours. When the Revival came—and one must remember its limited scope and not anticipate its dominance in the next century—this must to some degree have been a consequence of the godly clergy; it was, after all, an energizing movement within the Established Church. Yet there must have been more to it. What caused the sudden outbreaks of revival? Dissatisfaction with the moral climate and contempt for the spiritual emptiness of conventional religion certainly fanned the flames, as it had done in Germany and the Netherlands in the Pietist movement and in Lutheran communities in Catholic central Europe; but what struck the bright, fiery sparks (*y gwreichion golau tanllyd*) of which Pantycelyn wrote? A sense of emotional deprivation might come near it, with a changed attitude towards the individual and a loosening of the sense of authority. The year 1735 could fairly be thought of as the watershed, as indeed it was in Massachusetts and Connecticut, the revival later characterized by Jonathan Edwards in his *Faithful Narrative of the Surprizing Work of God*. It was on Palm Sunday that Howel Harris, as a 21-year-old schoolteacher in Talgarth, was overwhelmed by the admonition of the wholly uncharismatic vicar, Pryce Davies: 'If you are not fit to come to the Lord's Table, you are not fit to come to Church, you are not fit to live, you are not fit to die.' The following weeks he spent in anguished self-examination, guided by a rather mixed bag of seventeenth-century spiritual handbooks, and at the sacrament on Whit Sunday and later in private prayer at Llangasty church: 'I felt my heart melting within me, like wax before the fire, with love to God my Saviour.' (John Wesley, it will be recalled, had his experience of the 'heart being strangely warmed' in May 1738.) Daniel Rowland, then a curate at Llangeitho in south-east Cardiganshire, and later rhapsodically hailed by admirers as 'surely the greatest preacher in Europe' and 'perhaps the greatest Divine since the time of the Apostles', is said to have been converted in 1735 through hearing Griffith Jones, Llanddowror, preach. The young reformers frequently went too fast and too far for Griffith Jones, but there can be no doubting the inspiration of this measured enthusiast for the young leaders of the Methodist Revival; twenty years before them he was travelling outside his own parish and preaching, sometimes in churchyards, to crowds of many hundreds, and he combined in himself the spiritual Pietism of Spener and the more active and challenging aspects of Francke's development of Pietism. (His annual accounts of the work of his schools, the *Welch Piety*, owe a clear debt to the latter's *Pietas Hallensis*.) As an incidental, since his overriding aim was to save souls, he impelled a drive to literacy that brought the Welsh people to a level rivalled only in Scandinavia. In doing so he tilled the seed-bed of revival.

Harris himself was soon preaching to large crowds in the open air and forming the fellowship societies (*seiadau*) that became such an important constituent of Methodism. He had probably been told by

Griffith Jones about the religious societies pioneered by Anthony Horneck within the Church of England in the previous century, the inspiration for the Wesleys' Holy Club at Oxford in the early 1730s. By 1750 some 400 such societies had been formed by Welsh Methodism, nearly all in south and mid-Wales and, more by instinct than design, they formed the base of what grew into an integrated and hierarchical organization with rules, reports and disciplinarians. Harris formed close connections with the English awakening and spent a good deal of time in London and Bristol, remaining on generally good terms with the Wesley brothers, bringing George Whitefield into Wales and acting as his deputy in London. The Calvinist orientation of the movement in Wales was reinforced by Whitefield, but the intensity of the struggle with Arminianism belongs to the next century and in the earlier stages there was a good deal of co-operation between the revivalists, including Dissenters. John Wesley travelled a good deal in Wales but there appears to have been a tacit understanding that he would, as indeed language dictated, confine his activities mainly to English speakers. Relations between Harris and Rowland were another matter; they varied between warmth, invective and tearful reconciliation, but with a sense of rivalry always beneath the surface. They first met in August 1737 and both were by then drawing very large crowds to hear them preach frighteningly about judgement and hell: it was said that Harris described it as though he had been there. Harris's theology, however, was relatively unsystematic and a frequent source of friction; particularly suspicious was his contact with the Moravians and his espousal of much of their vocabulary, if not of their actual doctrine. Moravians were accused of the heresy of Patripassianism, or the belief that God the Father suffered in or as Christ on the cross, and the person of Christ, the dying lamb, with his wounds and his blood became a constant refrain. Pantycelyn's hymns reveal something of the same tendency in moderation, but adherence to the orthodox doctrine of the Trinity was of great importance to the other revivalists, as their emotional attachment to Christ could easily lead away from the Father, and somewhere on a side-road was the Arianism that separated Christ out into a creature, a much feared heresy that by the middle of the century had permeated the Carmarthen Academy, leading after 1780 to Unitarianism.

In 1748 an already unhappy situation was much worsened by Harris's infatuation with Madam Sydney Griffith, wife of the squire of Cefnamwlch in Caernarfonshire, and his unwise attempts to impose her as the movement's prophetess. The relationship was, almost certainly, not adulterous and was not quite believed to be so by his colleagues, but his letters to her have an undoubted erotic charge that sublimates itself in devotional imagery. Madam Griffith and Moravianism were too much and the movement split into Harris's people and Rowland's people; by 1752 Harris had withdrawn to Trefeca where he constructed a community, the 'Family' of his followers, somewhat on the pattern of Francke's Pietist institutions at Halle. The growth of the Revival movement was much impaired and did not really pick up again for ten years. Rowland had not travelled the country anything like as much as Harris—or as Pantycelyn—but had drawn people to him at Llangeitho, and sometime in 1762 the Revival was rekindled there, 'on the day that Mr W.Williams brought his book of hymns called *Y Môr o Wydr* (The Sea of Glass) to Llangeitho', with crowds dancing in rapture like David before the ark and spending whole nights in songs and praises. And now the preaching was of free grace and salvation through faith, messages of hope rather than of condemnation. Two lines from a hymn added to *Caniadau y rhai sydd ar y Môr o Wydr* by Pantycelyn two years later convey the sense of release:

> Euogrwydd fel mynyddau'r byd
> Dry yn ganu wrth dy groes . . .

[Guilt like the mountains of the world, turns to singing at thy cross . . .]

A somewhat more acerbic view is provided by the scholarly Arian Dissenting minister, David Lloyd of Llwynrhydowen, in a letter to his brother in April 1764:

The Methodists after having kept quiet for several years have of late been very active. Their Number increases, and their wild Pranks are beyond Description. The worship of the day being over, they have kept together whole Nights, singing, capering, bawling, fainting, thumping . . .

By May of 1763, Harris had returned and preached at Llechryd to 'I think, the largest congregation I ever saw, I suppose 12,000 all'—though Harris's statistics always need to be treated with caution. The remainder of the century saw the new movement, still be it remembered at least nominally within the Church of England, extending steadily rather than dramatically to other parts of Wales and indeed to London, with something over 200 chapels being opened between 1764 and the end of the century. Almost equally powerful revival movements occurred among the Baptists and Independents; indeed they grew more quickly than the Methodists in many parts of Wales in the second half of the century.

Some recent historians, beguilingly led by Gwyn A. Williams, have rather underplayed the role of the Revival in eighteenth-century Wales and have seen the later decades especially as a period of the stirring of reform if not revolution, and they can point both to considerable unrest in several parts of Wales, notably the corn riots, and to intellectual movements. The leaders of Methodism were themselves deeply conservative in political and social attitude (though in Pantycelyn's case acutely aware of contemporary *scientific* speculations), but in Dissent democratic and radical voices were heard before the end of the century. The Baptist minister Morgan John Rhys had been fired by the French Revolution, and in 1791 had gone to Paris to preach and to distribute Bibles; in the five issues of his *Cylch-grawn Cynmraeg* (The Welsh Journal, 1793) articles advocated emancipation of the slaves, proposed parliamentary reform, attacked ecclesiastical oppression, and based millenarian hopes on the French Revolution. He and others, like the antiquarian, poet and country doctor William Jones, Llangadfan (the 'Welsh Voltaire'), looked for hope to America and in 1794 Morgan John Rhys set off with the aim of establishing a Welsh homeland there. In London the Gwynedd-igion Society, which had succeeded the gentlemanly, not to say snobbish, Cymmrodorion, was a nursery of democratic ideas, and through John Jones (Jac Glan-y-gors) Tom Paine's views became available to the monoglot Welsh in *Seren Tan Gwmmwl* (Star under a Cloud, 1795) and *Toriad y Dydd* (Daybreak, 1797). Whether the significant radical Welsh thinkers of the French Revolution, Richard Price and David Williams, had any marked effect on Welsh-language writing remains more a matter of assertion than evidence.

Parallel with the reformist, questioning attempt to mould a Welsh society in dreams or in America, and the very real construction of a local, but nationally structured, system in Methodism, there had throughout the century been attempts, from very different premises, to resurrect a national identity. If the radicals looked to a Utopian future and the revivalists to a final eschatological resolution (though linked by typology to the whole of providential history), others, heirs of humanism touched by the Enlightenment, turned to the past.

Building on a general seventeenth-century English, and European, antiquarian interest in primitive Celtic elements and druidism, the systematic mind of Edward Lhuyd had established a base for Welsh antiquarian and linguistic scholarship at the beginning of the century; Theophilus Evans had sought Welshness in the supposed descent of the Celts from Gomer, son of Japhet, son of Noah (Gomer = Cymry); Lewis Morris applied his questing intelligence and scientific precision to demystifying Welsh linguistic and historical relics; Evan Evans (Ieuan Fardd), whose disposition, the obituary in the *Gentleman's Magazine* notes, 'was violent, especially when he expressed himself upon a subject which related to his country's wrongs', collected, translated and introduced early Welsh poetry in *Some Specimens of the Poetry of the Antient Welsh Bards* (1764). The work had a considerable influence on the Celtic revival in English literature, particularly on Thomas Gray, and was known in Germany to Hamann and Herder, though there and in France the influence was minimal compared with that of Macpherson's Ossian forgery. Wales's own forgery came with the fertile imaginings of Edward Williams (Iolo Morganwg), whose dreams of a golden druidic age kept alive in the hills of Glamorgan found their expression in his creation, recreation as he claimed, of the Gorsedd of Bards of the Island of Britain, the first assembly of which was held on Primrose Hill in London in 1792. A little to one side stands Goronwy Owen, reaching back to the Poets of the Princes and the Poets of the Gentry, but clothed in the Augustan aesthetics of the century—a regimen of rules and modes sympathetic to the formality of *cynghanedd*.

It is tempting to make free with the small change of literary history and to trace through Ieuan Fardd and Iolo Morganwg those pre-Romantic counters of primitivism, natural man, the Gothic, melancholy, ruins, 'golden age', and the attraction of wild scenery that marked much of European sensibility in the second half of the century. Wales, however, lacks even its Collins, Shenstone, Thomson or William Mason, and the influence of English and other travellers into Wales had no real way of feeding back into Welsh literature of the time. There was, for all purposes, no Welsh-language travel-writing, and Welsh poets had little or no opportunity to respond to the visual. The Morris brothers were indeed accomplished horticulturalists but, for most Welsh writers, landscape gardening, formal or picturesque, had nothing like the resonance it carried in English literature of the century. The novelist and poet Cawrdaf, born in 1795, was perhaps the first to have any real experience of works of art, and it is wholly characteristic that Thomas Jones's painting *The Bard* (1774), with its evocation of sublimity and powerful mountain landscape based on Thomas Gray's poem, should have been unknown to contemporary Welsh writers, though William Owen Pughe has his own sketches of Iolo Morganwg druidic costumes in his *The Heroic Elegies of Llywarch Hen* (1792). Nor was the natural world a source of inspiration in its sublimity or its beauty, though at one remove both Howel Harris and Pantycelyn were admirers of James Hervey's *Meditations among the Tombs* (1745–7) with its sentimental flowery imagery. Perhaps the single most striking feature of Welsh literature in the eighteenth century, at least before Iolo Morganwg, is the almost complete absence of the landscape, that intensifier of the human experience exploited from Rousseau to the Romantics. Agrarian communities in subsistence economies tend to be somewhat matter-of-fact about their surroundings. Any hieroglyphic interpretation is confined to the familiar topos of nature as a book revealing the handwriting of God and, notably for Pantycelyn, doing so in terms of contemporary scientific investigation combined with scriptural images. Nature is unconsciously encoded in scriptural language.

Yet it can be said that the biblical imagery mediated profound shifts in emotional patterns; they are less deliberately selected tropes than pictures lit by the flame of passionate experience. A different sensibility emerges in Welsh writing. It comes pre-eminently in two sources that lacked literary intent: the diaries of Howel Harris, and the hymns and some of the prose writings of Pantycelyn. Harris was writing for his own soul, Williams for the spiritual nourishment of the flock (others of his prose works are primarily didactic). Newtonian optics hovered on the edge of their consciousness, but both would have learned with mixed feelings that they also owed a considerable debt to Locke, the advocate of a rational religion. Yet it is the experiential emphasis of his philosophical method that makes available the language necessary for the Revival experiences, for the interior sensing that is so prominent in Pantycelyn's hymns, and even in the Rules for Methodist Societies in 1742 (*Sail, Dibenion, a Rheolau*) where members are urged 'to relate in the simplicity of our hearts all of evil and good that we see within us'. The two Lockian streams come together in the testimony of Pantycelyn's Martha Philopur in her 'Letter' (*Llythyr Martha Philopur*) once 'the light has dawned' for her: 'My senses are more acute . . . my reason and all my emotions are so harmoniously in order.'

It was at this time that significant sensationist words became available in Welsh in a psychological sense: 'argraff, argraffiad' (*impression*), 'cydymdeimlad' (*sympathy, fellow feeling*). Pantycelyn was the first to use 'nerf' (*nerve*) and the scientific language of empiricism, expounded notably by the Royal Society, speaks not just to Lewis Morris, but also to Pantycelyn. This baldness of language is, in the case of the reformers, reinforced by the Moravian Zinzendorf's advocacy of 'a negative aesthetic ideal', 'the artless language of the heart'. Thus the precepts of Wordsworth's preface to the second edition of *Lyrical Ballads* (1800/1) are anticipated, but supplemented by the common storehouse of biblical envisioning. 'The Scriptures', says Martha Philopur, 'flow into my memory unceasingly.'

Without urban structures, without country estates, without a scenic sense, Welsh immersed itself in the geography of Scripture.

BIBLIOGRAPHY

General

Linda Colley, *Britons. Forging the Nation 1707–1837* (London, 1994; first publ. New Haven, 1992).

John Davies, *A History of Wales* (London, 1993, and Harmondsworth 1994).

Leonard Twiston Davies and Averyl Edwards, *Welsh Life in the Eighteenth Century* (London, 1939).

Michael Hechter, *Internal Colonialism; the Celtic Fringe in British National Development 1536–1966* (London, 1975).

Trevor Herbert and Gareth Elwyn Jones (eds.), *The Remaking of Wales in the Eighteenth Century* (Cardiff, 1988).

Emyr Humphreys, *The Taliesin Tradition. A Quest for the Welsh Identity* (London, 1983).

Geraint H. Jenkins, *Literature, Religion and Society in Wales, 1660–1730* (Cardiff, 1978).

Idem, *The Foundations of Modern Wales, 1642–1780* (Oxford, 1987); this has a particularly full bibliography.

David J. V. Jones, *Before Rebecca. Popular Protests in Wales 1793–1835* (London, 1973).

Gareth Elwyn Jones, *Modern Wales: a Concise History* (Cambridge, 1984).

Donald Moore (ed.), *Wales in the Eighteenth Century* (Swansea, 1976).

Prys Morgan, *The Eighteenth Century Renaissance* (Llandybïe, 1981).

Stuart Piggott, *Ancient Britons and the Antiquarian Imagination. Ideas from the Renaissance to the Regency* (London, 1989).

Helen Ramage, *Portraits of an Island. Eighteenth Century Anglesey* (Llangefni, 1987).

Peter D. G. Thomas, *Politics in Eighteenth-Century Wales* (Cardiff, 1998).

David Williams, *A History of Modern Wales* (London, 2nd edn.,1977).

Gwyn A. Williams, *When was Wales? A History of the Welsh* (London, 1985, and Harmondsworth, 1985).

Idem, *The Search for Beulah Land. The Welsh and the Atlantic Revolution* (London, 1980).

Society and Economy

Michael Atkinson and Colin Baber, *The Growth and Decline of the South Wales Iron Industry, 1760–1880* (Cardiff, 1987).

Richard Brown, *Society and Economy in Modern Britain 1700–1850* (London and New York, 1991).

Harold Carter, *The Towns of Wales. A Study in Urban Geography* (Cardiff, 1965).

A. H. Dodd, *The Industrial Revolution in North Wales* (Cardiff, 3rd edn., 1971).

G. Nesta Evans, *Social Life in Mid-Eighteenth Century Anglesey* (Cardiff, 1936).

Idem, *Religion and Politics in Mid-Eighteenth Century Anglesey* (Cardiff, 1953).

J. R. Harris, *The Copper King: A Biography of Thomas Williams of Llanidan* (Liverpool, 1964).

David W. Howell, *Patriarchs and Parasites. The Gentry of South-West Wales in the Eighteenth Century* (Cardiff, 1986).

Melvin Humphreys, *The Crisis of Community. Montgomeryshire, 1680–1815* (Cardiff, 1996); of more than county interest and with an extensive bibliography.

Geraint H. Jenkins, 'The Cultural Uses of the Welsh Language

1660–1800', in Geraint H. Jenkins (ed.), *The Welsh Language before the Industrial Revolution* (Cardiff, 1997), 369–406.

J. Geraint Jenkins, *The Welsh Woollen Industry* (Cardiff, 1969).

Philip Jenkins, *The Making of a Ruling Class: the Glamorgan Gentry 1640–1790* (Cambridge, 1983).

A. H. John, *The Industrial Development of South Wales, 1750–1850* (Cardiff, 1950).

W. J. Lewis, *Lead Mining in Wales* (Cardiff, 1967).

Jean Lindsay, *A History of the North Wales Slate Industry* (Newton Abbot, 1974).

G. E. Mingay (ed.), *The Agrarian History of England and Wales*, vol. 6 (Cambridge, 1989).

William Rees, *Industry before the Industrial Revolution*, 2 vols. (Cardiff, 1968).

John Rowlands, *Copper Mountain* (Llangefni, 1966).

Thirsk, Joan (ed.), *The Agrarian History of England and Wales*, vol. 5 (Cambridge, 1984).

Religion

T. M. Bassett, *The Welsh Baptists* (Swansea, 1977).

Richard Bennett, *Howell Harris and the Dawn of Revival* (Bridgend, rev. edn., 1987), translation by Gomer M. Roberts of a work first published in Welsh in 1909, with notes and an extensive bibliography.

Eifion Evans, *Daniel Rowland and the Great Evangelical Awakening in Wales* (Edinburgh and Carlisle, Pa., 1985).

William Gibson (ed.), *Religion and Society in England and Wales, 1689–1800* (London and Washington, 1998); a source-book.

Derec Llwyd Morgan, *The Great Awakening in Wales* (London, 1988), translation by Dyfnallt Morgan of *Y Diwygiad Mawr* (Llandysul, 1981).

Folk Life

T. Gwynn Jones, *Welsh Folklore and Folk-Custom* (London, 1930).

Trefor M. Owen, *The Customs and Traditions of Wales* (Cardiff, 1991).

CHAPTER 2

HISTORICAL WRITING IN THE EIGHTEENTH CENTURY

GERAINT H. JENKINS

On the eve of the eighteenth century, a budding young scholar eager to deepen his understanding of his native past and perhaps toying with the idea of writing a history of Wales could not have been faced with more discouraging obstacles and handicaps. Indeed, he might well have despaired of ever being able to achieve his ambitions. He belonged to a marginal, barely visible people who dwelt in a relatively poor and underdeveloped land on the fringes of western Europe. His contemporaries, especially those of peasant stock, were despised and derided by the English, not least because the guttural patois on their lips seemed scarcely an appropriate medium for polite or intellectual discourse. In 1697 the playwright Sir John Vanbrugh referred to Wales as 'a Country in the World's back-side' and the satirist Ned Ward was scarcely more complimentary when he branded Wales and its people 'the very Rubbish of Noah's Flood'. Wales lacked a national cultural centre, a populous capital city, literary clubs and scientific academies where gifted and ambitious young people could gain intellectual stimulation. There were no Welsh universities to train young scholars in the craft of writing history and to help them recover and sustain the memory of the nation. Although no one actually claimed that the Welsh had sold their national birthright for a mess of English pottage when Union came about in 1536–43, it is clear that one of the indirect effects of assimilation was the assumption that Wales no longer had an independent history. 'Since the happy incorporation of the Welsh with the English,' declared the historian William Wynne, Fellow of Jesus College, Oxford, in 1697, 'the History of both Nations as well as the People is united.' By 1786 William Warrington could confidently claim that the Welsh had abandoned their 'wild spirit of independence' and were 'mingling in friendship with the English and enjoying

with them the same Constitutional Liberties; the purity of which,
we trust, will continue uncorrupted as long as their Empire shall be
numbered among the nations of the earth'. Robbed of their
history, the Welsh could not even recognize their separate existence. Bereft of their past, they seemed destined to remain a power-
less, obscure people. In a letter written to the English historian
Thomas Carte in 1745, Lewis Morris of Anglesey painted a
sombre picture:

> I am ashamed for my self and country of Wales, that we have neither
> the skill nor courage to write the history of our own ancestors, nay far
> from that, that few of us in these days (I don't know what hath
> bewitched us) take any pleasure in reading the histories those brave
> people have left us.

Late Stuart scholars who were fully capable of serving the
national interest of Wales by writing informed and intelligent
history lacked the confidence to undertake the task. Robert
Vaughan, the celebrated antiquary of Hengwrt, was severely up-
braided by an eighteenth-century critic for preferring to transcribe
and pore over manuscripts than 'whet the Cambrian sword'
on behalf of the 'glorious' history of the Welsh. Humphrey
Humphreys, the learned, Welsh-speaking bishop of Bangor at the
turn of the seventeenth century, timidly resisted the temptation to
write a robust history of his native land because the chronological
material at his disposal was 'so confused, false, and contradictory'.
He might have deserved more sympathy had he claimed that the
scattered nature of historical material, as well as access to it, had
dogged his path. The dispersal of valuable manuscripts during and
after the dissolution of the monasteries and the loss of many more
during the upheavals of the civil wars meant that scholars were
obliged to travel considerable distances in search of fragmented
archival sources. The labours of Robert Vaughan, William Maurice,
Cefn-y-braich, and John Jones, Gellilyfdy, had made good some of
the losses, but it was not easy, especially for men without breeding,
to gain access to private libraries where many documents were
vulnerable to the ravages of mildew, mice, rats, rain and fire. Hair-
raising tales of wanton irresponsibility on the part of landowners
were often told, and some unscrupulous scholars even pillaged the
major treasure-house of the Hengwrt library.

It must be emphasized, too, that Welsh landowners provided scant encouragement for historians. The rise of a tiny group of affluent and influential landowners—often styled 'The Great Leviathans'—had been accompanied by the demise of the traditional gentry families who had for the most part remained sensible of their roots and familiar with Welsh culture. The old Welsh squires, according to Ellis Wynne, continued to surround themselves with 'all manner of armorial bearings, banners, escutcheons, books of pedigrees, poems of antiquity, *cywyddau*'. But the new behemoths exhibited little enthusiasm for the history, language and literature of the 'mountain Welsh great or small', and none of them was disposed, rightly or wrongly, to claim that the blood of ancient Welsh princes coursed through his veins. Those with the longest rent-rolls and the greatest desire to advance their own economic interests were prone to deride 'clownish' speakers of Welsh and to dismiss historical manuscripts relating to Wales as fossils 'of little use [to] the commonwealth of real learning'. Although many of the gentry remained devoted to the study of genealogy and heraldry, the fact that they had lost their native language and their sense of Welshness meant that they were either unable or unwilling to bolster the historical heritage of Wales.

Given the lack of acknowledged centres of learning and the failure to enlist the support of the leading gentry, it was not surprising that the Welsh turned to the ivory towers of Oxford for inspiration. It was here that the polymathic scholar, Edward Lhuyd, keeper of the Ashmolean Museum, left an indelible impression on both his students and his correspondents. Lhuyd's massive erudition and rigorously analytical mind earned him an international reputation and his magisterial work, *Archaeologia Britannica* (1707), not only included a catalogue of Welsh medieval manuscripts and their whereabouts but also a clear demonstration of the common Celtic origin of Breton, Cornish and Welsh. Tragically, however, within two years of its publication Lhuyd was dead and it is hard not to wonder what heights he might have scaled had he lived longer. We can be certain that his preliminary studies of prehistoric antiquity and comparative philology would have been greatly refined and that his inspiration to historians, antiquarians and chroniclers would have been of enduring importance. But it was not to be. Following Lhuyd's unexpected and melancholy death, several of his cherished disciples who had been expected to carry his torch never realized their full potential as scholars. Some of them succumbed to hard liquor, while others fell foul of church leaders. In August 1709 William Lewes of Llwynderw, an outstanding genealogist, bewailed the death of Lhuyd and feared for the consequences for 'the poore remains of the Ancient Bryttains, whose Antiquity he has vindicated against those whose ignorance as well as malice have aspers'd and Calumniated'. Having lost its finest scholar, Wales no longer looked to Oxford for stimulation and leadership. Neither scholarly curiosity nor patriotic commitment was forthcoming and John Morgan, vicar of Matching in Essex, lamented the fact that 'there peeps not a penny paper from Jesus College' to aid the ailing heritage of Wales. Likewise, Thomas Hearne, the scholarly under-keeper of the Bodleian Library, found the Welsh at Jesus 'utterly for the discouraging of their own History'.

It is not in any way surprising, therefore, that aspiring Welsh historians on the threshold of the eighteenth century were filled with a deep sense of gloom. For a variety of reasons, the Welsh had been robbed of their historical traditions and their sense of national identity. In 1688 Thomas Jones, Wales's first professional almanacker, believed that the Welsh had come within a hair's breadth of being 'blotted . . . out of the Books of Records'. Unlike the Irish, who were haunted by their history, the Welsh were in grave danger of losing theirs forever.

Paradoxically, however, out of this deep pessimism grew a strong and abiding desire to revive the lost history of Wales and implant in the minds and hearts of the Welsh people new respect for the nation's language and antiquities. As the eighteenth century unfolded, appreciable numbers of cultural patriots and reformers gained sufficient confidence to transform traditional ways of life. Even though Wales lacked institutions of statehood and a tangible cultural infrastructure, it became possible to effect improvements. Socially and economically, Wales was better placed, especially from the 1740s onwards, to enter 'the age of improvement'. Industrial development, agrarian improvements, swelling trade, urban growth and better communications all helped to encourage greater prosperity. As the economy became more productive and diverse, signs of cultural change and renewal also became increasingly apparent. Wales spawned its own printing presses from 1718 onwards and the deployment of subscription methods, booksellers, agents and hawkers meant that books of all kinds became more widely available. Religious revivalism and the extension of educational facilities helped to encourage the reading habit, especially among pious yeomen-farmers, craftsmen and artisans. The striking demand for saving literature meant that enormous time and energy were invested in publishing devotional and doctrinal manuals, but as readers acquired a greater desire for self-improvement and independence of mind circumstances became much more favourable for the publication of works of historical study. Stirrings in this field owed much to the influence of lively middling sorts, many of whom were associated either with London-Welsh societies or with the bookish Morris circle, and their willingness to rediscover the traditional heritage and to graft upon it new myths and institutions greatly strengthened and enhanced the distinctive sense of identity of the Welsh people. All these factors had wide-ranging implications for the writing and interpretation of the history of Wales.

The first and most urgent task was to salvage as much as possible from the past in order to boost national confidence. The initial fillip came seven years after the death of Edward Lhuyd. In 1716 the history of the 'glorious' origins of the Welsh found a pungent protagonist in Theophilus Evans, author of *Drych y Prif Oesoedd* (A Mirror of the First Ages). A native of the parish of Llandygwydd in south Cardiganshire, Evans was a precocious (and perhaps angry) young man of twenty-three when he published what was to become the most popular history book in Welsh for two centuries. His principal aim was to defend the captivating medieval soap-opera, *Historia Regum Britanniae,* written by Geoffrey of Monmouth *c.*1136, against the pompous condescension and scepticism of English historians. Ever since William Camden's much acclaimed *Britannia* (1586), the credibility of Geoffrey of Monmouth's tale had been called into question, and by the late Stuart period his reputation was in tatters in scholarly circles in England. Representatives of the new science, whose voices became ever more clamorous following the founding of the Royal Society in 1660, were not disposed to take seriously any theories based exclusively on biblical narratives or 'monkish fables'. In effect, the so-called 'British History' had become a joke among Saxon sceptics. Welsh scholars were thrown on the

defensive and in his 'augmented and improved' version of David
Powel's narrative account of the history of Wales, William Wynne
(writing in 1697) failed to summon up sufficient courage to take up
the cudgels on behalf of Geoffrey of Monmouth. He simply stated
that the legend probably contained a kernel of truth and should
not be ignored. Such timidity did not impress Theophilus Evans
and, wielding his notoriously sharp pen, he celebrated Geoffrey's
tale with considerable enthusiasm and condemned his traducers
for spreading 'a farrago of trashy and insolent lies against the
Welsh'. If *Historia Regum Britanniae* was to be no more than a
footnote in English histories, Evans was determined to restore it to
a central place in Welsh perceptions and affections. He studded his
account with vivid tales, epic military victories and heroic defeats,
and for the first time in the history of the nation monoglot Welsh
readers were supplied with a printed account of the legendary feats
of Brutus, Beli and Brân, Arthur, and many others.

Theophilus Evans had also been much taken by the romantic
notions of the learned Breton monk, Abbé Pezron, whose
L'Antiquité de la nation et la langue des Celtes (1703) had been
translated into English by David Jones in 1706. Pezron's work had
helped to stiffen the cultural self-confidence of the Welsh by
tracing their genealogy to the origins of the ancient Celtae who
were descended from Gomer, son of Japheth, son of Noah, and
who emerged in Asia Minor, whence they spread over the rest of
Europe. Pezron's work gave birth to the notion of Celticism and
his work greatly impressed contemporaries, including Edward
Lhuyd. One can imagine the sheer joy which Theophilus Evans
derived from being able to inform his readers that their roots were
traceable to the Tower of Babel: 'here is the blood and race of the
old Welsh, as exalted as any earthly lineage could be'. Since
Evans's avowed aim was to defend the honour of the Welsh
nation, his work was unashamedly Cambro-centric, polemical
and partisan. Like so many eighteenth-century Hanoverians, he
sported dual identities. A cleric of gentle stock (his grandfather,
who had fought bravely for the cause of Charles I, had been called
Captain Tory), Evans was a fervent monarchist and an ardent
anti-Papist. But he was also a cultural patriot who used every
means within his power to defend the good name of the 'True
Britons' who were the first and rightful proprietors of the island.
His history was not aimed at erudite scholars or fashion-conscious

middling sorts, and no one should take too seriously his formidable scholarly apparatus of footnotes; he wrote instead for the
benefit of patriotic Welshmen who were likely to appreciate one-
dimensional narrative and a 'babbling' racy style. *Drych y Prif
Oesoedd* was so well tuned to the particular needs of a people in
search of their own national identity that it became a popular
classic. A second, amended edition was published in 1740 and
three other editions had appeared before the century had run its
course. At least twenty editions (including an English translation,
entitled *A View of the Primitive Ages*, in 1834) were published by
1900. This evidence speaks volumes for Theophilus Evans's gifts as
a story-teller and as a people's remembrancer.

Theophilus Evans's history had a considerable impact on the
public's perception of the past, and the 'British History' received a
further shot in the arm when *The History of Great Britain*, written
by John Lewis of Llynwene, Radnorshire, *c.* 1610, was posthumously published in 1729. In recounting the history of the Britons
from the earliest times to that of Cadwaladr, Lewis had rallied to
the support of Geoffrey of Monmouth and heartily condemned
sceptical historians like Polydore Vergil, William Camden and
George Buchanan. Lewis believed that Geoffrey's tale embodied
the secret character of the Island of Britain and that it contained
the key to a fuller understanding of the nation's past. It must be
said, however, that other scholars were singularly unimpressed by
the lack of critical discrimination which characterized the work of
supporters of Geoffrey of Monmouth. In a significant, but much
neglected volume entitled *The History of the Cymbri (or Brittains)*
(1746), the Presbyterian author, Simon Thomas of Hereford,
bracketed Geoffrey with 'Inventors of evil things, Forgers of Lies
. . . the Pest of mankind'.

But even this doubting Thomas could not catch the public
imagination to the degree achieved by the redoubtable Morris
brothers of Anglesey and the groups of scholars, savants,
antiquaries and poets whom they invited to become members of
the charmed Morris circle during the middle decades of the
century. Lewis Morris, the presiding influence over the Honourable Society of Cymmrodorion (founded in 1751), supplied the
stimulus for considerable activity in historical and literary circles,
and by bringing together (in correspondence rather than in person)
some of the best minds in Wales he encouraged much sounder

critical scrutiny. The voluminous Morris letters bear witness to the pleasure which this gifted coterie of scholars derived from the study of history. Although Lewis Morris seized every opportunity to correspond with English antiquaries and historians, he also kept a watchful eye on 'every smatterer in history' who committed the cardinal sin of denying the authenticity of the 'British History'. He was convinced that a large element of truth was embedded in Geoffrey of Monmouth's tale and insisted (wrongly as it turned out) that the chronicle known as *Brut Tysilio* or *Brut y Brenhinedd* was the Welsh source which Geoffrey claimed to have translated into Welsh. Morris set himself the task of rescuing the glorious Welsh heritage from 'the dirt that is thrown upon it' and he never wearied of reminding his correspondents that 'the labouring oar falls upon me to defend our ancient History and antiquities'. Convinced that even the most ragged Welsh manuscript was of greater value than every English historian (especially those who impugned Geoffrey of Monmouth), Morris delighted in seeking out and transcribing manuscripts and preserving 'old writings on vellum'. He fervently believed that he was the true heir of Edward Lhuyd and he devoted forty years of his life to the task of compiling material relating to Celtic remains in Europe, a volume which remained unpublished until 1878 but which, by all accounts, replicated the analytical rigour which had characterized the writings of Lhuyd. In spite of poor health and countless distractions, Lewis Morris was determined to strengthen scholarly activity in his native land. As the following letter, written to his brother Richard sometime in 1760, reveals, learning and patriotism lay at the very heart of his aims and objectives:

> These are extracts out of my *Celtic Remains*, which I could wish to see published, but I don't believe I shall be able to live so long. My materials are decayd and I suspect my lungs are hurt. However, I shall trudge on while I live, and if God pleases, I shall be of some service to my country, and to the cause of truth.

By example as well as precept, Morris inspired remarkable literary and historical research which, in turn, encouraged an enhanced sense of Welsh identity. In his day, he had no equal among his contemporaries as a critic of manuscripts and he left a permanent mark on Welsh historical scholarship.

The spirit of impartial historical inquiry and critical detachment which Lewis Morris and some of his colleagues employed was not, however, shared by every eighteenth-century Welsh antiquary. This was a period when creativity, fantasy and self-expression co-existed with scholarly erudition, and some scholars had a foot in both camps. The anguish and dilemma which this duality created was embodied in the career of Henry Rowlands, who was vicar of Llanidan in Anglesey from 1696 until his death in 1723. An industrious and enthusiastic antiquary, Rowlands corresponded regularly with Edward Lhuyd and once described the Oxford scholar as 'exquisitely learn'd and judicious'. But following Lhuyd's death Rowlands abandoned his mentor's new standards of criticism without a backward glance and, instead, found congenial inspiration in the study of druidism. Although Welsh Renaissance scholars in the sixteenth century had rediscovered writings on the druids in classical texts, the Welsh did not succumb to 'druidomania' until the eighteenth century. A fresh beginning had been made by the antiquary John Aubrey, author of the entertaining 'Lives'. As early as the 1690s he had discussed with Lhuyd the possibility that the stone circles at Stonehenge and Avebury might have been druid temples, but it was not until 1723 that William Stukeley, the first secretary of the Society of Antiquaries of London, wrote up his notes on the basis of fieldwork undertaken at those sites. Stukeley's researches remained unpublished until 1740 and scholarly attention was therefore diverted to Henry Rowlands's remarkable account of the misty past of his beloved Anglesey. This was *Mona Antiqua Restaurata* (The Restoration of Ancient Anglesey), published in Dublin in 1723.

Mona Antiqua Restaurata is an extraordinarily interesting volume: its 388 pages are packed with information on the origin of languages, the story of Brutus, the philosophy of the druids, the etymology of local place-names and words, and several striking engravings. The great merit of the work was that it bore testimony to Rowlands's astonishing powers of observation and his determination faithfully to record 'the marks and footsteps of Antiquity to this day'. He was deeply familiar with the topography of his native island and, as a field archaeologist, he lived up to the expectations of Edward Lhuyd. But his view of the past was principally governed by biblical testimony and he was much indebted to the bizarre and muddle-headed ideas presented in Aylett

Sammes's bulky volume, *Britannia Antiqua Illustrata* (1676).
Although Sammes was once memorably described by William
Nicolson as 'the most unaccountable and ridiculous Plagiary and
Buffoon that ever had his name upon the title page of any book
what so ever', his account of the post-diluvial colonization of
Europe and his map showing 'The Procession of the antient
Cimbri' along the road from Ararat to Wales captured the
imagination of Henry Rowlands and prompted him to endorse the
notion of the Hebrew origins of the Welsh language and also to
advocate the view that the 'pure and untainted' doctrines of
druidism had been brought to the island of Anglesey by 'one of
Noah's sons'. His book marked a new departure insofar as the
druids now entered the Welsh consciousness with a vengeance.
Rowlands believed that Anglesey had been the headquarters or the
'mother church' of the ancient druids in the period before the first
Roman invasion, and that the megalithic monuments which were
to be found in such profusion on the island had formerly served as
altars and temples for the druids, whose chief had exercised
'supreme Metropolitan powers' over a priestly hierarchy made up
of druids, ovates and bards.

For many years Henry Rowlands's speculative fantasies
remained unchallenged, and a second edition of *Mona*, published
in 1766, reiterated the case for acknowledging Anglesey's unique
status as the 'Canterbury' of British druidism. The banner of the
Society of Cymmrodorion displayed an ancient druid and one of
its presidents, Sir Watkin Williams Wynn II, delighted in every
opportunity to dress up in druidic garb at festive occasions. From
the 1770s onwards a succession of travellers and artists, as well as
local antiquaries, were captivated by so-called druidic remains. By
this stage no one was more passionately interested in druidism
than the brilliantly gifted and fiercely patriotic Glamorgan
stonemason, Edward Williams, who was better known both then
and now by his bardic name Iolo Morganwg. His contempt
for Henry Rowlands's far-fetched notions was boundless and
he described *Mona Antiqua Restaurata* as 'a confused Mass of
violations of history, audacious assertion, groundless conjecture,
superstitious tradition, false etymology, and a shameful ignorance
of the ancient manuscripts, and even the Language of Wales'. In
his view, the puny monuments in Anglesey did not brook comparison with the magnificence of Avebury, which was indisputably

'the grand seat of the Druids before the Roman invasion'. Moreover, he claimed to have documentary proof that the learning of the druids had been handed down from generation to generation and that he and Edward Evan of Aberdare—both proud Glamorgan men—were the last surviving representatives of the ancient druidic bards. During the latter decades of the century, at a time when he found both solace and inspiration in laudanum, Iolo put into practice what historians like to call 'the invention of tradition' by passing off his wonderful forgeries as the work of Dafydd ap Gwilym and presenting his people with a new and colourful vision of their history. Central to that vision was the revival of *Gorsedd Beirdd Ynys Prydain* (The Gorsedd of the Bards of the Isle of Britain), a druidic moot which assembled for the first time on Primrose Hill, London, on 21 June 1792. In his preface to William Owen Pughe's *The Heroic Elegies of Llywarch Hen* (1792), Iolo explained in fascinating detail the 'bardic mysteries' and 'deep Druidic lore' which lay behind the bizarre pageant which became the first modern national institution in the history of Wales and which, from 1819 onwards, became successfully incorporated in the newly revived eisteddfod ceremonies. Historians have often derided Iolo Morganwg's attachment to druidism and treated the *Gorsedd* as a piece of folly or a charade with little practical significance or consequences. But Iolo was convinced that the function of history was to re-create a past to suit the needs of the present. Invention, fantasy and bogus scholarship were all grist to his mill, and his immense knowledge of the history of Wales and unique familiarity with a wide range of literary sources meant that few were in a position to challenge or undermine his theories. Druidism was a theme which offered an ideal breeding-ground for idealists, dreamers and charlatans, and no one derived greater delight from manipulating the past for patriotic purposes than 'Old Iolo'.

   Much of the historical writing in Wales before the American Revolution was profoundly conservative in character and, in many instances, was deliberately designed to stiffen loyalty to Hanoverianism. Cultural renewal, however, created a basis for less traditional interpretations and the new emphasis on druidism, Celticism and especially Romanticism encouraged historians to be more adventurous and imaginative. No self-respecting nation can flourish without its heroes, both real and imagined, and it became increasingly fashionable to view the history of Wales as a perpetual struggle by chivalrous patriots against Saxon oppressors. Evan Evans (Ieuan Fardd) is best known for his major scholarly work, *Some Specimens of the Poetry of the Antient Welsh Bards* (1764), but his determination to foster a stronger sense of patriotism also deserves attention. Evans read the works of Gerald of Wales, Dr David Powel, Humphrey Llwyd and Edward Lhuyd, he bought or borrowed books and manuscripts on early British history, and he urged members of the Cymmrodorion and wealthy patrons to publish historical manuscripts lest they fall foul of 'a thousand accidents'. The lukewarm response he received and, more crucially, the 'evil eye' cast upon him by his non-Welsh ecclesiastical superiors fuelled his sense of grievance against the English. His celebrated poem, *The Love of our Country* (1772), was a thwacking rejoinder to those 'despicable scribblers' who 'peremptorily condemn our histories as fabulous and fictitious' and who derided the valiant deeds of Welsh princes. Evans depicted Owain Glyndŵr as a popular hero and a patriot rather than as a bandit rebel and, when the gentleman-scholar Thomas Pennant published his first volume of *A Tour in Wales* in 1778, sixty-seven pages were earmarked for an account of the military exploits of 'the hero Glyndwr' and the manner by which he sought to release the nation 'from the galling weight of the Saxon yoke'. Pennant's work was chiefly responsible for creating the reputation of Glyndŵr as a chivalrous national leader and as a patriot 'not in the roll of common men'.

The search for heroic periods in the Welsh past was also accompanied by rabid anti-monarchical sentiment. In his celebrated poem *The Bard*, in 1757, Thomas Gray had related how the last Welsh bard had hurled a curse on the invading armies of the ruthless King Edward I:

> On a rock, whose haughty brow
> Frowns o'er old Conway's foaming flood
> Robed in the sable garb of woe,
> With haggard eyes the Poet stood . . .

It became fashionable to pillory the name of Edward, the alleged perpetrator of the massacre of the Welsh bards shortly after the conquest of 1282, and the tale acquired even greater resonance when the likes of Paul Sandby and Thomas Jones, Pencerrig, produced striking paintings on the theme. Some of the wilder democrats in London-Welsh circles found it hard to resist the temptation to urinate on Edward I's grave at Westminster, and Iolo Morganwg's passionate commitment to the republican cause was strengthened both by his abhorrence of the tyrannical regimes of European monarchs and his contempt for 'Long-shanked Edward' and his brutal successors:

> Edward the first, who massacred the Welsh Bards, and whose memory will in Wales be for ever held in that detestation which is justly due to the names of an amazing majority of all the kings that this world has hitherto groaned under.

In the turbulent 1790s William Jones of Llangadfan, a prickly radical who bore more than a passing resemblance to his hero Voltaire, who scandalized local clergymen with his bawdy and blasphemous conversation, and whose correspondence was liber- ally sprinkled with references to tyrants, oppressors and fleecers, was moved to compose a robust Welsh national anthem, sung to the refrain 'Ac unwn lawen ganiad ar doriad teg y dydd' (And join in joyful song at the fair break of dawn), in which he deplored the treachery, conquest and pillage wrought by merciless invaders. Like many other Welsh Jacobins, Jones felt justified in beating the drum of patriotism in view of the anti-Welsh animus which characterized the works of English historians.

The search for heroes extended even to the New World. Although the epic tale of Madoc, son of Owain Gwynedd, who had tired of strife-torn Wales in 1170 and sailed with eight ships westwards to a new continent which later became known as America, had been familiar, at least to the erudite, since Eliza- bethan times, the legend lay dormant until the publication of the second edition of *Drych y Prif Oesoedd* in 1740. Theophilus Evans included not only extraordinary details regarding Madoc's journey but also new evidence of the existence of a tribe of Welsh-speaking Indians. The tale acquired political significance since it proved that Britain's claim on the treasures of the New World was stronger than that of Spain, and when war broke out with Spain in 1789 the Madoc legend excited the curiosity of the Welsh literati in London, and the hunt for the Padoucas (or the Madogwys, the Lost

Brothers) began in earnest. In 1792 John Evans of Waunfawr, Caernarfonshire, crossed the Atlantic and embarked on a life-threatening journey, worthy of Indiana Jones at his boldest, up the Missouri river, only to discover that the white-skinned Mandan Indians had no connections with Wales and certainly spoke no Welsh. Nevertheless, the legend of Madoc excited the imagination of historians, and manuscripts, letters and magazines bristled with elaborate *apologiae* on behalf of the truthfulness of the tale.

Not all scholars, however, were devoted to innovation and myth-making on a grand scale, and we should not ignore the assiduous labours of modest antiquaries and scribes who did not court publicity. Local history, for instance, derived much of its vitality from the painstaking studies of a multitude of chroniclers, genealogists and armorists who delighted in being 'strangely thrifty of Time past'. In the vale of Teifi, many-sided scholars, clerics and poets worked like beavers in transcribing literary treasures and prided themselves not only on their knowledge of the past but also on their love for 'the country and nation of the Britons'. The so-called 'Llandaff school' of antiquaries in Glamorgan, many of them Anglicans and High Tories, energetically searched for medieval records, inspected graves and tombs, sketched churches and other historic buildings, and fostered local pride in the history of the county. In many counties in north Wales, too, antiquaries, poets and scholars took a proper pride in the richness of the historical traditions of their regions. Building on the success of Henry Rowlands's work, John Thomas's strongly topographical *History of the Island of Anglesey* was posthumously published in 1775, while Nicholas Owen's rather bland and unexceptional *Caernarvonshire. A Sketch of its History, Antiquities, Mountains, and Productions* (1792) was a pocket book for inquisitive artists, tourists and travellers in search of the 'sublime'. Thomas Pennant's *A Tour in Wales* (1778–83), a work made all the more vivid and attractive by the drawings of his draughtsman Moses Griffith, displayed an impressive familiarity with the topography of the six northern counties of Wales and also included so much valuable historical material that Philip Yorke informed him that he had 'gathered the Welsh Harvest of History, so close, that there is scarce anything to Glean after you'. The best counterpart to Pennant's work in south Wales was David Williams's *History of Monmouthshire* (1796), a work studded with shrewd observations on the mixed fortunes of gentry families and on the process of industrialization in the county, but also marred by gratuitous animadversions on the Welsh language and tedious philosophical digressions. The same county was also well served by William Coxe, whose *An Historical Tour in Monmouthshire* (2 vols., 1801) was based on a 1,500-mile tour of the county, in the company of Sir Richard Hoare, in 1798 and 1799. Although Coxe's work was not strictly a history of the county, it contained a wealth of valuable and sharply observed detail, and served as a model for a spate of county histories published in the early decades of the nineteenth century.

Local historians also ventured into print in the second half of the eighteenth century. Lewis Morris drew on his skills as a surveyor and a steward as well as on his deep knowledge of local history in writing *A Short History of the Crown Manor of Creuthyn in the County of Cardigan* (1756) and a welcome edition of Sir John Wynn's celebrated *History of the Gwydir Family* emerged in 1770. Probably the most popular and well-thumbed volume was *A Geographical, Historical, and Religious Account of the Parish of Aberystruth* (1779), written, at the age of seventy-seven, by the credulous 'Old Prophet', Edmund Jones of Pontypool. Although Jones made no secret of his desire to use the book as a means of advancing the cause of the 'true religion' of Dissent in the parish and beyond, his work contained intriguing topographical and historical evidence, not least relating to extraordinary 'natural curiosities'. A much wider appreciation of the local historian's craft, however, was exhibited in Thomas Pennant's *The History of the Parishes of Whiteford and Holywell* (1796). With considerable subtlety, Pennant depicted the sharp contrast between the unchanging rural character of his native parish of Whitford and the brisk and noisy industrialization wrought in the neighbouring parish of Holywell by brass and copper works. Nor should we forget that much of Iolo Morganwg's zeal and love for history sprang from his warm attachment to his native county and in particular to the Vale of Glamorgan. His tiny cottage in Flemingston was packed with antiquarian and historical notes which, at least in his eyes, provided convincing proof of the primacy of Glamorgan and, as Southey put it, his own mastery of 'whatever lore of science or of song/Sages and bards of old have handed down'.

No discussion of historical writing in eighteenth-century Wales would be complete without reflections on the role of religion. Religion was an intrinsic part of the fabric of social life and for many people it provided the most genuine sense of the past and its meaning. Religious writers never tired of interpreting the past in spiritual and moral terms and no Christian needed reminding that life on earth reflected the divine will of the Almighty. God was at the helm and it was He who ensured that the virtuous were rewarded and that the wicked never went unpunished. All readers of history soon became familiar with the general pattern of backsliding and repentance, lapse and recovery which had characterized the behaviour of their ancestors. Throughout the century, the historical thinking of Anglicans and Dissenters alike was governed by the providential view of the past. Nevertheless, it could not be claimed that men of different religious persuasions saw the past in the same light. Although they were joined together by their common allegiance to the Protestant faith, there was much mutual mistrust and sometimes even hatred between Anglicans and Dissenters, and this was reflected in the manner in which they perceived their immediate past. The coming of toleration in 1689 did not necessarily or immediately lead to a greater spirit of tolerance and, in their treatment of the past, many loyal servants of the Church of England continued to publish crude and defamatory tracts about radical Puritans in Cromwellian times, especially when, in 1713, Edmund Calamy (supported by the Welsh Dissenter, James Owen) chronicled in censorious detail the sufferings and indignities heaped upon ejected Puritan ministers by persecuting Anglicans.

In their appeal to history, defenders of the established Protestant faith clung tenaciously to the theory, first propagated by William Salesbury and Richard Davies in Tudor times, that the true Christian religion had been planted in these islands by Joseph of Arimathea and that an untainted apostolic church had thrived until the sixth century when the abhorrent Popish faith was forced upon the Welsh at the point of the sword. Sixteenth-century Protestantism, therefore, was the ancient faith of the Welsh people in a new guise and, even in the eighteenth century, embattled Churchmen continued to insist that the Church of England, in its capacity as the legitimate heir of the old British Church and as the church which still commanded widespread popular loyalty, was 'the best and purest church upon earth'. Part Two of *Drych y Prif Oesoedd* by Theophilus Evans was a celebration of the pure, unsullied Christian faith which had flourished mightily in Britain in the time of the apostles and which would flourish again once the might of Rome was destroyed. Evans also detected close affinities between the old Britons and the Hebrew people, a theme which was vigorously pursued by Charles Edwards in *Y Ffydd Ddi-ffuant* (The Unfeigned Faith), one of the masterpieces of Welsh prose literature. The classic version of Edwards's work, published in 1677, was reprinted in 1722. It reminded readers of the piety and chivalry of their forebears and of the pressing need to recapture the pure evangelical faith which had been the hallmark of the early apostolic church. Edwards drew striking parallels between the experience of the Israelites and the Welsh, and he hinted strongly that God had a special mission in store for His chosen people.

History and religion also came together when the drama of personal regeneration, energetic missionary activity and intimate spiritual fellowship made a deep impression on the minds of followers of Howel Harris and Daniel Rowland from 1735 onwards. The zeal and enthusiasm which fuelled Methodism aroused strong passions, both for and against, and these became all the more acute as champions of the movement loudly claimed that here was a turning-point of critical importance in the history of Wales. The Methodist apologist *par excellence* was William Williams, Pantycelyn, the greatest of Welsh hymnologists. Although a Dissenter by upbringing and in many ways the literary heir of Puritanism, Williams became a propagandist on behalf of 'The Great Awakening'. In his hymns and prose works he skilfully deployed striking images such as 'heat', 'light' and 'power' in order to convey the passion, energy and commitment of God's elect. By contrast, pre-Methodist Wales was depicted by him as 'the Land of Sleep', where spiritual torpor and moral decadence prevailed. Williams's version of the past is best encapsulated in the following passage in which he paints a depressing picture of negligence, sloth and torpor:

Spiritual death, love of the world, arid disputations, self-regard . . .
night, night in all the churches . . . Ministers without talent, with no
experience of grace, without simplicity, without a contrite heart,
without faith . . . crawling like tail-wriggling serpents into houses, that

is to say churches, for gain, profit or bodily sustenance, feeding on the fleece of the flock, with no care of souls . . . But now the day has dawned, the Lord has breathed upon the dry bones, and they are moving.

Even when allowance is made for poetic licence and the fact that it was natural for enthusiastic, hyperactive young men to accuse their predecessors of lethargy, neglect and corruption, it is clear that Methodists seriously underestimated the debt which they owed to their forebears. Church historians vigorously denied that the trumpet blasts of twice-born evangelists had awakened a slumbering people, and Edmund Jones, 'the Old Prophet', tenaciously defended the good name of Dissent by rebuking Williams Pantycelyn for his 'shameless untruth'. Nevertheless, the Methodist 'myth' lived on and prospered hugely in the nineteenth century when a series of one-dimensional histories perpetuated the notion of 'Y Deffroad Mawr' (The Great Awakening). Indeed, for committed evangelical historians, it has remained an article of faith to the present day. Not only, therefore, did Methodism contrive to cut off people from their past by eradicating popular customs and recreations, it also constructed a myth which was designed to erase the memory of the time when Wales had allegedly lain 'in a dark and deathly sleep'.

Even as Methodist historians bore witness to the cataclysmic effects of their God-given mission, Dissenting historians set about deepening their understanding of the past as a means of protecting and strengthening their own identity. By the 1760s there was a growing desire to discover or rediscover old Puritan roots, and it is significant that five editions of Morgan Llwyd's books were published between 1752 and 1778, as well as two editions of the autobiography of the Quaker Richard Davies, and a Welsh translation of Edmund Bagshaw's biography of Vavasor Powell. Welsh Baptists, however, stole a march on their fellow Dissenters by publishing *Hanes y Bedyddwyr Ymhlith y Cymry* (History of the Baptists Among the Welsh) in 1778. Its author was Joshua Thomas, a Carmarthenshire farmer's son who served as Baptist minister at Leominster from 1754 until his death, aged seventy-eight, in 1797. Thomas was a man of great integrity and his work displayed a degree of impartiality and magnanimity not shared by his Methodist counterparts. Indeed, he was prepared to acknowledge that the Methodist movement had provoked a lively interest in religion and that in its wake 'knowledge of God has spread wondrously throughout Wales'. Conscious of being a snapper-up of unconsidered trifles and 'a Retailer of scraps', he published detailed accounts of Baptist churches, biographies of leading ministers and members, and accounts of the persecution they endured on behalf of the faith. His work, however, was heavily anecdotal, reliant on the oral testimonies of 'aged people' or 'godly old men', and stronger on accumulation than analysis. On the basis of oral evidence and 'common tradition', Thomas insisted that the first Dissenting church in Wales was the Baptist church established at Olchon, in the parish of Clodock on the borders of Herefordshire, Monmouthshire and Brecknockshire, in 1633. Olchon thus predated Llanfaches, the acknowledged mother church of Welsh Congregationalists, by six years, and no one succeeded in convincing Joshua Thomas that his claim for the primacy of Olchon could not be verified. Even so, over a period of thirty years he assembled a mass of invaluable material relating to the Baptists and produced unpublished English revisions of *Hanes y Bedyddwyr* and a two-volume 'Ecclesiastical History of Wales'. His careful and methodical researches, coupled with his gracious spirit, earned him the warm admiration of fellow Dissenters.

Although still awaiting their historian, eighteenth-century Congregationalists were also deeply conscious of their historical roots and of their debt to Puritan saints in the Cromwellian period. In the 1730s, elderly Dissenters still remembered the heroic labours of Walter Cradock (d.1659) and Methodist evangelists in north Wales were often dubbed 'Cradockites'. Radical figures like Morgan Llwyd, William Erbery and Vavasor Powell were revered by liberal thinkers as well as by old-style Calvinists. No Congregationalist was more aware of the Dissenting heritage than Edmund Jones, and his sermons and unpublished manuscripts are suffused with damning references to Papists, Arminians, Deists and 'blind malignant royalists'. He made no secret of his belief that the Cromwellian period had been a kind of golden age in the history of religion in Wales: 'Let O [liver] C [romwell] have but his due and he shall be owned to be a notable Instrument of providence raised up to be a deliverer to God's persecuted people.' Methodists often contemptuously referred to Dissenters as *Sentars Sychion* (Dry Dissenters) whose energies were devoted to sterile theological disputes but, in fact, their spiritual life was full of robust vitality and many of them were anxious, as their ancestors had been, to carry the banner of liberty of conscience.

The earlier reference to the telling of tales of Walter Cradock's exploits long after his death serves to remind us that the historical memory was not necessarily dependent on the printed word. A rich fund of narratives circulated orally, especially among humbler folk who had received no formal or regular schooling. For the bulk of the unlettered peasantry, the spoken word was the vehicle by which popular beliefs and customs, fables and myths were handed down from generation to generation. In the 1690s Edward Lhuyd's correspondents assured him that tales regarding Arthur, Taliesin and the Celtic saints had not perished among the common people, and in 1715 James Owen referred to the traditional custom of listening to 'monkish fables' recited on the hearth during long winter nights. Poets who sang of the Treason of the Long Knives and the Massacre of the Welsh Bards did not allow themselves or their hearers to forget the centuries of neglect and contempt which had blighted the lives of their ancestors. The art of genealogy, too, provided a framework for wistful memories of past glories. When Richard Warner climbed Cader Idris in August 1797 his guide, David Pugh, informed him that the founder of the Welsh people was 'an hero who flourished some ages before the Christian epoch; and he affirmed it appeared by an elaborate genealogy, which was made out about three years since, that his race had flowed in an uninterrupted stream for no less than three thousand years'. Rich oral traditions of this kind, some of which found their way into printed almanacs and ballads, helped to ensure the continuity of the Welsh identity.

In view of the absence of major national institutions and a recognizable and effective cultural infrastructure, it is hardly surprising that Wales never produced a Gibbon or a Hume in the eighteenth century. Although cultural patriots, romantic nationalists and myth-makers had injected new life, vigour and passion into the study of the past and created a stronger sense of the distinctive identity of Wales, it is a matter for regret that Iolo Morganwg never realized his cherished ambition of writing and publishing a massive six-volume history of Wales, a work which would surely have swept with great mastery over the centuries and helped to elevate Wales to a new status among the traditional non-historic peoples of Europe such as the Czechs, Slovaks, Catalans and Finns. Iolo had prepared a detailed prospectus of his proposed *magnum opus* and the awesome corpus of manuscripts now safely deposited in the National Library of Wales bears witness to the voluminous raw material he had transcribed and assembled. We can be certain that his history would have been quite different from anything that had hitherto been published.

Iolo himself believed that most previous volumes on the Welsh past served no useful purpose other than 'to hurl at an impatient Bookseller's head' and he could be scathing in commenting on the 'stuff' written by non-Welsh-speaking historians. He was sharply aware of how the historical memory could shape and colour the political and cultural values and ideals of his own generation. To him, history was not simply about the past; it was also the present and, to some degree, the future too. As we now know, there were errors and inaccuracies as well as deliberate fabrications in his vision of the Welsh past, but his peerless knowledge, searching intelligence and brilliant imagination enabled him to detect and appreciate historical patterns which other less gifted than he could never see. It is a major tragedy that a historian of such dazzling virtuosity never fulfilled his dream.

BIBLIOGRAPHY

T. M. Bassett, *The Welsh Baptists* (Swansea, 1977).

Geraint Bowen (ed.), *Y Traddodiad Rhyddiaith* (Llandysul, 1970).

J. H. Davies (ed.), *The Letters of Lewis, Richard, William and John Morris of Anglesey (Morrisiaid Môn) 1728–1765* (2 vols., Aberystwyth, 1907–9).

Frank Emery, *Edward Lhuyd F.R.S. 1660 –1709* (Cardiff, 1971).

Theophilus Evans, *Drych y Prif Oesoedd 1716*, ed. G. H. Hughes (Caerdydd, 1961).

G. M. Griffiths, 'John Lewis of Llynwene's defence of Geoffrey of Monmouth's "Historia"', *Journal of the National Library of Wales*, 7 (1952).

Trevor Herbert and Gareth E. Jones (eds.), *The Remaking of Wales in the Eighteenth Century* (Cardiff, 1988).

E. Hobsbawm and T. Ranger (eds.), *The Invention of Tradition* (Cambridge, 1983).

Emyr Humphreys, *The Taliesin Tradition* (London, 1983).

A. O. H. Jarman, 'Y ddadl ynghylch Sieffre o Fynwy', *Llên Cymru*, 2 (1952).

Geraint H. Jenkins, *Cadw Tŷ mewn Cwmwl Tystion: Ysgrifau Hanesyddol ar Grefydd a Diwylliant* (Llandysul, 1990).

Idem, *The Foundations of Modern Wales: Wales 1642–1780* (Oxford, paperback edn. 1993).

Idem, *Literature, Religion, and Society in Wales 1660–1730* (Cardiff, 1978).

P. Jenkins, 'From Edward Lhuyd to Iolo Morganwg: the death and rebirth of Glamorgan antiquarianism in the eighteenth century', *Morgannwg*, 23 (1979).

R. T. Jenkins, *Hanes Cymru yn y Ddeunawfed Ganrif* (Caerdydd, 1928).

R. T. Jenkins and H. M. Ramage, *A History of the Honourable Society of Cymmrodorion 1751–1951* (London, 1951).

Francis Jones, 'An approach to Welsh genealogy', *Transactions of the Honourable Society of Cymmrodorion* (1948).

T. D. Kendrick, *British Antiquity* (London, 1950).

Prys Morgan, 'The Abbé Pezron and the Celts', *Transactions of the Honourable Society of Cymmrodorion* (1965).

Prys Morgan, *The Eighteenth Century Renaissance* (Llandybïe, 1981).

Idem, *Iolo Morganwg* (Cardiff, 1975).

A. L. Owen, *The Famous Druids* (Oxford, 1962).

Hugh Owen (ed.), *Additional Letters of the Morrises of Anglesey (1735–1786)*, Parts 1–2 (London, 1947–9).

Stuart Piggott, *The Druids* (London, 1968).

Eiluned Rees, *Libri Walliae: A Catalogue of Welsh Books and Books Printed in Wales, 1546–1820* (Aberystwyth, 1987).

B. F. Roberts, 'Ymagweddau at Brut y Brenhinedd hyd 1890', *Bulletin of the Board of Celtic Studies*, 24 (1971).

Gomer M. Roberts (ed.), *Hanes Methodistiaeth Calfinaidd Cymru*, vol. 1, *Y Deffroad Mawr* (Caernarfon, 1973).

Gomer M. Roberts and G. H. Hughes (eds.), *Gweithiau William Williams Pantycelyn* (2 vols., Caerdydd, 1964–7).

J. G. Thomas, 'Henry Rowlands, the Welsh Stukeley', *Transactions of the Anglesey Antiquarian Society* (1958).

David Williams, *John Evans and the Legend of Madoc* (Cardiff, 1963).

G. J. Williams, *Agweddau ar Hanes Dysg Gymraeg*, ed. Aneirin Lewis (Caerdydd, 1969).

Idem, *Iolo Morganwg* (Cardiff, 1956).

Glanmor Williams, *Religion, Language and Nationality in Wales* (Cardiff, 1979).

Gwyn A. Williams, *Madoc: The Making of a Myth* (London, 1979).

Idem, *The Welsh in their History* (London, 1982).

CHAPTER 3

TWO PROSE WRITERS: ELLIS WYNNE AND THEOPHILUS EVANS

GWYN THOMAS

ELLIS WYNNE

Ellis Wynne is probably the most famous Welsh prose writer of the period between the Middle Ages and Daniel Owen (1836–95). He was born on 7 March 1671, in a substantial farmhouse called Y Lasynys, not far from Harlech in Gwynedd. He was the son of Edward Wynne of Glyn Cywarch, a mansion in the same locality. His mother was the heiress of Y Lasynys. There is no definite evidence to indicate where he went to school, though the fact that some Latin poems by him were found in the archives of Beaumaris Grammar School suggest that he may have been there. In 1692 he became an undergraduate student at Jesus College, Oxford. After graduation he seems to have moved back to Y Lasynys. In September 1698 he married Lowri Wynne of Moel-y-glo, near Harlech. She died on the birth of a son, and the son died soon afterwards. In February 1702, he married Lowri Lloyd of Hafod Lwyfog, in Nant Gwynant, not far from Beddgelert. They had nine children, some of whom died young. He was ordained deacon and rector in the Anglican church in December 1704—to be ordained deacon and rector within days in this way is rather unusual. He became rector of Llanbedr and Llandanwg, near Harlech until 1711, when he became rector of Llanfair, again near Harlech. He died in July 1734.

When one considers his small literary output it is rather surprising that he gained such eminence as a writer. In 1701 he published *Rheol Buchedd Sanctaidd*, a translation of *The Rule and Exercises of Holy Living* by the English divine Jeremy Taylor. His next work, and the one on which his fame is based, was *Gweledigaetheu y Bardd Cwsc* (The Visions of the Sleeping Bard), published in 1703. He also edited a version of the Book of

Common Prayer in Welsh (1710), and a short work on the catechism and a few prayers, hymns, and carols by him were published posthumously by his son, Edward, in a book entitled *Prif Addysc y Cristion* (A Basic Christian Education) in 1755.

The translation of the Bible into Welsh in 1588 became the basis of what developed into a modern tradition of translation, especially of devotional and religious works. Many of the religious books translated in the seventeenth century were books by Anglicans. Ellis Wynne's *Rheol Buchedd Sanctaidd* fits well into that tradition. It is, like several seventeenth-century translations, a book which aims at improving the morals and the lives of its readers. One or two quotations from Taylor's original work will give an impression of the book's contents.

In a section entitled 'Devotions for Ordinary Days' one, of many, prayers for the morning is this one:

> Guide me, O Lord, in all the changes and varieties of the world; that in all things that shall happen, I may have an evenness and tranquillity of spirit; that my soul may be wholly resigned to thy divinest will and pleasure, never murmuring at thy gentle chastisements and fatherly correction; never waxing proud and insolent, though I feel a torrent of comforts and prosperous successes.

The prayer in itself shows how different from ours were the religious ideals of the age.

These are two of his 'Arguments against Pride by way of consideration':

> 1. Our body is weak and impure, sending out more uncleannesses from its several sinks than could be endured, if they were not necessary and natural: and we are forced to pass that through our mouths, which as soon as we see upon the ground, we loathe like rottenness and vomiting . . .

> 3. Our beauty is in colour inferior to many flowers, and in proportion of parts is no better than nothing; for even a dog hath parts as well proportioned and fitted to his purposes, and the designs of his nature, as we have: and when it is most florid and gay, three fits of an ague can change it into yellowness and leanness, and the hollowness and wrinkles of deformity.

The considerations chosen by Taylor are meant to bring any pretensions to pride down to an extremely unpleasant level. We can immediately see a difference between this old view of life and ours if we consider that to cultivate the 'body beautiful' seems to be an ultimate goal of life in many western countries. All earthly life was, in theory, subservient to spiritual values for most seventeenth- and eighteenth-century divines.

Wynne's *Gweledigaetheu* was also based on an English work—two English works, to be exact. Both of these were English versions of a Spanish original, namely *Los Sueños* (The Dreams, or Visions) of Don Francisco Gomez de Quevedo Villegas (1580–1645). The Spanish work is a series of visions which provide Quevedo with a framework for satirizing various types of people. Sir Roger Lestrange (1616–1704) first published his adaptation of this work, *The Visions of Dom* [sic] *Francisco de Quevedo Villegas*, in 1667—earlier adaptations had appeared before this, in English and in French. Wynne used this version and another one, by John Stevens, *The Visions of Don Francisco de Quevedo Vellegass* [sic]: *The Second Part*, published in 1682. Some loose adaptations of passages of these works appear here and there in the *Gweledigaetheu*. Before the publication of his *Gweledigaetheu* Ellis Wynne had made known to some of his friends his intention of using Quevedo as well as other English works by, for instance, Tom Brown—one of the so-called London School of Burlesque Writers—and some of the work of Lucian, a classical author of Other World visions, in his work. He had also told them that he was resolved to adapt them all to the 'Humour of ye Welsh'.

In fact, in the seventeenth century in England, and to some extent in France, there was a genre of visionary literature about the Other World, especially about Hell. The visions served as a convenient framework for satire, usually of a fairly unsophisticated kind, and was used for political and religious purposes. In England, the framework was popular with Royalists and Anglicans. In their works it was usual to find Cromwell and his Roundheads and Nonconformist sects relegated to Hell. Wynne's *Gweledigaetheu* fits well into this mode of writing.

The *Gweledigaetheu* is a book of three dreams and three visions. The visionary dreamer is called Y Bardd Cwsc or Cwsg (The Sleeping Bard), a name which Wynne had picked up in his reading of old manuscripts. It is one of the bardic names of Rhys Fardd, a

fifteenth-century writer of political prophecy, a genre of writing
which abounds with obscure references. It is part of Wynne's
playfulness that he should have made his Bardd Cwsg meet the
'original' poet of that name in the Kingdom of the Dead. Wynne's
Gweledigaetheu begins with a poem addressed to 'The Reader',
exhorting him or her to consider well what he or she will read.
Then follows the first 'Vision of the World'.

One fine summer day the Bardd Cwsg makes his way to the top
of a mountain and, as the sun is near to setting, thinks how
fortunate, compared with his own country (Britain), are those
countries whose gentle plains he has glimpsed through his
telescope. He falls asleep and is snatched by 'tylwyth teg', a term
which is usually translated as 'fairies'. It is part of Wynne's
criticism of some pagan folk-beliefs that he should, like some
before him, have equated these with the spirits of the malicious
dead. He thinks his end has come when he is rescued by a shining
Angel. The Angel has been sent on a special mission:

> As your desire to see the course of the small world is so great, I have
> been directed to let you see it, so that you will realize how foolish is
> your discontent with your own estate and country.

He then takes him high to observe the course of the world
(including Britain), which is presented, metaphorically, as the City
of Destruction or the City of Doom. This city is divided into
streets, each under the rule of what Wynne regarded as four
cardinal sins—Pride, Pleasure, Profit and Hypocrisy. Each sin is
personified as a fair Princess. All these Princesses are the daughters
of Belial, 'the prince of celestial powers', who lives in a magic
castle in the air. The wide streets of the world run down to an
Unscaleable Wall, through which sinners will go into the Lower
Kingdom of Death. From there they will be cast down into Hell.
The geography of the city is in itself a metaphor for the power of
evil and wickedness. A small, narrow street in the city, running
counter to the streets of sin, completes the spiritual geography of
this world. This is the path of righteousness which leads to the
strait Gate of Everlasting Life. The moral significance of the wide
and the narrow in this first vision is, of course, based on the words
of Christ in the New Testament:

Enter ye in at the strait gate: for wide is the gate, and broad is the way, that leadeth to destruction, and many there be which go in thereat: because strait is the gate, and narrow is the way, which leadeth unto life, and few there be that find it. (Matthew 7.13–14)

The Angel's role in this First Vision—and, in this, his role is consistent with one of the main purposes of the whole book—is to give the Bardd Cwsg, and to give us, a closer look at the world and at sinners. It is this close scrutiny that reveals the ugliness and wickedness of things. In the First Vision the Angel tells the Bardd Cwsg, 'Come nearer to them'. What he sees, in this instance, is a ruined manor:

and in the Street of Pride we descended upon a great, wide, open-ended manor-house, that the dogs and crows had plucked its eyes, and whose owners had left for England, or France, to search there for what would have been a hundred times easier to find at home, so instead of the old charitable goodly country-folk that used to be, there is none now that keeps possession but the foolish Aunty Owl, or scavenging crows, or mottled magpies, or the like to proclaim the feats of the present owners.

Close scrutiny reveals actual details that undermine general assumptions and, in these visions, actual details disclose a world of wickedness.

The First Vision concludes with a battle between Belial and his forces (which include the Pope and Louis XIV of France) on the one hand, and Anne, the queen of England and head of the Anglican Church and the forces of righteousness, on the other. Having seen Belial being beaten, the Bardd Cwsg is woken by the tumult of the fray: 'and wholly against my will I returned to my drowsy sod, and how splendid, how pleasant it was to be a free spirit, especially in such a company, in spite of the danger'. There follows a song entitled 'Behold the Edifice'. The edifice in question is, in the first place, the world which has been defiled by sin. In the second place, it is the true universal and invincible church.

The Second Vision begins in winter, with the Bardd Cwsg musing about the brevity of man's life and the certainty of death. He falls asleep and is accosted by Master Sleep and his sister Nightmare. Master Sleep is there to guide him into the Lower Kingdom of Death, that is, the kingdom where sinners go—those who are meant for heaven would visit Death in his Upper Kingdom and would certainly see another aspect of him. Behind the gates of the City of Destruction, sinners enter the Chambers of Death and then go through the Unscaleable Wall. Above each door is written its peculiar form of death, for instance Hunger is superscribed on the door through which those who died of famine would come and Ambition is written over the door through which those who died of ambition would come. The Bardd Cwsg is given a sleeping potion and wakes up in a barren plain, where nothing but noxious creatures—serpents, tapeworms, toads and flies—thrive. Then there are figures gathering about the Bardd Cwsg, including his namesake who has, so he says, been left in peace in this land for nine hundred years. Among others there are Myrddin (Merlin) and Taliesin. These two were major half-mythical figures in the Welsh oral and literary tradition. Wynne treats them like buffoons, a fact which indicates that he was as sceptical of the mythical history of Wales (and Britain) as some of the more scientific historians of the sixteenth and seventeenth centuries—he was far more sceptical than Theophilus Evans, for example. Eventually the Bardd Cwsg and Master Sleep come to the Court of Death, an edifice of skulls cemented together with tears, sweat, phlegm and pus. Here Death himself—'an extremely narrow King'—was devouring corpses. Following this thoroughly unpleasant section is the sentencing of sinners, where Death dons his robes of shining scarlet and his three-cornered hat inscribed with the words Mourning, Moaning and Woe. Some of what occurs here is serious and some facetious. It is a facetious kind of satire that we see in the arrival of a Papist who addresses Death in this manner:

> 'Sire,' said he, 'let it be known to you that you have no right to detain me, or to interrogate me: I have remission of all my sins by the hand of the Pope himself; for my faithful service to him, he has given me permission to go directly to Paradise, without tarrying an instant in Purgatory.'

He is given short shrift.

More sinners are judged, until we come to seven—not named—who would cause such consternation in Hell that Lucifer, the king of Hell, has written a Miltonic letter to Death urging him to keep them on his side of the Chasm of Perdition. Death replies in a similarly lofty manner. We are now as anxious as the Bardd Cwsg to learn who these monstrous sinners are. It is a satiric and mock-heroic anticlimax to learn that they are Master Busybody, Master Libeller, Master Show-off and so on. They are thrown over the edge of the chasm and the Bardd Cwsg is so frightened by what he sees that he wakes up.

> And I was exceedingly joyful to find myself again amongst the living; and I resolved to live better and better, since a hundred years of affliction in the paths of righteousness were easier for me than having to glimpse again the horror of that night.

The Second Vision is followed by a song about the inevitability of death. Only belief in Christ, repentance, and a good life are of any avail if one is to avoid its bitter sting.

The Third Vision is 'The Vision of Hell'. It begins on a pleasant April morning. The Bardd Cwsg is on the banks of the river Hafren (Severn), amid the joys of nature, and from time to time reading parts of the Welsh translation of *The Practice of Piety*—a book not unlike Taylor's *The Rules and Exercises of Holy Living*. Thoughts of his former visions disturb him and he feels it his duty to write them down as a warning for others. He becomes drowsy and sleeps. As in the First Vision, the Angel appears and acts as his guide through Hell. This vision draws on a whole tradition of writing about the Other World, from classical sources, medieval visions and the seventeenth-century genre of visions already mentioned. The Bardd Cwsg describes, in detail, some of the tortures of Hell:

> I could see devils with pitchforks casting them [the damned] to fall head first on poisonous hackles made of sharp pointed barbs, to writhe by their brains; after a short while they threw them one on top of the other in litters, on to one of the burning rocks to roast like dry gorse. From there they were snatched far away to the top of one of the chasms of eternal ice and snow; then back to a vast torrent of boiling brimstone, to be submerged in conflagrations, and suffocations, and strangulations of unbearable stench; from there to the bog of flies to embrace infernal reptiles, far worse than serpents and vipers; then the devils would take scourges of fiery steel from the furnace, and would beat them till they

howled through the expanse of Hell, because of the terrible, unutterable pain; then they took red-hot irons to sear the bloody wounds.

The Bardd Cwsg is led through various cells in Hell, where he sees all kinds of sinners and all kinds of tortures. Some of these sinners we have seen before, in the First and Second Visions. Wynne is making it plain that Hell is their ultimate destiny.

There is an attempt at insurrection in Hell. Three armies —those of the Turks, the Papists and Roundheads—fill the plains of Hell, and even Cromwell himself breaks out of his kennel. They are put down. Lucifer holds court, and several sinners come before him to be condemned.

The Vision concludes with an infernal parliament to prepare a strategy to conquer what Lucifer calls: 'Britain and the isles about it [which are] the most dangerous kingdom to my government, and fullest of my enemies: And what is a hundred times worse is that now there is [in Britain] the most dangerous queen of all . . .' (Note that Britain, which the Sleeping Bard wished to leave in order to see better realms, is now revealed to be the best of all countries and he realizes how foolish he was to be discontented with his 'own estate and country'.) Various sins offer themselves as Lucifer's lieutenant in Britain: Cerberus, the devil of tobacco; Mammon, the devil of money; Apollyon, the devil of pride, and so on. None of them is chosen. The one whom Lucifer chooses is Hawddfyd (Easy-time) for, says he, it is 'success and ease, plenty and lack of any cares' that best breed fodder for Hell.

The Vision ends with a description of the basis of Hell, the giant figure of Sin with its three faces, a savage face turned towards heaven, a fair and pleasant face towards the world to entice its people to come under its spell, and a terrible face towards Hell.

The book ends with a song on the tune called 'Heavy Heart'. Most stanzas begin with the refrain that the heart is heavy when it thinks on Hell. The last stanza urges the reader to consider the eternal terrors presented and to turn to Christ who will keep his soul from all of them.

The *Gweledigaetheu* has a clear moral purpose: it is meant to save the souls of sinners. But this purpose does not mean that the book is uniformly solemn, though there are large sections of it which display a high seriousness. The serious aspect of the book comes from a long Christian tradition of moralizing, especially as that tradition was represented in the devotional and didactic Welsh books (and translations) of the seventeenth century. The following may serve as an illustration of this aspect of the book: a taverner approaches Lucifer to complain that he had been placed with apothecaries and poisoners in the cell of 'Wet Murder'. Does not a taverner have to make a living? Lucifer responds:

Behold, what evil have we here that you did not have at home, save only the punishment? And to tell you the plain truth here, the infernal heat and cold were not unknown to you either. Did you not see an ember of our fire in the tongues of blasphemers, and the scolds fetching their men home? Was there not much of our inextinguishable fire in the mouth of the drunkard, in the eye of the malicious, and in the crotch of the whore? And could you not see some of the infernal cold in the kindness of the waster, and certainly in your own amiability towards them whilst they had anything, in the drollery of the spiteful, in the praise of the jealous and the libeller, in the promises of the lewd, or in the legs of the good companions freezing under your tables? Is Hell strange to you, when you kept Hell at home? Away you hellhound to your penance.

But there is in the book, as well, a verve and wit and a many-registered vivacity of language which sharpens the satire and enhances its comic aspect. Wynne is especially adept at making sin and sinners disgusting or laughable. The following serve as examples. The first is taken from the First Vision:

From there we went [to a place] where we could hear a loud noise, and thumping and prattling, and crying and laughing, and shouting and singing. 'Well, here's Bedlam sure enough,' said I. After we had gone inside, the affray was over, and one prostrate on the floor, another throwing up, another dozing above a hearthful of dented flagons, and pieces of pipes and cups: and after examination [we found] that it was a carousal among seven thirsty neighbours, a tinker, and a dyer, and a smith, a miner, a chimney-sweeper, a poet, and a priest—who had come to preach sobriety, and to show by his own example how disgusting a thing is drunkenness. And the recent squabble had begun with the argument and contention between them as to which of the seven best liked a pot and pipe; and the poet had won the laurel over all—except the priest, and he, out of respect for his cloth, was given the last word, and accounted the best of the good companions . . .

There is a kind of surreal reasoning in this section which makes the disgusting episode comic and all participants laughable.

The next quotation is taken from the Vision of Hell and refers to
a cell of whores. They attempt to patch up their ugliness. One of
them speaks:

> 'Hell, and double Hell to that mad bull of a nobleman who first began
> to seduce me . . . if he had not, by fair and foul, ploughed the field, I'd
> not have become an open cell to all, and not have come to this infernal
> cell.' . . . After masturbating, others went from hole to hole on heat,
> and pulled devils beneath their feet; sometimes those fled from them,
> and sometimes gave them fire for fire, they would bore them with
> chisels of white-hot steel until they had enough grinding, with their guts
> sizzling and frying.

This passage shows us that there was nothing prim about this
puritanical eighteenth-century rector, and that his word-register
was more than adequate to deal with a multitude of situations.
Here the coarseness of the language is employed to generate a
savage disgust that would not be unworthy of Jonathan Swift.

The *Gweledigaetheu* is a book of forceful satire presented from
within a defined moral framework. The writing is opinionated, but
masterful in its creation of a variety of effects, and Ellis Wynne is
probably the most wide-ranging stylist of all Welsh prose writers.

THEOPHILUS EVANS

Theophilus Evans was another opinionated Anglican clergyman.
He was born in 1693 in a farmhouse called Penywenallt, near
Newcastle Emlyn, Carmarthenshire. There is no record of his
attendance at the grammar school in Carmarthen, though he may
have been educated there. In August 1717, he was ordained deacon
and shortly afterwards was appointed curate in Defynnog,
Brecknockshire, and then in Llanlleonfel, where the antiquarian
Moses Williams was vicar. In 1718 he was ordained rector of these
two parishes. His subsequent appointments were as follows:
1722–8, rector of Llandyfrïog, near his home town; 1728–38,
rector of Llanynys and Llanddulas, Brecknockshire; in 1738 he
became vicar of Llangamarch, a living which he retained until
1763, even though he was also appointed in 1739 to the living of St
David's, Brecon. He resigned the living of Llangamarch (in favour

of his son-in-law) in 1763, but stayed on in Brecon until his death in 1767. He married Alice Bevan from Glamorgan and they had five children. Theophilus Evans's career in the Church seems to have been a successful one. One interesting incident in this career involves William Williams, Pantycelyn, who became one of the leaders of the Methodist Revival of the eighteenth century. In 1740 Williams was appointed curate of Llanwrtyd, Llanfihangel Abergwesyn and Llanddewi Abergwesyn and was responsible to Theophilus Evans. In 1743 his bishop refused to permit Williams full ordination, because of his Methodist beliefs. Theophilus may well have had something to do with this refusal.

Apart from his main work, *Drych y Prif Oesoedd* (A Mirror of the First Ages), Theophilus published sermons, a book entitled *A History of Modern Enthusiasm from the Reformation to the Present Times* (1752), and several translations of religious works, mainly of a disputatious nature, as the original title of one of them will suggest—*A serious call to the Quakers inviting them to return to Christianity*. If he had not written the *Drych* Theophilus Evans would have been long forgotten.

The *Drych* was first published in 1716, when the author was twenty-three years of age. A second, expanded and changed edition was published in 1740. From the number of times the book was published between the author's time and the beginning of the twentieth century it seems to have been a popular work, probably the most popular history book in Welsh since the translation of Geoffrey of Monmouth's Latin work, *Historia Regum Britanniae* (History of the Kings of Britain), composed in the Middle Ages.

In fact, the *Drych* has more in common with Geoffrey's work than it has with history books of the twentieth century for, between Theophilus Evans's time and ours, people's concept of 'history' has changed. Whilst it is probably true that only pedantic historians are concerned with facts about the past and facts only, we take it for granted that respectable historians should get their facts right, that they will have researched whatever sources that are available from the period they are studying. Having done this we expect them to make something of them, to present some kind of thesis, to provide some insight into life in the past. It may well be that the historian's own personality or his nationality and, almost certainly, issues of his own age will colour his attitude to the past and may shape his interpretation of it, but we would expect an interpretation of the past to be based on ascertainable evidence examined in a comprehensive, not a selective, manner. Even so, two historians may look at the same facts and interpret them in different ways. This is probably too idealized a concept of the modern historian. Some of them, of course, openly admit adherence to an ideology and approach the past with attitudes shaped by that ideology—a person may be a Catholic historian or a Marxist historian and may find confirmation for his ideology in the past. Theophilus Evans certainly approached the past with his own interpretation of Christianity, that is, he approached it with a ready-made pattern. Unlike any self-respecting modern historian, of whatever ideology, he had not the means to examine the past in any detail. The careful scrutiny of archaeology and the meticulous searching for documents and sources of information from the past were not among his preoccupations. His 'research' work was nothing like that of the modern historian: for information about ancient times he depended on the Bible and on the evidence of Classical authors; for information about more recent times he turned to the work of Geoffrey of Monmouth and others whom he regarded as historians—writers like James Ussher, Sir John Prys, Humphrey Llwyd, David Powel and others (including Polydore Vergil who had dared to question the reliability of Geoffrey of Monmouth). In his Introduction to the *Drych* of 1716 he says that he consulted his 'Authors' in 'the great, splendid Library belonging to the Free-school of Shrewsbury Town'.

There are two parts to the *Drych*. Part I deals with the antiquity of the Britons, the coming of Christianity to Britain and how this pristine Christianity had been defiled by Catholicism—until it was revived by the Protestantism of the sixteenth century. (This backward look to a pure Christianity, untarnished by the influence of Rome and the Pope, is a version of what has been called 'the Protestant ecclesiastical theory' which first appeared among Welshmen at the time of the Reformation.) In this part, history is interpreted as a revelation of God's will, in exactly the same way as it is interpreted by the prophets of the Old Testament and by early Welsh historians such as Gildas and 'Nennius'. When a nation obeys the will of God, it prospers; and when it disobeys the will of God, great calamities befall it. This is hardly a fashionable interpretation of history today, but it is not as *outré* as is often taken for granted. It is one of the great assumptions of Jewish and Christian thought over many centuries: as a nation (or an individual, for that matter) sows, so shall it reap. It is a moral (rather than, say, an economic or a political) interpretation of history, and some would claim that it is as tenable as most other interpretations.

Part II of the *Drych* defends episcopalianism, the baptism of children, Anglican liturgy and Anglican (and Christian) virtues.

As a historian we have seen that Theophilus Evans adopts, however consciously, a particular attitude towards the past. That attitude had been instilled by his upbringing, his religious education and by his reading. His uncompromising Anglicanism was instilled in much the same way. If we judge his time by its literature and by recorded events it appears that many people were then much preoccupied with religious sectarianism. He, like others of his time, thought that Christian salvation came by belonging to the right church. It follows that matters of liturgy, of the manner of baptism, of many things that may seem to us minutiae of belief were, to him, of eternal importance.

Then there was Theophilus Evans's strong sense of his Welshness and of the nobility of his own people. Nowadays a historian's nationality is not supposed to be of any great consequence in what it is hoped is his objective search for historical evidence. In fact, the study of history has hardly been more nationalistic than in the twentieth century—we have only to consider how Germany or the colonizing countries have used 'history' to realize the truth of this. Theophilus Evans's 'nationalism' is of the uncamouflaged variety.

So far, we have drawn attention to three elements in Evans's presentation of history: his moral interpretation of it, his Anglicanism, his Welsh 'nationalism'. We shall now examine some passages of the *Drych* to see in more detail how he actually wrote his history.

To relate the tribulations and oppressions of the Welsh is a mournful topic, in all ages and countries since Languages were mixed in the Tower of Babel: I can assert with confidence that they are more unfortunate with their earthly possessions than any other nation under the Sun. They were once a glorious race, but mostly more valorous than cunning. But we can still boast this, although we were conquered by the

Romans and the English, we still have our original language if not
altogether whole and complete, yet purer than any other nation in the
world. *They shall keep their Language, but lose their Land*, according to
Myrddin [Merlin]. And if we had not offended God as we did by our
heinous sins, we would not have lost our Land either. And because we
moved the Almighty to wrath, *We have been left few in number, whereas
we were as the Stars of Heaven for Multitude, because we did not obey
the voice of the Lord our God.* Deut. 28.62.

It will certainly seem rather odd to most twentieth-century readers
that this is called 'history'. Surely this is myth of some kind, that is, a
tale that is not literally true, though it may convey an important
truth? Today it may be so, but for many in the eighteenth century
this was literal biblical truth; it was history. We can clearly see the
influence of the Old Testament attitude to history in this paragraph,
just as clearly as we can see Theophilus Evans's 'nationalism' and
his care for his mother tongue. Theophilus Evans insists that the
British became Christians at a very early date:

> Let everyone say what they will to the contrary, we have clear evidence
> from the Most Eminent Teachers to prove that Christianity came here
> early, yes during the youth of the Church. [Here he quotes Gildas, a
> British historian of the sixth century to support his assertion.] . . . Many
> men of learning are of the opinion that Joseph of Arimathea was the
> first who preached salvation in Britain.

Further on he adds:

> Everyone supposes that the Claudia that Paul mentions (2 Tim. 4.21)
> who, among others, was taken to Rome with Caradoc was a Welsh
> woman. And if that is true (and everyone says it is) she could have
> encouraged Paul to go to preach to her fellow-countrymen the British.

Through all this he cites his 'authorities' and sets out his
arguments point by point—this was a common practice of his. He
concludes, carefully: 'I cannot find any more to say, but I state
that many think that Paul and Joseph of Arimathea preached in
Britain.'

What was brought to Britain was the true 'catholic' faith, which
had nothing to do with Popery. This was the true faith that the

early Welsh saints defended. Having referred to Saint Teilo, a saint whom he places about AD 500, Theophilus has this to say: 'His cleric was Samson, who became the Archbishop of Brittany; and Aidan, who so bravely withstood Popery when Augustine was sent by Pope Gregory to preach to the English . . .' When did the Welsh become Papists? 'Our ancestors' only gradually yielded to Popery:

> They were persuaded to accept one article [of faith] now and then, until they finally accommodated the whole rubbish of Popery: And that happened (in my estimation) about the ninth Century: But there is no doubt that the British yielded to Popery about the tenth century of the Christian era . . .

Wales came out of this 'darkness' with the Reformation and with the translation of the Bible into Welsh:

> And from then on knowledge of God went forth extensively among our nation, and the Christian religion was restored to them, as it was in the first Church, when all was within an Evangelical order.

And with the Anglican Church things would have been as they were in the true and first Church had not some been enticed out of it by the plague of schism. We can see that this is a peculiarly 'Anglican' view of British history.

Classical historians—Tacitus, for example—did not think it amiss to quote the words of historical characters, or to embroider descriptions of events, especially of battles. Homer and Virgil, whose influence pervaded the Classical education of the seventeenth and eighteenth centuries, also gave graphic descriptions of events, places and battles. Theophilus Evans follows this custom. He is quite often a lively presenter of history. The sides of Caesar's ships had as many British arrows in them 'as the back of a hedgehog has bristles'; the Roman emperor Severus 'was as full of wrath as a frog is full of poison'; with the invasions of the English the face of Britain was 'more like . . . a volcano like Etna than a fruitful country as it had been before'. These examples have been taken from the 1716 edition. In the 1740 edition they are far more numerous. In fact, the 1740 edition is more colourful, more dramatic, and more direct than the edition of 1716.

Some portions of the 1740 edition have been quoted often to show the quality of Theophilus Evans's style. This section about the fall of the Roman Empire is one of them:

> This kind of unruliness (and this without respite over many years) soon caused the whole of the Roman Empire to rock and disintegrate; like a great ship coming apart, when waves and contrary winds snatch it. Or, like a wide field of wheat being trampled and torn by a herd of swine, unless there be a secure fence about it. Thus Rome and all its might was one piece at a time shattered utterly, because of the many splits within it, and the savage attacks of the barbarians around it. And as a large extensive hall with many rooms cannot fail to be ruined, when it is inhabited by weaklings, so, in like manner, when the soldiers were unruly, and changing masters so often, that is, elevating whoever seemed fit to them to be emperor, and with the slightest quarrel resigning again, it is no wonder that no supreme ruler could keep so many countries in subjection in such circumstances.

Another much quoted passage is his vivid description of the Battle of Bath (Brwydr Baddon):

> And they all met on a mound near Caer Baddon, or Bath in Somerset; namely the traitor Pascen and his men, the English under Eppa and Cerdic two of the chief leaders of the host and on the other side Uthur Bendragon and his hosts, and Nathan Lwyd and his men from Wales. Then after their men had gathered on both sides, began the most savage battle ever perhaps between the Britons and the English. There one could see arrows flying from one host to the other, like a shower of hail together, when a cross wind moves them to and fro. Oh, what a sorry sight would it be to see some with their bowels out; the war-steeds becoming wild in the entrails and innards of others. An occasional dart in the eye socket, and the man still alive becoming mad with pain. The occasional dart in the mouth, half of it this side and half the other side of the neck. Another dart in the brow deeper than its barb, and the brain drivelling out. Another dart falling on the brass breastplate or shield, and sounding hollow like a bell. And a few darts exactly in the heart, stopping the pain in an instant. And on top of all this, instead of physicians to tend their wounds, war-steeds running wild here and there over the wretched wounded; breaking the bones of some, smothering others, knocking out the brains of some, and the hearts and entrails of others.

This is as violent as some of Homer's descriptions. Some have praised the vividness of the writing, drawing as it does on an education where rhetoric (training in the use of words to achieve various effects) had such an important role. But one tends to ask whether these effects are too exaggerated to be plausible, so that they become more comic than tragic. At times Theophilus Evans is straining too hard to achieve his effects—or so it seems to this modern reader.

Some passages are less self-conscious than these, and more effective because the emotion is more real and less rehearsed. Theophilus Evans's passage on the cross in a section on instruments of torture used against Christians is a case in point:

> The Cross deserves to be considered first, not only because it is one of the oldest instruments of execution, but also because it is on the Cross that our Saviour himself was hung to die. And it is not strange that Christians have been persecuted so often in this manner, for if it is thus that they dealt with the owner of the house, how much worse will they deal with his kindred? Two things were accounted terrible in putting to death in this way. The Pain, and the Disgrace. 1. Pain; because whoever suffered was nailed through his feet and hands; and these are the parts where the extremities of the arteries are, and therefore they are more sensitive to pain than any other part. And besides this, the Feet and the Hands are the parts furthest from the Heart, the source of the body's life; so whoever was put to death would be a long time dying. 2. It was a shameful death, only dealt in pre-Christian times to Traitors and Slaves.

Another passage where Theophilus Evans's feeling for true Christian values is expressed with a quiet intensity is this one, which deals with the manners of the first Christians:

> Their care to contribute to the needs of the poor brethren was great. They would not eat the greatest delicacies with any enjoyment if it was known that one of the brethren was in need. Can we be joyful (they said) when our brother is sorrowful? Can we be easy in our hearts, with our brother in pain and affliction? Can we eat and drink, with our brother needy and unprovided? Will the Lord allow us to treat our fellow-soldier in this way, when he is of one faith with us? Will he be allowed to die of hunger, whilst we live in the midst of plenty? Glory to thee Lord Jesus, who has taught us better things.

Theophilus Evans was a historian in the old Classical manner; he was influenced by his reading of the Classics and of other more recent historians. He was, it may seem to us, rather gullible even for his own period, though from time to time he does express some reservations about some characters and events. But they have to be pretty odd for that to happen! He is a colourful reciter of his history, and can enliven descriptions with homely sayings or striking—or sometimes strained—comparisons and metaphors. He was, as we have seen, a committed Welshman and an Anglican, and was opinionated in much the same way as many of his contemporaries, but his *Drych* also shows that he had a strong realization of the true values of Christianity. In the end his history reveals something of his own character, it shows some individuality, and that is at least one feature of a memorable work of literature.

BIBLIOGRAPHY

Ellis Wynne
Text
Patrick Donovan and Gwyn Thomas (eds.), *Gweledigaethau y Bardd Cwsg* (Llandysul, 1998).

Studies
Garfield H. Hughes, 'Tom Brown ac Ellis Wynne', *Journal of the Welsh Bibliographical Society*, VII (1950–3), 144–50.
R. M. Jones, *Angau Ellis Wynne* (Llandybïe, 1968).
Saunders Lewis, 'Y Bardd Cwsc' and 'Gweledigaeth Angau', in R. Geraint Gruffydd (ed.), *Meistri'r Canrifoedd* (Caerdydd, 1973), 206–16, 217–24.
D. Tecwyn Lloyd, 'Ellis Wynne o Lasynys', in Geraint Bowen (ed.), *Y Traddodiad Rhyddiaith* (Llandysul, 1970), 247–60.
Derec Llwyd Morgan, 'Darllen "Cwrs y Byd"', in J. E. Caerwyn Williams (ed.), *Ysgrifau Beirniadol X* (Dinbych, 1997), 257–66.
Gwyn Thomas, *Y Bardd Cwsc a'i Gefndir* (Caerdydd, 1971).
Idem, *Ellis Wynne* (Cardiff, 1984).

Theophilus Evans
Text
Samuel J. Evans, *Drych y Prif Oesoedd* (Bangor, 1902), 1740 edition.
Garfield H. Hughes, *Drych y Prif Oesoedd* (Caerdydd, 1961), 1716 edition.

Studies

D. Ellis Evans, 'Theophilus Evans ar hanes cynnar Prydain', *Y Traethodydd* (1973), 92–113.

Garfield H. Hughes, *Theophilus Evans a Drych y Prif Oesoedd* (Llandybïe, 1963).

R. T. Jenkins, 'Theophilus Evans ar "Modern Enthusiasm"', *Yr Apêl at Hanes* (Wrecsam, 1930), 35–46.

Bedwyr Lewis Jones, 'Theophilus Evans' in Dyfnallt Morgan (ed.), *Gwŷr Llên y Ddeunawfed Ganrif* (Llandybïe, 1966), 30–46.

Idem, 'Theophilus Evans' in Geraint Bowen (ed.), *Y Traddodiad Rhyddiaith* (Llandysul, 1970), 262–75.

John Gwilym Jones, 'Gwerth *Drych y Prif Oesoedd* fel hanes', in J. E. Caerwyn Williams (ed.), *Ysgrifau Beirniadol IV* (Dinbych, 1969), 83–97.

Prys Morgan, 'Y ddau Theophilus: sylwadau ar hanesyddiaeth', *Taliesin*, 19 (1969), 36–45.

David Thomas, 'Cysylltiadau hanesyddol a llenyddol Theophilus Evans', *Y Llenor*, xviii (1939), 46–56.

Idem, 'Drych y Prif Oesoedd', *Y Traethodydd* (1951), 117–25.

CHAPTER 4

THE MORRIS BROTHERS

GERALD MORGAN

It would be good to believe that the extraordinarily talented quartet of literary brothers from Anglesey, Lewis, Richard, William and John Morris, were appreciated for their genius in their lifetime, but that was hardly the case. John (1706–40) died young of fever on board ship, leaving only a handful of letters. Richard (1703–69), founder of the Honourable Society of Cymmrodorion, lived a frantically busy life as a civil servant in London, and William (1705–63) remained in Anglesey, Collector of Customs at Holyhead, known only to a small circle of littérateurs and gardeners. Lewis (1701–65) alone achieved some measure of fame, and not a little notoriety; he was the Crown's representative in the Cardiganshire lead-mining industry, attempted to found the first Welsh magazine, surveyed much of the Welsh coast for the Admiralty (1737–48), and saw some of his poems published in *Y Diddanwch Teuluaidd* (1763) only two years before his death. Yet he never completed what he felt was his major work, the encyclopaedic *Celtic Remains*: half was published a hundred years after his death, and the other half remains in manuscript. Of the poets and scholars he taught and encouraged, Evan Evans (Ieuan Fardd) did not fulfil his potential, and Goronwy Owen emigrated to America, while others sank virtually without trace.

It was only in the twentieth century that the publication of the letters of the Morris brothers, and those of their nephew John Owen and many letters by others in their circle of acquaintance, brought them recognition. More than a thousand letters survive from the four brothers and their nephew, most of them written to each other, and many of them long and vivid. Many hundreds of other letters have been lost, almost certainly for ever. The Morris letters are remarkable not only in themselves, but for the very suddenness with which they seem to have come into being. Correspondence was not a Welsh-language skill in the sixteenth and seventeenth centuries; there is nothing in Welsh to compare with the late medieval Paston letters in English, or the correspondence of Dorothy Temple in the seventeenth century. Barely a handful of letters in Welsh survive before Richard Morris went to London at the age of twenty and began to write home. It is fairly easy to explain why there should have been so little correspondence in Welsh during the seventeenth century: the gentry and their associates (such as the clergy) received a completely Anglicized education. Similarly, hardly any Welsh-language documents survive among the thousands of seventeenth-century wills made by Welsh men and women, although the probate authorities were content to accept them. During the eighteenth century, however, hundreds of Welsh-language documents appear among the probate records, especially in the diocese of Bangor. There was a rejuvenation of the language in written practical use which is not easy to explain.

How the Morrises themselves learnt to read and write is still a mystery, for they tell us little about their education. Their father, Morris Prichard (1674–1763), must have been a key figure. A farmer and cooper, he could write vigorous Welsh. Certainly his sons were raised literate in both Welsh and English. It seems unlikely that they attended the grammar schools at Beaumaris or Bangor, since they had little Latin and less Greek, while the grammar-school curriculum of the time was almost entirely Classical. The brothers only knew enough Greek to be able to use the Greek alphabet to disguise minor obscenities, or in Lewis's case to conceal comments which he did not wish his wife to see. The Bible was part of their culture, and they knew the contemporary minor poets of Anglesey and Caernarfonshire who preserved, and composed in, the strict metres of Welsh poetry, in which Lewis particularly became skilled.

The Morrises and their friends were especially fortunate that the postal service had improved by their day, and that they could call on Richard as a civil servant and on their parliamentary acquaintances for 'franks', which enabled many of their letters to be sent free of charge. It was certainly easier to correspond than to travel, especially once William had settled in Holyhead (visiting Ireland once), Lewis in Cardiganshire (with one prolonged visit to London) and Richard in London, visiting Wales only once in fifty years, to rescue Lewis's manuscripts after his death. In their

unmarried youth, of course, things had been different: William
had sailed to Liverpool and worked there, Lewis surveyed much of
the Welsh coast, John joined the Navy and died in Gibraltar, while
the teenage Richard escaped from Anglesey to London.

It is not surprising, given the improved postal service and
extended literacy, that the eighteenth century was an age of great
letter-writers in England. Nor is it unexpected that the best
correspondents of the age, such as Horace Walpole, wrote quantities of letters which remain highly readable. Horace Walpole, son
of a prime minister and a wealthy dilettante, had both leisure to
write and connections to supply him with gossip and scandal, in
which he delighted. He wrote as a man conscious that his letters
would be circulated and appreciated. Walpole was the wealthy son
of a famous politician, and hobnobbed with the quality. Of the
Morrises, only William had much leisure; Lewis was constantly
preoccupied with many distractions, and Richard with over-
working. All three had pressing family problems and varying
degrees of financial worries, and William and Lewis spent much
energy on that enemy of correspondence, gardening, as well as
many other hobbies. The only Welsh letter-writer who approached
the style of Walpole is Lewis Morris when writing to his friends,
especially Edward Richard and William Vaughan. Then, he forgot
family business, largely abandoned verbal pugilism, and concentrated on entertaining the recipient.

By and large however we cannot expect in the Morris correspondence the same degree of literary self-consciousness typical
of the finest letters of Walpole or Samuel Johnson. For much of
the time the brothers wrote as they thought, hurling a virtual
stream-of-consciousness onto the paper with no overall regard
for form, paragraphing but rarely, and knowing that oblique
references, hints and undertones, which today escape or exasperate
us, would be understood. However, as well as a thousand vivid
asides and brief comments, more extended passages show how self-
consciously artistic they could be. Here is William on an Anglesey
scandal, writing in Welsh which is a brilliant meld of medieval and
biblical and which loses much in translation:

> Jones, [vicar] of Llanvair and Llanbedr [is] an empty fellow. I'll tell you
> a comic tale of him and old uncle Owain Parri the carpenter. Owain
> lives in a house of Mr Meyrick's called Glyn Llanbedr, and with him

there lodges Jones the priest, and one night Owain heard a noise, and suspected that the maid was going in to the priest, so he silently arose and stood in a corner close to the man's room. Before long Owain saw the maid come stealthily forth and go to her own bed, so Owain returned to his wife. In the morning when he rose, he said to her, 'Siân, this girl can no longer stay in my house, since she is fornicating with the priest; I saw her in the small hours of the night coming in her shirt from his room.' Then Siân called on the servant-maid, and the priest too came to the place. Then both maid and priest swore oaths that Owain had seen a vision, that he could not be believed, and so between them and his wife, the poor wretch had to hold his tongue. But in the fullness of time he had the pleasure of seeing the birth of a thumping baby-priest, to the satisfaction of all parties. (tr.)

Lewis, too, could be a master of narrative when he chose, as when he relates to Edward Richard a disaster which smote him in the middle of a long and serious illness:

On the 22nd at 10 at night being in a violent sweat in the height of my fever, the chimney of my bedroom took fire, which in a few minutes blazed up to the clouds, or several yards high at least with great noise. It threw lumps of fire on a thatched house adjoining and down the chimney even all over the room and under my bed. As it pleased God my servants were not gone to bed, they followed my directions, and immediately my room was all afloat, and the fire extinguished. I was as little able to bear water as fire, but bear both I was obliged.

The letters of the Morrises, their nephew John Owen (d.1759) and their circle, are a well-spring of supple, vigorous language, whether English or Welsh, for the brothers were masters of both. Some of their correspondents, on the other hand, preferred one language or the other. When writing to each other the brothers frequently switched from Welsh to English and back with infuriating inconsistency. Here, for example, is Richard gossiping:

Rhodri Mawr has left Portsmouth, now resides in town with gwraig fechan bach [a tiny little wife/woman]. Grumbles horribly at the Commissioner putting dyn mwyn synhwyrol [a sensible mild man] over his head . . . Told me the other day he was to dine with Brych in town, ond nid oes goel arno mwy nag ar din dyn bach.

This macaronic style is typical; so is the use of nicknames, which the brothers loved to coin for their acquaintances, especially scurrilous ones: Rhodri Mawr was an early Welsh king, whose name is used mockingly; and 'brych' = afterbirth. They also loved earthy expressions, like that last clause of Richard Morris's, which translates as: 'he's no more to be depended upon than a baby's bum'. Unfortunately J. H. Davies and Hugh Owen, the editors of the Morris letters, felt constrained to censor them, thus depriving them of some of their colour and bite.

Nevertheless, reading these letters suddenly makes it possible to sit at a Welshman's elbow and listen to him grumbling, rejoicing, reminiscing, laughing, exclaiming, gossiping, moralizing and, perhaps above all, coughing. Like their father, the Morrises coughed heroically, and like most men and women of their time they suffered a great deal of ill-health with very little in the way of real medicine. Lewis complained of his condition:

> my teeth acking, my face swolln, my mouth in a manner shut, my stomach craving, my lungs refusing most things—every inch of me afflicted with the rheumatism, the whole system of my fluids being stagnant.

Lewis was enormously fat in later life, and could jest about it in describing his young, pregnant second wife—'my wife is coughing fiercely, and her belly is as big as mine' (tr.); William was even blunter, writing to Lewis: 'Siôn the Weaver next door has a slack-bellied short-legged black pig; I think of you every time I see it, you'd never believe how fat and decrepit it is' (tr.). All three brothers grew fat, though William protested at the accusation:

> Is a man fat who can walk five or six miles before dinner, through bog and brake and frost, his gun on his shoulder, following wild duck, partridge, woodcock, bittern, crows, thrushes . . . swans and wild geese?

Despite such mocking, the brothers took great delight in writing and reading their correspondence. William commented to Richard: 'One of my greatest pleasures is reading in their letters my intimates' gossip, sharing their secrets at a distance, since I have been separated from them' (tr.). William in particular chose correspondence as a means of satisfying what Lewis called 'the itch of scribbling'. He kept a shorthand diary, now lost, which may have helped recall the many vivid details with which he filled his pages. He knew too how to convey intimacy:

> There's hardly any stir in my little house, only a lad and a girl, and an elderly maid, a dog, a tabby, a turtle dove, and four tame rabbits, and half a dozen hens in a cage, and plenty of mice . . . . (tr.)

> Here I am starting to answer your letters while dinner roasts over a slow fire . . . (tr.)

> Siani and Angharad are playing cards with their friends . . . in our sister's house, and the maid has had leave to go to the *noson lawen*, so here's not a soul in the world but me and the dog and the grey cat and the dove cooing. (tr.)

He delighted in portraying himself as the dunce of the family, supposedly lacking the swift wit and brains of his brothers. Yet his botanical and horticultural skills made him a respected correspondent of the leading British scientists of the day, and Hugh Davies's important *Welsh Botanology* (1813) almost certainly owed much to William's groundwork.

Gardens and gardening are a constant theme in the correspondence, more especially of William and Lewis, since Richard dwelt in the city. Lewis boasted of his fruit: 'I never saw my apple trees looking so well as they do. Solomon in all his pride was a fool beside them.' He enjoyed the pastoral aspect of his country life:

> Forty-five people were here yesterday harvesting my rye, and some peas. Breakfast was bread, cheese, milk and whey. For dinner, flummery and milk and bread-and-butter, but supper was the big meal, a brewpanful of beef, mutton, carrots, potatoes and broth with wheatflour dumplings, and twenty gallons of small beer and twenty gallons of ale, with the strings in the red wooden fiddle and a fiddler playing to them when they'd filled their bellies, and out to the barn on the wooden floor, dancing till they sweated freely, with a jugful of beer at their knees, and tobacco for every one. This is the life! (tr.)

William, the botanist, took gardening even more seriously, when he was not engaged in restoring Llanfigel church, leading the music in Holyhead church or doctoring the complaints of the local sick. He delighted in his apples:

lemon pippin, golden pippin, golden renet, Holand pippin . . . black
pippin, Conway darling (Called by some Chester permain), summer
queening, billasin, Royal George, French russetting, Kent codlin,
summer belabon, nonpareil . . .

Unlike Lewis, he gives quite a full description of his own garden,
which must have been one of the most remarkable in Wales:

There was never a more foolish fellow than I am, trying to raise an
orchard on sea-rock, and yet I have wonderful fruit, owing to cross
shelters. Let me see how many have I, 24 or 25, including the walls,
espaliers, elm, lime, and beech hedges, and these to break the violence of
the north-east and south-west winds, which blow up and down the
garden, which unluckily is a slope facing the north-east, and divided
into 3 gardens, with 3 or 4 steps descending to each of the 2 low'st. The
southerly and westerly winds does me no harm, the garden being narrow
and well hedged with quick, elm, elder, etc. My willow holt comes on
bravely, you can scarcely see the belfry from the Custom House.

Hares were a frequent menace to William's horticulture:

Never in my life have I lost so much to a hare as I've done this year,
coming to my garden as it did every night for two months. Finally I was
so angry that I called out my neighbours with their whippets and
hunting-dogs and clubs . . . and I had the pleasure of eating it at my
table, and I never tasted better. (tr.)

In their outlook on the world the Morrises were typical men of
the Enlightenment, cherishing constitutional stability and deplor-
ing political agitation and religious enthusiasm. They combined a
professed detestation of the English and a fierce Welsh patriotism
with complete loyalty to the Hanoverian dynasty and the union of
Wales with England. Politically they were British nationalists. As
Richard expresses it: 'Great Britain was never so famous among
the nations as she is today; she is victorious in every quarter of the
world, and the boasting arrogance of the false French has been
humbled in the dust' (tr.). The 1745 insurrection under Charles
Stuart held no appeal. To William, the Scots invaders were 'a
bunch of bare-arsed Highlanders' (tr.). Such loyalty did not, however, prevent Lewis Morris from commenting, after the death of
the Prince of Wales in 1751, that he was a fool. Their Christianity

was a faith the brothers took for granted, commenting that every misfortune was God's will, and that the dead were happily released from this vale of tears. William expressed this general scepticism well enough:

> 'Tis a great gift of Providence that the more we see of the world, the worst every honest considerate man must like it . . . the bulk of mankind is compos'd of knaves, fools, and now and then by meere chance an honest fellow, but they are cursed scarce in these parts.

He particularly detested Methodists:

> Is John Wesley a saint? I heard his brother preach the other day in a tavern doorway, and either he was mad or supposed everyone else to be so, like one preaching to a gang of ignorant and irreligious pagans. (tr.)

Nevertheless he saw the virtues of the Anglican Griffith Jones's circulating schools, and defended them vigorously. This tolerance he even extended to Catholics, remarking when in Ireland that the wealthy Lord Trimblestown 'is now soliciting some liberties . . . for the Papists. What matter which Christianity for an honest man?'

Lewis, while willing enough to take the Church of England for granted, loathed the Anglo-Welsh bishops. Of the bishop of Bangor, he opined that the man was 'filthy, stinking and useless'. He refers to the English as 'those Vermin [who] had the Management of all the Island under them till Hen. 8th's Time', and to English clergymen in Welsh livings as being 'as fit for the Business, as an Elephant to breed Goslings'. As for religion in London, Lewis commented:

> Religion in this country is quite out of taste, it is such an old fashiond thing. I am positive if Mahomet had any dareing fellows to preach him here, he would gain ground immediately, or any merry religion like that.

Richard Morris shared these basic attitudes with his brothers, although both he and William were much more mild-mannered and tolerant than the irascible Lewis, and William at least much more pious. Richard in particular, as was natural in a Londoner, knew the English better, and could say 'we retain the greatest regard for the English nation in general and their Language'.

Though Richard was not the first Welshman to see that London was, in that age, the only cultural capital Wales had, he did more than anyone to exploit that truth, establishing the Honourable Society of Cymmrodorion in 1751 with the enthusiastic support of his brothers. Traditional Welsh literary culture was suspended uneasily between the age of the manuscript and the printing press. The presses of London, Shrewsbury and Carmarthen were successful in circulating a mass of religious literature, almanacs and ballads, but classical Welsh poetry and medieval prose remained buried in libraries. One of the brothers' many achievements was to copy and circulate this literature, and encourage others to do likewise, especially Evan Evans (Ieuan Fardd), the greatest Welsh literary scholar of the age. William wrote with mixed pride and envy:

> True, I have a number of Dafydd ap Gwilym's cywyddau that Lewis lacks; I have twenty-seven altogether, but [Lewis] in Gallt Fadog has eleven score of them! What a pleasure it would be to see them in print, it's a shame that so many of them are lewd. (tr.)

Lewis Morris was determined to break out of this bind, bringing a press to Bodedern in Anglesey and publishing in 1735 the first and only number of a Welsh-language periodical, *Tlysau yr Hen Oesoedd*, but after that the press lay idle. Lewis in particular was patronizingly scornful of the efforts of other less sophisticated figures (Dafydd Jones of Trefriw, Huw Jones of Llangwm) to publish Welsh poetry, and it was no thanks to him that much of his own best poetry was eventually printed in *Y Diddanwch Teuluaidd* (1763).

Intellectually, Lewis Morris was the most ambitious of the brothers. Polymathic in his interests but lacking intellectual discipline, he combined real insight with vain speculation. Fascinated by place-names, he commented acutely that 'no words [are] more ancient than names of waters and mountains'. He rightly ridiculed the claims made on behalf of Macpherson's Ossianic poems, and when it was suggested to him that the *tomenni* or artificial hummocks which occur frequently in the Welsh countryside were Roman altars, he replied by distinguishing between those mounds which were motte-and-bailey castles and those which were 'the Tombs of Gt. Men among the Brittains, perhaps before they were a province to the Romans'. In more expansive mode, he wrote a brilliant letter analysing the *penillion telyn* or folk-verses which still give readers of Welsh such delight.

On the other hand, Lewis believed passionately that the medieval Welsh translation of Geoffrey of Monmouth's *Historia Regum Britanniae* (History of the Kings of Britain) was really the original from which Geoffrey had worked, and that the Celtic languages were the source from which other European languages had borrowed extensively. It was not Lewis Morris but his protegé Evan Evans who, despite many handicaps, was able to present the world with the first published edition of early Welsh poetry, giving the texts with both English and Latin versions, as well as the first history of Welsh poetry, all in his *Some Specimens of the Poetry of the Antient Welsh Bards* (1764). Nor was it peppery Lewis but sensible William who summarized so succinctly the qualifications needed to be a Celtic scholar:

> Sufficient wealth. A head, with a share of brains. Learning, especially in Welsh, Celtic and other ancient languages. Time to study them, with little else to hinder him. An honest heart . . . A bold spirit, under control. A burning desire to carry him far and near to visit every antiquity. Good nature, and what else? A thousand other things.

Richard Morris experimented with verse in his youth, and William knew his *cynghanedd*, but Lewis was the family's poet, writing in both English and Welsh. His English verse is pleasant enough, particularly his ballad 'The Fishing Maid of Hakin', while his Welsh verse tends to the scabrous. He produced an elegy to a London whore ('known to every Welsh gentleman'), and his 'Cywydd y Pais' (the Petticoat Poem) is lewdly effective. He also experimented with a kind of rhetorical-comic writing, particularly to please his friend William Vaughan, the vigorously Welsh-patriotic squire of Nannau, MP for Merioneth and president of the Cymmrodorion.

As far as his busy life allowed, Richard Morris shared in the copying and circulating of Welsh literature, both classical and popular. He did his best for the folk-publishers Dafydd Jones and Huw Jones, and made the Cymmrodorion buy generous numbers of books published by subscription, though they often remained unsold to the members, so Richard must often have been out of pocket. He was the first layman to be given the task of editing the Welsh Bible and the Book of Common Prayer when the Society for the Promotion of Christian Knowledge decided on a new edition to be published in 1745. Richard brought a high standard of orthography and editorial accuracy to this and the subsequent edition of 1752, and he ensured the republication of the Book of Common Prayer in a sumptuous illustrated edition (1770). William enthusiastically supported Richard's work on the Bible:

> Truly this is a wonderful work, you can now lie on your couch in ease! There has never been so much fighting over books in Anglesey, people have been ready to tear Parson Ellis's eyes out for a copy. (tr.)

Lewis painted a fine word-picture of Richard:

> Richard is a true son of his father, he does not love advice, but knows it to be good, and would follow it if it came by chance. Positive, precipitate, indefatigable, quick enough and ingenious, but too credulous; loves his country to excess, and for that reason his countrymen, who all impose upon him that he deals with, and he chuses to deal with them because they are his countrymen, and I would for my part sooner deal with a Turk or a Jew than with a London Welshman. He owns they are rogues, but like the hare he loves to lie near the dog kennel. I am afraid that foolish meeting of Cymmrodorion will make an end of him, for he stays there till one, two, three or four in the morning, and sometimes comes as far as his door... and there sleeps till the watch awake him, or did use to sleep drunk on the vault for four or five hours and afterwards cough for a month.

Lewis's words have infuriated London Welshmen to this day, but he delighted in such savage opinions, commenting for example that Aberystwyth town was 'full of Hottentots'.

Even the mild William was capable of inhuman comment when the subject was Goronwy Owen. The brothers were certainly driven to exasperation by Goronwy, whose poetry thrilled them with its promise of a new greatness in Welsh literature, and whose drunken, careless ways infuriated them. Lewis summed up their attitude: 'What poet ever flew higher? What beggar, tinker, or sowgelder ever groped more in the dirt? A tomturd man is a gentleman to him.' William, hearing that Goronwy's wife and child had died on their voyage to America, wrote: 'What splendid news that Elin, Goronwy's wife, has gone to heaven and her little son with her, so that the muse will have peace to sing' (tr.). Such a comment would have been typical of Lewis, but comes surprisingly from the gentle William who, for example, urged the kind treatment of children rather than the harsh discipline which he had heard that Lewis inflicted on his children.

Children and family affairs naturally occupy a share of the correspondence, though the brothers' attitudes to women and children could be cavalier enough. Richard in particular never mentions the names of his first two wives (he had four), and John Morris offered sardonic comment on the way his brother had married without bothering to tell anyone else:

> You speak of your Llewelyn and Meirian! Has the Devil found a weakness in the gentleman? Where should I have heard of them? It's not possible that you can be married, and have children, without my ever hearing of it. You must have acquired them by chance (I ask my sister-in-law's pardon if I'm wrong, but how do I know who she is?). (tr.)

William, who married late, was as casual as Richard: 'I confess I am somewhat to blame that I had not told you of my alteration, which I would have done had I not thought you dead or indifferent . . .' (tr.). One would scarcely credit from this that William was in fact a doting husband who mourned long after his wife's death, and never remarried, though he did not enjoy his loneliness. Richard was certainly fortunate in his third wife, to whom he refers with the greatest affection, writing for instance to his father: 'I'm blessed that I have a wife who cares for me with such tenderness, otherwise I could never hold up' (tr.).

Lewis married twice, the second time when he was fifty to a woman half his age for whom he came to express respect, despite his usually sardonic tongue, for her courage and ability; his nephew John Owen, who lived with the family for a while, christened her 'the Captain' in his letters to his other uncles. Lewis commented with remarkable gentleness on Richard's third wife, telling him: 'Make much of your wife, for I find her to be good and innocent, with none of the stubbornness and spirit of contradiction which affects most women of every class . . .' (tr.). Lewis himself certainly displayed stubbornness and contradiction, and when separated from his wife on his long and litigious visits to London, he could both show his concern for her and be unfaithful. John Owen came to hate his uncle, and left a vitriolic description of his London lechery:

> he's been lodging out of town with an old Welshwoman, and one night he came to an agreement with the maid for what she might do, and next morning the two got up at five . . . and went to it, with the girl spread out on a table, but as bad luck would have it another lodger got up before time, went downstairs and found him screwing her sorely, so he [sc. the lodger] did nothing to hinder them, but passed out through another door without being seen. I've only just heard this, and it's true—what an old lecher!—and yet there's no one honest in the world beside himself—all are whores, strumpets and thieves. (tr.)

The brothers' comments on childbirth could be coarse in the extreme. Using a favourite expression, William wrote to Richard expecting to hear of a birth to Lewis Morris's wife Anne, 'I had expected to hear before now from Penbryn that his wife was on the straw', i.e. in labour like a cow. Nevertheless, William appreciated Margaret's courage in having ridden from Cardiganshire to Anglesey and back in an advanced state of pregnancy. As we have already seen, John Owen could be even coarser than his uncles. He observes of his cousin Margaret (Lewis's daughter) and her husband-to-be Robert Lance: 'I hear from others that Robert dangles his cock after cousin Margaret, and she's as hot for the deed as a dog for butter' (tr.). Lewis's disparaging comments on women may exasperate his modern readers, but he was maddened by his foolish daughter Peggy, who seems to have inherited much of his character but little of his intelligence. He could actually write to his wife, commenting on Peggy (who was her stepdaughter), expressing the common prejudice of his sex and many ages:

> You know what kind of a thing a woman is when her tail is ripe. She, like other animals, will jump at any animal that offers; all reason and sense is then gone. But it is not quite so with man in general, though it is with some. Man will hearken to reason . . .

Peggy paid swiftly for her folly, dying young, apparently of venereal disease caught from her husband.

Children, as ever, could be sources of despair and sadness as well as delight. Richard Morris doted on his children, especially his son Richard: 'Little Dick Morris is here on my knee wriggling and hindering me from writing . . .' But tragedy followed:

Yesterday at six in the evening my dear boy Dicci died, the dearest child under the sun. He was taken with a violent purging, which continued for 12 days, till at last he died convulsed, all the apothecary's medicines could not stop it. We must have a couplet in *cynghanedd* on his tomb, under the lines for Llywelyn. What shall I say?

Lewis responded to the request with a moving poem. He was himself familiar with loss, writing from London to his wife:

[I heard] an account of our poor child's death, which gives me very great concern, especially as the whole weight is upon your self, and that it is not in my power to administer you any comfort in your trouble.

Like Richard, Lewis could indulge paternal feelings:

The boys are home from school, and within a quarter hour I was playing the fiddle for five of my chicks, the eldest but ten years old, with another at his nurse's breast and it seems another in the oven.

William commented to Richard on Lewis's patriarchal nature when he had a letter from the latter: 'There were three Lewis Morrises present, father, son and grandson, which plenteousness gave not a little contentment' (tr.).

*   *   *

Letters convey the untidiness of real life in a way that art does not usually seek to imitate, and the deaths of their writers frustrate us, because their life-stories are not rounded as tidily as those of characters in plays or novels. Of the brothers, William is the one who most successfully conveys his love of life. When he brews mead, he invites Lewis to come to Anglesey to share it; he enjoys sea-bathing; he boasts of his acquaintances in Britain, Ireland and New York; he delights in his visit to Phoenix Park, Dublin ('the most heaven-like place I have ever been in' though 'I did not

meet . . . any as good a botanist as myself, except one Dr Jenkins');
he rejoices in his garden:

> Dear Brother, the weather is summery, my garden is lovely, its dress
> green, with multicoloured flowers, and their scent rising like a mist
> from the islands of the east—who could bear to sit about in the house?
> Yet I must take a pen in hand for this occasion, though my eyes are in
> pain from reading St John's Day accounts . . . (tr.)

William's sudden decline in health therefore comes rather
unexpectedly to the reader. Although suffering from this and that,
and especially the cough, he seems to have been suddenly overwhelmed in 1763: 'My teeth are out of all order. Some drawn, 4
loose and very painful, and the rest of them are not sensitive either
to hot or cold.' There follows a long description of his aches and
pains including his balding greying pate, his eyesight and stye, his
throat, boils, constipation, piles, left thigh and right knee. His
shoulder hurt, and he put on it a poultice of Burgundy pitch, wax
and frankincense, commenting with his old humour 'if it's no
better, at least it's no worse'.

But it was worse. William's last letter tells Lewis of the death of
their father, and briefly of his own complaints, which brought his
death within a few days (29 December 1763). Both Lewis and
Richard wrote anxiously enquiring the fate of William's manuscripts, but within eighteen months Lewis too was dead (11 April
1765), and on that occasion Richard made his one and only return
journey to Wales in fifty years, to save his brother's papers, which
with his own are now in the British Library. Richard himself
remained alone of the four brothers for another fourteen years,
writing letters quite frequently until 1771, but little survives from
his last years. He died in December, 1779.

Even had we not a single Morris letter, the brothers would have
left their mark on Welsh life and letters, thanks to the valuable
manuscript copies of medieval literature they made, the encouragement they gave to other writers and scholars, to Lewis's
poetry and Richard's editing of the Bible. But it is their letters, not
simply in their volume but in the quality of so much of the
material, that make them unique. The correspondence is of course
a quarry, not itself a work of art. The letters provide endless
material for social historians, but their literary significance lies in

the brilliant expression of that material, the neologisms, the humour, the vigorous dialect, the literary allusions, the wistful nostalgia expressed in a language so pungent or so subtle as to defy translation—yet one must attempt it once more, citing William's wry consideration of his widowerhood:

The flesh murmurs in your ear, I swear, that the Bible is a fine thing, but a virtuous wife much finer. The spirit whispers in opposition that 'tis better to marry the Bible than an empress; you tell me I must search, but search I will not. There's a calf of a woman who's caught me in a net and yet refuses to feed on me, and were I to hang myself I could not escape her clutches. Ten to one but I'd be happier with my own two chicks than were I to get some feather-headed eligug [guillemot], but who knows? Were she young, there'd be getting of children, and I'm old to deal with them. If the maiden were old, I'd be as well off without her as with her. There would have to be one of the middling kind somewhere, but here is no such thing. (tr.)

Nowhere in Welsh literature before the novels of Daniel Owen, and scarcely even then, do we encounter such rich variety of human nature as in the letters of Lewis, Richard and William Morris.

BIBLIOGRAPHY

J. H. Davies (ed.), *The Letters of Lewis, Richard, William and John Morris of Anglesey (Morrisiaid Môn) 1728–1765* (Aberystwyth, 1907, 1909).

R. T. Jenkins and Helen M. Ramage, *A History of the Honourable Society of Cymmrodorion, and of the Gwyneddigion and Cymreigyddion Societies (1751–1951)* (London, 1951).

Charlotte Johnston, 'The Morris Letters', *Transactions of the Anglesey Antiquarian and Field Club* (1993), 19–38.

Bedwyr Lewis Jones, 'Rhyddiaith y Morrisiaid' in Geraint Bowen (ed.), *Y Traddodiad Rhyddiaith* (Llandysul, 1970), 276–92.

Tegwyn Jones, *Y Llew a'i Deulu* (Tal-y-bont, 1982).

Hugh Owen, *Additional Letters of the Morrises of Anglesey (1735–1786)*, *Cymmrodor*, xlix (1947–9); Hugh Owen also produced invaluable indexes to the four volumes of letters, originally in the *Transactions of the Anglesey Antiquarian Society and Field Club* (1942, 1943 and 1944), also printed separately.

Idem, *The Life and Works of Lewis Morris (Llewelyn Ddu o Fôn) 1701–1765,* (Llangefni, 1951).

D. Lleufer Thomas, 'Lewis Morris in Cardiganshire', *Cymmrodor*, xv (1901), 1–87.

Dafydd Wyn Wiliam, *Cofiant William Morris* (Llangefni, 1995).

Idem, *Lewis Morris: Deugain Mlynedd Cyntaf ei Oes 1700/1–42* (Llangefni, 1997).

Idem, *Cofiant Richard Morris (1702/3–79)* (Llangefni, 1999).

J. E. Caerwyn Williams, 'Cymraeg y Morrisiaid' in *Llên a Llafar Môn* (Llangefni, 1963) 132–59.

CHAPTER 5

GORONWY OWEN:
NEOCLASSICAL POET AND CRITIC

BRANWEN JARVIS

The two most important eighteenth-century Welsh poets have, for all the deep differences between them, one very important thing in common: they share a Christian view of the nature and purpose of poetry. For both Goronwy Owen and William Williams, Pantycelyn, the muse is a Christian muse. William Williams advised would-be hymn writers never to write unless they felt themselves to be under the influence of the Holy Spirit: 'Peidio gwneud un Hymn fyth nes y byddont yn teimlo eu heneidiau yn agos i'r nef, tan awelon yr Ysbryd Glan' (Never to compose a single hymn until they feel their souls to be close to heaven, under the inspiration of the Holy Spirit). For Goronwy Owen, who saw his primary function as a poet to be the fashioning of songs of praise, 'Poed i wau emynau mawl', inspiration comes from one muse only, the Christian muse:

> Un Awen a adwen i
> Da oedd, a phorth Duw iddi.
>
> [One Muse do I know
> She is good, and has God's protection.]

The two poets are of course very different. Goronwy Owen harboured a lifelong intense antipathy to the Methodists, their ideas and their culture. His concern for literary scholarship, his care for precision and accuracy of expression, are the antithesis of much of Pantycelyn's approach to writing poetry. Pantycelyn, who was careless of mere words, was both Romantic and utilitarian in his approach; Goronwy Owen embraced the aesthetic and traditional ethos of classicism. The two in fact have little in common beyond their contemporaneity (they were born within

five years of each other) and their rootedness in a consciously
Christian tradition in which religion provides both the initial
inspiration and the ultimate purpose for writing.

This chapter on Goronwy Owen begins by mentioning
Pantycelyn because, in spite of the disparity between the two, there
is much to be gained by placing Goronwy firmly within the all-
encompassing tradition of Christian poetry. This, after all, is
where he placed himself. It is usual to regard him as a neoclassical
poet, an Augustan writer. He undoubtedly is such a writer, but we
should guard against too exclusive a use of these labels. The
congruity between Goronwy Owen and Pantycelyn too, however
broad and generalized, reminds us that literary labels are often far
too narrow.

In the case of Goronwy Owen, it is particularly important to
avoid over-use of labels. He has always been seen by literary
historians as part of a movement. He is a member of the 'school of
Welsh Augustans'; a 'founder of the literary renaissance of the
eighteenth century'; a 'link in the chain of tradition'. All these
things are true; but he is also a poet and prose writer marked
by his own singular experiences and by deeply held personal
convictions.

His prose and his poetry show us two different facets of his
relationship with the Church. In his letters, we come vividly face to
face with the reality of his daily life as an impoverished curate.
Goronwy Owen had entered the service of the Church from a
lowly family background in Anglesey. His father, Owen Gronw, is
described as an 'eurych', a word which originally meant a crafts-
man in metal, but which by Owen Gronw's time described a man
of inferior status who was little more than a tinker. Owen Gronw
had some knowledge of poetry, however; he was a country
rhymester, of a type much maligned by Goronwy Owen in later
years. However, he possessed a bardic grammar, and his son was
undoubtedly first introduced to strict-metre poetry, at however
rudimentary a level, during his Anglesey childhood. His mother
Siân Parry was, says Goronwy, a fine speaker of Welsh who was
'careful to correct an uncouth, inelegant phrase or vicious
pronunciation'. From such poor, but not altogether unpromising
beginnings, Goronwy Owen was sent to Friars School, Bangor, to
be educated. Here he received a thorough grounding in Latin, and
learned some Greek too. His earliest extant poems are written in

Latin. Juvenilia they may be, but they show considerable technical ability. The foundations of Goronwy Owen's classicism, in both style and content, were undoubtedly laid at Friars School. He went up to Oxford during the summer of 1742, but appears to have stayed there for one week only.

With only a secondary education behind him, Goronwy Owen entered the service of the Church. The formal requirements for ordination in the eighteenth century were very few. So loosely supervised were arrangements that highly unsuitable men were sometimes appointed curates. So, Archbishop Secker in 1758 called for great care in making such appointments, 'because men of bad character, or men not in Holy Orders, may intrude'. The ranks of the clergy were overpopulated by men of inadequate education and little or no sense of vocation. Goronwy Owen does not fit this particular mould. Though his formal education ended at a comparatively early age, his scholarly bent and thirst for learning set him apart from many of his fellow-clergymen. His poetry shows that he was keenly aware of the nobility of his calling, and his letters reveal that he applied himself to his duties with a serious sense of purpose.

The general overmanning in the Church, and his own lack of influence among the higher ranks of the clergy (though his mentors the Morris brothers did their best to help him) partly explain the fact that Goronwy Owen remained a curate for nearly all his working life. It was not until middle age that he gained the status of rector. By that time he was serving in what was then a far-flung corner of the Diocese of London: St Andrew's, Brunswick County, Virginia. He died there in 1769, at the age of forty-six. His period in America was in reality his second exile. The first, which left its profound mark on his work, was his unwilling and bitterly regretted exile in England. His first curacy was in the Oswestry area, a position to which he was appointed after failing to secure a curacy in his home parish of Llanfair Mathafarn Eithaf. Via Donnington, Walton and Northolt he arrived in Virginia, without ever setting foot again in his beloved Anglesey. He was forever to be denied the living in Wales that he longed for.

Goronwy Owen lived out his life as a curate in poverty. He was constantly in debt and frequently relied upon friends, particularly Lewis Morris, to come to his aid. During his first curacy he was briefly imprisoned in Shrewsbury gaol for debt. As the years wore on, he and his wife Elinor (Elin) made the situation worse by their drinking habits. As William Morris, who worried much about what he saw as a tragic dissipation of Goronwy Owen's talent, remarked: 'Ond ydyw resyndod mawr fod dyn a ga'dd y fath dalent gan ei Greawdr yn ei chuddio mewn succan?' (Is it not deeply to be regretted that a man who received such talent from his Creator should hide it in ale?).

The minimum paid to a curate in his time was twenty pounds per annum—a woefully small sum. The usual stipend was around forty pounds, but to earn this sum Goronwy Owen, when he moved to Walton, was obliged to keep school in addition to his other duties:

> Thirty–five pounds is the sum which my Patron has promised me; but I understand that he will be somewhat better than his word. He will give me not a farthing more from his own pocket; but there is here a free school, which every Curate before me has been given, and which I shall have unless he fails to give it to me. It pays thirteen pounds a year, apart from a house in the burial ground to live in, and if I get it, my position will be worth more than forty pounds a year. (tr.)

In the event, he hated keeping school, and the incumbent of the parish made heavy demands upon him. In Walton, as in all the other places in which he served, Goronwy Owen fell into debt and became deeply disheartened.

These, then, were the Church's outward gifts to Goronwy Owen: poverty, exile, lack of recognition, heavy duties. Yet, though individual clerics and bishops are sometimes castigated by him, not once does he rail against the Church as an institution. He remained her loyal and proud servant. His famous phrase 'fy mharchus, arswydus swydd' (my revered, terrifying calling) sums up his attitude. From a literary standpoint, it is significant that Goronwy's complaints about his life as a priest, and indeed his life in general, are to be seen in his letters. Poetry was for him, morally, stylistically and aesthetically, an elevated medium, and it is in his poetry that we come face to face with his highest thoughts and aspirations. This high seriousness is apparent in Goronwy Owen's best-known poem, 'Molawd Môn' (Praise of Anglesey), which is in reality much more than a paean of praise to Anglesey. In the context of his love for his native island, and of his failure to

gain earthly happiness in her bosom, he reflects upon the significance of the life he has lived, and of his 'two callings' as priest and
poet. This poem, Goronwy Owen's *apologia pro vita sua*, is
conceived in religious terms. He seeks to justify and explain his
life's work, in both spheres, in the context of his relationship with
God.

His treatment of the priestly theme is notable for three things: its
emotional intensity; its deep sense of personal humility, to the
point of subsumption of self into the Godhead; and its careful
intellectual justification of the nature of priesthood. The line in
which he describes his calling as 'terrifying' has already been
quoted. He also refers to the onerous intensity of the priest's cares:
'dwys yw y boen'. The burden of priesthood lay heavily upon him.
Goronwy Owen is also insistent that any respect or reverence due
to him as a priest derives from God: 'O cheir parch, diolch i'r Pen'
(If there is reverence, it is thanks to the Head). The priest is merely
God's instrument on earth. He is set apart from his fellow men not
by any innate virtue, but by the nature of his vocation: he is called
not merely to try to live a life of exemplary purity, but to justify
himself through his deeds. Goronwy Owen feels himself called not
merely to be good; he is to do God's work.

It is the seriousness of Goronwy Owen's adherence to his calling
which is remarkable. He is equally serious about the religious basis
of his poetic vocation: 'Gwae ddiles gywyddoliaeth' (Woe to the
making of [morally] redundant poems). Goronwy follows his
beloved Milton in his belief that God is the fount of all true poetry:
the Muse is God's Muse. This theme is explored more fully in his
cywydd 'Bonedd a Chyneddfau'r Awen' (The Lineage and
Characteristics of the Muse), where he refers to the nine muses of
Homer before stating that for him there is only one. This is the
muse of the Old Testament: she was with Adam and Eve in
Paradise, and with Moses, David and Solomon.

The poem which Goronwy Owen mentions more frequently
than any other in his letters is the *cywydd* written on the most
serious and terrifying of all orthodox Christian themes: the Day of
Judgement. This poem, 'Cywydd y Farn Fawr', was for him an
undertaking of profound personal importance, its significance
undiminished by the fact that Judgement Day poems were a
common feature of the contemporary literary scene. He was also
acutely aware of his own mortality at the time of writing it:

'gwybyddwch clâf a thra chlâf o'r Cryd oeddwn pryd y dechreuais y Cywydd, ac hyd yr wyf yn cofio meddwl am farw a wnaeth i mi ddewis y fath destyn' (You should know that I was ill, very ill with ague when I started the cywydd, and as far as I remember it was thinking about dying which made me choose such a subject).

'Cywydd y Farn Fawr', for all the importance that Goronwy Owen attached to it, is not altogether successful as a poem. It lacks the vivid dramatic power of another strict-metre Welsh poem on the same theme written by the fifteenth-century poet Siôn Cent, a copy of which was in Goronwy Owen's possession. Dr Lewis Edwards, an important figure in nineteenth-century Wales, drew attention to its two most important defects: a lack of imaginative power and the weakening of the emotional impact upon the reader by its over-concern with the general, 'for we sympathize with men individually'. None the less, the poem, particularly in its middle passages, has great rhetorical force. In the vigour of its vocabulary and in its crashing consonantal sound-patterns, it manages to convey the awesome reality of the subject-matter for the people of the age:

Hyll ffyrnbyrth holl uffernbwll
Syrthiant drwy'r pant draw i'r pwll;
Bydd hadl y wal ddiadlam
Yrhawg, a chwyddawg a cham;
Cryn y gethern uffernawl
A chryn, a dychryn y diawl . . .

[The hideous furnace mouths of the entire pit of hell
Fall through the depths into the abyss;
The impassable wall will lie in ruins
Henceforth, all bulging and crooked;
The hellish family of demons trembles
And the devil himself trembles and takes fright . . .]

This is poetry which transcends neat categorization. In its forcefulness and sense of drama, it does not sit easily with much of the 'polite' poetry of the eighteenth-century neoclassical tradition. Similarly, 'Molawd Môn', particularly in its soaring final passages, is not confined by its outward adherence to traditional patterns. The poem ends, as do many elegies in the Welsh classical tradition, with a committal of the soul to God's care. Goronwy Owen borrows the classical device for a poem which considers his own death. Usually, the device is a mere formality, a neat way to end a poem on the passing of an individual. In Goronwy Owen's hands, it is no such thing. Into this final part of the poem, he pours heart and mind. All his longing for Môn (Anglesey), which he has seen as unattainable Paradise, all his earthly pain and suffering are, ultimately, of no import in the face of a joyful heavenly union with God. The world, including Môn, will be consumed by fire, but in the security and safety of heaven, 'in the fortress of the stars', he will be home at last, with no possibility of exile: 'heb allael ymadael mwy'. The poem, throughout, is concerned with placing man and his burdensome sojourn upon earth in the context of God's eternity.

Goronwy Owen, then, in his greatest poems, cannot satisfactorily be described solely as an Augustan poet. The poems are too powerful, too transcendent, too profoundly concerned with the poet's own heart and soul. In other poems, however, he offers a model of Augustan thought and style. Poems such as 'Awdl y Gofuned' (The Wish), 'Arwyrain y Nennawr' (The Garret), 'Cywydd y Maen Gwerthfawr' (The Precious Stone) and 'Cywydd y Gwahodd' (The Invitation) all, in their different ways, deal with the ideal life; a life which is disciplined, domestically ordered, civilized and lived in reasonable plenty. It is a life in which nature is subservient to man's demands upon it. On the surface, the poems have a calm air. Occasionally, however, one is struck by the tension which lies beneath the surface. The ideal life is not to be easily attained: like Môn, it remains, for Goronwy Owen, a dream which cannot easily be fulfilled. There is a poignant irony in these 'wish' poems when one considers how very different the reality of Goronwy Owen's daily life was. In 'Awdl y Gofuned', his earnest wish is that the tribulations of his daily life may be left behind:

A pheidio yno â ffwdanus—fyd
Direol, bawlyd, rhy helbulus.

[There I may escape this tiresome world,
Disordered, dirty, too full of troubles.]

'Awdl y Gofuned' is one of his early poems. It was written in 1752 at Donnington when Goronwy Owen was still, in the matter of writing Welsh classical strict-metre poetry, something of an apprentice. 'No wonder that my Gofuned should be faulty in blindly copying after so inaccurate a pattern,' are his words in a letter to William Morris, the 'pattern' in question, for which 'inadequate' would be a better word than 'inaccurate', being 'a stanza or two of it, made by Ieuan Brydydd Hir on Melancholy that Mr. Morris [Lewis] had sent me as a specimen'. Goronwy Owen's confusion regarding the technical requirements of the *awdl* is not to be wondered at: it is a reflection of the fact that he was part of an ongoing movement of rediscovery and redefinition of Welsh classical forms.

Goronwy Owen's 'wish' is for a quiet living in Môn, with reasonable duties, and, importantly, a shady garden, where he may read the works of ancient poets. He wishes to listen to the singing of birds above him, and to the happy chattering of his two small sons. It is, of course, a highly conventional picture, and this conventionality is important. It shows that Goronwy Owen could write in a thoroughly Augustan mode, and that, in his work, he married eighteenth-century neoclassical thought and imagery with Welsh classical forms. While the poem's debt to contemporary English writers seems, to the modern reader, very marked, it is noteworthy that Goronwy Owen himself considered it to be thoroughly Welsh in content as well as in form. In one of the poem's most interesting passages, he makes of the classical ideal a conscious choice, and contrasts it with two fashionable ideals which he thinks of as being English: the appeal of nature, wild and picturesque, is one, the appeal of the exotic is the other:

> Deued i Sais yr hyn a geisio;
> Dwfr hoff redwyllt, ofer a ffrydio
> Drwy nant, a chrisiant (a chroeso)—o chaf
>   Fôn im; yn bennaf enwaf honno.
>
> Ni wnaf f'arwyrain yn fawreiriog
> Gan goffáu tlysau, gwyrthiau gwerthiog,
> Tud, myr, mynydd, dolydd deiliog—trysor
>   Yr India dramor, oror enwog.
>
> [Let the Englishman have what he desires;
> The appeal of wild-running water, a stream

Which wells up through a gorge, like crystal; (he is welcome)
If I have Môn; chiefly I name her.

I shall not fashion my song of extravagant words;
Celebrating treasures, rich marvels,
The land, seas, mountain, leafy meadows; the riches
Of far-flung India, famed land.]

Wild nature and the exotic are admired ideals in the Romantic
tradition. Goronwy here seems to be making a conscious rejection
of both.

The wish for an ideal life is understood rather than stated in the
lively 'Arwyrain y Nennawr', sometimes known in English as 'The
Garret Poem'. It is a poem which begins in complaint, and ends in
a philosophic acceptance of the author's lot. Goronwy Owen
wrote it in London in 1755, when he was in very straitened circumstances and dependent on the goodwill and charity of the
Cymmrodorion, that society of exiled supporters of Welsh poetry
and scholarship of which he was a corresponding member.
Richard Morris, ever looking for a way to help Goronwy Owen
and to ease his path as both priest and poet, had invited him to
London to help in the running of the Cymmrodorion and to
minister to a Welsh congregation there. The proposed arrangements do not seem to have materialized and Goronwy Owen spent
some time living in a garret, in conditions of great poverty.
'Arwyrain y Nennawr' is a description of his daily life in the garret,
but it turns ultimately into something far more. As in 'Molawd
Môn', the poet places his earthly plight in the context of a higher
spirituality and draws profound, and indeed brave, sustenance for
his soul from his contemplations.

The poem's chief appeal, however, does not lie in its
philosophical musings or in its biographical content. It is the
vivid descriptions—in *cynghanedd*—of eighteenth-century London
street-life which strike the reader. We are here in the world of
Hogarth's vivid images of London low life, and in the tradition too
of the Welsh prose writer Ellis Wynne's satiric portrayal of
'Pleasure Street'. All is hideous noise, drunkenness, prostitution,
and courtiers, lawyers, churchmen are no better than the rabble,
for they too are seen to be in the business of unprincipled and
deceitful doings with their fellow men. In the face of such dross,

Goronwy Owen is grateful that, literally and morally, he is, even in his poverty, able to rise to higher things: 'Dedwydd im gell a'm didol' (I am fortunate in the cell which keeps me separate). Like all serious social satire, 'Arwyrain y Nennawr' is written from a position of moral apartness.

'Cywydd y Gwahodd' is written in a far happier vein. For once, Goronwy Owen seems close to attaining that ideal life which he so much desires. Richard Morris's efforts on his behalf finally led to his securing a curacy for him just outside London, at Northolt, where Goronwy Owen settled in reasonable comfort. So delighted is he by his improved circumstances that he invites William Parry, a fellow member of the Cymmrodorion and Deputy-Comptroller of the Mint, to visit him. The idealized picture of life at Northolt painted by Goronwy Owen is, like the life he portrayed in 'Awdl y Gofuned', very much in the Augustan mould. It is a life not of extravagance but of a controlled and reasonable plenty. Its pleasures are gentle and civilized:

> Ceir profi cwrw y prifardd,
> A 'mgomio wrth rodio'r ardd;
> Cawn nodi, o'n cain adail
> Gwyrth Duw mewn rhagorfraint dail . . .

> [You shall partake of the poet's beer,
> And converse as we stroll in the garden;
> We shall take note, from our fine abode,
> Of God's miracle in the supreme beauty of the leaves . . .]

The beauty of the flowers in the garden must, however, serve as a warning. It is late summer, and, for all their present beauty, they are about to fade away and die. So is it with us, says the poet to his friend. It is an age-old theme, but for Goronwy Owen, writing from within the Augustan tradition, originality counts for little. What matters is that the theme is well applied, and that it is memorably and succinctly expressed. In this, Goronwy Owen succeeds admirably, and the poem, for all its conventionality, is deeply touching, particularly in the context of the poet's life history. Like 'Arwyrain y Nennawr' it is a courageous poem; Goronwy Owen was putting a brave front on circumstances which, though improved, were still very far from the ideal which he craved.

In these three poems, part reality, part wish, Goronwy Owen escapes from one of the dangers of Augustan poetry of this kind. The accessibility of the ideal life, its attainable circumstances, can place severe limitations on the poet's vision. He is confined by the very orderliness of life. Goronwy Owen, however, is released by it. Once his life on earth is, as it were, controlled, he is imaginatively free to consider other matters. In all three poems, he uses his vision of the ideal life as a stepping-stone to higher and wider spiritual considerations. For all its earthly desirability, the Augustan vision is always, for him, inadequate *sub specie aeternitatis*.

Nowhere is this made clearer than in 'Cywydd y Maen Gwerthfawr' (The Precious Stone), a poem written on a fashionable eighteenth-century theme. The jewel sought is contentment. Contentment, for Goronwy Owen, was always far out of reach. It was not simply a matter of impoverished material circumstances. He was a difficult, stormy, restless and often self-centred man, always craving for something he did not have. It is this perception of the poet's own life and personality which lends to this poem, as to the others in this group, a sad irony.

The poem's objective air, however, in true Augustan fashion, means that the poem itself is disciplined and unsentimental. The poet's search for contentment, though diligently pursued, ends in failure:

> Chwilio ym man amdani
> Chwilio hwnt heb ei chael hi.
>
> [Searching for it high and low
> Searching far without finding it.]

Goronwy Owen is guided in his conclusions by two things: one is Solomon's wisdom, the wisdom of a king blessed with power and earthly riches who yet considered that all on earth is mere vanity; the other is the teaching of the Gospels that it is in heaven that true happiness may be found:

> Duw'n ein plith, da iawn ein plaid,
> F'a'n dwg i nef fendigaid.
>
> [God with us, we are fortified by Him,
> He brings us to the blessedness of heaven.]

In this, in spite of all the differences between them, Goronwy
Owen shares the same ultimate belief as Pantycelyn: this earthly
life is of little import compared with the eternal realities of the
world to come.

Goronwy Owen's poetry is in some ways less easily categorized
than his critical beliefs. Although ostensibly classical, it is
sometimes seen to have features which can be regarded as pre-
Romantic. His criticism, however, is almost purely in the classical
mould. That classicism derives from several sources.

His discovery of the classical tradition of Welsh poetry is the
most important single theme of Goronwy Owen's letters. Though
the rudiments of that tradition had been passed on to him in his
youth, his scholarly involvement in the rediscovery and interpretation of the strict-metre poetry of the past came about largely
through his involvement with the Morrisian circle. After some
earlier instruction by William Elias, a native of Clynnog who later
settled in Anglesey, it was Lewis Morris who guided him through
the intricacies of *cynghanedd* and who introduced him to the
various stanza forms of traditional metrics. The progress of
Goronwy Owen's training as a Welsh poet can, in part, be traced
through the letters. His period at Donnington is marked by an
energetic attempt to master the strict metres and to put newly
gained knowledge to immediate use in compositions of his own.
These lines, written to William Morris in February 1753, show very
well the process of education at work. Goronwy Owen had asked
Lewis Morris for examples of all the twenty-four classical metres:

> This is a favor I've been a begging of Mr. Lewis Morris this whole
> twelve month and above without any effect. One example or two in a
> letter would soon make me acquainted with 'em. I suppose you either
> have or may borrow Gramadeg Sion Rhydderch. I remember my father
> had one of 'em formerly, and that is the only one I ever saw, and as far
> as I can remember, it gave a very plain, good account of every one of
> 'em, viz., Cywydd Deuair Hirion (or the like) a fesurir o 7 sillaf, &c.,
> &c. All the measures I know at present are Englyn Unodl Union,
> Cywydd Deuair Hirion, Gwawdodyn Byrr, and Englyn Milwr and I
> protest I know no other. The two last, Mr. Lewis Morris brought me
> acquainted with . . .

However, the process developed into something far greater than
the simple introduction and furnishing of examples which these

lines describe. The letters record a multi-layered process. There is the basic poetic training which has been noted; Goronwy Owen's commentary on his own compositions; his discussion of his correspondents' reactions to his poetry; his evaluation of the strict metres as vehicles for various kinds of poems; and his involvement with the rediscovery of the poetry of the past through the scholarly effort of this circle in the field of manuscript collection. In his letters and poetry, we see a poet, critic and scholar developing before our eyes. This individual 'birth' takes place against the wider eighteenth-century renaissance in Welsh poetic learning of which he formed a part. Through his connection, largely epistolary, with the Morrisian circle and the Society of Cymmrodorion, Goronwy Owen developed a far-reaching critique of traditional poetry.

What, then, are the main features of this critique? Goronwy Owen is much exercised by the suitability of *cynghanedd* and the various metric forms for the production of certain kinds of poetry, and he is not always of the same mind: 'Do you think that horrid jingle called Cynghanedd . . . essential to poetry?' he asks at one point; he talks of 'the fetters of *cynghanedd*, which our language groans under' and declares to William Morris that 'ye freer and less confin'd to *cynghanedd* the metre is, the better a poem must be'. This railing against *cynghanedd* is to be taken in the light of Goronwy Owen's long-considered aim in the field of metrics: the discovery of the most suitable vehicle for the creating of epic poetry in Welsh. He recognizes that *cynghanedd* is more suitable to lyric than narrative poetry, but in spite of his strictures on the use of it he is led ultimately to the conclusion that, in Welsh, the *cynganeddion* must be used 'for without them it were no Poetry'. For him, *cynghanedd* was too deeply ingrained in the Welsh poetic tradition to allow it to be jettisoned. Whether or not Goronwy Owen knew of the opinions of the Welsh Renaissance grammarian Gruffydd Robert, who had considered this same question two centuries earlier, is not known. Gruffydd Robert reached a far more radical conclusion and advocated writing without *cynghanedd* in 'the same kind of metres as the Italians use'. The vernacular alternative uppermost in Goronwy Owen's mind is, however, English blank verse, and side by side with poetry written in *cynghanedd*, this appears to him to be a thoroughly unsatisfactory medium:

> I would never wish to see our Poetry reduc'd to the English Standard,
> for I can see nothing in *that* that should entitle it to the Name of
> *Poetry*, but only the number of Syllables (which yet is never
> scrupulously observ'd) and a choice of *uncommon*, or if you please
> Poetic words, and a wretched Rhyme, some times at the end, and in
> blank Verse, i.e. the best kind of English Poetry, no Rhyme at all.
> Milton's Paradise Lost is a Book I read with pleasure, nay with
> Admiration, and raptures . . . you'll find me ready to subscribe to
> anything that can be said in praise of it, provided you don't call it
> *Poetry.*

For Goronwy, a highly-wrought and specialized form of language
was a *sine qua non* of poetry; without it 'poetry would be but a
mere formal, swelling & pompous prose'.

Goronwy Owen concludes that the main stumbling-block to the
writing of epic poetry in Welsh is not *cynghanedd* itself, but the
inadequate length of lines in the traditional stanza forms, and
indeed the shortness of complete poems. Poetry in Welsh is too
restricted by the length of 'Verses and Poems':

> our longest lines not exceeding ten syllables (too scanty a space to
> contain anything *Great* within the compass of *Six* or *Seven* Stanzas, the
> usual length of our '*Gwawdodyn Byrr*'), and our longest Poems not
> above Sixty or Seventy Lines, the standard Measure of *D. ap Gwilym's*
> '*Cywyddau*'; which is far from being a length adequate to a Heroic
> Poem.

When Goronwy Owen wrote this, in February 1753, his knowledge of traditional poetry was still very partial. By May of the
following year he had, by means of a manuscript collection sent
to him by William Morris, deepened his acquaintance with the
Gogynfeirdd, those poets of the court and aristocracy of the twelfth
to the early fourteenth centuries, some of whom are also known as
the Poets of the Princes. In succeeding centuries, the concise form
of the *cywydd*, based on a rhyming couplet with seven syllables in
each line, was to gain overwhelming ascendancy over other strict-
metre forms, and developed into a highly polished and sophisticated instrument. However, as Goronwy Owen rightly perceived, it
is not a form suitable for lengthy narrative or epic-type poetry. In
the work of the *Gogynfeirdd*, he found a different and far more
suitable potential pattern. The *awdl* of the *Gogynfeirdd* was a richly

decorated poem composed mainly of lines of nine and ten syllables on a unitary rhyme, with a number of passages of this type frequently linked to make one fairly long poem. The poetry is often very difficult, but it has a majesty and sweep which appealed particularly to Goronwy Owen.

He was especially impressed by the work of Gwalchmai, who wrote of the brave exploits of Owain Gwynedd:

> Compare Gwalchmai's "Arddwyreaf hael o hil Rodri" with the most jingling piece of Dd ap Gwilym or any of his cotemporaries and give the latter the preference if you dare . . . Cywydd is a measure particularly adapted to love affairs, and the smoother the cynghanedd glides, the more soothing and engaging it is to the fair Sex, and to the easy & effeminate of either Sex. But it is no ways suitable to express the martial heat and ardor of an Owain Gwynedd at the head of his victorious Army . . . I protest Gwalchmai seems to me to have said as much, and as much to the purpose in this little Awdl, as Homer has done in his voluminous Iliad.

For all his delight, and for all the promise he saw in seeking to emulate the work of the *Gogynfeirdd*, Goronwy Owen failed to produce the Welsh epic poem of his ambitions, or indeed anything approaching it. The closest is 'Cywydd y Farn Fawr' (The Great Judgement), which has the grandeur of subject-matter and a number of the stylistic devices of Greek and Latin epic poetry. The importance of Goronwy Owen's dealings with the subject of epic poetry does not lie with the poetry produced; it lies in his critical considerations and in the defining of the ambition itself. His ideal and many of his critical ideas were adopted by poets of succeeding generations with enthusiasm if not always with good sense, and were to prove, particularly through the eisteddfodic tradition, highly influential until well into the nineteenth century.

Goronwy Owen's critical ideas are not of course restricted to the matter of finding the best medium for epic poetry. His discussion is wide-ranging and includes matters of style and content. He is always searching for the elevated and the grand. The comments on Dafydd ap Gwilym's poetry which have just been quoted show why his work, though admired for its technical dexterity, did not gain Goronwy Owen's complete approval. It lacked seriousness and grandeur or, to use one of the most important critical words of Goronwy Owen and his contemporaries, it lacked 'sublimity'.

'Tho' I admire (and even dote upon) the sweetness of his poetry, I have often wish'd he had raised his thoughts to something more grave and *sublime.*' Of all the poetry he had read, Goronwy Owen's opinion (in May 1752) was that 'the grandest, sublimest piece of poetry in the universe' was Milton's *Paradise Lost.*

His admiration for *Paradise Lost* is partly rooted in fashion. His adulation of Milton, and the critical terms he employs to describe his poetry, echo similar opinions expressed by many others. Indeed, during the thirty years from about 1730 to 1760, admiration for Milton was at a very high peak, and Goronwy Owen was part of that movement. In this context, it is important to note one thing. Milton wrote on Classical models and with constant reference to Classical themes; his basic subject matter is, however, biblical, and his basic theme, the nature of good and evil, is fundamental to Christian morality. These aspects of his work find an echo in Goronwy Owen's work, in particular in 'Cywydd y Farn Fawr'. His inspiration for that poem, he tells us, was biblical rather than Classical: 'nis gwn edrych o honof unwaith yn Homer na Virgil, ond y ddau Destament yn fynych' (I do not know that I looked once in Homer or Virgil, but in the two Testaments frequently).

These words also point to another aspect of Goronwy Owen's opinions on poetry: that subject-matter is frequently, and indeed inevitably, derivative. Writing of Homer and Virgil he remarks: 'Meddwl yr oeddwn nad oedd neb a ddichon ysgrifennu dim mewn Prydyddiaeth, na cheid rhyw gyffelybiaeth (neu Parallel) iddo yn y ddau Fardd godidog hynny' (I thought that there was no one who could write anything in poetry without there being some similarity (or parallel) to it in these two magnificent poets). His immediate point is that other sources exist; the underlying assumption however is that poetry is by nature imitative. This fundamental tenet of neoclassical thought was further strengthened in Goronwy Owen's case by his being part of the eighteenth-century uncovering of the riches of the Welsh poetic past. Paradoxically, the neoclassical creed of 'follow the ancients' had for him a new and exciting dimension. When he seeks to advocate Gwalchmai, for instance, as a source and pattern, he is breaking new ground and thinking afresh about the possibilities of poetry in Welsh.

Goronwy Owen believed that 'the conceptions and ideas of all mankind always were and ever will be pretty much alike'.

Throughout the ages, poetry had been produced by men of judgement and good sense and had been cherished by those similarly endowed. The ideal of 'the poetry of good sense' is less limited than it sounds. For Goronwy Owen and his contemporaries, it meant distrust of over-reliance on the workings of the imagination and the emotions, but not a denial of these qualities. One of Goronwy Owen's best-known poems, his elegy to his infant daughter Elin, illustrates this. The personal circumstances were intensely sad, for he loved his children dearly. The motivation for the poem is not the same as for his fine elegy to Marged Morris, mother of the Morris brothers and a woman to whom Goronwy Owen, as a boy, had owed much. That elegy, in true Welsh classical fashion, is more of a celebration than a lament. Though there is sadness at her passing, that has happened in the fullness of time and after a life well-lived. Her life had been dedicated to the upbringing of her remarkable family and to the service of others as a nurse and knowledgeable herbalist. It is a personal poem, but it is also in the nature of being a public tribute, and it is marked by its sense of balance and objectivity.

It is patently a poem of 'good sense'. So too is Goronwy's elegy to Elin. There is no doubting a father's grief. He is in unrelievable pain, 'yng nghur digysur', and feels himself to be a prisoner of his longing for her: 'yn gaeth o'm hiraeth am hon'. Interspersed with such direct expressions of grief however are lines of light and loveliness when he describes his small daughter. She is 'liw sêr' (of the colour of the stars), her child's talk is golden, 'oedd euriaith mabiaith o'i min', she is a warm-smiled angel, 'angyles gynnes ei gwên', who greets her father with a lively and joyful delight, 'afieithus, groesawus swn'. The elegy, for all its poignancy, is composed and controlled, partly by the author's self-disciplined approach to his emotionally charged subject-matter, partly by the formal demands of *cynghanedd*, and partly by its varied tone.

His grief is also disciplined by his Christian beliefs. The final lines of the poem have a soaring grandeur as Goronwy Owen expresses his conviction that, in heaven, all shall be well and his daughter shall wear a crown in the company of angels. As with others of the poems dealing with matters nearest his heart, he controls earthly grief and longing by placing them in the context of God's eternity. Thus there is in his work a potent fusion of the Christian and classical spirit which shows the poetry of 'good sense' at its finest. We see the shaping of personal experience by the distilled wisdom of the ages and by the controlling context of eternal verities.

When poetry is conceived of in this elevated way, it is no wonder that poetry of a lower order is little regarded. Goronwy Owen, although he composed one or two strict-metre pieces in a lighter vein, dismisses with contempt the offerings of unsophisticated folk poets. His mentor Lewis Morris had a more catholic vision of the nature of poetry, and himself composed poems based on the simple, lyric patterns of poetry in the manner of 'hen benillion', which were traditional free-metre stanzas on age-old subjects, in a direct and unassuming style. This lyric tradition stretches from the eighteenth century through the nineteenth, when it was influential in the development of such poets as Alun and Ceiriog, and on to the early twentieth century with the poetry of such popular lyric poets as Crwys and Eifion Wyn. It is a tradition which, while lacking in 'sublimity', has an undoubted and lasting appeal to popular taste. Even when folk poetry was, in this form, at its best, Goronwy Owen would have none of it. Still less did he appreciate the offerings of the 'rhyme taggers' which appealed to 'the sand boys and the spinning girls' ('y llangciau tywod a'r merched nyddu'). Poetry, for him, was the preserve of men of high learning:

> I never wrote anything (designedly) for children, no, nor fools, nor old women, and while my brains are sound, never shall . . . Whatever I wrote was design'd for men, and for men of *sense* and *ingenuity* . . .

The qualities of intellect and disposition required to make a poet were, in Goronwy Owen's opinion, inborn. He quotes with approval the dictum *Poeta nascitur, non fit*, but nevertheless explains that an early poem is deficient because it is 'the mere foetus of uninstructed nature'. While nature is of the essence, so too are application and learning: 'Er na ddichon dysg *wneuthur* prydydd, eto hi a ddichyn ei wellhau . . .' (Though learning cannot make a poet, yet it can improve him). In practical terms, the emphasis on 'improvement through learning' is far more important in Goronwy Owen's case than the emphasis on the gift of nature. His letters record in detail the making of a poet. Through them we can watch the process of conscious and deliberate acquisition of learning at work.

This process of learning and development is the major concern of his letters. Taken as a whole, the letters reflect the seriousness and high-mindedness of his poetic and critical output. However, they do on occasions allow us a glimpse of another Goronwy Owen. Critics have often referred to the realism, even the bawdiness, which coexist with the refinement of neoclassical poetry and with the seriousness of neoclassical thought. Lewis Morris is an excellent example of the two faces of the early and mid-eighteenth century. On the one hand we have his regard for true scholarship and his concern for poetry as high art; on the other the raw earthiness of some of his poetry and letters. Occasionally, in his letters, Goronwy Owen too can write in this vein. The most famous is the letter written on board the *Trial* when it was becalmed at Spithead, before its fateful journey to America. The voyage, for Goronwy Owen, was to prove profoundly tragic: his wife and one of his sons succumbed to the illness which was rampant on board ship and were buried at sea. For the time being, however, he was in good spirits and the letter he wrote to Richard Morris is vivid, vigorous and very far removed from the politeness of such poems as 'Awdl y Gofuned' or 'Cywydd y Gwahodd'. However, underlying it is a sense of social satire:

Sailors are hideously filthy men. May God protect me, every one has taken to himself a harlot from amongst the she-thieves, and they do no work but are in drivelling fornication in every corner of the ship. Five or six of them have caught the hot-arse disease, which is hardly mentionable, from the women, and there is no doctor here at all except me, who has a copy of Dr Shaw with me, and following that I try to patch things up with the old remedies which are in a chest here. I sometimes fear to catch it myself from being amongst them . . . Do you recall how this blockhead of a captain promised that my wife could have one of these thieves as a maidservant during the voyage? There is one of them in this cabin, but to serve the prick of that man, not to attend my wife, was she brought here. There never lived a worse beast than the master. For the last fortnight, we have been forced to drink stinking water or choke (for there is not a drop of small beer in the ship) and to look at him drinking his wines and his beer between him and his whore, licking his cursed chops to whet our desire and saying 'It is very good'. What, say you, will become of us before the end of the voyage? (tr.)

While the letter, ostensibly, is not written to make a moral point, its unapologetic realism is biting in its effect. Goronwy Owen remained committed to his priestly calling.

In this letter, Goronwy Owen is very much in the tradition of the Welsh prose writer Ellis Wynne, whose *Gweledigaetheu y Bardd Cwsc* (Visions of the Sleeping Bard) he much admired. This vivid social satirist, who was, like Goronwy Owen, an Anglican priest, wrote Welsh prose of great vigour, with no concessions to any enervating sense of politeness. Ellis Wynne's influence on Goronwy Owen is not confined to some of his prose passages. His influence on 'Arwyrain y Nennawr' has already been discussed. 'Cywydd y Farn Fawr', too, which presses a highly powerful and dramatic style to the service of a deeply moralistic theme, is in the same tradition as Ellis Wynne's 'Gweledigaeth Uffern' (Vision of Hell). It should not be supposed that, because they talk so much of poetry, Goronwy Owen's letters have no literary pretensions or antecedents in themselves. On the contrary, his letters are frequently carefully considered pieces which owe much to contemporary fashions in the art of writing prose.

The many memorable passages of Welsh prose in Goronwy Owen's letters point to the one thing which underpins all his literary output and which gave impetus to his scholarly and critical interests: his abiding love for the Welsh language and his profound emotional and intellectual involvement with it. The conscious embracing of one's mother tongue, indeed the very existence of that tongue as an objectively considered entity, an entity which is to be explored, protected, buttressed, and proudly used and displayed, is a phenomenon which may appear strange to English readers. For Goronwy Owen, as for other members of the Morrisian circle, and indeed as for poets and scholars in other generations, this impulse is not, as it is for most English men of letters, a largely unconscious matter; it is a driving force which is recognized as having its own important existence.

Thus Goronwy Owen is always concerned to maintain clarity, dignity and right usage; he is also concerned to use the resources of the language to the full. What he has to say on the subject is influenced by general neoclassical attitudes to language, by the ethos and interests of the eighteenth-century scholarly and antiquarian movement, and by his own instinct, and indeed genius, for language. He is always concerned, in his own words, with

'retrieving the antient splendor of our Language . . . laying open its
worth and beauty to Strangers'.

Of the intrinsic 'worth' of the Welsh language he has no doubt.
Fairly early in his deliberation on the matter of producing epic
poetry in Welsh, he is concerned that difficulties lie in the matter of
finding suitable metrics. Linguistic resources, on the other hand,
are no problem at all: 'Our language undoubtedly affords plenty of
words expressive and suitable enough for the genius of a *Milton*
. . . Our language excells most others in Europe . . . ' This is a
theme to which he returns: 'For our language, I'm certain, is not
inferior for copiousness, pithiness, and significancy, to any other,
antient or modern, that I have any knowledge of.' The critical
vocabulary used is that of the neoclassical school; the conviction
arises from his personal delight at the riches he found in earlier
Welsh poetry.

He insists, however, that these riches must be jealously guarded
and promoted by men who are equal to the task. Any weaknesses
are due to the limitations of individuals, not to the limitations of
the language itself: 'If we had some men, of genius and abilities, of
my way of thinking, we should have no need to despair of seeing it
in as flourishing a condition, as any other antient or modern.' He
is thus unsparing in his criticism of all those who use or encourage
'market Welsh', including the lexicographer Thomas Richards of
Coychurch, who had augmented his version, published in 1753, of
Dr John Davies's famous *Dictionarium Duplex* (1632) by including, among others, Glamorgan dialect words:

> Dictionaries are or should be made to understand Authors by, and to
> teach us to write correctly in imitation of 'em, and not to acquaint us
> with the different corruptions that words may be perverted to by the
> lisping prattle of Nurses and Children, and vicious phraseology and
> pronunciation of Clowns and Rusticks.

When Goronwy Owen, in 1753, was elected one of the first
corresponding members of the London-based Society of Cymmrodorion, he was delighted at being numbered among a company
of men dedicated to furthering the Welsh language, its literature
and antiquities. Lewis Morris, in his introduction to the constitution, states that the society's 'principal End' was the 'Cultivation

of the *British* Language and a Search into Antiquities'. Goronwy Owen later prepared the Welsh version of the constitution, and was moved to compose an *awdl* to the Honourable Society of Cymmrodorion in London 'ac i'r hen odidawg Iaith Gymraeg' (and to the ancient and magnificent Welsh Language). The Society was to play a pivotal role in the furtherance of Welsh language and literature (a role which is discussed elsewhere in this book). Goronwy Owen's ideas and poetry were to be widely disseminated in the future largely through the offices of his fellow-members. In his *awdl*, he refers to '[ein] heniaith wiw, frenhinol' ([our] ancient, worthy, kingly language). It is a language, he says elsewhere, which must receive all the succour necessary to maintain it as a language able 'to converse with Princes'. This language of kings and princes was the one which he, and the Society, were moved to serve.

BIBLIOGRAPHY

Editions
J. H. Davies, *The Letters of Goronwy Owen* (Cardiff, 1924).
Isaac Foulkes, *Barddoniaeth Goronwy Owen* (Lerpwl, 8th edn., 1924).
Robert Jones, *The Poetical Works of the Rev. Goronwy Owen with his Life and Correspondence* (London, 1876).
W. J. Gruffydd, *Cywyddau Goronwy Owen* (Casnewydd, 1907).

Studies
Glenda Carr, 'Goronwy Owen', *Anglesey Antiquarian and Field Club Transactions* (1969–70), 137–63.
Branwen Jarvis, *Goronwy Owen*, (Cardiff, 1986).
Bedwyr Lewis Jones, 'Goronwy Owen' in J. E. Caerwyn Williams (ed.), *Ysgrifau Beirniadol II* (Dinbych, 1966), 92–108.
Idem, 'Lewis Morris a Goronwy Owen' in J. E. Caerwyn Williams (ed.), *Ysgrifau Beirniadol X* (Dinbych, 1977), 290–308.
Bobi Jones, 'Goronwy Owen' in Dyfnallt Morgan (ed.), *Gwŷr Llên y Ddeunawfed Ganrif a'u Cefndir* (Llandybïe, 1966), 129–36.
John Gwilym Jones, *Goronwy Owen's Virginian Adventure: His Life, Poetry and Literary Opinions* (Williamsburg, Virginia, 1969).
Saunders Lewis, *A School of Welsh Augustans* (Wrexham and London, 1924).
Idem, 'Goronwy Owen', reprinted in R. Geraint Gruffydd (ed.), *Meistri'r Canrifoedd* (Caerdydd, 1973), 259–75.

Alan Llwyd, *Gronwy Ddiafael, Gronwy Ddu: Cofiant Goronwy Owen, 1723–1769* (Cyhoeddiadau Barddas, 1997).

Griffith T. Roberts, 'Goronwy Owen', *Yr Eurgrawn*, 161 (1969), 88–95, 119–28.

Transactions of the Honourable Society of Cymmrodorion (1922–3), special supplement including articles by J. H. Davies and John Morris-Jones.

W. D. Williams, *Goronwy Owen* (Cardiff, 1951).

CHAPTER 6

CELTICISM AND PRE-ROMANTICISM: EVAN EVANS

FFION LLYWELYN JENKINS

The significance of the short-lived Celtic movement in eighteenth-century literature, which is often dismissed as little more than a literary detour on the way to a grander destination, is considerable. Its importance lies in the way in which Celticism bridged two far more widely recognized literary phenomena: the Augustan and Romantic movements. Far more than a passing fancy dismissed in favour of weightier Romantic concepts, the Celtic movement can be viewed as an essential conduit between neoclassical dependency upon tradition and classical precedent, and the more imaginative expression of the turn of the century.

The Celtic movement has added significance to the student of Welsh literature as a unique point of connection between the Welsh and English literary tradition—the bridge between Augustan and Romantic literature also spanned Offa's Dyke. At no other time during the eighteenth century does the connection between Welsh and English literature have such a profound reciprocal effect. The Celtic movement, inspired by the discovery of fragments of early British literature, gave new material to poets disenchanted by tired Augustan forms and platitudes, and at the same time boosted literary activity among contemporary Welsh poets and writers. Celticism provides us also with a rare instance of Welsh literature gaining widespread recognition in England, being acknowledged as authentically ancient, of international stature and even as a forerunner of the modern English literary tradition.

Alongside the powerful neoclassical movement, however, any other eighteenth-century literary trend must seem dwarfed. Celticism is no exception. The Celtic movement gathered force steadily throughout the first half of the century, but enjoyed only a brief period of prominence, becoming fashionable around 1750 and running out of steam by 1770. Furthermore, the movement produced only one work that can be said to be truly important to the development of Welsh literature: Evan Evans's *Specimens of the Poetry of the Antient Welsh Bards*. Celticism has, however, left an enduring mark on the world of scholarship and antiquarianism. The contribution of Evans's collection of early poetry to our understanding and appreciation of subsequent Welsh literature is immeasurable, and in itself justifies more than a passing glance at Celticism in studying eighteenth-century Welsh literature.

As a movement, Celticism in Wales and England is virtually inseparable. Indeed, the interdependence of Celticists in Wales and England was such that the movement can only properly be discussed with reference to both. The term 'Celtic movement' refers to the small but influential group of mid-eighteenth century writers who used material derived from early British literature and history in their work. The reward for searching out the elusive facts and fragments of poetry that survived from the early British period was considerable: new inspiration and sense of poetic direction, a renewed confidence in the native literary tradition and, above all, the tantalizing possibility of discovering an authentic native epic worthy of comparison with the classics of Virgil and Horace.

The raw material that inspired the Celtic movement (bearing in mind that the term 'Celtic' in this context cannot be precise, since the eighteenth century could, and did, regard anything dating from medieval times as 'Celtic') consists of a body of early Welsh verse copied from mainly private collections. By far the largest part of this body, including ten short poems by Aneirin from *Y Gododdin* and other influential poems such as 'Arwyrain Owain Gwynedd' by Gwalchmai and fragments by Gruffudd ab yr Ynad Coch, was brought together in one seminal work. This was the collection (the *Specimens*) copied and translated by Evan Evans, the central figure of the Celtic movement in Wales. Preliminary work was also done by Lewis Morris in his *Tlysau yr Hen Oesoedd* (1735), contributing to the growing interest in early poetry. The Celtic movement itself produced a number of studies of the verse in Latin, English and Welsh, and further translations of the early poetry by leading poets such as Thomas Gray, as well as several original works. These, in Welsh and English, are characterized by themes of primitivism, early civilization and histories and legends relating to the early British period.

Though considered minor in significance in comparison with
neoclassicism or the Romantic movement, Celticism was embraced
with enthusiasm by its exponents and, though its roots were firmly
in the Welsh tradition, that enthusiasm was perhaps most evident
in England. Certainly, by the mid-eighteenth century, Celticism
was the very latest thing on the English literary scene. Fashionable
writers like Horace Walpole and 'Monk' Lewis wrote novels full of
Gothic horror and anachronism, while more serious literary
creatures wrote histories, letters and poems in which the desire to
unveil the Celtic period, historically and culturally, was prominent.
A canon ranging from Evans's *Specimens* and the *englynion* 'I Lys
Ifor Hael' (To the Court of Ifor the Generous), through Thomas
Gray's *The Bard* to Horace Walpole's novel, *The Castle of Otranto*
(1764), is a highly diverse assortment of works out of which to
blend a coherent literary movement. In the last half of this century
of paradox and literary eccentricity, however, such difficulties are
perhaps to be expected.

Welsh antiquarians knew that the key to the period was in their
hands, or rather in many private libraries scattered throughout the
country. Steadily, Lewis Morris was acting as the prime mover,
collecting and copying fragments of verse, and inspiring (or
sometimes coercing) others to do likewise. The laborious work
progressed slowly. It had begun with the publication of Edward
Lhuyd's *Archaeologica Britannica* in 1707 and Morris's own
Tlysau in 1735 and would, no doubt, have progressed more rapidly
had Welsh scholars made better use of the printing press, the
potential of which was understood but never fully exploited. Thus,
important works like Morris's *Celtic Remains*, on which he
finished working in 1757, was not published until 1878, and then
only partially. Likewise, much valuable information and research
work, both new and old, languished in manuscript. Indeed, for
much of the latter half of the eighteenth century Welsh scholars
worked painstakingly in libraries, their work unknown and largely
unanticipated by English writers eager for such material.

The curiosity concerning the Celtic period in both Wales and
England during this period had its roots in two phenomena that had
developed during the first half of the century: the decline of Augustan
literature and the growth of antiquarianism. It is worth spending a
little time examining those trends that, when combined, caused a
generation of poets and scholars to rediscover the Celtic period.

The term 'Augustan', commonly used to describe the literature of the period 1680–1740, encompasses the work of Dryden, Pope, Addison, Swift and Johnson, with Goronwy Owen as its main exponent in Wales. The work of these writers shares the characteristics of poetry of the Augustan reign in classical literature (27 BC–AD 14), the age of Virgil, Horace, Ovid and Tibulus. Both periods are characterized by 'civilized' literature, expressing rational concepts of a general nature, often through set literary forms. The more comprehensive term 'neoclassicism', however, extends further to bridge the gap with Romanticism, covering the period between 1680 and 1784. Such terms are by their nature imprecise; nevertheless, neoclassicism incorporates the work of writers who, in addition to looking back to the golden age of Rome, also turned to the giants of their own tradition for inspiration. The Welsh neoclassicists naturally returned to the golden age of Welsh poetry, to the work of the Poets of the Princes and Dafydd ap Gwilym, using and developing the forms of *englyn* and *cywydd*, and reviving the declining art of *cynghanedd*. In England their counterparts revisited the work of Milton, Spenser and Chaucer, their most illustrious predecessors.

Neoclassical ideas still current towards the end of the period include the emphasis on the art of writing as a craft that could be improved upon and perfected. This is a development of the Miltonic concept of God-given poetry. Neoclassicists believed, it might be said, that inspiration (*yr awen*) was God-given, but the poetry (*y gerdd*) belonged to man. It is to the neoclassicists also that we owe the re-emphasis on poetic forms of previous centuries, demonstrated to good effect by both Goronwy Owen's and Evan Evans's use of the *cywydd*, and Edward Lhuyd's reworking of the pastoral genre. In England too, the pindaric ode was developed by Gray, and the heroic couplet became so widespread through its use by poets like Dryden and Pope that it came to characterize the period.

Neoclassicism parts ways with Augustan literature not over issues of form, but over issues of content. The seventeenth and early eighteenth centuries saw a strong focus on religious poetry dealing with moral and philosophical topics. Milton, for instance, wrote *Paradise Lost* in order to interpret God's great design to ordinary men:

> . . . What in me is dark
> Illumine, what is low raise and support;
> That to the height of this great argument
> I may assert eternal providence,
> And justify the ways of God to men.

Neoclassicists gradually brought the focus back to human kind, a philosophy neatly summed up by Pope in *An Essay on Man*:

> Know then thyself, presume not God to scan,
> The proper study of mankind is man.

The neoclassical emphasis on mankind led to the general discussion of man's commonality that persisted for most of the eighteenth century. Neoclassical poetry painted a general portrait of man and nature in relation to God. In consequence, the use of the imagination was necessarily conservative throughout the period. Imagination, on the whole, was considered to be dangerous, an instrument of immorality and excess that was to be used solely as adornment of the subject.

Naturally enough, reaction against these conventions and rules formed the starting-point for the Romantic movement, with its joyful rediscovery of the imagination. The Romantic emphasis on man in nature, and on individualism, brought new subject-matter and new ideas to the fore, including natural religion, paganism, the emotional link between man and his environment, and the power of imagination to release the poet from the confines of society and social bonds. It is inconceivable that such a reversal in poetic thinking could happen so rapidly without the influence of some intervening factor, and that factor was undoubtedly Celticism.

In Celticism we see the development of some of the most important Romantic concepts: the isolation of the poet in 'I Lys Ifor Hael' and *The Bard*; the wildness of early society with the correspondingly wild and imaginative descriptions of nature from the original poetry; the exploration of druidism and paganism; and the use of imagination to complete the unfinished jigsaw formed by the manuscript evidence. Goronwy Owen, William Wynne and Evan Evans in Wales, and in England, Thomas Gray, William Collins and William Mason, belonged to the tail-end of neoclassicism, between the Augustan and Romantic movements.

Often referred to as pre-Romantic, their work betrays an uncomfortable clash of ideas, at times bearing a much closer resemblance to Romantic than to Augustan or neoclassical literature. Evan Evans, for instance, stands out among the Morrisian circle for his emphasis on nature, demonstrated well in his poem 'Hiraeth y Bardd am ei Wlad' (The Longing of the Poet for his Country).

It appears to be symptomatic of this shift away from neoclassicism that writers became anxious to find new sources of inspiration. However, the tendency to turn to history for fresh material persisted and, having exhausted the Classical period, the Celtic era became a magnet for poets, writers and scholars alike. However briefly, literary activity and antiquarianism became entwined, the one providing the impulse to write, the other providing the raw material from which to draw inspiration. Indeed, such was the similarity between the two types of activity in this period that Thomas Gray, for instance, could approach Celticism through poetry—writing possibly the best-known Celtic poem, *The Bard*, in 1757—and then move on to a series of essays accompanied by translations, eventually abandoning poetry completely in a seamless transition.

For the Celtic movement to flourish, it needed material upon which to feed. Providentially, the growing antiquarian movement was able to supply that material. Antiquarianism was itself a branch of the mainstream theory of history which was constantly developing throughout the seventeenth and eighteenth centuries. History in the seventeenth century was a popular subject, that is to say that a large proportion of the literary population read history books out of interest and for entertainment. Factual, analytical history was not designed to win widespread popular acclaim, so instead, historians produced easy-reading history, easy to understand and to enjoy. This rightly suggests that factual accuracy was not the main priority; rather, historians strove to create readable literature.

Denys Hay, in his book *Annalists and Historians – Western Historiography from the VIIIth to the XVIIIth Century* (1977), relates an anecdote about a seventeenth-century historian that suggests that primary sources were not then highly regarded:

Father Daniel went to see the volumes in the Royal library, spent an hour among them and declared he was very satisfied. Happy man! He himself said the citing of Manuscripts did great credit to a historian, that he had seen many, but that reading them was more of a labour than it was worth.

However, historical philosophy changed radically during the eighteenth century, mainly due to the work of historians such as Hume, Bolingbroke and Voltaire. These authors refused to accept the seventeenth-century definition of what history should encompass, and sought to escape the narrow vision of their predecessors, who saw history as a catalogue of wars and court conspiracies. Hume's most revolutionary idea was that the patterns of the present could be discerned through studying the past. It was not a new idea, but one that had lapsed in historical philosophy. This led directly to the idea that all examples of man's behaviour were grist to the historian's mill. This in turn led to the acceptance of primary sources, and of literature as a primary source. Thus, Hume used private material—autobiographies, letters, poems—as historical material in his work.

At the same time, another historical movement was gaining strength through the work of innovative scholars such as Edward Lhuyd. This kind of writing also became popular, although it had little in common with the histories of authors such as Father Daniel. Lhuyd's work was antiquarianism, a branch of scholarship. History was regarded as a kind of popular literature, and it was the role of the former, not the latter, to trace extinct civilizations and assess the social conditions of the past.

In the eighteenth century therefore we see the two separate branches of seventeenth-century history—popular history and antiquarianism—coming together so that the historian became both chronicler and scholar. The mix is not perfect in its early days; in Hume's early work, the essays on human behaviour are separated from the historical chapters, but the general trend was to produce more thorough and all-encompassing history books.

The increasing emphasis on historical interpretation and the growing need for more primary sources (letters, poems and the like) explains in part one of the more puzzling eighteenth-century trends, and one closely connected with Celticism—literary faking. It seems paradoxical that, in the very age when the modern ideal of accuracy in history was making an appearance, James Macpherson, Thomas Chatterton, Thomas Gray and Iolo

Morganwg were writing literature based on fake history or faking the work of earlier writers.

No doubt the intense scrutiny of the authentic material, and the genuine desire for more, played a part, as did the overall lack of knowledge about the period: historians had previously dealt almost exclusively with a fairly narrow field, that of modern British history from the beginning of the Tudor dynasty onwards. There were exceptions, naturally, but it would appear that early British history received little or no attention, mainly because the lack of information about the period was an insoluble difficulty for Hume and others. The historians of the period considered early British history to be barbaric, and this dark period extended from the Middle Ages back to Celtic times. David Punter, in his book *The Literature of Terror*, refers to the eighteenth century's 'foreshortened sense of past chronology', which neatly sums up the sense in which any past event beyond what was familiar became caught up in a vague impression of primitivism. Because of this, the field was well and truly open to fakery, and the rewards for a successful fake were great, as Macpherson was to discover.

With its emphasis on evidence, and an acceptance of literature as a primary source, antiquarianism flourished in Wales. Building on the foundations of Edward Lhuyd's research, interest in the work of the early Welsh poets increased rapidly, and the work of recording and copying the work of these *Cynfeirdd*, preserved in manuscripts, began. It was this activity that set the foundations of the Celtic movement and linked the development of history and poetry more closely than ever before, since it was through poetry in the main that historic fact about the dimly lit Celtic period emerged.

The printing press also became an essential factor in the discussion and dissemination of early literature. It was not now sufficient to copy examples of early literature out of manuscripts in private libraries. Celticists throughout Britain demanded proof of their existence. The printing press was the only means of satisfying the general demand. This facet of antiquarian activity increased in Wales towards the end of the seventeenth century and throughout the eighteenth century, as versatile scholars such as Lewis Morris and Evan Evans took an active interest in the field. Gradually, these men became convinced of the importance of publishing the early works, though Welsh poetry was never to enjoy the attention lavished on its fake rival, James Macpherson's Scottish epic.

In the face of the decline of Augustanism, Celticism offered poets a way forward, supported by the heightened activity in the antiquarian field during the same period. The appeal of the surviving fragments of early British poetry, and the early British period in general, is not hard to see. Within a single movement, Celticism encompassed several of the most compelling literary themes of the mid-eighteenth century.

The first of these, and the starting-point for the whole movement, was the emergence through antiquarian research of several fragments of authentic early British poems. Enthusiasm for the genuine Welsh article was somewhat blunted by the emergence, in 1760, of James Macpherson's poems, attributed by him to the fictitious Scottish poet, Ossian mac Finn. The whole literary scene, in Wales as in England, was set alight by the 'discovery', with curious and ecstatic letters flying to and fro from London to Edinburgh. At first, men of letters like Thomas Gray were inclined to believe the forger's tale:

> I am so charmed with the two specimens of Erse poetry, that I cannot help giving you the trouble to enquire a little farther about them, and should wish to see a few lines of the original, that I may form some slight idea of the language, the measures, and the rhythm . . . Is there any more to be had of equal beauty or at all approaching to it?

In comparison with Macpherson's work, specifically attuned as it was to the eighteenth-century ear, Evans's specimens, short and incomplete were an anticlimax, though genuine, and it took some time for their very different merits to be appreciated. Evans himself felt the injustice, and delivered some scathing comments on his rival's work in his 1764 treatise 'De Bardis Dissertatio'. The critics' eventual enthusiasm for genuine discoveries sprang from the fragments themselves, and in turn speeded up the process of uncovering more of them.

The second factor in the popularity of Celticism also relates to history. The relatively new emphasis on literature as a primary source of evidence meant that any such material excited more interest than before. The Celtic fragments were not only strangely wild and beautiful, they also provided information about a different civilization, and this was fully appreciated. Thus the appeal was twofold: the poetry itself was inspirational, and it also revealed a society wherein the poet played a central and valued role. The decline of poetry in the early eighteenth century in Wales had left poets particularly insecure. The antidote to such feelings was to draw inspiration from a culture in which the role of the poet was far more integral to society. Celticism offered an opportunity to do just that, at a time when poets in Wales (as in England) were struggling to maintain the poetic tradition. It must indeed have been welcome to hark back to a time of supreme poetic confidence, when royal poets sang in royal courts without doubting the supremacy of the song or of the tradition from which it sprang. Though unable to understand the poetry in the original Welsh, the portrayal of the poet as a leading figure in society also had fundamental appeal in England. Poets could be more sanguine about the decline of a tradition dating back to Classical authors if there was an alternative native British tradition with which to identify.

Linked with this desire to unearth a strong and continuous native tradition beginning with the earliest British poets (and there is some evidence that English poets sought to extend this line back to druidism) and preserved in manuscripts, was the search for a native epic. For, from an eighteenth-century point of view, the quality of the epic provided a means of assessing the quality of the tradition from which it sprang. The classical epics set the standard that Milton aspired to reach, and proof was needed that an old Welsh or Gaelic epic could measure up to the same standard. At the same time, contemporary Welsh poets felt the pressure to produce an epic in the vernacular to demonstrate the richness of the language—a task to which no mid-eighteenth-century poet seemed equal. Goronwy Owen especially devoted considerable effort to exploring the resources of the Welsh language, notably in 'Cywydd y Farn Fawr', to assess its suitability for an epic work (*arwrgerdd*). Consequently, the excitement of the Welsh scholars on discovering for the first time part of what seemed to be a genuine Welsh epic was overwhelming. That excitement was captured in a letter from Lewis Morris to Edward Richard in 1758:

who do you think I have at my elbow, as happy as ever Alexander thought himself after a conquest? No less a man than Ieuan Fardd, who hath discovered some old MSS lately that no body of this age or the last ever as much as dreamed of. And this discovery is to him and me as great as that of America by Columbus. We have found an epic Poem in the British called Gododin, equal at least to the Iliad, Aeneid or Paradise Lost.

The discovery of Aneirin's poetry had answered the prayers of the Welsh scholar-poets and, in their eyes at least, had proved once and for all the pedigree and stature of the Welsh poetic tradition.

The convergence of these contemporary themes made the appeal of Celticism unsurprising and, for a short period, almost universal. Between 1750 and 1760, when Evan Evans was collecting his *Specimens,* Thomas Gray was painstakingly researching the early British period for an essay named *Cambri,* and virtually every scholar in Wales and England had read the standard works dealing with the period. As we have seen, facts about the Celtic period were few and far between, and writers were heavily dependent on a handful of key works, widely read, that encapsulated the sum of eighteenth-century understanding of the Celtic period. These works repay a closer look, and were as formative in their way as the fragments of poetry.

The three primary sources most often referred to are the works of Tacitus, Caesar and Giraldus Cambrensis. Caesar, Roman politician and brilliant military leader, was also a writer who recorded in detail his infamous campaigns in the *Commentarii.* His successful campaign against Britain is chronicled in *De Bello Gallico,* together with a description of the Celts. Caesar also paints a vivid picture of the druids as priests and poets, and emphasizes their elevated position within Celtic society. He writes that the role of the druid was to

officiate at the worship of the gods, regulate sacrifices, private as well as public, and expound questions of religion. Young men resort to them in large numbers for study, and the people hold them in great respect . . . During [pupils'] novitiate it is said that they learn by heart a great number of verses; and accordingly some remain twenty years in a state of pupilage. It is against the principles of the Druids to commit their doctrines to writing . . .

The *Commentarii* were almost wholly translated into English by the seventeenth century, but every schoolboy had read them in the original Latin.

Cornelius Tacitus, the renowned historian, wrote the equally popular *De Analogia* which contains an account of Roman Britain, together with the famous passage describing the druids' defence of Anglesey against the invading Roman army:

> On the shore stood the forces of the enemy, a dense array of arms and men, with women dashing through the ranks like furies, their dress funereal, their hair dishevelled, and carrying torches in their hands. The druids around the host, pouring forth dire imprecations, with their hands uplifted towards the heavens, struck terror into the soldiers by the strangeness of the sight; insomuch that as if their limbs were paralysed, they exposed their bodies to the weapons of the enemy, without an effort to move.

This passage instilled in its eighteenth-century audience a vivid impression of the mystical power of the Celtic priest-poets. It also accounts for the recurrence of long white beards and flowing robes etc. in descriptions of early poets. Gray's *The Bard* is typical, and betrays the influence that Tacitus had on his vision of the Celtic bard:

> On a rock, whose haughty brow
> Frowns o'er old Conway's foaming flood,
> Robed in the stable garb of woe,
> With haggard eyes the poet stood;
> (Loose his beard and hoary hair
> Streamed, like a meteor, to the troubled air)
> And, with a master's hand and prophet's fire,
> Struck the deep sorrows of his lyre.

Giraldus Cambrensis' *Itinerarium Cambriae* was another favourite source for Celticists. Cambrensis (Gerallt Gymro) of course, had the advantage of knowing Wales well, and the eighteenth century took careful note of his record of Welsh legends and customs, especially those pertaining to the druids. He was considered an authority on the national character of the early Welsh people.

These provided what was the closest the eighteenth century had to authentic evidence about early Celtic times, and contemporary historians and antiquarians drew heavily on these sources. The most well-known of the secondary sources, based on those first-hand accounts, was Thomas Carte's *A General History of Britain* whose section on Welsh culture was written with the help of Lewis Morris. This work was published between 1747 and 1755, the first volumes coinciding with the rapid growth in interest in Celticism. The first volume of Carte's *History* contained a discussion of druidism and an article on Welsh literature, drawing on Morris's expertise. The second volume contained the popular and false historical myth of Edward I's massacre of the Welsh bards. Carte's *History* also provides us with the best contemporary record of standard works on this subject: William Camden's *Britannia* (1586) (containing additional information about druidism and about the Brythonic and Gallic languages), Sir John Prys's *Historiae Britannicae Defensio* (1573), Jean-Babtiste Fennel's *Religion des Anciens Gaulois*, Siôn Dafydd Rhys's *Cambro-brytannicae Cymraecaeve Linguae Institutiones et Rudimenta* (1592), and David Powel's *The History of Cambria* (1584). Other standard works in the Celticist's library would have been Percie Enderbie's *Cambria Triumphans* (1661), and John Davies's *Antiquae Linguae Britannicae . . . Rudimenta* (1621). This formed a respectably sized canon on Celticism, serving as the basis for the Celtic movement in England and Wales. The steady trickle of studies of the period was both an encouragement for, and the product of, growing interest in the early British period among writers and poets.

Celticism was an unusual episode in literary history by any standards. Few movements have been so fuelled by enthusiasm and been consumed so quickly by another, of more durable appeal. Few movements also have combined the efforts of historians and antiquarians so successfully with the talents of contemporary writers. Indeed, in the true spirit of eighteenth-century versatility, the two activities were often undertaken by the same people.

The concept of developing the writing of poetry as an art was a comparatively new one in England, but was an integral part of the Welsh poetic tradition, a fact noted by Thomas Gray in his research work. As a result, poets like Goronwy Owen and Evan Evans became interested in history and antiquarianism as they collected information about early Welsh poetry and poets to feed their craft. Indeed, it becomes increasingly difficult to distinguish between poets and antiquarians in this period, so knowledgeable were the poets about the literary history and traditions of the past.

It seems inevitable that the search for authentic material by English writers should eventually reach Wales and the Welsh scholar-poets in their antiquarian pursuit. It is proof of the remoteness, from an English standpoint, of Wales in the eighteenth century that this connection did not happen until 1760, and then almost by chance. That chance brought together the most prominent figures in the Celtic movement in Wales and England, Evan Evans and Thomas Gray, both scholar-poets, to form a connection that boosted the literary activity on both sides of Offa's Dyke. It was indeed a pivotal connection in the history of Celticism, and stands out as a prime example of the way in which the Celtic movement developed in a pattern of reciprocal influence by the Welsh and English literary cultures.

Evan Evans (1731–88), protégé of Lewis Morris, was the focal point of the Celtic movement in Wales. Eccentric and unstable, a creature of his time, he was chronologically and temperamentally suited to become the poet at the heart of the transition between the neoclassical and Romantic movements in Wales. Evans, like Goronwy Owen, earned his living as a priest. Born in Lledrod, Cardiganshire, he met Lewis Morris—whose mantle as the foremost authority on early Welsh literature he was to inherit—early in life. Morris added the study of Welsh literature and poetic forms to the admirably thorough education Evans received at Edward Richard's school at Ystrad Meurig. Morris also introduced Evans to Goronwy Owen and William Wynne, other leading poets of his generation, and coined the name by which he was known in literary circles, Ieuan Brydydd Hir (Ieuan the Tall Poet), in affectionate reference to his unusual height. Evans progressed in 1750 to Merton College, Oxford, and then to work as a curate. During this period he wrote poetry, and searched for manuscripts of early Welsh poetry at the behest of Lewis Morris. He spent periods of time in England, reading in private libraries, including time spent transcribing the Red Book of Hergest in the library of Jesus College, Oxford, and it was during these fruitful periods that Evans made contact with the Celticists in the English universities and beyond. Evans's integrity as a scholar was in stark contrast to that of some of his contemporaries. In all his work, he adhered to the instruction given to him at the start of his career by Lewis Morris:

As I apprehend your chief Employment at first will be copying old
Welsh manuscripts. If you meet with any dark passage or bad poetry,
you had best leave blanks till you can compare it with other
manuscripts, or write with black lead pencil. Let your Letters be very
strong and distinct in your copy. A small matter well wrote is better
than much ill wrote.

And a 'small matter' written by Evan Evans was indeed better than
'much' written by a less scrupulous scholar. His copies were a safe
basis for comparison, and set a high standard for the future. The
same scrupulous standards were also applied to his translations. In
the preface to his *Specimens*, he wrote:

As to the translation, I have endeavoured to render the sense of the
Bards faithfully, without confining myself to too servile a version, nor
have I, on the other hand, taken liberty to wander much from the
originals, unless where I saw it absolutely necessary, on account of the
different phraseology and idiom of language.

Evans understood, as Edward Lhuyd and Lewis Morris had
before him, that the most important task of all for Welsh
antiquarians was to collect and compile the early texts that were
hoarded in private libraries throughout the country, and to publish
their contents for the benefit of a much wider audience. However
well understood, though, was the need for publication, Evans
made little progress in publishing his findings, and in 1760, at the
height of the Celtic movement, his 'specimens' and the treatise on
them, 'De Bardis Dissertatio', were still in manuscript form. 1760
was the year the poetry of 'Ossian' was published in Scotland,
causing a tremendous stir in Wales and England. We can only
conjecture what might have happened had Evans published the
Welsh treasures first.

However, the much needed spur to publish eventually came
from England, from that most English of poets, Thomas Gray.
Gray was born in Cornhill, London, in 1716. Educated at Eton
and Peterhouse, Cambridge, he turned in the highest social
circles—though he was not from a particularly wealthy or noble
family—through his close friendship with Horace Walpole, son of
the then prime minister, Sir Robert Walpole. Gray settled in
Cambridge, living a scholarly life of research and poetry, and

making his mark as author of 'Elegy Written in a Country Churchyard' in 1751. That poem betrays Gray's confusion as a poet at the tail-end of the neoclassical movement, and stands out as an early pre-Romantic work because of its emphasis on the solitariness of the poet figure, and its rejection of Augustan generality in favour of individualism.

Shortly after publishing the 'Elegy', Gray's research led him to consider a sketched history of English poetry, left unfinished by Alexander Pope. That led him to begin work on a study of early British poetry as a possible forerunner of the modern poetic tradition. The study, *Cambri*, was finished in 1758, and at that time, Gray had no idea that such treasures were being unearthed by Evans in Wales. He was, however, familiar with the name of Lewis Morris as a leading antiquarian, from his contribution to Thomas Carte's *History*. Carte records his debt to the Welshman in a note to the first volume:

> These are the words of a very judicious Welsh antiquarian (Mr. Lewis Morris) perfectly well versed in the writings of the old british poets, who refers me to Dr. John David Rhys' grammar . . .

This note is reproduced verbatim in *Cambri*, and bears testimony to Gray's first contact with contemporary Welsh scholarship. However, he did not pursue the tantalizing lead until two years later, in 1760, when a friend sent him some of James Macpherson's fake Erse poems. Gray's enthusiastic welcome for these poems showed that his desire to read early poetry was far from extinguished. His reaction to Macpherson's poetry is also intriguing in that it demonstrates his need as a poet to believe the Erse poems genuine, whilst his academic mind forces him to remain, rightly, sceptical. In a letter to Thomas Wharton in June 1760, he says:

> If you have seen Stonehewer he has probably told you of my old Scotch (or rather Irish) poetry. I am gone mad about them. they are said to be translations (literal & in prose) from the Erse tongue, done by one Macpherson, a young Clergyman in the High-lands. he means to publish a Collection he has of these Specimens of antiquity, if it be antiquity: but what plagues me is, I can not come at any certainty on that head. I was so struck, so extasié with their infinite beauty, that I

writ into Scotland to make a thousand enquiries. The letters I have in
return are ill-wrote, ill-reason'd, unsatisfactory, calculated (one would
imagine) to deceive one, & yet not cunning enough to do it cleverly. In
short, the whole external evidence would make one believe these
fragments (for so he calls them, tho' nothing could be more entire)
counterfeit: but the internal is so strong on the other side, that I am
resolved to believe them genuine, spite of the Devil & the Kirk . . .

The same letter shows that Gray's attention had also turned to
Wales, but Evans's work is dealt with almost as a footnote:

The Welch poets are also coming to light: I have seen Discourse in Mss.
about them (by one Mr Evans, a Clergyman) with speciments of their
writings. this is in Latin, &, tho' it don't approach the other, there are
fine scraps among it.

It is interesting to note that the genuine work of the Welsh
Cynfeirdd did not please as much as Macpherson's fakeries. It
should not surprise, however, since Macpherson's poems were
products of the eighteenth century, aimed at the contemporary
palate. Evans's work, though, stood the test of academic scrutiny,
and he was not taken in by the Ossianic enthusiasm. In his Welsh
preface to his essay, 'De Bardis Dissertatio', he wrote:

Certainly I would not be taking this task upon me, except for the
tauntings of the English, that we have no poetry that it pays to show to
the world: and that one of the inhabitants of the Highlands of Scotland
has translated a quantity of the work of an old Poet; or rather has
adorned and tidied some later work; and has laid it out in his own
name. (tr.)

The 'Dissertatio' was inserted as the preface to his collection of
early texts in Latin translation. It had been shown to Gray by an
acquaintance with Welsh connections, in the light of his enthusiasm for things Celtic, since Gray had commissioned a friend to
search for precisely that kind of material. The friend was Daines
Barrington, a judge on the Welsh circuit who took an active
interest in antiquarianism and was a celebrated naturalist. In 1757,
Barrington was appointed to the counties of Anglesey, Caernarfonshire and Merioneth, and doubtless came into contact with

the leading Welsh scholars and poets. He was himself a prolific writer, though not of the first rank, and his circle of friends included Horace Walpole, James Boswell, Dr Johnson and Bishop Percy, as well as Thomas Gray. Through his numerous contacts in Wales, Barrington met Evan Evans and, in 1760, took a manuscript copy of his work to show Thomas Gray in Cambridge. Evans recorded the development in a letter to Richard Morris in April 1760:

> I have waited on Mr Justice Barrington at Caernarvon with the Dissertation on the Bards, who approved of it. He has taken it and a copy of Nennius, both bound together to London . . . he advises me by all means to translate more of the ancient Bards after the same manner I have done those odes I sent you, and make a small book of it by itself, which he says will sell well. He says that Mr Gray of Cambridge admires Gwalchmai's Ode to Owen Gwynedd, and I think deservedly. He says he will show the Dissertation to Mr. Gray, to have his judgement of it, and to correct it when necessary.

Gray's interest in the work finally convinced Evans to do what Lewis Morris had been urging him to do for years—to gather together the fruits of his research, translate and publish it. Barrington did indeed show Evans's work to Gray and maintained a link between them, eventually paying for the publication of the *Specimens* in 1764, all at the request of Thomas Gray. Evans acknowledged the influence of these English scholars in the introduction to the *Specimens*:

> I have with great reluctance, been forced by some of my English friends, who were desirous to know something of the nature of our poetry to attempt a translation of an Ode of Taliesin, and I have of my own accord translated an ode of Gwalchmai the son of Meilir, who flourished about the year 1157, who has wrote a very spirited one on one of the victories of prince Owain Gwynedd.

Evans further demonstrates Gray's influence by referring to *The Bard* throughout his own poem, 'A Paraphrase of Psalm 137'.

Evans's willingness to allow Gray to correct his work demonstrates the eminence of the English poet. It is hardly surprising that he should therefore have had such an encouraging effect on Evans, who was not known for his diligence. Gray did indeed look over the essay and the translations before they were published, giving Evans the benefit of his research into the Celtic period, and himself an opportunity at last to read authentic verse by the early poets. Evans's volume contained translations of the work of Owain Cyfeiliog, Hywel ab Einion, Dafydd Benfras, Aneirin, Taliesin and many others. The effect of the connection between Evans and Gray was mutually beneficial, for among Evans's translations, Gray gathered material for his poems/translations, 'The Death of Hoel', 'Caradoc' and 'Conan' and, most famously perhaps, 'The Triumphs of Owen'. In the translated fragments, Gray and his contemporaries found the inspiration and the new themes they sought: the supremacy of the poet; the image of the poet as priest and as warrior; and the elevated position of the poet in society. The scholars in Wales gained confirmation of the quality of the lost poetry and of the former glory of the ailing Welsh tradition.

Evans's *Specimens* was the culmination of the Celtic movement in Wales, and firmly established him as an important scholar. Unfortunately, intervention by Lewis Morris, Thomas Gray or someone of similar influence seemed necessary to encourage Evans in his scholarly work, for, although he wrote a great deal of his best poetry after 1764, he never produced another major work. Evans subsequently led a transient, unsettled life and in order to try to escape his debts he enlisted in the army in 1768, only to be released four days later when his superior officers discovered that he was a priest. At the time, it was rumoured that Evans was showing signs of insanity. Evans then led a nomadic life, moving from parish to parish in England and Wales until 1771. In that year, he received the patronage of Sir Watkin Williams Wynn, who gave him an annual income and the run of his library at Wynnstay. This was one of the most productive periods of Evans's life, from the point of view of copying manuscripts, but in 1778 he incurred the displeasure of Sir Watkin, and he relied thereafter on the kindness of friends, as he was too old and too notorious to hope for preferment within the Church. Despite poverty, this was the period in which he wrote many of his most memorable poems, including the *englynion* 'I Lys Ifor Hael' (1780). Evan Evans died in Lledrod in 1788.

The main exponents of Celticism in Wales and England, Evan Evans and Thomas Gray, also both demonstrate in their poetry how Celticism became the way forward to Romanticism, although neither poet can be said to have followed that path to the end. So closely do Celticism and early Romanticism fit together that the two are often indistinguishable. The Celticists revelled in the primitive qualities of Celtic society, in particular the heroic nature of the poets and the contrast it presented to the rational neo-classical world-view. Here was something different, an alternative form of society from which to learn, and with which to challenge the oppressive shadow of neoclassicism. The vivid fragments that inspired Gray, Evans and their contemporaries were none the less incomplete, thereby encouraging the use of imagination to supply what history and literature could not. Thus, Gray's *The Bard* not only draws on historic legend from Thomas Carte's book, and on Tacitus' description of the druids, it also paints a scene embellished by the fruits of Gray's own imagination, producing a fantastical ode, quite unlike his previous work, which was, on the surface at least, cast in neoclassical mould. Gray chooses to portray his Celtic bard in an anti-establishment stance, challenging the king himself. This was revolutionary in terms of the previous neoclassical tradition, in which the poet had spoken to society and for society. It is perhaps far-fetched to claim the solitary, shy Mr Gray as the first of the great Romantic rebel-poets, but the first moves in an anti-establishment direction are there to be seen.

Evans, too, used and developed those elements in the early poetry that held special appeal for him. Loyalty and homage to a master had always been features of the Welsh poetic tradition and these are apparent in Evans's early request poems (*cywyddau gofyn*). That loyalty, however, seems a corrupt version of the stronger tie between poet and prince or nobleman which held fast from the *Cynfeirdd* onwards through the heyday of Welsh poetry. One might say that the loyalty in the later *cywyddau gofyn* was born out of need, and out of the poets' economic dependence upon the noblemen to whom the poems are directed. The work of Aneirin and Taliesin, however, is startlingly different. In the early poems copied by Evan Evans, the unquestioning loyalty of poet to prince is born of love, and reflects a mutual respect and full acknowledgement of the relationship between leadership and poetry in that society. Poets in those early times lived and died with their prince, and the bond between them has a resonance that lends the poetry its emotive appeal. That early bond is echoed in the brooding melancholy of Evans's *englynion* 'I Lys Ifor Hael'. By rekindling that genuine and dignified bond between poet and dead master, Evans creates an enduringly great poem. The poem has added significance in that the focus on the poet's isolation, and the dark, melancholic mood heralds the departure from neoclassicism and foretells the Romantic sensibility to come.

Another remarkable feature of Celticism was the way in which it brought together two very different cultures at different points in their development. English poets and writers found the fact behind the attractive fiction in the work of Welsh literati, and this both legitimized and inspired their work. In Wales, the interest in the native heritage shown by English scholars and writers provided an almost immeasurable boost to the work of collating and presenting the early manuscripts, and went some way towards imparting to Welsh poets a regained sense of importance and self-esteem.

Celticism thus held a singular appeal for the mid-eighteenth century. In its stark contrast to neoclassicism, Celticism released poets from the shackles of convention, allowing the imagination free rein and freeing Evans and his contemporaries from an influential literary movement in decline.

BIBLIOGRAPHY

Original Works
Evan Evans, *Some Specimens of the Poetry of the Antient Welsh Bards* (Montgomery, 1764).
Aneirin Lewis (ed.), *The Correspondence of Thomas Percy and Evan Evans* (Baton Rouge, 1957).
Roger Lonsdale (ed.), *The Poems of Gray, Collins and Goldsmith* (New York, 1969).
James Macpherson, *Ossian* (London, 1763).
Hugh Owen (ed.) *Additional Letters of the Morrises of Anglesey (1735–86)* (London, 1947).
Paget Toynbee and Leonard Whibley (eds.), *Correspondence of Thomas Gray* (Oxford, 1935).

Critical Works
Marilyn Butler, *Romantics, Rebels and Reactionaries* (Oxford, 1981).
Thomas Carte, *A General History of England* (London, 1747–55).
Saunders Lewis, *A School of Welsh Augustans* (Bath, 1969).

David Punter, *The Literature of Terror* (London, 1980).

Pat Rogers, *The Augustan Vision* (London, 1974).

E. D. Snyder, *The Celtic Revival in English Literature 1760–1800* (Cambridge, USA, 1923).

Fiona Stafford, *The Sublime Savage* (Edinburgh, 1988).

Articles

Arthur Johnson, 'Gray's use of the Gorchest y Beirdd in "The Bard"', *Modern Literary Review*, 59 (1964).

Idem, *Thomas Gray and 'The Bard'* (Cardiff 1966).

W. P. Ker, 'The Literary Influence of the Middle Ages', Cambridge History of English Literature, vol. 10 (Cambridge, 1913).

CHAPTER 7

IOLO MORGANWG

CERI W. LEWIS

Of all the major historic regions of Wales, only Glamorgan can justifiably claim to have fostered, not merely one, but two great and richly diverse literary traditions. It must not be assumed, however, that both traditions, notwithstanding the fact that they are often intricately intertwined, are firmly based on well-attested historical foundations. On the one hand, there is the undeniably authentic tradition, which is represented by the compositions of a long and talented line of bards and vaticinators who sang in both the strict and free metres; by the works of the region's prose writers and translators; by the scholarly activities of its historians, hagiographers, heraldic bards, lexicographers, grammarians, and professional scribes, whose devoted labours preserved for generations to come the literary treasures of a bygone age; and by the generous patronage extended to bards, littérateurs and antiquarians alike by many of Glamorgan's cultured, literature-loving gentry, whose exemplary munificence frequently provided the indispensable economic basis for so many important literary and scholarly activities. Modern scholarship has convincingly demonstrated that it was an uncommonly rich and dynamic tradition, for which there is an abundance of incontrovertible evidence in early, authentic manuscripts and texts.

On the other hand, there is the essentially fictitious but, nevertheless, very colourful and extremely enchanting 'tradition' that began, from approximately the last decade of the eighteenth century onwards, to capture the imagination and to arouse the enthusiasm of a new generation of Welsh scholars and men of letters who were then becoming increasingly prominent in Welsh literary and cultural circles in both Wales and London, a city which exercised considerable influence during that period on the literary life of the Principality. This is the 'tradition' that was created by the extraordinarily fertile imagination of Edward Williams (1747–1826), who is better known by his bardic name of Iolo Morganwg. This romantic poet and antiquary is unquestionably the most remarkable and most complicated figure in the whole history of Welsh literature. Although he had received no formal education in school or college, he was in his day a man of impressive erudition and of quite extraordinary versatility. In his early years he was a particularly gifted romantic poet, in both Welsh and English, and throughout his long and astonishingly productive life he remained an ardent romantic dreamer and visionary.

His remarkably numerous papers, letters, diaries and documents, which are now preserved in the famous Llanover collection of manuscripts in the National Library of Wales, Aberystwyth, testify clearly to the extraordinary range of his scholarly interests. For it must be emphasized that the forged strict-metre poems he attributed to the great medieval Welsh poet, Dafydd ap Gwilym (*fl.* 1340–70), and the great corpus of spurious matter—chronicles, triadic sequences, proverbs and apophthegms of some of the 'famous' Welsh sages of old, bardic statutes, and the like—which he succeeded in publishing early in the nineteenth century in parts of *The Myvyrian Archaiology of Wales* represent only a comparatively small proportion of his indefatigable labours. His early and sustained contact with the cultured and manifestly talented fraternity of bards that had emerged in the Uplands (*Blaenau*), the northern part of Glamorgan, and his close association with many of the intelligent and well-informed local historians, littérateurs, grammarians and lexicographers who had been inspired by the scholastic and antiquarian revival whose initial impetus had been provided by the scholastic activities of Edward Lhuyd (1660–1709), brought Iolo Morganwg early in his career into the main stream of eighteenth-century Welsh scholarship and helped to lay the foundations of his own impressive erudition. As a result of his wide and tireless researches, he acquired a knowledge of the contents of extant Welsh manuscripts unsurpassed by that of any of his contemporaries, especially after the untimely death in 1788 of Evan Evans (Ieuan Fardd), the gifted eighteenth-century antiquary from Cardiganshire. Not surprisingly, therefore, Iolo eventually developed into the outstanding authority of his day on the history of Welsh literature, especially from the fourteenth century onwards, and on many aspects of the nation's history. Throughout the greater part of his long life he diligently studied and transcribed the old manuscripts and a wide variety of books and articles that threw some light on those subjects. His volume *Cyfrinach Beirdd Ynys Prydain*, which was published posthumously in 1829, shows beyond any doubt that he had a firmer grasp of the old bardic learning and of the contents of the early bardic grammars than any of his contemporaries. Indeed, it is not until the advent of Sir John Morris-Jones (1864–1929) that we find a Welsh scholar who can reasonably be compared with him in this field. Iolo's interests, however, were not confined to literature, history or Welsh prosody, for he also acquired a very detailed knowledge of such subjects as architecture, sculpture, botany, geology, agriculture, horticulture, theology and music, and in his later years he was not averse to lecturing occasionally on metallurgy in the school his son, Taliesin, had opened in the new industrial town of Merthyr Tydfil. The keen and highly intelligent interest he took in various scientific disciplines is occasionally reflected in his literary work. So, for example, the interesting, but undeniably eccentric, analysis of the Welsh metrical system which was published in *Cyfrinach Beirdd Ynys Prydain* and which became known variously as '*Dosbarth Morgannwg*' (the 'Glamorgan Classification') or '*Hen Ddosbarth*' (the 'Old Classification') was based on the system devised by the renowned Swedish botanist, Carolus Linnaeus (or Carl von Linné, 1701–78), for the identification and classification of plants.

Iolo's expertise was recognized by the Board of Agriculture in 1796, for in that year he was invited by the Board to prepare detailed descriptions of the land and farms in Glamorgan and Cardiganshire. At a later period, he assisted Walter Davies (Gwallter Mechain, 1761–1849) when the latter was actively collecting material for the two detailed reports, sponsored by the Board of Agriculture, on the state of husbandry in both north and south Wales. Those reports were published in 1810 (reprinted 1813) and in 1815 respectively, and the one that dealt with conditions in south Wales owed much to Iolo Morganwg, who wrote commendably detailed descriptions of the condition of the farms and of the agricultural customs and techniques that were popular at that time in the region, and he occasionally suggested, in his own inimitable manner, all kinds of changes and improvements. He also wrote many diaries containing a wealth of interesting observations on the many things that had attracted his attention as he travelled at various times, on foot, through different parishes—the roads and highways, the villages, the small market towns, the farms, gardens and orchards, the local industries and dialects, and some of the main features of the social, economic and religious life of the region that had aroused his interest. In these reports and diaries, and in the long and detailed letters Iolo sent from time to time to various friends and acquaintances—especially the correspondence that belongs to the period when he was wandering through north Wales diligently searching for literary material that might be published in *The Myvyrian Archaiology of Wales*—we are presented with vivid and extremely interesting descriptions of the various aspects of Welsh life that flashed before his eyes. And these descriptions, it must be emphasized, were written by an uncommonly knowledge-able Welshman who claimed, with considerable justification, that he had travelled on foot through every parish in Wales as well as many parishes in England, a percipient scholar who had a firmer grasp of the literary, cultural and historical traditions of Wales than virtually any of his contemporaries, a man of wide learning who knew of the famous figures who had lived at various times in the past in every part of Wales that he visited. He conversed not only with those farmers and gentry who earnestly aspired to improve agricultural techniques in their local communities, but also with the poets, the literati and those select few who diligently collected or transcribed Welsh manuscripts and took a keen inter-est in Welsh literary developments and activities. Moreover, his work contains some valuable references to the industrialization that was slowly but inexorably spreading over various parts of the northern Uplands of Glamorgan during his lifetime, references which reveal the firm grasp Iolo had succeeded in acquiring of such subjects as geology and some of the related sciences.

The reports, diaries and letters he wrote also reveal quite clearly that he had a detailed knowledge of the religious life of Wales as a whole, of the history and vicissitudes of the old Nonconformist chapels and denominations, and of the way in which the older Nonconformity had affected the literary and cultural life of the counties of south Wales. Indeed, it has been claimed that Iolo has bequeathed to us more valuable material for the understanding of the main features of Welsh life in the late eighteenth and early nine-teenth centuries than has any other Welsh writer of that period. The historical importance of these detailed and interesting descrip-tions is further enhanced by the fact that they do not, on the whole, reflect any marked bias on the author's part, for he does not seem to have been greatly affected while he was writing them by those strange romantic whims and powerful psychological inhibitions that so often afflicted him and inevitably gave rise to many distortions and prejudiced judgements whenever he dealt with the literary history of his native Glamorgan or with the organization, practices and esoteric lore of the professional bards.

Iolo's manuscripts show also that he took a highly intelligent interest in almost all aspects of the discipline that is nowadays called 'the study of folk-life'—an interest in old buildings and the salient features of their architectural design, period furniture, tools and instruments, the victuals that were popular in bygone ages, old customs, games and pastimes associated with the various seasons of the year, folk-songs, old methods of tillage, religious beliefs, ancient proverbs and expressions, idioms of speech, the local dialects, technical terms, ancient beliefs and legends and, to some extent, the clothes and costumes worn in earlier periods. English writers such as Samuel Taylor Coleridge and Robert Southey were amazed at the extent of his knowledge in this field and were deeply impressed by the amount of material he had carefully gathered over the years. Although it would be foolish to deny that other Welsh scholars and antiquarians, such as John Jones of Gellilyfdy, Edward Lhuyd, Lewis Morris, Peter Roberts or William Davies, Cringell, for example, had taken some interest in various aspects of these studies before him, no one had previously exhibited as wide an interest as did Iolo Morganwg and he was almost certainly the first to explain how individuals and learned societies should set about organizing the study of folk-life on a systematic basis. In 1820, when he was in his seventy-third year and only six years before his death, he strongly advocated the establishment of a Welsh corresponding 'Academy' that would not only encourage and foster the study of Welsh literature, history and antiquities, but also actively undertake the work that is nowadays being done in the Museum of Welsh Life in St Fagans—not only the systematic study of folklore and of the Welsh dialects, but also the history and development of all rural industries and, to quote his own words, 'ancient traditional songs Tales Music &c. Ancient Practices in Agriculture, in rural and domestic economy, &c.' He was the first Welshman to grasp fully the fundamental importance of the study of folk-life in *all* its manifold aspects. It is no exaggeration to state that the contribution made by Iolo Morganwg to this particular discipline was one of seminal importance.

The same percipience is evident in his linguistic studies, for the modern scholar is frequently astonished to discover that Iolo had succeeded, even occasionally in his forgeries, in explaining the meaning or, sometimes, the derivation of words that had apparently baffled every one before his day. He was also clearly ahead of all his contemporaries in the intelligent interest he took in Welsh dialectology. Throughout his long life he assiduously collected and recorded in his notebooks old words and dialectal expressions, not only in his native Glamorgan or during his acutely observant wanderings through Carmarthenshire, Pembrokeshire, Cardiganshire, Gwynedd and Powys, but also in such regions as Ewias (in Herefordshire), Blaenau Gwent and Gwynllŵg (Wentloog), where the Welsh language has, alas, virtually disappeared in our day. His papers contain many interesting lists of dialectal words and technical terms connected with various rural crafts, names of birds, animals, insects, flowers, plants, trees, fruits and herbs, words denoting various colours and sounds, idioms, proverbial expressions (as we have already seen), special forms of address, and much else besides. His zeal and curiosity knew no bounds. Nor was it dialectal words alone that aroused his interest, for he collected over a long period the obsolete vocabulary he had seen in the old strict-metre verse, in Middle Welsh prose texts, and in various contemporary publications, such as *Blodeu-gerdd Cymry* (1759) or *Diddanwch Teuluaidd* (1763). Nor did he overlook the works of the celebrated Welsh hymn-writer, William Williams (1717–91), Pantycelyn, which provided him with many instructive examples of words that occurred in the contemporary Carmarthenshire dialects.

After he had studied Edward Lhuyd's *Archaeologia Britannica* (1707), he set about coining Welsh words on the pattern of those he had seen in Cornish and Breton, for he was firmly convinced that there was a close relationship between those two languages and the dialects of Glamorgan and Gwent, to which he naturally devoted a great deal of attention throughout the greater part of his life. He also coined Welsh words on the pattern of those with which he was familiar in Latin and French, languages which he read with considerable ease. His manuscripts contain many lists of words and technical terms he himself had coined in the firm belief that there was an urgent need for them in Welsh if the language was to become the medium for discussing a wide range of technical subjects, including geology, mining, mathematics, geography, theology, philosophy, logic, astronomy, prosody, rhetoric, literary criticism, agriculture and horticulture. No one had previously coined so many Welsh words and technical terms of this kind, and a number of these new linguistic formations deserve the highest praise.

Inspired by the treatise *A Dissertation on the Welsh language, Pointing out it's Antiquity, Copiousness, Grammatical Perfection, with Remarks on it's Poetry*, which one of his former teachers, John Walters, of Llandough, near Cowbridge, published in 1771, Iolo set about amassing a substantial corpus of linguistic data with a view to writing a volume on a broadly similar theme, and one of his manuscripts contains an interesting list of nineteen 'Heads of subjects to be considered in the Critical Essay of ye Welsh Language'. It was obviously Iolo's intention to discuss a fairly wide range of subjects in this work, including *inter alia* the historical connection between the Celtic languages, methods of enriching and embellishing the standard literary language, the main phonological features of Welsh, the various types of compound formations it contained, the main distinguishing features of the various Welsh dialects, the best method of creating a standard oral language, the principles that should be adopted when coining new Welsh technical terms in the arts and sciences, the function of prefixes and affixes in Welsh, 'its figurative Grammar, Rhetoric, poetry', and so on.

He was already collecting data for inclusion in this work about 1770–1, when he was only twenty-three or twenty-four years of age, and it is noteworthy that another of the numerous subjects he intended discussing in it was a comparison of 'the venedotian, Silurian and Dimetian Dialects . . . which is the purest, most regular . . . the different Beauties, defects, coruptions [*sic*] &c. of each considered, with a concise Grammar of each'. This was undoubtedly one of the matters to which he devoted a great deal of attention as he travelled on foot through every parish in Wales, listening intently to the speech of the local inhabitants and carefully recording in his notebooks every unusual word or interesting expression he heard in the local communities. He was greatly perturbed by the possibility that some dialects could completely vanish, even during his own lifetime, before they had been systematically recorded and analysed. It is hardly surprising, therefore, that his manuscripts

contain numerous references to the importance of Welsh dialectology, and here again we come across ideas and suggestions that are
remarkably modern in nature. One example of this is his intention
of writing a grammar based on the colloquial speech of ordinary
folk in his own native province, together with a detailed comparison with the speech heard in other parts of Wales. His intention,
however, was never fulfilled: once again, as with so many other
scholarly projects he had in view, he was building castles in the air,
an inherent failing to which his wife referred in a letter she sent him
during one of his not infrequent absences from home. But, in fair-
ness to Iolo, it must be emphasized that even today, although over
170 years have elapsed since his death, no detailed study of this
nature has been undertaken by any Welsh scholar.

But however enlightened or advanced some of his ideas on this
subject may have been, it would be wrong to assume that Iolo
applied to his researches into the Welsh dialects the scientific methods and techniques that are adopted by responsible modern dialec-
tologists. Some of his comments and conclusions reflect his strong
personal prejudices; nor can it be denied that there are serious lacu-
nae in some parts of his analysis, which is hardly surprising when
we consider the manifold tasks he had to undertake while pursuing
his profession as a stonemason in various parts of Wales and
England. Nevertheless, in spite of these deficiencies, the general
picture he presented of the geographical distribution of the Welsh
dialects was far more interesting and detailed than any that had
previously been given by any Welsh scholar. He fully realized that
the dialectal pattern was considerably more complex than the
simple twofold division between north and south that earlier writers on the subject had stressed *ad nauseam*. Eventually, he came to
the conclusion that there were four main dialects of equal status,
namely, the Gwentian (which embraced the speech of both
Glamorgan and Gwent), the Dimetian, the Powysian and the
Venedotian, but he also stressed that there were important and significant subdivisions, which he endeavoured to identify, within
these four main dialects. In his view, the dialect of Monmouthshire
and east Glamorgan in his day came 'the nearest of any of the
present vernacular Dialects to the Ancient literary dialect'.

Although he manifested some interest in the phonology of the
dialects, it was vocabulary that unquestionably received his greatest attention. As early as 1776, when he was only twenty-nine, he

claimed that he had accumulated a more detailed collection of Welsh words than had any other living person and, as any one who is familiar with the contents of his manuscripts and papers will readily confirm, that was no empty boast. To the end of his life, he continued to add to his very substantial collections of words taken from the various dialects, frequently indicating, as he did so, to which part of Wales various words and distinguishing dialectal features belonged. In this task he made intelligent use of old political and administrative units, especially when it was deemed that the existing shire boundaries were not wholly adequate as markers for the geographical distribution of some word or some dialectal feature or other. Nor did he overlook the influence that may have been exerted by old centres of learning and by those towns that had previously played an important political role in a particular region. These were subjects on which Iolo could expatiate with some authority, and this aspect of his work clearly reflects his historical acumen. Undoubtedly, Iolo's contribution to this subject, notwithstanding some obvious faults and deficiencies, constitutes an important milestone in the history of Welsh dialectology.

No less noteworthy is the part he played in the religious life of his day, for he took a keen interest in theological matters. He became acquainted with some of the leading Unitarians of his day, such as Joseph Priestley, Andrew Kippis, Theophilus Lindsey and Thomas Belsham, and he played a not insignificant role in establishing the Unitarian denomination in south Wales. He was certainly one of those responsible for creating the Unitarian Association in that region in 1802, the so-called 'Cymdeithas Dwyfundodiaid yn Neheubarth Cymru' (South Wales Unitarian Society), and the 'Rules and Ordinances' (*Rheolau a Threfniadau*) that were published the following year were undoubtedly the product of his gifted pen, as the various drafts that occur in his manuscripts amply confirm. He wrote hundreds upon hundreds of hymns, some of which were published in 1812 in a volume entitled *Salmau yr Eglwys yn yr Anialwch*, with a second edition appearing in 1827. Another collection of his hymns was published under the same title in 1834, and both collections appeared in one volume in 1857. However, this represents only a small part of his prodigious output as a hymn-writer, for almost 3,000 unpublished hymns by him occur in manuscripts that are today deposited in the National Library of Wales, Aberystwyth. These have been bound in volumes by his son, Taliesin. Although there are, it must be emphasized, some notable exceptions, most of these hymns make very tedious reading. Rarely do they convey the profound religious experience, the intense passion, or the abundant mental fertility contained in the hymns of William Williams, Pantycelyn, for ex-ample, nor do they contain the radiant vision, the mystic symbolism and striking imagery found in the work of Ann Griffiths (1776–1805), nor yet the exquisitely sweet melancholy and artistic refinement of expression that characterize the compositions of Thomas William(s) (1761–1805), minister of Bethesda in the Vale of Glamorgan. In his hymns, Iolo was far too fond of moralizing and giving expression to his intensely held theological beliefs and to his burning desire for social justice. His predilection for obsolete vocabulary contributed yet further to the distinctly prosaic quality of many of these compositions. His other contribution to hymnology reflects his musical ability: his unpublished papers and manuscripts contain a very large collection of tunes he composed at various times to accompany his hymns or some of the lyrics he had written on non-religious themes. This provides us with yet another example of his astonishing versatility. He learned to play the flute at a comparatively early age and, to quote his own words, he had received some instruction from his mother 'in the Theory and vocal practice of music', a subject that continued to interest him until the end of his life. This interest was unquestionably one of the things that inspired him to collect the folk-tunes, together with the accompanying lyrics, which he heard during his peregrinations through every parish in Wales.

The political aspect of this remarkable man's career has aroused the interest of many latter-day historians. During the various periods in the 1770s and 1790s when he practised his craft as a stonemason in London and its environs, he became acquainted with such celebrated radicals as Thomas Paine, Thomas Hardy, David Williams, John Horne Tooke and some Americans of a similar political persuasion. He read avidly the writings of Rousseau and Voltaire, and revelled in the pulsating excitement of the years that immediately followed the outbreak of the French Revolution. He exulted in the fall of the Bastille, and during the period 1791–5, when he was in his mid- and late-forties, he frequently attended the meetings of those Radical societies in London that openly sympathized with the ideals of the French Revolution, which he regarded as the dawn of a new and glorious age for mankind. He took great pride in the title 'Bard of Liberty' and roundly condemned in both his Welsh and English verses the iniquities of the *ancien régime* and the oppression of the masses by despotic monarchs, rapacious nobles and corrupt priests. He firmly believed that once these latter had been effectively divested of their power and influence the peoples of the world could and would live together in perfect accord and that war, which in the past had been so frequently caused by the selfish dynastic ambitions of kings and princes or by the territorial greed of aristocratic governments, would vanish for ever from the face of the earth. He derived from the doctrine of 'the natural rights of man' the unshakeable conviction that all men are equal and that they should live a life of Christian brotherhood, a theme which recurs in more than one of his numerous hymns. Not surprisingly, he was a vigorous opponent of the slave-trade and a staunch advocate of the abolition of slavery itself. True to his convictions, he refused to accept what, in those days, was a fairly substantial sum of money that had been bequeathed to him by his brothers, who had emigrated to Jamaica, because the money, in his view, had been acquired through the back-breaking toil of numerous Negro slaves in the plantations of that country. 'No! I cannot touch their money,' he declared. 'It is the price of blood—it is the purchase of humanity's birthright; rather would I starve, than be fed on the contaminated gains of that *detested slave-trade!*'

Nevertheless, he could be astonishingly inconsistent in other respects. Although he frequently condemned emperors, kings and princes, he dedicated his two volumes of English verse, *Poems, Lyric and Pastoral*, which were published in 1794, five years, it should be noted, after the fall of the Bastille, 'to his Royal Highness George Prince of Wales'. Moreover, although he roundly condemned war and quoted verses from the Bible to prove that it was absolutely impossible to justify war on any grounds, he nevertheless addressed a poem in English to the Glamorgan Volunteers in which he called upon all patriotic Britons to unite and decisively crush *by force of arms* any one who attempted to oppress them.

No less surprising, perhaps, is the fact that there is not a distinctively Welsh aspect to his political ideas. Iolo, as we shall see, regarded himself and his fellow Glamorgan bards as the inheritors of a long and uncommonly rich tradition that extended back to the period of the druids. He took great pride in both the richness and the unbroken continuity of that ancient tradition, and it is not unreasonable to assume, therefore, that this would have instilled in him a powerful awareness of the distinctive identity of the Welsh people, whose bards had fostered and nurtured such an awareness throughout the centuries. Moreover, during the time he spent practising his craft in London, he became closely associated with many members of the Cymmrodorion and Gwyneddigion Societies, which had been formed in the eighteenth century by London Welshmen partly to allay the intense longing they frequently experienced in their exile for their homeland. Their writings and many of their activities clearly show that they were intensely aware of their inherent Welshness and it might therefore be expected that this would have had a significant influence on Iolo's interpretation of the importance of the French Revolution for the inalienable rights of the people of Wales.

Jean-Jacques Rousseau, whose writings had made a deep impression on Iolo, had proclaimed the principle of self-government when he asserted that every individual who is subject to the will and whims of another is essentially a slave. This principle directly challenged all the existing monarchical and aristocratic systems of government. Obviously, no government could be wholly legitimate unless it was subject to the will and directives of the people it claimed to govern. This basic principle was fully accepted by many of the radical thinkers with whom Iolo came into contact during the periods he spent in London, but he never applied it to his own country. Although he was fully aware of the oppression and injustices that existed in Wales in his day, he did not formulate a specifically Welsh reaction to them. The liberty he so frequently extolled in both his Welsh and English verses was conceived by him in 'universalist' terms. He genuinely sought freedom for *all* men from the tyranny and oppression of monarchs, aristocrats and priests; it was with the rights of men in general and not with those of Welshmen in particular that he was pre-eminently concerned. The explanation for this may lie in the fact that he failed to perceive a meaningful connection between the national identity he saw—more clearly than the vast majority of his contemporaries—in the long and rich bardic tradition and the political identity of the Welsh people. Or, as some scholars have suggested, it is possible that in his political thinking, notwithstanding the warm romantic glow that suffused so much of his literary output, he was pre-eminently a creature of the Enlightenment.

No account of Iolo Morganwg's wide interests or of the extremely valuable contributions he made to so many diverse fields would
be complete without a brief reference to his outstanding creative literary gifts, for he was an important Romantic poet in his own
right, one who has a special place in the history of free-metre Welsh
verse by virtue of the joy and verve that suffused his poetry whenever he sang on the themes of love or nature, or when his muse was
inspired by the gentle, unadorned simplicity of rural life. Indeed,
some of the forged strict-metre *cywyddau* attributed by him to
Dafydd ap Gwilym, and for long accepted as part of that four-
teenth-century bard's authentic canon, and some of his exquisitely
beautiful compositions in the free metres must be listed among the
outstanding products of the Welsh muse in the eighteenth century.
Many of Iolo's contemporaries recognized his genius, and before
his death on 18 December 1826, at the age of seventy-nine, he came
to be highly esteemed by a new generation of Welsh scholars and
men of letters who were determined to do all they reasonably could
to publish what they genuinely considered to be the fruits of his
wide and indefatigable researches. This is not to imply that they
were totally blind to his faults and foibles—his fierce temper, which
could quite easily be aroused, his disagreements and tempestuous
quarrels, even with his closest friends, and his peculiar habits and
eccentricities, which no one could satisfactorily explain. That sober
historian, Theophilus Jones (1759–1812), of Brecon, who was
noted for his balanced judgement and equanimity, referred to him
as 'Mad Ned'.

None of his contemporaries, however, and no one for almost a
hundred years after his death realized that he was a daring, highly
accomplished and astonishingly prolific literary forger, a fact
which Iolo, with a blend of literary expertise and artful cunning,
succeeded in concealing, not only from his closest friends and
acquaintances, but also from his intelligent son Taliesin, who was
unquestionably the apple of his eye and who had seen him labouring day after day, night after night, for many years over his books
and papers in the tiny cottage in Flemingston which was his home.
None of them fully realized that within Iolo Morganwg there dwelt
a talented demon who had driven him on relentlessly throughout
the greater part of his long life.

The latter-day literary historian can now tell, by examining and
analysing Iolo's voluminous writings, that there was a marked

duality in his personality. On the one hand, there was the extremely industrious and percipient literary scholar, the well-informed historian and the keen and highly intelligent observer, who was fully capable, on occasions, of discussing dispassionately various aspects of the literary, social, economic and religious life of Wales. Here was the knowledgeable scholar who had formed a clearer picture of the development of Welsh literature from the fourteenth century to his own day than any of his contemporaries. His work contains the first intelligent attempt, as far as we are now able to determine, to discuss the history of the professional guild of bards. The large corpus of material he gathered in a systematic and commendably scholarly way from various sources that threw some light on this subject was later skilfully used by him in his writings and pronouncements on the teachings and organization of the ancient druids, which aroused the interest of so many scholars and literati both in his own day and in the years that followed. Some of his literary forgeries reveal that he had discovered important facts and developments which had to be rediscovered by university scholars many years after his death. He grasped the significance in the history of the Welsh bardic order of the important eisteddfod that had been held in Carmarthen, probably in 1453, under the patronage of Gruffudd ap Nicolas of Dinefwr, and he fully understood the function of the two eisteddfodic assemblies that had been held in Caerwys in 1523 and 1567. Only a scholar who had fully understood the purpose and significance of these bardic gatherings could have forged as successfully as Iolo did those documents that provided the basis for his volume *Cyfrinach Beirdd Ynys Prydain*. He made a detailed study of the old bardic grammars and triads and of the statute that is traditionally associated with the name of Gruffudd ap Cynan. He fully understood the fundamental difference between the syllabic strict-metre verse and the poetry composed in the accentual free metres that became increasingly popular in Wales from the sixteenth century onwards. He also devoted some attention to that most difficult of subjects, the accentual patterns of strict-metre verse. He had perceived also some of the important stages in the development of that intricate system of consonantal alliteration and internal rhyme known in Welsh as *cynghanedd* nearly a century and a half before Sir Thomas Parry published an important and illuminating paper on this subject in 1936 in the *Transactions of the Honourable Society of Cymmrodorion*. He

found also an analysis of the poetry of the Continental troubadours and *trouvères* in the work of a French scholar and quickly
perceived that there was some resemblance, both as regards theme
and treatment, between this verse and that composed by Dafydd ap
Gwilym. But it is now generally believed that the first scholar to
detect this similarity was Professor E. B. Cowell of Cambridge in
1878, whose work was later developed and expanded by Dr Th. M.
Chotzen, librarian of the Peace Library at The Hague, Holland,
and by Sir Ifor Williams, of Bangor, for, as usual, Iolo never bothered to publish what was really a very important literary discovery.
He saw quite clearly that Tir Iarll (lit. 'The Earl's Land'), the district which included the parishes of Llangynwyd, Betws, Cynffig
and Margam, was the most important nursery of the bardic culture
and literary life of Glamorgan from a comparatively early period—
and certainly from the fifteenth century onwards—a fact of great
importance, which the late Professor G. J. Williams, the outstanding authority on the literary history of the region, had to rediscover, after many years of intensive research, in the twentieth century.

But, as Iolo was firmly convinced that a substantial corpus of
poetry composed by bards who came from this district had unfortunately vanished, he proceeded to fill the void thus created in
Glamorgan's literary history by frequently asserting in his manuscripts that 'Cadair Tir Iarll' was in origin the 'Chair of King
Arthur's Round Table', which had been transferred, it was
claimed, from Caerleon to Llangynwyd, an assertion which was
embellished by the invention of many colourful stories. It was with
a similar purpose in view that he took some of the characters whose
names he had come across in old pedigree charts and transformed
them in his writings into poets, grammarians and prose writers of
considerable merit. It was precisely for the same reason that he was
impelled to claim that Rhys Goch ap Rhicert ab Einion ap
Collwyn, a very shadowy figure about whom virtually nothing is
known, was the gifted predecessor of the Welsh Romantic poets
who sang during various periods in the succeeding centuries; and it
was the same motive that impelled him to create many romantic
characters, such as Ieuan Fawr ap y Diwlith, and to invent a large
number of romantic tales, which captured the imagination of many
Welsh people in the nineteenth century. He fully realized that it was
south Wales that had fostered the richest Welsh prose tradition,
that it was in that part of the country that many important

medieval Welsh manuscripts had been transcribed, and that it was during the sixteenth and seventeenth centuries that they had been transferred, frequently in very obscure circumstances, to north Wales. Moreover, he realized, after many years of detailed and intensive study, that Llywelyn Siôn (1540–1615?), who was born at Llangewydd in Laleston, near Bridgend, was 'a transcriber by trade, for there are in Glamorgan several copies of the same work in his handwriting'. Iolo was probably the first to realize this, and it was to some extent in recognition of the sterling efforts made by this professional scribe to preserve a number of important Welsh manuscripts from oblivion that he claimed it was Llywelyn Siôn who had arranged in systematic form the 'Mysteries of the Bards of the Isle of Britain', a claim for which there is no historical foundation. He also attempted to trace the origin of the measure known in Welsh as *englyn unodl union*, which, he suggested, had developed from the Latin elegiac couplet. This interpretation was offered many years later by Sir John Rhŷs and by the celebrated English poet, Gerard Manley Hopkins, and it was widely accepted for some time until it was decisively rejected by Sir John Morris-Jones in his scholarly volume *Cerdd Dafod* (1925).

It is hardly surprising, as he was the outstanding authority of his day on the literary history of Glamorgan, that Iolo devoted much attention to the bardic life of his native province. He traced, with a fair degree of accuracy, the lineage of the chief bards of the region from one generation to another from the fourteenth century down to his own day and, in doing so, he noted the chiefs-of-song (or master-poets) in various periods, together with the names of their bardic disciples. This is a remarkable achievement when we consider the period in which he lived. Similarly, he traced the lineage of the leading bardic teachers in north Wales from the period of Dafydd ab Edmwnd in the fifteenth century to the days of Rhys Cain, Gruffudd Hafren and various other bards in the seventeenth, when the professional guild of bards, for all effective purposes, came to an end in north Wales. He realized also that the indigenous bardic tradition was pre-eminently an oral one prior to the fifteenth century, a fact he skilfully used whenever he attempted to account for inconsistencies in his literary forgeries. He displayed considerable perspicacity in his discussions of the old bardic grammars and of the men whose names are traditionally associated with them. He traced carefully the development of the measure known as *cywydd*

deuair hirion in Welsh, and he noted the short example of that popular measure in the bardic grammar that is traditionally associated
with the names of Einion Offeiriad and Dafydd Ddu of Hiraddug,
an example (devoid of regular *cynghanedd*) which, in his view, must
be attributed to a period earlier than the one to which Dafydd ap
Gwilym belonged. Therefore, he concluded, it must have been
Dafydd who was largely responsible for popularizing the measure.
His volume *Cyfrinach Beirdd Ynys Prydain* shows quite clearly that
he had an impressively firm grasp of the contents of the old bardic
grammars. Only a talented scholar who had acquired a deeper
understanding of the esoteric lore of the old chiefs-of-song than
anyone else in the eighteenth century could have formulated the so-
called 'Glamorgan Measures' (*Mesurau Morgannwg*). For Iolo
claimed that the metrical system he himself had largely created consisted of the measures used by the bards of the Isle of Britain in
ancient times, and he ingeniously argued that this system, by virtue
of its venerable antiquity, should be accorded a far more privileged
place in the bardic tradition than that established by Dafydd ab
Edmwnd (*fl.* 1450–97) at the eisteddfod held at Carmarthen about
the middle of the fifteenth century.

Astonishingly, some of the great flashes of insight mentioned
above are to be found in Iolo's literary forgeries, which are replete
with many of his romantic dreams and theories, a fact which clearly testifies to the remarkable duality in his personality. For if, on
the one hand, we sometimes find in Iolo's writings, as the examples
given above amply confirm, the percipient and unprejudiced scholar who clearly understood the significance of the literary facts he
had discovered, we also encounter, on the other hand, a man whose
great erudition and penetrating insight were frequently vitiated by
the queer convolutions of an unusually perverse mind. Only rarely
did his abnormally over-active imagination have any firm contact
with historical reality. Impelled partly by deep-rooted psychological complexes, whose origins can probably be traced to the powerful influence exerted on him during his early formative years by a
possessive and rather haughty mother, who always treated Iolo as
her favourite child, and partly by a desire, which gradually developed into an overwhelming passion, to enhance the prestige and
glory of his native Glamorgan as the cradle and repository of all
that was best and most splendid in the nation's cultural heritage, he
felt constrained to rewrite many aspects of the literary history of

Wales, and to this end he was constantly driven to distort what he actually knew about the true historical and literary traditions of his native province. For example, having detected, as was noted above, the resemblance in both theme and treatment between some of the compositions of Dafydd ap Gwilym and the works of the Continental troubadours and *trouvères*, he proceeded to propound the ingenious theory that the bards who sang in Glamorgan in the twelfth century regularly visited the Norman castles in the Vale and that it was there that these poets first became acquainted with the modes and compositions of the troubadours. But Iolo was not content to let the matter rest there. He transformed one of the grandsons of a famous Glamorgan chieftain, namely, Rhys Goch ap Rhicert ab Einion ap Collwyn, into a poet, whose twelfth-century love-songs, it was claimed, provided an excellent example of the love poetry that was one of the most distinctive features of the bardic life of Glamorgan throughout the succeeding centuries and reflected the enriching influence of the Continental troubadours. Twenty poems were attributed to Rhys Goch ap Rhicert in the volume *Iolo Manuscripts* (1848), edited by Taliesin ab Iolo, poems which the talented arch-romantic from Flemingston many years earlier had claimed he had discovered in a manuscript-book that was then in the possession of one of his teachers, John Bradford (1706–85), of Betws Tir Iarll, an antiquary and poet who was a prominent figure in the literary renaissance that took place in the northern Uplands of Glamorgan during the first half of the eighteenth century. It was further claimed that Rhys Goch ap Rhicert had employed the original Welsh metres in his poetry and that, in response to the initial stimulus provided by the new poetic modes of the aforementioned Continental bards, an important and highly talented romantic school of poets had flourished in the Vale in the twelfth century. This early romantic movement, it was asserted, was pre-eminently represented by the enchantingly beautiful love poetry of Rhys Goch ap Rhicert, who could therefore be regarded, according to Iolo Morganwg, as a forerunner of Dafydd ap Gwilym, acknowledged to be the greatest of the medieval Welsh bards. There is no real historical warrant for any of these claims. It has been established beyond any reasonable doubt that, of the twenty poems attributed to Rhys Goch ap Rhicert, fifteen were composed by Iolo himself, a remarkable tribute to his great creative genius, while the remainder were compositions he had skilfully refurbished from five old poems he had seen in unpublished Welsh manuscripts. All these compositions contain many words and expressions that are uniquely characteristic of Iolo's work, and there is really no evidence to suggest that the historical Rhys Goch ap Rhicert ever composed a single line of poetry. Iolo's manuscripts contain scores of poems, some of which are enchantingly beautiful compositions, written by the inspired arch-romantic himself and later attributed by him to various bards, some of whom were figments of his own imagination, from the fifteenth century down to the eighteenth, solely with a view to providing some 'substance' for his oft-repeated claim that a talented and influential romantic school of bards had once flourished in his native Glamorgan. And sometimes, as we have seen, he refurbished in a commendably skilful manner poems with which he was familiar. Another typical example of this latter practice is the famous poem 'Bugeilio'r Gwenith Gwyn' (Watching the Blooming Wheat), which has been associated with the name of Wil Hopcyn (1700–41), a poet from Llangynwyd in Tir Iarll, Glamorgan, of whom very little is known.

These forgeries provide us with some instructive examples of the way this romantic dreamer treated the literary and historical material with which he became familiar. He was constantly driven by an overwhelming desire to incorporate his dreams and theories in scores of poems, tales and documents of various kinds. In order to give greater 'substance' to the glorious Glamorgan he saw so clearly in his own abnormally fertile imagination, he created a wealth of romantic tales associated with places in both the Vale and the Uplands, locations which, as a result, came to be regarded by the vast majority of his contemporaries and by succeeding generations of his literature-loving compatriots as being hallowed by tradition. He altered the names of parishes and villages and, by so doing, he endowed many of them with a mystique entirely of his own creation. He conjured into being many new poets and saints. He rewrote and doctored the old documents relating to the Welsh bardic order, giving the new version a peculiar slant to accommodate and promote his theories and assertions, and he manufactured a great collection of triads, documents, chronicles and statutes, in which he invariably incorporated statements and descriptions designed to provide a 'factual basis' for his many theories and claims. No other county in the whole of Wales has been treated or

remodelled in this way. It cannot be denied that Iolo corrupted
many important historical sources and thus misled many scholars,
not only in his own day, but also for many years after his death.
Local historians dealing with the history and literary traditions of
Glamorgan frequently have to grapple, therefore, with problems
that do not arise in the other Welsh counties. Many works on various aspects of Glamorgan's local history that were published in
the nineteenth century and the early part of the twentieth accept
some of Iolo's fabrications as though they were sober history. This
is not surprising, for the poems, tales, proverbs, aphorisms, triadic
sequences, chronicles and documents of various kinds that he published were accepted without challenge by the vast majority of his
contemporaries and by most Welsh scholars until late in the nineteenth century; and even then, when some doubts were at last
expressed regarding the authenticity of this substantial literary output, Iolo Morganwg's personal integrity was never seriously
impugned.

Even today, although well over a century and a half has elapsed
since his death, comparatively little of Iolo's voluminous literary
output has been published (see the bibliography appended to this
chapter). Fortunately, this large collection—for Iolo never
destroyed any scrap of his writings on so many diverse fields—was
never dispersed. It has remained intact to this day, for all the manuscripts and papers, which were carefully preserved by his son, are
now deposited in the National Library of Wales, in the Llanover
collection. That is singularly appropriate, for Iolo Morganwg was
the first of the sons of Wales to advocate the creation of such an
institution. It is probably the most remarkable collection of manuscripts and papers deposited there. Any person studying these writings for the first time is likely to be bewildered by the strange twists
of this highly gifted eccentric's mind.

It is impossible to understand how that mind worked without
referring to some salient facts in his life. Iolo himself maintained
that he had written an autobiography, and in 1824, some two years
before his death, he confidently assured his friends and acquaintances that it would be published in November that year. No credence should be attached to this, however, for it is probably yet
another example of the confidently asserted, but wholly unreliable,
claims that occur so frequently in his papers and correspondence.
Nevertheless, he did write many autobiographical essays, but they

must always be treated with the greatest caution. There is no foundation for some of the statements they contain, and even when they
are factually correct, the data can be presented and coloured in
such a way as to give the reader a very misleading impression. Also,
to complicate matters yet further, many of Iolo's statements, even
when it can be shown that they are generally false, contain a hard
kernel of truth, as do many of his literary forgeries. Any one who
attempts to write a biography of Iolo Morganwg is therefore
embarking upon an extremely hazardous undertaking.

Within the space of one short chapter it is difficult to provide a
comprehensive account of his very colourful and, at times, tumultuous career—his work in many different localities as a skilled
stonemason; his efforts to become a business man in Cardiff and a
farmer in Gwynllŵg (Wentloog), efforts which eventually ended in
Cardiff gaol, where he was imprisoned as a debtor from August
1786 to August 1787; the period he spent as a shopkeeper in
Cowbridge; his extraordinary wife, who, like his talented mother,
took a keen interest in literary matters; the years he spent pursuing
his profession as a stonemason in Kent and London, where he met
Dr Samuel Johnson and impressed such leading figures in the literary world as James Boswell, Robert Southey and Samuel Taylor
Coleridge by his great erudition; his wanderings in Bristol, Bath
and various parts of southern England, and through all the Welsh
counties, searching for early manuscripts; his astonishing feats as a
pedestrian; his journeys through south Wales as a representative of
the Board of Agriculture and as one of the assistants of Walter
Davies (Gwallter Mechain), when the latter was preparing his
detailed reports on the state of agriculture in both north and south
Wales; his frequent visits to private libraries in north Wales as one
of the editors of *The Myvyrian Archaiology*, published in three volumes in London between 1801 and 1807 and containing a valuable
collection of Wales's early prose and poetry; his hopes that, with
the publication of his two volumes of English verse, he might be
able to settle down in London as a literary figure, publishing books
and articles and contributing regularly to the London reviews and
periodicals; his important contribution to the religious life of south
Wales in his day; his life in London during the exciting years that
followed the outbreak of the French Revolution, when he became
acquainted, as we have seen, with some of the more prominent radicals and agitators; his close connection with the London Welsh

societies and the popular Welsh Provincial Societies; and the vital part he played in the movement to make the eisteddfod a national institution and an essential feature of the literary life of Wales. Nor should one overlook his enthusiasm and exuberance whenever he began to expatiate in congenial company on what he considered to be the glorious literary past of his native province, and the great reputation he won for himself as a talker and raconteur, 'the Dr Johnson of every company', as he has appropriately been described; his occasional lapses into utter irresponsibility, which may have been a manifestation of the schizophrenia from which he probably suffered; his fierce temper and his bitter quarrels, even with erstwhile friends; his devastating sense of humour; his extremely peculiar habits; and his passionate advocacy of the democratic ideals that were becoming increasingly popular in the latter part of his life.

Although it is impossible to discuss all these aspects of his career, interesting as they undoubtedly are, in the space of one short chapter, some salient facts in his early life must be noted, for a psychologist or psychoanalyst would probably attribute the amazing duality and the marked egocentricity that characterize so many of his writings and activities to some deep emotional experience that had affected him in his childhood or youth. Born in the hamlet of Pennon in the parish of Llancarfan, Iolo Morganwg, who was the eldest son of Edward William and Ann Matthew, lived for the greater part of his life in the little village of Flemingston (Trefflemin) on the other side of the river Thaw. He claimed that his father, who was a stonemason, belonged to one of the old Welsh families and that he was descended from the same family as Oliver Cromwell, namely, the Williams family of Whitchurch and Llanishen. It is impossible, however, to prove this conclusively, and it may be yet another figment of Iolo's extremely fertile imagination. But it was his mother who was unquestionably the great formative influence in his life. She could legitimately claim to be descended from a decayed branch of the famous Mathew family of Llandaff and Radyr. It is uncertain how the druidic democrat reacted to this, but there can be no doubt whatsoever that the romantic dreamer that lurked in Iolo's extremely involved personality was intensely aware of his mother's illustrious ancestry. This awareness partly helps to explain the strange convolutions of his mind. Ann Matthew had been reared, from about the age of nine, by her relatives, the celebrated Seys family of Boverton, and had received the kind of education that was in those days imparted to young ladies of gentle breeding and connections. Then, as she had no fortune she could call her own, she condescended to marry a simple stonemason, a man who had no pretensions to any kind of social status. Local village life held little interest for her, and her neighbours generally considered her to be somewhat self-important, aloof and disdainful to those she considered to be her social inferiors. A woman of manifestly frail physique, she was rarely content except when she was in the company of Edward, her eldest son and her favourite, reading and talking to him about the English books she had studied and about the gentle, refined life she had experienced in her early years.

Although he eventually became an avid reader, Iolo received no formal education at school, college or university, and he claims in one of his autobiographical essays that he first learned to read by watching his father cutting inscriptions on gravestones in the local cemeteries. It is important to remember, however, that it was neither grammar school nor university, both of which were heavily Anglicized institutions, that could create a *Welsh* scholar in those days, but rather the old traditional learning. It was the local historians and antiquarians, the grammarians and lexicographers, the products of the antiquarian revival of the eighteenth century, who laid the foundations of Iolo Morganwg's impressive erudition. He claimed that it was a bard called Edward Williams, from Llancarfan, who first taught him the basic rules and elements of Welsh strict-metre verse, and early in his life he came into contact, as noted above, with the cultured and talented fraternity of bards that had emerged in the Uplands in the northern part of the county, bards such as Lewis Hopkin, from Hendre Ifan Goch in the parish of Llandyfodwg; John Bradford, from Betws Tir Iarll; Rhys Morgan, from Pencraig-nedd; Dafydd Nicolas, from Aberpergwm; and Edward Evan, from Aberdare. This new generation of poets had succeeded in acquiring, to some degree, the more important elements of the old bardic learning and skills, and it was Iolo's early and prolonged contact with them that accounts, in a very large measure, for his learning, his extensive knowledge of the literary traditions of Wales, and his mastery of the intricate rules of Welsh strict-metre verse. This started a new period in his life, for although he had already studied printed volumes on Welsh prosody, it was through his contact with this close-knit fraternity of bards in the

Uplands of the county that he acquired a firm grasp of that undeniably difficult and intricate art. Later in his life, he was able to manufacture what he claimed was the old genuine system of Welsh metrics, a system which had been devotedly preserved and fostered by the bards of Glamorgan throughout the centuries and one markedly different from that established by Dafydd ab Edmwnd in the eisteddfod held at Carmarthen towards the middle of the fifteenth century. This was the metrical system published in *Cyfrinach Beirdd Ynys Prydain*, a remarkable achievement which no other Welsh bard or scholar of that period could have accomplished.

Although Iolo never went to school or university, he had plenty of opportunities in his youth to study the volumes that would normally be found in the private libraries of eighteenth-century scholars. There was a flourishing Book Society in Cowbridge, and Iolo was patronized by a number of the literature-loving gentry and clergy of the Vale, some of whom were descended from the old noble families that had settled there many years earlier—the Carnes, the Bassetts, the Turbervilles, the Gamages and others. A detailed analysis of his papers and manuscripts reveals that already in his youth he had studied the works of many prominent English historians, especially their volumes on early British history, a subject which held an abiding fascination for him. By a later period in his life, he had acquired an excellent personal library, which included not only copies of historical works, but also books on an impressively wide variety of subjects, including volumes on the eastern religions and philosophies and the works of some of the most famous English poets and prose writers. Moreover, he read and studied avidly many of the important reviews and periodicals of his day. It is difficult to imagine how all these books, together with a very large collection of papers, notes and manuscripts, could be contained in his little thatched cottage in Flemingston. Iolo Morganwg had made, therefore, from a fairly early period in his life a detailed study of many subjects, both literary and historical, and there is much to support the claim that he eventually became the most widely read scholar in the whole of the Principality in his day. There can be no doubt that he had acquired a more detailed knowledge of the contents of extant Welsh manuscripts than anyone else until the present century.

No account of the early influences that contributed to his development as a Welsh scholar should overlook the informal guidance he received in his youth from a neighbouring clergyman, John Walters, rector of Llandough, near Cowbridge, and vicar of the neighbouring parish of St Hilary, who published a monumental English–Welsh dictionary. John Walters remained one of his greatest friends, and it was he who probably encouraged Iolo to learn Latin, French and, possibly, Greek. Another talented clergyman, Thomas Richards of Coychurch, unquestionably the greatest scholar to arise in Glamorgan in the first half of the eighteenth century and compiler of *Antiquae Linguae Britannicae Thesaurus: being a British, or Welsh–English Dictionary*, which was published in Bristol in 1753 (with a second edition appearing in 1759), instilled in Iolo a deep and passionate interest in both lexicography and dialectology, two subjects which played a prominent part in his scholarly activities to the very end of his life. It was a combination of all these influences that laid the foundations of Iolo's wide learning, and it was in response to these influences that he set about collecting or transcribing old Welsh manuscripts, copying all the important poetry and prose he could discover during his wanderings through every parish in Wales, noting the outstanding features of the local dialects, collecting proverbs, expressions and technical terms, and recording obsolete vocabulary from the old bardic verse. At the heart of all his scholarly activities was his search for the former literary glories of his nation, and especially of his native province, a search which gave rise to, and was also partly the result of, many strange ideas and abnormal impulses. No attempt to explain the burning passion that governed him throughout the greater part of his long and exceptionally active life should ignore the importance of this early and highly exciting period in his career.

Even at this comparatively early stage in his life, his work reflects the strange and extraordinarily powerful impulse that drove him on relentlessly to the very end, for he found it impossible to transcribe any text, whether it was in prose or verse, without altering it in some way, or without adding material of his own to various parts of it. It is not easy to detect what purpose he had in mind when making these textual emendations or additions. They seem to have been the product of a deep psychological impulse to tamper and to forge, and they were not intended for publication at this early stage in his career. Nor was Iolo in any way prompted by considerations of pecuniary gain, for he remained a comparatively poor man throughout the greater part of his life. This impulse, as far as we can now tell, first manifested itself when he was making a detailed analysis of Thomas Richards's Welsh–English Dictionary so that he could acquire a more thorough knowledge of the old bardic vocabulary, much of which was obsolete. The work contained illustrative quotations from the compositions of the old bards. Even during this early period, Iolo found it impossible to resist the urge to coin, in accordance with his own pet linguistic theories, a large number of new Welsh words with illustrative quotations by him, which he attributed to various bards whose compositions he had seen in unpublished manuscript sources. Some of these quotations provide us with the earliest examples of his work as a Romantic poet. He then proceeded to attribute to those bards whole compositions—not merely lines and couplets—which he himself had written. Undoubtedly, the outstanding examples of these are the strict-metre *cywyddau* that were later included in the first edition of the work of Dafydd ap Gwilym, which was published in 1789 under the auspices of the London-based Gwyneddigion Society. Not content with this, he then proceeded to fabricate a substantial corpus of prose documents of various descriptions, a task which became his main literary activity from then on until his death many years later.

Literary forgery was by no means uncommon in the eighteenth century. One thinks immediately of James Macpherson (1736–96), the Scottish poet and translator, who published verse he claimed to be translations of the legendary third-century Gaelic poet Ossian; or Thomas Chatterton (1752–70), 'the glorious boy who perished in his pride', who was the author of spurious 'medieval' verse he ascribed to a fifteenth-century monk called Thomas Rowley; or William Henry Ireland (1777–1835), who forged manuscripts that contained, so he claimed, some of the works of Shakespeare; or, finally, that remarkable character from the south of France who called himself 'George Psalmanaazaar' and, while claiming to be a native of Formosa, invented a language, an alphabet, a religion, a 'history' and 'time-honoured' customs for the inhabitants of that distant island about which precious little was known in western Europe at that time. Daring and inventive as they were, however, none succeeded in enriching the literary heritage of his nation as Iolo Morganwg so triumphantly did. Nor can the view that it was their activities which provided the initial impetus for Iolo's literary deceptions be accepted, for his earliest forgeries, as has already been emphasized, were glossaries and were compiled in his youth when he was studying the contents of the Welsh–English Dictionary mentioned above. The urge to forge seems to have been a natural, a wholly uncontrollable one.

Iolo's life history seems to suggest that he was constantly being driven by deep-rooted urges which had their origin in an abnormally powerful influence exerted on him by his mother in his early formative years. In assessing that influence, it is important to remember that she could claim—so Iolo often asserted, and there is much to confirm this—to be a descendant of one of the greatest of the fifteenth- and sixteenth-century bardic families of Tir Iarll, the family of Rhys Brydydd, Gwilym Tew, Lewis Morgannwg and Tomas ab Ieuan ap Rhys, of the line of Einion ap Collwyn, a family which had made an outstanding contribution to the bardic life of the region over the centuries. Iolo became firmly convinced, therefore, that he was a descendant of these famous and talented chiefs-of-song who, as was commonly believed from the sixteenth century onwards, had inherited the learning and traditions of the ancient druids. The great influence exerted on him by his mother explains to a large degree the urge that later impelled him to claim that it was only in Glamorgan, his native province, that these ancient druidic traditions had been preserved in their primordial purity. In the latter part of his life, he became deeply conscious, too, of a 'messianic' calling. For after the death of his friend and fellow-bard, Edward Evan of Aberdare, in 1798, Iolo became overwhelmingly convinced that he was the last surviving descendant of the ancient British druids and that it was, therefore, his divinely preordained duty to reveal and to explain to his contemporaries, as well as to countless generations who were as yet unborn, the rich esoteric lore and the arcane ceremonies and practices of his illustrious forebears. This deep-rooted conviction drove him on to express himself in unusual ways, while the fact that he had never been to school or university played to some extent on his mind, gave rise at times to an element of exhibitionism and caused him frequently to over-romanticize the past. The beliefs and passions that regularly governed his mind and his literary activities strongly suggest that the literary historian has to reckon with something far more deep-rooted than a desire to imitate other eighteenth-century forgers.

His work reveals, too, a strong element of egocentricity: everything, in the final analysis, revolved around Iolo Morganwg himself. As he was at pains to emphasize at the end of a number of those literary forgeries that were eventually published, it was he who had discovered those manuscripts that contained poems and various prose texts none of his contemporaries had ever seen. Again, in an article he published in *The Gentleman's Magazine* in 1789 he proudly informed its readers that he and Edward Evan of Aberdare were the only living descendants of the '*Ancient British Bards*', an expression which created quite a stir in the minds of many eighteenth-century literati in both Wales and England. The egocentricity that characterized his personality and so much of his literary output became increasingly marked after the death of Edward Evan in 1798, for naturally Iolo then became overwhelmingly convinced that he could legitimately claim to be the only living person who had a detailed knowledge of the great druidic traditions that could be traced back to the ancient Brythonic and Celtic past. In that respect, he, Iolo Morganwg, was truly unique, a stance he frequently took in his manuscripts and in the voluminous correspondence he addressed to his friends and acquaintances.

The propensities referred to above were probably stimulated by the fact that he began to take laudanum (tincture of opium) when he was about twenty-six years of age in order, in his own words, '[to] relieve a very troublesome cough'—actually, he suffered from severe bouts of asthma—and it seems that he continued to take laudanum, 'often in very large doses of even 300 drops at a time', until his death fifty-three years later. Not surprisingly, the first composition in the two-volume collection of his English verse, *Poems, Lyric and Pastoral*, which was published in 1794, is an encomium 'To Laudanum'. One of his friends, David Williams, the founder of the Royal Literary Fund, advised him that he 'depended too much on Opium, Foxgloves, etc.' Informed medical opinion believes that this addiction could have a marked influence on the minds of romantic dreamers and cause them to see visions. It is said, for example, that Sir Walter Scott conceived *The Bride of Lammermoor* during a drugged trance induced by an overdose of laudanum, and it is significant that he, like Iolo Morganwg, over-romanticized the past and was prone to fabricate mystifying fables about the genesis of his own works. Clearly, there is much to substantiate the view of one medical expert that addiction to laudanum over a long period could stimulate the 'image-making faculty' of romantic dreamers. But it seems that this effect can only be produced in those people who are endowed with great imaginative faculties. As Alethea Hayter has emphasized in her masterly study, *Opium and the Romantic Imagination*, 'Opium . . . cannot give the power of vivid dreaming to those who have not got it already, and to those who have, the dreams and reveries that it brings will be mixed from the paints already on the palettes of their minds—there will be no colours entirely new, beyond the spectrum'. That neatly summarizes the effect which the long and sustained practice of taking laudanum probably had on Iolo Morganwg, 'the greatest of the Welsh romantic dreamers', as he has appropriately been described.

In assessing the various factors that prompted Iolo to fabricate such a substantial body of spurious literary material, in both prose and verse, it is quite misleading to maintain, as some literary historians have done, that his sole purpose throughout was to enhance the prestige and glory of his native Glamorgan. This was certainly *not* the initial impulse, for it must be emphasized that the illustrative quotations in the glossaries already referred to are ascribed to poets from all parts of Wales, and even to some of his early contemporaries in north Wales, such as Lewis Morris (1701–65) and Goronwy Owen (1723–69). He could safely make these ascriptions, for they were not intended for publication. In a later period in his life, however, the romantic past and literary glories, as Iolo viewed them, of his native province, which he loved so dearly, became inextricably bound up with his dream-world. He set about rewriting the history of Glamorgan and proudly announced his intention of publishing a 'superb' history of the province in several volumes. To that purpose, he had studied in great detail everything relevant to the subject he had been able to discover in both printed books and manuscripts and, as has already been emphasized, he eventually became the greatest authority in his day on the history and literary tradition of Glamorgan. His work, however, was frequently marred by that disturbing duality referred to above. The scholar within him could readily grasp the significance of the facts and data he had so diligently and painstakingly assembled, and he sometimes maintained, with apparently sincere conviction, that they should not be tampered with or distorted in any way; but the romantic dreamer and visionary that also lurked within him could not refrain, at times, from twisting, colouring or embellishing the evidence that had been collected so that it 'substantiated' the picture of the golden past he was so anxious to create and present to his contemporaries. Perhaps nothing illustrates more clearly the remarkable duality in his personality than the fact that he was able, sometimes, to examine critically some of his own literary forgeries and express doubts about their authenticity! Hardly less astonishing is the fact that he would occasionally go on a pilgrimage to places he himself, by means of his fabrications, had associated with great figures of the past. And it was in order to provide some evidence for the past he saw so vividly in his imagination that he began manufacturing a very substantial body of literature in both prose and verse, much of which was ascribed to poets and authors of an appreciably earlier period, or to figures that were merely figments of his own uncommonly fertile imagination.

But this extraordinary literary activity constituted only a part of that golden romantic past he saw so clearly in his imagination. Iolo had rebelled fairly early in his life against the idea, which was very prevalent in the first half of the eighteenth century, that the indigenous bardic tradition had been preserved in its purest form in north Wales and that the dialects spoken in the southern regions of the Principality were corrupt and markedly inferior forms of Welsh. His rebellion against this view, a notion which incensed him greatly and ultimately instilled in him a burning antipathy to most north Walians, led him to rewrite the old authentic documents relating to the Welsh bardic order. In undertaking this task he tried to demonstrate that no reliance could be placed on the texts preserved in north Wales and that it was the bards of his own native province who had inherited the old authentic traditions as they had been preserved and fostered in King Arthur's court in Caerleon. For he ingeniously argued, with a wealth of colourful and interesting detail, that the vital task of fostering Welsh literature had been one of the main preoccupations of King Arthur and his valiant knights as they sat around their celebrated Round Table in the company of the renowned sixth-century bards Taliesin, Aneirin and Myrddin. Under Iolo's magic wand the ancient bardic statute became the 'Statute of the Round Table'. He took the word *gorsedd* and gave it an entirely new meaning. It originally meant 'mound of earth, tump or knoll, hillock, tumulus', and it occasionally occurs in the Laws of Hywel Dda to denote a court or tribunal or judicial assembly held in the open air. Characteristically, Iolo took this word and used it to denote a special gathering of bards. But the bardic documents he had fabricated at a fairly early stage in his

career were later skilfully reframed by him so that they could support the druidic theories that increasingly preoccupied him from
about 1788–90 onwards, and the word *gorsedd* came therefore to
acquire a distinctly druidic connotation.

For when he was in his early forties the druids, the priests and
sages of the ancient Celtic and Brythonic world to whom there are
many references in the works of the Classical authors, began to
play an increasingly important part in Iolo's romantic dream-
world. Ever since the sixteenth century, when both British and
Continental historians began to analyse the evidence contained in
the works of the Classical authors concerning the beliefs, function
and activities of this arcane priesthood in Gaul and Britain, the
druids had come to be regarded as the ancestors of the Welsh
bards. In his celebrated *Mona Antiqua Restaurata*, which was published in 1723, Henry Rowlands (1655–1723) had maintained that
Anglesey, described as the 'dark island' (*ynys dywell*) by the bards,
was the metropolitan seat of the druids in Britain. In his work
Commentarii de Scriptoribus Britannicis, the greater part of which
was compiled by approximately 1540, but which was not published
until 1709, John Leland (*c.* 1503–52), the famous English antiquary, had maintained that the *druidæ*, *bardi* and *vates* mentioned
by the Classical authors were the ancestors of the Welsh bards, who
had thus inherited the traditions and esoteric lore of the great sages
of western Europe in the pre-Christian epoch. Other sixteenth-century scholars and antiquarians, including the Englishman John
Bale in his work *Scriptorvm Illustrivm Maioris Brytanniæ* . . .
Catalogus, a second edition of which was published in 1557, gave a
distinctly religious twist to this belief, by arguing that the bardic
traditions could be traced back to the days of the descendants of
Noah who had settled in western Europe, and that it could therefore be maintained that the druids had inherited the resplendent
traditions of the great biblical patriarchs. These ideas, albeit modified in detail, were enthusiastically received by such historians as
Lambarde, Holinshed, Camden, Harrison and White, and by many
Welsh students at the universities of Oxford and Cambridge. This
druidic myth coloured and conditioned much of Welsh thought
from the sixteenth century onwards. Then, towards the end of the
seventeenth century, that talented and commendably industrious
Welsh antiquarian, John Aubrey (1626–97), gave this highly influential myth a further important twist in his work *Monumenta*

Britannica by propounding the theory that the ancient circles of standing stones located in Avebury and Stonehenge and in some other parts of Britain were really the remains of the ancient druidic temples. The same basic ideas are to be found in the works of that celebrated eighteenth-century antiquary, Dr William Stukeley (1687–1765), *Stonehenge*[:] *A Temple Restor'd to the British Druids* (1740) and *Abury, A Temple of the British Druids* (1743).

In the eighteenth century, the druids became romantic figures of great fascination, a learned and courageous priesthood that had resisted the cruel oppression of the Roman Empire, valiant champions of freedom, as can be seen in *Liberty* (1736), the long poem by James Thomson (1700–48), and in the *Ode to Liberty* by William Collins (1721–59), two notable forerunners of the Romantic Movement in Britain, as well as in a number of works published during the French Revolution. Many of the opponents of the war against France came to regard the druids as pacifists and as members of an ancient order that had propagated the principles of liberty, equality, fraternity, justice, peace and benevolence. This idealization of the druids influenced the work of some English Romantic poets, such as William Blake (1757–1827) and William Wordsworth (1770–1850), but no one was more profoundly affected by it than Iolo Morganwg, who became firmly convinced that in all these details about the ancient druids there was a faithful portrayal of his own ancestors. Moreover, he associated these ideas with the teachings of Jean-Jacques Rousseau (1712–78) and other celebrated French thinkers concerning man's condition in primeval times, the great 'Golden Age', as it was sometimes called, prior to his being corrupted and debased by civilization, science and art. Iolo thus became, as we have seen, an enthusiastic supporter of those political and social ideals that led to the outbreak of the French Revolution. Furthermore, he became firmly convinced that the ancient druidic traditions had been preserved, safeguarded and devotedly fostered in Glamorgan, especially in the northern Uplands, where, as he maintained, they had found a safe and permanent retreat after these traditions had tragically been destroyed in all the other regions of Wales by the internecine wars of the Middle Ages. The Welsh language, he proudly asserted, was 'the only druidic language in the world', a fact which obviously conferred upon it a unique distinction. He further claimed that he had in his possession *authentic* manuscripts containing detailed and reliable evidence that shed valuable light on early bardic teaching and practices, which the people of Wales, and especially the professional bards in his native Glamorgan, had proudly inherited.

Furthermore, Iolo argued that this ancient tradition was an oral one and that this largely explained how the druids had succeeded in retaining, as he expressed it, 'pure notions of religion and morality' and 'rational principles of government'. With great ingenuity, he referred in many of his writings to the closely guarded secrets of the druids, such as the mysterious symbol (*nod cyfrin*) of the ineffable name of God. He maintained that 'God created the world by the melodious threefold utterance of his Holy Name and the form and figure of that Name was /|\ , being the rays of the rising sun at the equinoxes and solstices conveying into focus "the eye of light"'. Iolo also devoted much attention to the vestments of the druids, to their time-honoured rituals, their beliefs and teachings, their esoteric lore and mythology. These themes preoccupied him to the end of his days and he continually added new elements to his intricate and ingeniously formulated 'druidic system', including ideas he had discovered in books on the Jewish cabbala (an ancient Jewish mystical tradition based on an esoteric interpretation of the Old Testament), on Hinduism, Brahminism, theosophy and mysticism. His private library in Flemingston contained, as has already been noted, many books on these themes, a fact which provides yet further proof of his extraordinarily wide range of interests and knowledge.

Wales—and Glamorgan in particular—so the argument ran, was extremely fortunate in that it had succeeded in retaining the old institution that had devotedly fostered throughout the centuries this resplendent druidic tradition, which included the triadic method adopted by the bards of imparting instruction to young novitiates. That institution, so Iolo claimed, was the *Gorsedd* of the Bards of the Island of Britain (*Gorsedd Beirdd Ynys Prydain*). The gathering of the bards, or the eisteddfod, which thus acquired a distinctly druidic connotation, had traditionally been held, according to Iolo, in a *gorsedd*, within a circle of stones in the open air, for the eighteenth-century antiquarians, as has already been emphasized, regarded the old stone-circles found in various parts of Britain as ancient druidic temples, where the chief druid, whom Iolo called the 'priest of nature', would officiate and preside over the various rituals. It was Iolo's intention that the *Gorsedd* should superintend *all* aspects of Welsh national life—literary, cultural, religious, moral, political and social—for he firmly maintained that this had always been the function of this ancient institution, and it appears that he proposed to include in a volume he hoped to publish a 'Plan for an accommodation of the Ancient Bardic Institution to the Present Times'. Not surprisingly, he became a staunch Unitarian for, according to some of the Classical authors, the ancient druids held firmly to the belief that there is only one God. Therefore, it was argued, after the advent of Christianity to Britain, the bards had become firm Unitarians. In Glamorgan, this had been the general practice, according to Iolo, down to his own period, and in the various *Gorseddau* that he arranged in his native province the singing and recital of Unitarian hymns constituted an important part of the ceremonial. When Cymdeithas Dwyfundodiaid yn Neheubarth Cymru was formed in Neath in 1802, preparations were made for holding a bardic *Gorsedd* on Mynydd y Gaer in the vicinity. Moreover, it was assumed that a Unitarian minister became an *ex officio* member of the ancient 'Order of Druids' without being required to undergo any rites of initiation. It is also significant that the secret symbol /|\ was printed on the title-page of the collection of Iolo's hymns, *Salmau yr Eglwys yn yr Anialwch*, which was published in 1812.

But the *Gorsedd* also had unmistakable political connotations, for the druids depicted by Iolo had established their own distinctive 'rational principles of government', which harmonized, to a marked degree, with the stirring ideals that led to the French Revolution. Naturally, therefore, Iolo and a number of his associates in the London-based Welsh societies became enthusiastic supporters of the European revolutionary movement, and it is surely significant that the motto of the first *Gorsedd* held on Primrose Hill in London on 21 June 1792 was 'Freedom' (*Rhyddid*). At the opening ceremony, Iolo read his English poem 'Ode on the Mythology of the Ancient British Bards', in which he extolled the goddess of Liberty and called for an end to slavery and the abominable slave-trade. Iolo also maintained that his famous poem, 'Breiniau Dyn' (The Rights of Man), for which he had used the title of the well-known work by Thomas Paine, was formally declaimed within the circle of twelve stones that had been laid out, with another placed in the middle to serve as the *Maen Llog* (Logan Stone). It is hardly surprising, therefore, that the state authorities came to regard the

Gorsedd with considerable suspicion and, at times, with some alarm, and when it was planned to hold a *Gorsedd* on the Garth Mountain in Glamorgan, in June 1798, the local magistrates intervened and the Glamorgan Volunteers soon arrived on the scene, ordering the assembled bards to disperse lest they should 'attract the French invader'. They also threatened to go to Iolo's small cottage in Flemingston and conduct a thorough search of his papers.

It was also intended that the *Gorsedd* should patronize a wide variety of sports and athletic activities. Iolo obviously believed in Juvenal's well-known advice: *Orandum est ut sit mens sana in corpore sano* (You must pray for a sound mind in a sound body). The old Welsh treatise on 'the twenty-four feats of skill and prowess' was rewritten and transformed by Iolo into a bardic document. He firmly believed that a *Gorsedd* should last for a full week and that the last day should invariably be devoted to old Welsh games and athletic pursuits.

But the basic work of the *Gorsedd* was to preserve and foster the ancient bardic traditions, which were to be declaimed regularly and ceremoniously at every meeting, for Iolo fully realized that it was by oral transmission that the practices and esoteric lore of the professional bards had been preserved throughout the centuries. Verse compositions on set themes that effectively highlighted these ancient traditions and beliefs were also to be recited, orations on bardic topics were to be delivered, and arrangements were to be made for the admission of suitable candidates to the three druidic orders. These latter were to be the official instructors or teachers, and they were required to hold secret conclaves where they could discuss and formally settle various matters pertaining to the ancient traditions and to their professional craft. It was also their responsibility to organize future developments. But final approval for all this had to be sought and obtained in a public *Gorsedd*, for these were not the meetings of a secret coterie of bards but public assemblies held 'in the face of the sun and in the eye of light' to teach the people of Wales their national history and literature and to instruct them in the basic principles of bardism. As Iolo was constantly at pains to emphasize, ' The publicity of their actions was a leading consideration'. He was adamant that the *Gorsedd* was not in any way a secret society and that there was no contemporary connection between it and freemasonry.

In order to provide some 'substance' for this remarkable druidic world, he proceeded to manufacture scores upon scores of documents and miscellaneous notes, including a very large number of triads, which he steadfastly maintained had been ceremoniously recited by the professional bards in the *Gorsedd* assemblies held in days of yore, for Iolo had perceived quite clearly that some of the old authentic Welsh triads had a mnemonic purpose: they had been composed so that pupils or young novitiates could more easily memorize the most important elements of the instruction that had formerly been imparted orally in the bardic schools. He composed Triads on the Art of Poetry, Triads of Wisdom, the Law Triads, which he associated with the name of Dyfnwal Moelmud and in which he endeavoured to portray customs and practices in the so-called 'Golden Age' (a truly remarkable achievement), Triads of Bardism, Theological Triads, and so on. This vast collection provides us with yet another example of his incredible industry and wide learning.

Nor did all this astonishing literary output exhaust his creative ingenuity. He invented an alphabet, called '*Coelbren y Beirdd*' (literally, 'Signboard of the Poets'), which was used, so he maintained, by the Britons and the ancient druids. This alphabet, according to Iolo, had been preserved and safeguarded throughout the centuries by the bards of his native province. Its letters, he maintained, were ingeniously based on the mystic sign /|\ and were cut on a wooden frame, not unlike an abacus. There were twenty characters, with twenty more variations representing elongated vowels and mutations. Each of these consisted of straight lines, so that, as in the ogham alphabet, the letters could be more easily cut or carved. As one description points out:

> The characters were often cut on each face of a square strip of wood and thus a four-lined stanza or, more regularly, an *englyn*, could be carved on each strip. These strips could have their ends rounded and fitted into a pair of upright battens so as to form a gate-like frame that could carry a number of verses or *englynion*. The frame was known as a *peithynen*, a word coined by Iolo, possibly from the Latin *pectinum*, meaning a comb or a rake. Occasionally, the strips would be three-sided to accommodate three-line verses, or *englynion milwr*.

Iolo maintained that this strange alphabet, which constituted an important part of the armamentaria of the ancient druids and of the British and early Welsh professional bards, had survived only in Glamorgan, where so much else pertaining to the ancient bardic traditions and practices had been retained. A number of examples dating from the nineteenth century have been preserved, and the alphabet (or, at least, a part of it) has sometimes been incorporated in the decorative carving on prize eisteddfodic chairs.

As a skilled and highly experienced mason and stonecutter, Iolo would naturally have taken a great interest in epigraphy and in the art of lettering, and he may have got the idea of the *peithynen* from two independent sources: (i) from the 'clog almanack', which consisted of a square piece of wood with characters inscribed on each face, a picture of which was included in *The Natural History of Staffordshire* (1686), by Dr Robert Plot, keeper of the Ashmolean Museum and secretary of the Royal Society; and (ii) from his study of the work of the Danish scholar, Olans Wormius, on the runic alphabet, another striking example of his extremely wide range of interests.

Perhaps the clearest manifestation of the way in which Iolo's ingenious forgeries and confident pronouncements influenced many of his contemporaries and conditioned Welsh thought at the end of the eighteenth century and throughout the greater part of the nineteenth is the importance accorded to Glamorgan by scholars and learned antiquarians of that period. Whereas in the earlier part of the eighteenth century Glamorgan had been regarded as a province of no great significance in the literary history of Wales, a province which had been 'entirely drained of its valuable antiquities', as one prominent literary figure from north Wales writing in that period expressed it, its manuscripts 'buried among the rubbish of old libraries unheeded', and its dialectal vocabulary hardly worthy of the attention of any reputable lexicographer, by the end of that century it was increasingly being regarded by knowledgeable antiquarians and literary historians as probably the most important, and unquestionably the most fascinating, region in the whole of Wales. Scholars in Wales and England alike reacted to Iolo's writings and fabrications with immense enthusiasm. The account of the *Gorsedd* that was published in 1792 made a deep impression on a number of French literati and intellectuals in Paris, while Iolo's Welsh friends and acquaintances in London were of the opinion that it was probably the most important contribution any individual had ever made to Welsh studies, for the work had effectively demonstrated that Wales was one of the great nations of the world, a nation with a rich and glorious history stretching back to patriarchal days. These people felt it was their bounden duty to encourage and assist Iolo in every possible way, so that he might complete his detailed English study, 'The History of the Bards', which he himself regarded as the most important work of his life, one to which he had devoted many years of intense labour. They therefore offered him a salary so that he could live in London and devote the greater part of his time to scholarly pursuits. Unfortunately, Iolo declined this generous offer, and so the work to which he himself attached such great importance was, alas, never completed. Nor were the gentry of his native Glamorgan less solicitous of their moral obligation in this regard, for under the leadership of the famous Traherne family of St Hilary—and later of Coedrhiglan, near Cardiff—they generously provided him with an annuity to enable him to complete all the works he had begun, including his great projected 'History of Glamorgan', a work in which Iolo intended incorporating many of his ingenious forgeries. In his later years, the new Provincial Societies (*Cymdeithasau Taleithiol*), the first of which had been founded in Carmarthen in 1818, about eight years before his death, tried hard to persuade him to prepare his 'History of Wales' for publication, a work which, according to Iolo, comprised several volumes. There can be very few Welsh scholars who have received greater acclaim and encouragement from their contemporaries than the arch-romantic from Flemingston. Little did these people realize that the various works about which they had frequently heard Iolo speak with such unbridled enthusiasm were nowhere near completion, although it must be emphasized that very many portions or fragments survive, and a large number of title-pages occur in his unpublished manuscripts. Clearly, Iolo Morganwg, even in the twilight of his long and extraordinarily industrious life, was still building castles in the air.

Although there had been from time to time a few earlier, generally tentative, expressions of doubt or misgiving, it was not until the end of the nineteenth century and the beginning of the twentieth that a new and better-informed generation of Welsh scholars was able to explode the whole druidic myth and expose the numerous literary forgeries, by applying new and stringent linguistic tests that had only become possible once the long history of the Welsh language during the successive stages of its development had been systematically and scientifically explored. For Iolo Morganwg was probably the most daring and accomplished literary forger the world has ever seen, a forger of great genius and erudition, whose dreams have powerfully influenced the ideas of many generations of Welsh people down to our own day. The National Eisteddfod, as we are familiar with that institution today, is very largely his creation.

Although Iolo's writings and fabrications undoubtedly added a number of substantial complications to the study of Welsh history and literature, since they seriously contaminated many important currents of Welsh scholarship for the greater part of a century, they cannot be entirely disregarded, for they often contain, as might reasonably be expected from an author of such great erudition, a hard kernel of truth. That both literary traditions—the historically authentic and the romantically fictitious—referred to at the beginning of this chapter became so intricately intertwined in Iolo's writings, and that they were at many points so mutually enriching, testifies not only to his wide erudition, but also to the range and power of his great creative genius, which has aptly been compared with that of a highly talented romantic novelist like Sir Walter Scott. The picture of Glamorgan presented in his numerous historical essays, a picture replete with colourful detail, memorable incidents, engaging characters of varying social status, and interesting anecdotes, is unquestionably one of the great creations of the Romantic period in Welsh literature. That kaleidoscopic panorama, which held such an abiding fascination for many of Iolo's cultured, literature-loving compatriots during the latter part of his lifetime and for many years after his death, coupled with the warm romantic glow that suffused so many of his compositions in both prose and verse, contributed in no small measure to the growth and development of Welsh national consciousness in the nineteenth century.

BIBLIOGRAPHY

Works by Iolo Morganwg or publications which contain some compositions by him (in chronological order)

Dagrau yr Awen neu Farwnad Lewis Hopcin (Pont-y-fon [Cowbridge], 1772). A facsimile of the original was published in L. J. Hopkin-James, *Hopkiniaid Morganwg* (Bangor, 1909). See also pp. 347–54.

Barddoniaeth Dafydd ab Gwilym, ed. Owen Jones and William Owen (Llundain, 1789).

The Heroic Elegies and Other Pieces of Llywarch Hen, ed. William Owen (London, 1792).

Poems, Lyric and Pastoral (2 vols., London, 1794).

The Myvyrian Archaiology of Wales, ed. Owen Jones, William Owen and Edward Williams (3 vols., London, 1801–7). The entire contents were reprinted in one volume in 1870.

Salmau yr Eglwys yn yr Anialwch (2 vols., Merthyr Tydfil, 1812 and 1834). The two volumes were published together in Aberystwyth in 1857.

Cyfrinach Beirdd Ynys Prydain, ed. Taliesin Williams (Abertawy, 1829).

Coelbren y Beirdd, published in the name of Taliesin Williams (Llandovery, 1840).

Iolo Manuscripts. A Selection of Ancient Welsh Manuscripts . . . with English Translations and Notes by . . . Taliesin Williams (ab Iolo) (Llandovery, 1848).

Dosparth Edeyrn Davod Aur, ed. John Williams (ab Ithel) (Llandovery, 1856).

Barddas, ed. John Williams (ab Ithel) (2 vols., i Llandovery, 1862; ii London, 1874).

Casgliad o Hen Ganiadau Serch: yn cynnwys rhai a briodolir yn gyffredin i Rys Goch ab Rhiccert ab Einion ap Collwyn, ed. J. H. Davies (Caerdydd, 1902).

Gwaith Iolo Morganwg, ed. T. C. Evans (Cadrawd) (Llanuwchllyn, 1913).

Blodeugerdd o'r Ddeunawfed Ganrif, ed. D. Gwenallt Jones (Caerdydd, 1936; new edn., with a revised introduction and more texts, 1947; 5th edn., 1953).

The Oxford Book of Welsh Verse, ed. Thomas Parry (Oxford, 1962).

The Triads of Britain, compiled by Iolo Morganwg, translated by W. Probert, with an Introduction and Glossary by Malcolm Smith (London, 1977).

Y Gwir Degwch[:] Detholiad o Gerddi Serch Iolo Morganwg, selected by Tegwyn Jones (Gwasg y Wern, 1980).

Cerddi Rhydd Iolo Morganwg, ed. P. J. Donovan (Caerdydd, 1980).

Biographical (in chronological order)
Elijah Waring, *Recollections and Anecdotes of Edward Williams, the Bard of Glamorgan; or, Iolo Morganwg, B.B.D.* (London, 1850).
T. D. Thomas, *Bywgraffiad Iolo Morganwg, B.B.D.* (Caerfyrddin, 1857).
Islwyn ap Nicholas, *Iolo Morganwg[:] Bard of Liberty* (London, 1945).
G. J. Williams, *Iolo Morganwg – Y Gyfrol Gyntaf* (Caerdydd, 1956).

Some critical studies (in chronological order)
John Morris-Jones, 'Gorsedd Beirdd Ynys Prydain', *Cymru*, X (1896), 21–9, 133–40, 153–61, 197–204, 293–9.
Idem, 'Derwyddiaeth Gorsedd y Beirdd', *Y Beirniad*, I (1911), 66–72.
Ifor Williams, 'Rhys Goch ap Rhiccert', *Y Beirniad*, III (1913), 230–44.
G. J. Williams, 'Cywyddau cynnar Iolo Morganwg', *Y Beirniad*, VIII (1919), 75–91.
Idem, 'Cywyddau'r Ychwanegiad at waith Dafydd ap Gwilym', *Y Beirniad*, VIII (1919), 151–70.
Idem, 'Rhys Goch ap Rhiccert', *Y Beirniad*, VIII (1919), 211–26, 260.
Idem, 'Yr Eisteddfod a'r Orsedd', *Y Llenor*, I (1922), 131–8.
Thomas Shankland, 'Hanes dechreuad "Gorsedd Beirdd Ynys Prydain"', *Y Llenor*, III (1924), 94–102.
G. J. Williams, 'Gorsedd Beirdd Ynys Prydain', *Y Llenor*, III (1924), 162–71.
Idem, *Iolo Morganwg a Chywyddau'r Ychwanegiad* (Llundain, 1926).
Idem, 'Iolo Morganwg', *Y Llenor*, XV (1936), 222–31.
Idem, *Iolo Morganwg*, annual lecture of the BBC in Wales (Cardiff, 1963).
Idem, *Edward Lhuyd ac Iolo Morganwg. Agweddau ar Hanes Astudiaethau Gwerin yng Nghymru* (Caerdydd, 1964).
Ceri W. Lewis, 'Iolo Morganwg', in Dyfnallt Morgan (ed.), *Gwŷr Llên y Ddeunawfed Ganrif* (Llandybïe, 1966), 207–15.
G. J. Williams, 'Brut Aberpergwm: a version of the Chronicle of the Princes', in Stewart Williams (ed.), *The Glamorgan Historian*, IV (Cowbridge, 1967), 205–20.
Idem, 'Wil Hopcyn and the Maid of Cefn Ydfa', translated from Welsh by Mrs E. E. Williams, in Stewart Williams (ed.), *The Glamorgan Historian*, VI (1969), 228–51.
Prys Morgan, *Iolo Morganwg* (Cardiff, 1975).
Brinley Richards, *Golwg Newydd ar Iolo Morganwg* (Abertawe, 1979). This book contains many incorrect conclusions and must be read with extreme caution.
Prys Morgan, 'The historical significance of Iolo Morganwg', *Transactions of the Port Talbot Historical Society*, III, ii (1981), 59–68.
Gwyn A. Williams, 'Iolo Morganwg: bardd rhamantaidd ar gyfer cenedl

nad oedd yn cyfrif', in Geraint H. Jenkins (ed.), *Cof Cenedl*, V
(Llandysul, 1990), 57–84.

Geraint and Zonia Bowen, *Hanes Gorsedd y Beirdd* (Cyhoeddiadau
Barddas, 1991).

Geraint Bowen, *Golwg ar Orsedd y Beirdd* (Caerdydd, 1992).

Dillwyn Miles, *The Secret of the Bards of the Isle of Britain* (Llandybïe, 1992).

Ceri W. Lewis, *Iolo Morganwg* (Caernarfon, 1995). This book contains a
full bibliogaphy.

Paul Baines, *The House of Forgery in Eighteenth-Century Britain*
(Aldershot, 1999).

CHAPTER 8

WILLIAM OWEN PUGHE AND THE
LONDON SOCIETIES

GLENDA CARR

The lexicographer William Owen Pughe describes himself at the age of seventeen setting off to London because, as he says, the city was 'in our rustic conversations, the primary point in the geography of the world'. Many young Welshmen over the centuries have made the same journey, full of hope and ambition. As it happened, William Owen Pughe did not fare too badly in the city but many of his compatriots were less fortunate. It was to succour the families of these luckless exiles that societies such as The Honourable and Loyal Society of Antient Britons were founded. The charitable activities of this particular society, founded in 1715, included the setting up of a school in Clerkenwell for the sons of Welsh parents. The Antient Britons met only once a year, on St David's Day, when they listened to a sermon and made a collection for the upkeep of the school. Not surprisingly, this rather feeble effort did not adequately provide for the educational and cultural needs of the London Welshmen. It was ostensibly the desire to meet these needs that fired a few patriotic Welshmen to found the first society to bear the name of the Honourable Society of Cymmrodorion.

The guiding lights of the Cymmrodorion were the versatile Morris brothers of Anglesey, especially Richard Morris, who has been called the father of the society. The history of the society can be divided into three periods: the first from its founding in 1751 until 1787; a second spurt between 1820 and 1843; and the modern period from 1873 to the present day. However, for present purposes we need concern ourselves only with the early period. There is no doubt that the lack of diligence on the part of the Antient Britons was one of the main incentives behind the founding of the new society. Its constitutions stress the need for it to set its house in order as the charitable activities of the Antient

Britons had been 'of late entirely neglected by the Great, and but little regarded by any for want of proper Regulations'. Charity, then, was the primary motive to which lip-service, at least, was paid. The society had its 'Poor's Box' to alleviate any distress suffered by members and their families in London and to help them return to Wales should family commitments call them there. But there were less altruistic motives as well. The enterprising Welshmen who had come to London had not entirely forgotten their language and many of them longed for an opportunity to converse with their compatriots in Welsh. It was natural for them to foregather to water their roots and to weep over their ale for the fatherland that they had so willingly left. Such meetings were inevitably inclined to become rather jolly as is reflected in the song with which the society greeted the enrolling of a new member and which refers to the draining of cups to their very dregs. That such activities were not unusual can be seen in the fact that the society's constitutions provided the means of controlling any excessive behaviour on the part of the members: the chairman had the right to admonish anyone found guilty of 'drunkenness, profane Cursing or Swearing, using any obscene or irreligious Expressions in his Discourse'. Conviviality at times threatened to overshadow philanthropy: in a letter to his brother William in September 1755, Lewis Morris describes a visit to one of the society's meetings which went on until two o'clock in the morning—'Sad work!' Goronwy Owen was present, extremely drunk, and others who did nothing but argue: no wonder that Lewis says that things had to improve 'ag onide ffarwel Gymrodorion' (for otherwise, farewell Cymmrodorion).

The Morris brothers had their own agenda for the society anyway. At that time, Wales had no focal point for its intellectual activity: no university, no national library, no national eisteddfod. In the Cymmrodorion Society the brothers hoped to provide a focus for Welsh culture, and the constitutions which they drew up stated unashamedly that its main aim was neither social nor philanthropic but rather 'the Cultivation of the British Language, and a Search into Antiquities'. To this end the society took over the library and museum of the charity school in Clerkenwell Green. The members were charged an annual fee of 10s 6d after 1777 'for the support of Welsh publications', and the society aimed to buy every book published in Welsh and 'as many British Manuscripts as can be procured at a reasonable Price'. The Morris brothers, with their own insatiable love of knowledge, had also drawn up a very ambitious and wide-ranging list of subjects to be discussed in the meetings. However, one wonders what a certain Evan Pugh, soapmaker of Bishopsgate Street, would make of a discussion on 'Gildas, Nennius, Asserius Menevensis, Giraldus Cambrensis, Galfridus Monemuthensis, Ponticus Virunnius; and other ancient Writers among the Britains, who wrote our History in the Latin Tongue', and indeed whether the Revd Thomas Pardoe, DD, principal of Jesus College, Oxford, would have made the effort to come up to London to hear the proposed paper on 'Manurement of Ground with Marl, Sand and Lime and Methods of Manuring'.

Catering for a society whose members had only one thing in common, namely the fact that they were Welsh, proved to be a problem, especially for the clever Morris brothers who did not seem to realize that not all the members were as well-informed as they were. The rank and file of the society included a great many tradesmen and craftsmen. Amongst them were some interesting occupations, such as a 'bees-man', a chocolate-maker (translated by Richard Morris as *cocolatydd*), a scarlet dyer and a stocking presser. The snobbish brothers (themselves the sons of a cooper, albeit a cultured one) tried their best to disguise the humble background of their fellow-members 'that every English fool may not have room to laugh in his sleeve and say "such a society indeed"'. However, there were professional men among the members and the list of Corresponding Members is even more impressive as it includes Evan Evans (Ieuan Fardd), Goronwy Owen, Paul Panton and many others who made a genuine contribution to the advancement of Welsh literature and culture. The first Cymmrodorion Society came to an end in 1787. It did not really recover from the death of its 'father', Richard Morris, in 1779. The aspirations of its founders were not realized, and in retrospect its achievements do seem rather disappointing. However, the society had won the respect of Welshmen everywhere and it did provide a focus for the cultural life of the nation. The London Welshmen were regarded as arbiters in literary matters, and this trend was to continue when other societies came to take the place of the original Cymmrodorion.

'As the Cymmrodorion did not embrace that part which practically encourage such customs of Cymmru as Pennillion singing, in the latter part of 1770 the projected Gwyneddigion was set on foot'. This is how W. D. Leathart, chronicler of the history of that society, describes the founding of the rather more plebeian Gwyneddigion. They were truly an offshoot of the Cymmrodorion as the founding members came from the earlier society. These were Robert Hughes (Robin Ddu yr Ail o Fôn), who had left his native Anglesey for London to become a clerk to Ratcliffe Sidebottom, barrister in Essex Court, Temple; John Edwards (Sion Ceiriog); and the man who became the doyen of the new society, Owen Jones (Owain Myfyr). The latter had left Llanfihangel Glyn Myfyr to be apprenticed to a London furrier and before very long had his own successful business in 148 Upper Thames Street. In 1776, William Owen (he had not yet adopted the surname Pughe) arrived in London and seems to have earned his living either as a solicitor's clerk or as proof-reader for some of the London publishers. It is difficult to believe that William Owen Pughe spent six years in London without being drawn into the net of Welshmen in the city, but this is what he says in the introduction to the first edition of his Welsh dictionary:

> I had continued in this great city until about the year 1782, without knowing that any other person in it, besides myself, ever thought of the Welsh language, or of its literature. Then it was that chance threw me in the way of ROBERT HUGHES, the poet and judicious critic.

It was Robert Hughes who drew Pughe into the circle of the Gwyneddigion, thereby changing the course of his life. His name is recorded as one of the newcomers to the society's meeting on 5 May 1783, together with Edward Jones (Bardd y Brenin), who was to make a valuable contribution in the field of Welsh folk-music. The gifted and diligent Pughe soon drew the attention of Owain Myfyr, and although he was basically a shy man, he was soon playing a prominent part in the activities of the society, becoming secretary between 1784 and 1787, rising to president in 1789. The society had more to offer Pughe than companionship: he was amazed to discover, as he said, its 'treasures of British manuscripts of which I did not know before that we had one in the whole metropolis'. By about 1784 he was working on the early Welsh poets before progressing to the Poets of the Princes, studies which later formed the basis of *The Myvyrian Archaiology of Wales*. With the demise of the first Cymmrodorion Society the Gwyneddigion took over many of their responsibilities, as well as their valuable library, which included Richard Morris's books and manuscripts. Pughe was appointed one of the librarians.

The Gwyneddigion did much to promote the eisteddfod in its early days. During the eighteenth century, informal gatherings which could loosely be termed eisteddfodau had been held in Wales, and the Cymmrodorion had already tried to make these meetings more respectable and dignified by offering prizes and patronage. It was natural now for the organizers to turn to the Gwyneddigion for the same support. Unfortunately, the society's dealings with the eisteddfod began rather inauspiciously. The local organizers of an eisteddfod held in Corwen in May 1789 had found it difficult to judge who was worthy of the main poetry prize. They decided to ask the Gwyneddigion to act as adjudicators. The contenders were Walter Davies (Gwallter Mechain), Thomas Edwards (Twm o'r Nant) and Jonathan Hughes. There were soon rumours that Walter Davies had seen the subjects beforehand (it was supposed to be an improvized effort) and that he had had a chance to revise his poem before sending it on to the Gwyneddigion. Letters have survived which show that this was indeed true, and that Walter Davies had actually written to Pughe and Owain Myfyr to curry favour. Owain Myfyr admitted that the Gwyneddigion had been rather embarrassed to have been asked to adjudicate at all, as only Pughe and one other member knew anything about the strict metres in Welsh. Walter Davies's wiles worked and he was awarded the prize, but not without considerable jealousy and backbiting on the part of Thomas Edwards and his supporters.

Another eisteddfod was to be held in Bala in September 1789, with the full support and patronage of the Gwyneddigion. This time, Walter Davies attempted to influence Owain Myfyr only and particularly asked him not to involve anyone else. William Owen Pughe, however, was drawn into the stratagem and Walter Davies won another prize. Overwhelmed with gratitude to his patrons in London, he sent Owain Myfyr the gift of a hare, only to be told that the hare and its accompanying letter had come to grief in transit and on no account was he to acknowledge publicly any acquaintance with the officials of the Gwyneddigion again, for fear of rumours of favouritism. It was too late. The poets knew what was going on and the Gwyneddigion lost the support of the rank and file. They were to feel that loss keenly when they tried to enlist support for *Barddoniaeth Dafydd ab Gwilym.* The Morris brothers had been collecting the poems of Dafydd ap Gwilym diligently over the years. After their death, Owain Myfyr enlarged the collection, copying all the known poems in his own bold and distinctive hand. He had been working on this project for ten years before he met William Owen Pughe. As early as 1773 he appealed to Edward Williams (Iolo Morganwg) for help, and received more than he had anticipated in return. At first, Owain Myfyr's main helper was Robert Hughes, but from 1784 onwards the work fell more and more into the hands of Pughe. Just as the work was nearing completion Iolo Morganwg dropped his bombshell and, in March 1788, sent Pughe a thick wad of poems which he claimed were the work of Dafydd ap Gwilym, adding that there were plenty more where they came from. The volume was too far advanced for these poems to be included in the main body of the book and they had to be added as an appendix. By now, we know that the notorious 'Cywyddau'r Ychwanegiad' were nearly all forged by Iolo, as well as at least two others in the main body of the book. *Barddoniaeth Dafydd ab Gwilym,* 'compiled by Owen Jones and William Owen', was launched in March 1789 and a plentiful supply was taken to Bala in September, as the editors had already realized that an eisteddfod was a good place to sell books. But they had reckoned without the grievances and suspicions of the poets, who had not forgotten the sight of Walter Davies smugly walking off with more than his fair share of the prizes. Owain Myfyr preferred to talk of the lack of appreciation and welcome for the book in terms of casting pearls before swine. However, what with lack of support from the poets and some surprisingly feeble and careless marketing and book-keeping on the part of that usually astute man of business, the venture was not a success and Owain Myfyr, personally, lost a good deal of the money which he had invested in it.

The editors of *Barddoniaeth Dafydd ab Gwilym* did not claim that the collection contained all the poems written by Dafydd ap Gwilym, nor did they claim that there were no textual errors. They were very aware of the pitfalls which awaited any editor and they knew, too, that poems preserved orally from one generation to the next were bound to show discrepancies. Unfortunately, they also lacked the necessary scholarship to detect forgeries when they met them. Others were more astute, and quick to point out their suspicions to Owain Myfyr. David Thomas (Dafydd Ddu Eryri) drew his attention to patterns in the strict metres used in the poems sent in by Iolo which differed from those used by Dafydd ap Gwilym. But all this happened about seventeen years too late and, by then, more of Iolo's forgeries had found their way into *The Myvyrian Archaiology of Wales.*

The publication of *Barddoniaeth Dafydd ab Gwilym* marked the beginning of a whirl of literary activity for William Owen Pughe. He had been collecting materials for a Welsh–English dictionary for quite a while and had visited many of the private libraries in Wales in the course of his researches. In the meantime, however, he had been concentrating on the early heroic poetry, and in particular the Llywarch Hen englynion. The fruit of these studies was published as *The Heroic Elegies and other pieces of Llywarch Hen.* Although the volume is dated 1792, a more likely date of publication is the first half of the following year. Some of the preparatory work had been done by Richard Thomas from Ynyscynhaearn in Eifionydd, who had died a young man in 1780 and had left a valuable collection of manuscripts to the Gwyneddigion. Pughe felt that Richard Thomas had been 'too anxious in aiming at elegance' in his translation of the Llywarch Hen poems, and so he himself tried to give what he thought was a more literal version. This was not a success. In places the translation is pure nonsense, and as a whole bears little relation to the reading of the poems with which we are familiar today in the light of recent scholarship. This is not entirely Pughe's fault as he worked mainly from copies of the text, many of which were inaccurate. This was a problem which was to plague him all through the years he worked on the early texts, in this volume, in his dictionary and in *The Myvyrian Archaiology.* It was often difficult to gain access to the private libraries of the great houses of Wales to check the original manuscripts, even if their whereabouts were known. But in the *Heroic Elegies* Pughe added to his problems by experimenting with the orthography, a whim which was to make him many enemies as his enthusiasm for such innovations grew. The most interesting aspect of the *Heroic Elegies* was possibly the long section on 'Bardism' included in the volume. This was most probably the work of Iolo Morganwg, or was written by Pughe and heavily influenced by Iolo. In it the bards and druids are portrayed as pacifists and radicals who seem to have much more in common with the end of the eighteenth century than any early heroic age.

The *Heroic Elegies*, whatever its shortcomings, certainly enhanced William Owen Pughe's reputation among the literati of London. He became a member of a coterie of intellectuals with whom he associated or corresponded, men such as Robert Southey, Walter Scott, Sharon Turner, John Leyden and Richard Heber. He met many of these when he was elected Fellow of the Society of Antiquaries in 1793. In 1794, Cymdeithas yr Ofyddion (the Ovates) was founded. Although it obviously owes its fanciful name to the bardic dream of Iolo Morganwg, its aims were unimpeachable. It hoped to publish not only the earliest Welsh texts but others which could have a more general appeal, such as the Welsh laws, the Mabinogi and the works of the physicians of Myddfai. These would be published in the society's own journal, which was originally called *Walian Register* before it was changed to *Cambrian Register*. The first number appeared in 1795, edited by William Owen Pughe; there was a second one in 1799 and a final one in 1818 before it expired for lack of support.

The Morris brothers often complained of the need for a comprehensive dictionary in Welsh which would furnish polymaths such as themselves with the varied vocabulary necessary to discuss their interests. They were difficult to please and ready to find fault with other men's efforts to fill this gap. Moses Williams, who had worked with Edward Lhuyd in the Ashmolean, had appealed for their help in compiling a dictionary but had been given short shrift by Lewis Morris, 'knowing him incapable of carrying on ye work'. William Morris complained that John Davies of Mallwyd's *Dictionarium Duplex* was deficient in the terms that he needed to discuss natural history. Lewis was just as scathing about Davies: 'he knew no animals except his own cattle and fowls'. The fact was that Lewis Morris rather fancied himself as a lexicographer, among other things, and was encouraged by his brothers in this respect. William Morris promised that he would supply him with the most wonderful botanologium that the world had ever seen. However, the brothers had too many irons in the fire and it was left to others to write the dictionaries. William Gambold compiled a Welsh dictionary between 1707 and 1722, but failed to publish it for lack of support. In the Morris letters, we read of the attempts

of Gambold's son to sell his father's manuscripts to another
lexicographer, Thomas Richards, but in the end they came into the
possession of John Walters, who published his English–Welsh
dictionary between 1770 and 1794. Thomas Richards, however,
had seen his own Welsh–English dictionary published in 1753,
with a second edition in 1759. This was basically a Welsh version
of John Davies's dictionary with the addition of words already
collected by Edward Lhuyd and the fruits of his own researches.
This work again failed to gain the approval of the critical Lewis
Morris: Richards was 'not equal to the task . . . laborious, but very
ignorant'.

This, then, was the situation when William Owen Pughe set
about the task which he claimed that his 'prudent friends'
described as 'so unprofitable a sacrifice of time, as the collecting
together the words of a nearly expiring language'. Such gibes, far
from deterring him, actually spurred him on to greater efforts. He
was fortunate, too, in his colleagues at the time. Although serious
rifts and even enmity later grew between him and Owain Myfyr
and Iolo Morganwg, they were a great support to him when he
began on his enormous task. Iolo Morganwg, in spite of his
idiosyncracies, had an incomparable knowledge of the Welsh
manuscripts, gleaned on his tireless journeys around the libraries
of Wales. Others, too, were ready to supply Pughe with lists of
specialist terms which they themselves had collected: Dafydd Ddu
Eryri, for instance, sent him a collection of names of birds and
fish. In the introduction to the first edition of his dictionary, Pughe
thanks all those who had helped him in different ways; he
acknowledges the labours of those who had toiled in the field
before him, he thanks all those who had supplied him with
'various communications', and mentions in particular Paul Panton
of Plas Gwyn in Anglesey and Thomas Johnes of Hafod Uchdryd
in Cardiganshire for allowing him generous access to the treasures
in their private libraries. His warmest thanks, however, go to
Owen Jones: 'Of him it may be truly said, that he has extended
greater patronage towards preserving the literary remains of
Wales, than any other person, in ancient or modern times.'

Geiriadur Cynmraeg a Saesoneg: A Welsh and English Dictionary
was originally published in parts, the first section appearing in
June 1793. This extended only as far as the letter *C* and cost six
shillings, and, with the prospect of five more parts to follow, many

of those who had awaited its appearance with interest found that it would be dearer than they had expected. There were other disappointments as well. Pughe had experimented further with the orthography, substituting ç for *ch*; z for *dd*; *f* for *ff*; *f* for *ph*; and v for *f*. Pughe was aware that his experiments with the orthography would be criticized. In a letter to Gwallter Mechain he says:

> There is another thing I ought to be afraid of—your critics will be setting their faces against the orthography—for I have disencumbered it of four double letters, namely ch, dd, ff, ph—Mrs Prudence advised me to stop short here.

The second part was published in June 1794, and we know from letters which have survived that many who had bought the first part did not bother to buy any more. By December 1795, the whole of the first section of the first edition had been published but, to add to its problems, the next part did not appear for five years, and it was 1803 by the time the whole dictionary had appeared. At the same time, Pughe's idiosyncratic *Grammar of the Welsh Language* was also published, both as part of the dictionary and separately. An abridged version of the dictionary was published in 1806, this time in the standard orthography at the request of the publisher. He was Evan Williams, a Cardiganshire man whose business was in the Strand, and he had had financial losses with the first edition. A second edition of the abridged version appeared in 1836, and a second edition of the full version in 1832 in the standard orthography. A third edition, revised by Robert John Pryse (Gweirydd ap Rhys), was published in 1866.

One of the first things to strike the reader in Pughe's dictionary is the way in which he reduces the words into very simple elements in an attempt to explain their etymology. More obvious still is the fact that Pughe's word divisions have no connection at all with the known derivation of the word. These elements actually seem to be primitive sounds rather than words. However, in an appendix to his dictionary, Pughe not only refers to them as 'elementary words' but says that they are all 'the appropriate or fixed symbol of one simple idea'. He even claims that 'a e i o' can be regarded as a sentence and translates it as 'going is he into out of'. Sir John Morris-Jones referred scornfully to Pughe's belief in these primitive elements as 'the principle of ba, be, bw'—a very apt description, as *ba*, *be* and *bw* were among the elements which Pughe claimed formed the basis of the Welsh language, together with *ib*, *ich*, *og*, *wff*, *yg* and other equally uncouth sounds. The Latin influence in Welsh is also ignored in words such as *pererin*, and, rather than acknowledge its origins in *peregrinus*, Pughe prefers to derive it from two elements, *per* and *er*, giving its primitive meaning as 'that has a course through', and only secondarily as 'a pilgrim'. Pughe was perfectly aware of the Latin element in Welsh and readily admits that Welsh has a great many words 'in common' with Latin but, as he claims in the appendix to the dictionary,

> these words can be satisfactorily proved not to have been borrowed by the Welsh from the Romans; neither could the latter people be indebted to the Britons for them. Therefore, the affinity, existing between the two languages, must be attributed to a common origin of such words, and preserved in each from a period anterior to the commencement of the history of either nation.

Where did these eccentric ideas come from? The theory that there was a common origin to all languages was very popular up to the eighteenth century and many still believed that there was once a mother tongue which had been shattered in the Tower of Babel. But by Pughe's day, that theory was losing ground as detailed studies of Sanskrit as well as modern languages began to reveal the inter-relationship of the Indo-European family of languages. Edward Lhuyd, too, had compared the Celtic languages in a scientific way, thereby later earning the accolade from Sir John Rhŷs that he was 'in many respects the greatest Celtic philologist the world has ever seen'. However, rather than tread in the solid footsteps of such scholars, Pughe chose to follow the lunatic fringe. To a large extent the blame for Pughe's erroneous theories can be laid at the door of Paul-Yves Pezron (1639–1706), a Breton who published his *Antiquité de la Nation et de la Langue des Celtes...* in Paris in 1703. The English translation appeared three years later. Pezron had decided that the primitive mother-tongue was Celtic, and gave the Celts an ancient and noble lineage extending through the mists of time as far as Gomer the son of Japheth. It is more than possible that Pughe could have read Pezron's work in translation: Gwallter Mechain, for example, made copious notes on *The Antiquities of*

Nations. However, it is more likely that there was an intermediate link between Pughe and Pezron in the form of Rowland Jones (1722–74) from Llanbedrog in Llŷn. He was a lawyer by profession, but chose instead to devote his later years to writing several highly fanciful books on the supposed origin of languages. Lewis Morris, as usual, was full of criticism, and this time his judgement was pretty sound when he said:

> I am too grave to make a joke of any poor man touched in the head, and as he acquired a good fortune by his former Industry, it is fit he should lay it out as he pleases in whims and fancies provided that he hurts nobody . . . But alas! poor Ro. Jones the Attorney can produce nothing but an empty froth!

Unfortunately, Rowland Jones's whims proved to be more harmful than Lewis Morris ever imagined and did much to hinder linguistic scholarship for several generations, once William Owen Pughe had adopted his theories. Jones proclaimed the esoteric information that Gomer the son of Japheth had not been present at the momentous diaspora in the Tower of Babel, and that his descendants had thereby managed to retain their language in its original unspoilt form. Rowland Jones, like Pezron, believed that this unsullied language was Celtic, and that not only Welsh but Latin, Greek and English were derived from it. He had gone even further than William Owen Pughe, claiming that Welsh was so pure and primitive a language that not only did each syllable have a definite meaning, but individual letters also. He claimed that the letter *O* was the primary letter, being 'the alpha and omega, and as the indefinite circle of time and space, comprehending all nature'. The poet Goronwy Owen, too, although he had received a traditional schooling in the Classical languages, had been dazzled by the idea of the primitive elements of language: 'You know Monsieur Pezron's rule,' he said, pleading that some 'able hand' might come to reduce 'the compound words into the simples, and derivates onto their primitives'.

William Owen Pughe did more harm than his predecessors by allowing his confused ideas to influence the orthography of the language. In a letter to Iolo Morganwg, he stated that his aim was 'to introduce a purity of orthography deduced from etymological reasoning'. Not only did he interfere with the doubling of the letters *n* and *r*, a problem in Welsh at best, but, as we have already seen, he also attempted to rid the language of the digraphs *ch*, *dd*, *ff*, *ng*, *ll*, *ph*, *rh* and *th*. He was not the first to try to do this: John Prys, Gruffydd Robert, Milan, Siôn Dafydd Rhys and John Jones, Gellilyfdy, had all dabbled with the orthography long before him, and had met with no more success. As Professor R. T. Jenkins said, 'no doubt it would be "easier" to write *ovyz* for *ofydd* (or in English *nolij* for *knowledge*)—but people just won't'. Pughe's attempts to abolish the digraphs were rejected, but the way he resurrected archaic forms and distorted the grammar resulted in making his fellow Welshmen more confused than ever about their spelling. The debate about the orthography was to continue long after his death, and it was left to Sir John Morris-Jones to clear up the mess in the end.

In 1735, Lewis Morris had set up a printing press in Holyhead and published what he hoped was to be the first of many numbers of a journal containing excerpts from early Welsh texts. Because of lack of support it proved to be the only one. But the dream was not forgotten, and with the founding of the Cymmrodorion in 1751 interest was rekindled. Evan Evans (Ieuan Fardd), a feckless man but a brilliant scholar, did a great deal of collecting and copying of the ancient manuscripts. In 1764 his anthology, *Some Specimens of the Poetry of the Antient Welsh Bards*, was published containing a selection of poems extending as far back as Aneirin. Ieuan would have been the ideal person to have edited more of the early texts but his wayward nature spoiled all hopes of this. William Owen Pughe, a far more stable and dependable character although lacking Ieuan's genius, had been interested in the early Welsh poems since his youth, having read Rhys Jones's volume, *Gorchestion Beirdd Cymru neu Flodau Godidowgrwydd Awen*, as a boy. These anthologies were the first fruits of the interest that arose in Celtic in the eighteenth century. Men of letters began to clamour for more, and when more did not materialize they began to voice their doubts about the existence of further works and about the authenticity of those already in circulation. The forgeries of men such as Macpherson and Chatterton did little to allay their suspicions. Realizing this, Sharon Turner published *A Vindication of the Genuineness of the Antient British Poems* in 1803, in which he tried to prove the authenticity of the early texts. He argued that the way in which they had been neglected pointed to an honest, if regrettable, insouciance rather than any attempt to deceive. As he says: 'No friendly chest—no ruinous turret—no auspicious accident—has given them to us. No man's interest or reputation is connected with their discovery. Their supporters are therefore at least disinterested.'

It was indeed from purely altruistic motives that Owen Jones (Owain Myfyr) was fired to begin on the enormous and thankless task of copying the early manuscripts. As we have already seen, the editing was later taken over by William Owen Pughe, while Owen Jones dug deep into his capacious pockets to support the work, and *Barddoniaeth Dafydd ab Gwilym* had appeared in 1789, followed by *The Heroic Elegies of Llywarch Hen* in 1792/3. An advertisement for the latter contained an interesting promise: that the works of other poets 'who flourished anterior to the death of the last Prince Llywelyn' were to be published in separate volumes, and that the works of Taliesin would appear before the end of 1793. They did not. However, around this time Owen Jones and Pughe had a change of heart and they decided to adopt a less ambitious scheme. There were many willing hands at the beginning: Iolo Morganwg, Gwallter Mechain, Dafydd Ddu Eryri, Richard Fenton (the historian from Fishguard) and others all offered to help, but they gradually began to lose interest, leaving Pughe, Iolo and Owen Jones to shoulder practically the whole project in the end.

The new plan was to publish a large volume containing several texts rather than a series of shorter individual ones. The original title chosen for the volume was *The Welsh Archaiology*, but his colleagues wished to honour Owain Myfyr and pay tribute to his generous patronage by incorporating his name in the title. Owen Jones, although he was a brash man in many ways, was also rather embarrassed at being self-made and self-taught. 'Myfyr will not have his name announced lest he should be sneered at by some people,' said Pughe to Iolo in a letter in 1798. And he persisted in his stance, so that when the first volume was published in 1801 the title inside the book was *The Welsh Archaiology*. The unusual spelling 'Archaiology' had been decided by Paul Panton, who had been so generous a patron to the editors that they could hardly argue with any of his whims. At the very last moment, Owen Jones relented to the appeal of his friends and the title was changed on the cover and title-page to *The Myvyrian Archaiology of Wales*, thereby honouring two of the great patrons of the work.

The task of traipsing around the private libraries of Wales to copy the manuscripts was entrusted to Iolo Morganwg, a prodigious walker, who would disappear without trace for weeks on end, leaving William Owen Pughe to cope with anxious enquiries from his distracted wife. It fell to Pughe, too, to urge Iolo to keep to the task in hand and not be diverted by other interesting manuscripts which were not relevant to the *Archaiology*. The printer was causing them problems as well because of his slowness: in one letter, Pughe begs Iolo to send him more material 'to keep Griffiths' Gwasg Malwen [Snail Press] a-going, in order not to leave him any excuse for saying he stops on our account'. However, Iolo did have some real problems of his own: it was no easy task to gain admittance to some of the private libraries. This was not surprising. Many libraries had been shamefully pillaged by unprincipled copiers, and in other cases the misplaced generosity of the owners meant that priceless manuscripts were being passed nonchalantly from hand to hand in the neighbourhood of the great houses, often never to return. It was almost too late by the time the owners of libraries such as Hengwrt realized the extent of their losses, and when they did eventually clamp down on would-be copiers it made the task of bona fide researchers very difficult. The delays caused by the negotiations now required to gain access to the manuscripts made the editors in London very uneasy. Already there were some signs of the rift which was later to develop between Owen Jones and Iolo. Pughe feared that Iolo might offend Owen Jones so much that the enterprise would suffer. His concern is obvious in the letter which he sent Iolo in May 1800:

> you must know that in consequence of your dilatory spirit O. Myfyr is become quite fractious in not seeing you in London. For goodness' sake do not be the means of his becoming tired of the path (to glory) wherein he now treads, for Welsh literature will not find another such a supporter.

As it happened, Owain Myfyr's journey along the path to glory was nearing its end. It is estimated that he spent more than a thousand pounds on the publishing costs alone of *The Myvyrian Archaiology* and a great deal more on supporting Iolo Morganwg and William Owen Pughe while they were working on the volume. Altogether it is reckoned that he spent between four and five thousand pounds on the venture—an enormous sum at that time. However, after the first two volumes were published in 1801, Owen Jones began to experience financial losses in his business, although he did manage to back the third volume which appeared in 1807. He had also got married in late middle-age and had a young family to consider. William Owen Pughe's circumstances had changed as well: he had inherited an estate in Wales and was no longer so dependent on his literary work to support him and his family. The affairs of the estate and his increasing involvement with the strange prophetess Joanna Southcott and her mission meant that he had less time to spend on his researches. Iolo Morganwg was sulking. This was the beginning of the rift that Pughe had feared would develop between him and Owen Jones. It was not Iolo's 'dilatory spirit', however, that was to destroy their friendship in the end but a dispute about money. Iolo believed that Owen Jones had reneged on his promise to pay him fifty pounds a year for life. To be fair to Owen Jones, there is evidence that he carried out his promises honourably while he could. Iolo, however, always ready to consider himself to be the victim of injustice, nursed his grudge for years until it had become distorted in his over-active imagination. As early as 1806 he was writing to Gwallter Mechain about Owen Jones's 'mental depravity', and by 1821 he was abusing his former patron in no uncertain terms in a letter to Evan Williams, the publisher, referring to him as 'more than half Idiot and more than two halves of a swindler'.

Owen Jones and William Owen Pughe really had more reason to attack Iolo than he had to attack them. His forgeries were to mar the *Archaiology* as they had spoilt *Barddoniaeth Dafydd ab Gwilym*. He had forged the 'Triads of Dyfnwal Moelmud' and the triads attributed to the 'Bards of the Isle of Britain' as well as 'Brut Aberpergwm', 'Brut Ieuan Brechfa' and 'Doethineb Catwg Ddoeth'—titles which to us today seem so redolent of Iolo that it is surprising that he got away with it at all. William Owen Pughe, that most honest and gullible of men, would not have dreamt of suspecting any fraud because there was no guile in his own naive nature. But Owen Jones was also duped and he was nobody's fool. The reason was that neither of them had the scholarly insight of men such as Moses Williams and Ieuan Fardd, who might have detected discrepancies not immediately obvious to the less observant reader. However, there was no reason to suspect Iolo at the time. He had shown the world his unparalleled knowledge of the texts in his treatise 'A Review of the Present State of Welsh Manuscripts' in the *Archaiology*. The original version of this treatise is more interesting than the published one for, in it, Iolo discusses the notorious literary forgers, Macpherson and Chatterton. He almost finds fault with them for not having sufficiently convincing manuscripts to support their claims, adding what is to us now, with hindsight, a very sinister comment: 'It is no difficult thing to manufacture very fine Poems and impose them on the public for works of great Antiquity.'

In spite of Iolo's forgeries and some very amateur editing by modern standards, the *Archaiology* was an important contribution to Welsh literature, as it brought the early texts within reach of the public. However, many were disappointed that some of the most attractive and sought-after texts had not been included, namely the Four Branches of the Mabinogi and the Romances. Their absence was all the more surprising as it was well known to his contemporaries that William Owen Pughe had been working on them for some time. There is evidence that he had intended from the beginning to devote a separate volume to them alone. He had already published the text of *Pwyll Pendefig Dyfed*, with a translation, in *The Cambrian Register* in 1795 and 1799. He was urged to persevere by Walter Scott, Sharon Turner and Robert Southey, who were eager to see all the tales published. Southey had already read some of Pughe's translations and had commented: 'Owen has translated them admirably in so Welsh a syntax and idiom that they convey the full manner of the original', which suggests that Southey's knowledge of Welsh was superficial to say the least. Pughe published the text of *The Dream of Macsen Wledig* in *Y Greal* in 1806; *Pwyll Pendefig Dyfed* was published in *The Cambro-Briton* in 1820–1, and *Math fab Mathonwy* in the *Cambrian Quarterly Magazine* in 1829. The public did not want to see the Mabinogi and Romances in piecemeal form and urged Pughe to collect them all in one volume. It is obvious from his letters that he was doing his utmost to achieve this, but with little success: he had offered his collection to two publishers, Longman and Murray, and had been rejected. He had tried to collect subscribers but the response was slow. By 1827, he was reduced once more to publishing his material piecemeal. By 1830, Pughe's son Aneurin Owen was showing a keen interest in the work. Pughe himself had moved from London to live near his son on his estate near Denbigh, and it was decided to publish the work in that town. Pughe was now over seventy and in failing health. In 1832 there was an announcement in the *Cambrian Quarterly Magazine*:

> at this moment the public is on the very tiptoe of expectation for the promised appearance of an edition of the Mabinogion or Babinogion under the auspices of the first Celtic scholar of the age.

This promise was not fulfilled. Pughe's tireless labour on the Mabinogi can be seen today in neat manuscript bundles in the National Library of Wales. But the Mabinogi did reach the public shortly afterwards: in 1838, Lady Charlotte Guest's translation first appeared. William Owen Pughe had died in 1835. With his death a whole era came to an end. No longer did Wales turn to London for guidance on literary matters; a new generation was arising in Wales itself, a more educated and self-confident generation which was to build on the foundations laid by those tireless and generous pioneers who really did prove that there is some truth in the Welsh proverb 'Gorau Cymro, Cymro oddi cartref' (The best Welshman is the exiled Welshman).

BIBLIOGRAPHY

The following is a short bibliography of the main sources used in this chapter. A fuller bibliography can be seen in Glenda Carr, *William Owen Pughe* (Cardiff, 1983).

Primary Texts
The main manuscript sources are NLW 13221–63 (letters, poetry, transcriptions and personal papers of William Owen Pughe including the unpublished translations of the Mabinogi); NLW 21280–6 (Iolo Morganwg's papers); BL Add. MSS 9848–50 (papers of the Gwyneddigion Society); BL Add. MSS 14866–15089 (papers of the charity school in Gray's Inn Lane, London, and papers of the Morris brothers); BL Add. MSS 31062–110 (collection of poetry copied by Owen Jones and his nephew, Hugh Maurice).

Owen Jones and William Owen, *Barddoniaeth Dafydd ab Gwilym* (Llundain, 1789).

O. Jones, E. Williams and W. O. Pughe, *The Myvyrian Archaiology of Wales* (London, 1801–7).

William Owen, *The Heroic Elegies and other pieces of Llywarch Hen* . . . (London 1792).

Idem, *Geiriadur Cynmraeg a Saesoneg: A Welsh and English Dictionary* . . . *to which is prefixed a Welsh Grammar* (1793–1803).

Studies

R. T. Jenkins and H. M. Ramage, *A History of the Honourable Society of Cymmrodorion 1751–1951* (London, 1951).

Prys Morgan, *The Eighteenth-Century Renaissance* (Llandybïe, 1981).

G. J. Williams, *Iolo Morganwg a Chywyddau'r Ychwanegiad* (Llundain, 1926).

Idem, *Iolo Morganwg* (Caerdydd, 1956).

Idem, Chapters I, III and VIII in Aneirin Lewis (ed.) *Agweddau ar Hanes Dysg Gymraeg* (Cardiff, 1969).

CHAPTER 9

FOLK POETRY AND DIVERSIONS

RHIANNON IFANS

> The true genius and spirit of a people are best seen from their Diversions.

So wrote Thomas Percy in a letter to Evan Evans (Ieuan Fardd) in 1762. For the later observer, discontinued folk practices are often puzzling, and the diversions enjoyed by eighteenth-century stalwarts are echoes of a world with which we have largely lost touch. Yet, this world left us with an inheritance of free-metre poetry which once buttressed the social life of the community by helping it to stage its recreations and rituals.

Amongst these recreations and rituals are the celebrations associated with seasonal change. The old Celtic year ran from 1 November to 31 October and it is *Nos Galan Gaeaf* (All-Hallows Eve) which marked the end of one year and the beginning of the next. The next significant date on the rural calendar was mid-winter, when at one time the Saturnalia rites were observed in ancient Rome to commemorate the fabled rule of King Saturnus, who developed new methods of farming and improved the very fabric of his country Latium. This celebration took on a new meaning when the Christian Church declared that it would honour the birth of Christ on 25 December, to coincide with the Saturnalia and taking over from it as a communal celebration.

Christmas Day was the first day of the *gwyliau*, holidays. This meant attendance at an early-morning church service referred to as *y blygien*, a dialect form of *plygain*. These services were most popular in north Wales, in the Banw and Efyrnwy valleys and the upper reaches of the Tanad and Dyfi valleys. Carollers were called upon to sing a specific type of Christmas carol. These were strictly orthodox poems, containing purely scriptural materials, and they played an important part in the religious education of a semi-literate people. The most renowned of these carollers are two seventeenth-century poets, Edward Morris of Cerrigydrudion, Denbighshire, and Huw Morys of Llansilin in the same county. Their work sets the pattern for the carols of later centuries.

By the second half of the eighteenth century, *plygain* had taken on the meaning of a religious service of a specified type held at any hour and on any day during the period between Christmas Day and the old New Year on 13 January. The *plygain* service was staged in the local parish church and, as a rule, the carollers conducted themselves with decorum, although Dafydd Cadwaladr of Dinas Mawddwy accuses them in 1784 of lacking in sobriety and earnestness:

> Rhai yn hyderu, 'rwy'n pennu pam,
> Gael cwrw am y carol.

[Some trust, I determine why, that they will be given beer for their carol.]

Some carols proffer twenty stanzas, sometimes more, of theology. They begin at the Virgin Birth (although many begin in Genesis with the creation of the world and its subsequent fall), move on to various stories from the life of Christ, ponder his death on the cross, his resurrection, his ascension, and finally the glories of heaven. They also stress the need for man to wonder at God's glory and at his infinite mercy in providing sinful mankind with a redeemer. There is a strong emphasis on exhorting the community to repent and to strive to live a holy life. The early carols do not address the individual. It is not the individual's conscience that must be awakened but the communal conscience. The poet, the singer and his audience are as one.

These assemblies of carol-singers were male-dominated. Carols, which were not always sung in unison, were not intended for participation by the audience. The most popular mode of presentation was by a male trio, unaccompanied; this method could accommodate an inspired performance where one voice began the carol and the other parts joined in, perhaps at the end of a certain musical phrase.

Plygain carols were sung to the popular tunes of the day, for example 'Ffarwél Ned Puw', 'Crimson Velvet', 'The Belle Isle March' and 'Gwêl yr Adeilad' (See the Building). Words and tune fitted each other perfectly in accentuation and emphasis; add to that a complex alliterative system, matched by a complicated rhyming pattern, and it is no wonder that the populace found the melodic quality of these carols truly satisfying. Nevertheless, the literary achievement of some of these carols is minimal. Although the syntax of some sentences is intricate and in spite of many lines of *cynghanedd*, they do not carry the marks of elevated poetry. However, they were widely disseminated. They were published in printed books, almanacs and pamphlets, recorded in manuscripts, and were circulated by oral transmission, bestowing on Wales a unique legacy of *plygain* carols unparalleled in any other part of the world.

Welsh wassail-songs form another body of eighteenth-century poetry and have their origins in pagan fertility rites. They were sung on at least seven occasions during the year, and although four of them fall within the Christmas season itself (at Christmas, at the New Year, while accompanying the Mari Lwyd, and while hunting the wren on Twelfth Night), the other three occasions (at Candlemas on 2 February, on May Day, and as a marriage custom) have no association with Christmas.

A group of men would meet to list houses that would allow them access. Rural parishes presented the revellers with many problems, although these difficulties were of the light-hearted variety, as John Edwards of Cae-môr's prick-song attests. His first embarrassment was an incident with the local miller, his second an encounter with a company of ghosts, followed by the indignity of falling into a black dingle. From one adversity to another he staggers on at dead of night over hills and mountains until, suffering from cuts and bruises, a nose-bleed and a state of shock verging on lunacy, he eventually reaches his goal.

At the door, other difficulties might follow. Convention demanded that the wassailers call on the head of the household to get up from his bed and open the door to welcome them in. Complaints concerning the wretched journey, harsh weather, the state of the roads, all helped to press their case. One anonymous caroller sings:

> Ein dannedd sy'n clecio a'n gwynt ni ar ffaelio,
> Y tafod yn stytio, ar drigo 'rŷm ni.

[Our teeth are chattering and we are out of breath, our tongue is stuttering, we are about to die.]

Their songs focused on the prospect of a warm fire, good food, plentiful beer and lovely women to keep them company. Mean-minded householders were held in contempt and many insolent rhymes were composed to ridicule the grudging hand. It was indeed false economy to withhold favours from a company of wassailers. Carols sung in answer to the supplicants are also numerous. Some counter the wassailers' pleas of discomfort by taunting them with the accusation that they were all conspicuous by their absence at harvest-time. Why should a poor farmer, who can ill-afford to feed his own family, supply their wants at Christmas?

In contrast, one early eighteenth-century carol teasingly maintains that the householder, a paragon amongst men, has tarried at home for the sole purpose of fulfilling the wassailers' needs. He proposes to cater for the whole company single-handed:

> Mi leddis fuwch oedd hŷn na'm nain
> A honno oedd fain ei senna',–
> Chwi gewch ran o gig ei phen
> I gadw i chwi lawen Wylia.
>
> Wel, dyna swper i chwi yn barod,
> Nis gwn i am ddiod beth a wna.
> Mynna i ddŵr a'i ddrincio yn tŷ,–
> Ni chewch chi mo'r tagu yma.

[I have killed a cow which was older than my grandmother, one with skinny ribs, you may have a little head-meat to make merry this holiday.

Well, your supper is ready, although I do not know what to do for drink. I will fetch water and drink it in the house—you will not be allowed to thirst here.]

On leaving the house a further song was sung in recognition of the goodwill and liberality of the host. Its prime concern was to give thanks for the strong liquor enjoyed and to emphasize the convivial atmosphere that it generated. Many songs mention the probability that strong beer, weak legs and starry eyes will not see the revellers home and, in the same breath, they resign themselves good-naturedly to the inevitability of spending the night in a ditch. This banter is in fact a cunningly worded refusal, and it is the wassailers themselves who will decline the refreshments of their potential benefactor.

Poems of this nature are purely in jest. However, there was a serious aspect to some later wassail-songs that did not initially belong to the genre. Lewis Morris of Anglesey states in 1717 that he took part in the ritual with worthy intentions:

> Er mwyn y Gogoned daionus ei weithred
> Rhowch ddrws yn agored er nodded i ni;
> Gollyngwch ni i'ch annedd i ganu gogonedd
> I rinwedd yr hafedd Dduw heini.

[For the sake of the beneficial acts of the Glorious, allow us an open door for our protection; allow us into your home to sing glory to the virtue of the sunny, nimble God.]

He was not in pursuit of beer, but of true worship. The sixteenth and seventeenth centuries had provided Wales with a large body of religious free-metre poems expounding the Christian faith and extolling the virtues of adhering to its maxims. Most ordinary eighteenth-century men and women would be acquainted with the stanzas of Vicar Prichard, published in *Canwyll y Cymry* (1681; The Candle of the Welsh People), which were metrical renderings of basic Christian precepts. Most of his stanzas had been learned by heart and it is no wonder that they influenced the content of Christmas wassail-songs. The usual type of Christmas wassail-song celebrated the flourishing of the agricultural world without reference to God, but these 'modified' carols attributed every success and all prosperity to Almighty God and to his providence. They encouraged all and sundry to honour the birth of the Messiah at Christmas, and prompted the community to reflect on his mercies to mankind, in particular his atoning death on the cross. No mention is made of wine, women or song, although spiritual gifts, brotherly love and a biblical life-style are prayed for.

Initially, the wassailers visited all the houses in their district promoting the well-being of the neighbourhood in three respects: the longevity and fecundity of the parishioners; the fertility of the land and its prolific harvest; and the prosperity of the poultry and animal kingdom. In preparation for the time when their life on earth draws to a close, the caroller confers his warmest blessings on the householder and his family. The hope of being reunited in paradise always features last in the sequence of blessings and brings the ritual to an acceptable close.

One would have expected the custom of bringing in the New Year to have produced an abundance of eighteenth-century free-metre songs, but the only extant Welsh free-metre New Year wassail-song dating from the eighteenth century is a carol by Dafydd Jones, sung on New Year's Eve on entering the house and the dance. Dafydd Jones specifically notes that he is there by invitation. He glorifies God for sending a Saviour at Christmas, and merges the custom of 'letting-in' the New Year, which had been kept with great riot and licence by the pagans, with the Feast of the Circumcision observed on 1 January, the eighth day after Christmas, in commemoration of Christ's circumcision noted in Luke 2:21, 'when eight days were accomplished':

> Ar gyfer hyn enwaedwyd Iesu
> Yn ôl y ffasiwn i'w chyffesu;
> Rhown ninna chwedyn fawl barchedig
> Lawn galonnau, lân galennig.

[It was at a time corresponding to this time that Jesus was circumcised after the fashion that was acknowledged; let us also therefore give reverent praise from full hearts, a true New Year's gift.]

Dafydd Jones denies coming to the house to beg food and drink. His chief concern was the praise of God the Saviour. Adam had worked mankind's damnation, Moses had by divine inspiration written God's law for our instruction, but it was Christ's own heart-blood that healed us from our affliction, and for that we should rejoice for ever.

A worse fate has befallen the custom known as *Y Fari Lwyd* (probably best translated as 'Grey Mary' or even 'Grey Mare', rather than 'Holy Mary'). No eighteenth-century versions of this type of song, nor reports of its occurrence in that century, have survived and only vague references to its origin in some dark period in the history of Wales are extant.

Another form of Welsh wassail-song is the Wren Hunt song. The earliest Welsh record of hunting the wren is found in the work of Edward Lhuyd (?1660–1709), who noted in his *Parochialia* that it was customary in Pembrokeshire to carry a wren in a bier on Twelfth Night, as a gift from a young man to his sweetheart. All surviving versions of this song date from the nineteenth and twentieth centuries, but it may be assumed that wren-cult rites were observed during the eighteenth century in Wales as well as further afield. That the wren songs are to be found predominantly in the coastal regions of Wales suggests that they might be imports from other Celtic countries or from Scandinavia. Whatever their origin, the ritual itself involved hunting a wren, encasing it in a wren-house adorned with ribbons, and carrying it in procession from house to house on a bier.

The community gained from this pageant. Each home acquired a wren's feather or limb as a symbol of the luck bestowed on them for the coming year. As king of the birds it was believed that the wren had supernatural powers, and it was because of its sovereignty that the wren was hunted; sacrificing a king produces fertility. By bearing the wren in procession through the community, the ritualists scattered prosperity and fecundity. The wren ritual, as described by Edward Lhuyd, is associated with courting couples, and in particular, perhaps, with their fertility.

Over the centuries the Church has consecrated many feastdays to Mary. One of these, which today bears the title *Gŵyl Fair y Canhwyllau* (Mary's Festival of the Candles), is held on 2 February and is known as Candlemas. Originally this feast commemorated the purification of Mary as dictated in the law of Moses, Leviticus 12:2–4. However, many of Wales's professional poets referred to it as *Gŵyl Fair Forwyn ddechre gwanwyn* (The Feast of the Virgin Mary at the beginning of spring), and its association with the increasing light and new life of springtime made it an appropriate occasion for celebration by wassailing. The eighteenth century produced an abundance of free-metre Candlemas poems, mostly from Anglesey and Caernarfonshire. References to some Merioneth, Denbighshire and Flintshire place-names suggest that the custom may also have been familiar in those areas of Wales, and songs written by Merioneth-based poets seem to confirm this view.

Wassailing at the Feast of the Virgin Mary at the beginning of spring was done over many days. One poet boasts of not having been home since Monday evening and of having no intention of doing so until the coming Saturday. The celebration lasted many days in order to take in many locations, reaching its climax on the evening of 2 February.

Candlemas songs fall into two categories, the religious and the secular. The religious carols underline the fact that Jesus's coming

was the result of a virgin birth; Christ had no human father but
was conceived by Mary by the power of the Holy Spirit. One of the
carols portrays Joseph doubting the Immaculate Conception of
Christ. In a Welsh adaptation by William Evans in 1768 of the
English song 'The Cherry Tree Carol', Joseph becomes jealous of
the fact that Mary is pregnant by one other than himself and
refuses to reach out to pick an apple for her. As if to prove Mary's
chastity the apple tree lowers its boughs for her to choose her own
fruit. In the penultimate stanza, Joseph and Mary are reconciled.

Little emphasis is put on the custom of purification itself in the
Welsh carols. During the eighteenth century, attending church in
order to be purified following the birth of a child took place after
about a fortnight, when the new mother went to church to give
thanks for the birth of her child and for her own life. She would
then be declared clean. The carols sung at the Feast of the Virgin
Mary describe Mary's visit to the temple carrying Jesus Christ in
her arms. Dafydd Jones sang in 1760 of the angels there assembled
chorusing 'Hosanna', and he describes the scene as dozens of
candles light up Mary's progress. Great regard is shown in the
same carol for Simeon, the aged and devout Jew who took the
infant Christ in his arms in the Temple at Jerusalem and spoke the
words known as the *Nunc Dimittis* (Luke 2:25–35). The role of
Anna daughter of Phanuel (here referred to as Hanna) in the
pageant is noted—that in her old age she met Mary and the child
Jesus in the Temple, and together with Simeon she worshipped
him, recognizing him as the expected Messiah. Finally, in the
closing stanzas, the poet returns to praising Mary, who has now
come into great peace and fulfilment in a glorious heaven.

Siôn ap Siôn has a respectful regard for the angel Gabriel who
visited Mary to announce to her the conception of Jesus Christ.
Although Mary is described in his song as being troubled in spirit
following the angel's revelation, the kindly Gabriel comforts and
encourages her. She is not to fear; she has been favoured by God,
and her son will be an eternal and sovereign prince, conceived by
the power of the Holy Spirit.

But it is the secular songs written for the celebration of the Feast
of the Virgin Mary which give us an insight into the parallel pagan
ritual. In 1783, Dafydd Thomas (Dafydd Ddu Eryri) opens his
Candlemas Eve carol with an invitation which, translated, reads:
'Come to Betws Bach to be my drinking-companion . . .

Swallowing this peculiar beer and liquor will bring about a long
drunkenness.' 'Dry sobriety' will not be tolerated and the stage is
set for a drunken get-together. No mention is made of either Jesus
or Mary. In spite of the invitation proffered, admittance is
reserved for those who are successful in the verbal rally, using free-
metre stanzas, conducted on either side of the locked door. The
carollers outside want admittance, the householder and his
company inside are unwilling to allow them access. Whether they
gain entry or are refused at the door depends on who wins the
contest of words.

The arguments are similar to those tendered at Christmastide:
adverse weather conditions and an unhelpful countryside thwart
the ambitions of the wassailers; poverty and spite make the
householders hold them at bay. An anonymous carol dated 1717
narrates the story of six companions, each struck down by ill
fortune as they travel to a certain home to celebrate this feast.
Having told of the troubles which befell his friends, the author
continues:

> Nid wy' fy hun, chwaith, dda fy nhrefn,
> Bûm ar fy nghefn yn yr eithin;
> Yr wy' fi'n llawn o ddagra a gwaed
> O wadna 'nhraed i'm corun.

[Nor am I, either, in fine form. I've been on my back in the gorse; I'm
all blood and tears from the soles of my feet to the crown of my head.]

The emphasis, not surprisingly, is on drink, although lighted
candles also feature in these secular songs. Monetary payments are
less important than at Christmastide and there are no extant
stanzas refusing admittance to any company of carollers, although
one carol boasts of a party of more than twenty men. Intimidation
and threats may have contributed to the wholesale admittance of
the carollers.

'Answering carols' list all sorts of reasons and excuses for not
welcoming the carollers inside. Dogs who nip visitors about the
ankles are a danger, as are inconsiderate maids who urinate in
puddles where visitors are likely to tread. Poverty is also cited, and
where there was no poverty, ill luck would reign:

Mae yma borcyn yn y nen
Yn beder llen ragorol.
Fe aeth yn ofer i chwi eich traul,
Fe fethad cael yr ystol.

[There is here a salted pig hanging from the ceiling, in four excellent
sections. But your effort has been in vain as we have failed to acquire a
ladder.]

Reproaches are often the order of the day. Black marks are
awarded to the wassailers for their lack of concern at other
important times in the agricultural calendar. When the
householder was knee-deep in water at peat-cutting time no one
helped him, and they were not to be seen when the time came to tie
corn in sheaves to dry; yet with a bold face and regrets they knock
on his door requesting fine food and drink at the Feast of the
Virgin Mary. All they deserve is a quart of sour gruel. Both sides
prolong the agony until the householder's side admits defeat in the
poetic battle of wits. On submission, the joviality then continues
indoors.

There is one distinction between the ritual as observed in
Anglesey and that in Caernarfonshire. In Caernarfonshire, it
seems that no accumulative songs were sung during the observance
of this custom. Were the accumulative songs unique to the
Anglesey custom? Along with *dychmygion* (puzzles), they were
sung there as part of the contest that raged between the
householder and his party on the one side, and their unwelcome
visitors outside the door on the other.

Accumulative songs are highly amusing test-pieces designed to
entertain the audience and test the performer's memory, his
concentration and his mastery of a long list of between nine and
twelve unfamiliar objects, for example *petrisen ar y pren pêr* (a
partridge in a pear-tree). The number of objects increased with
each new stanza, making it more difficult for the singer to reach
the end of the stanza without drawing breath and with his dignity
intact. No matter how long the stanza, no matter how difficult the
syntax or how complex the enunciation, there was to be no
cheating. If actions amounting to a semi-dance were required in
concurrence with the singing exploit, then its accomplishment
brought even greater acclaim. The following extract, from a letter

written by Dafydd Thomas (Dafydd Ddu Eryri) to Edward Jones (Bardd y Brenin) in April 1799, suggests that such songs were performed at the Feast of the Virgin Mary:

> I humbly apprehend that it is now too late to send anything towards completing your Book, otherwise I might send you some kind of a Copy of Naw Gafr gorniog, which after a long and diligent enquiry I found at Caernarvon . . . It appears that it was sung on noswyl Fair, that is to say during the contest for the house.

Dychmygion are rather different. These ask puzzling questions, although the answers are simple in hindsight. Literary riddles of this kind were first recognized as a genre on the publication of a collection of Arabic riddles by Hajji Kjalifa in the fourteenth century. The following extract, in the hand of Richard Morris, is a well-known example from the early eighteenth century:

> Danfoned imi afal heb ynddo yr un dincodyn,
> Danfoned imi gapwl heb na phlu nac esgyrn,
> Danfoned imi fodrwy heb na thro na chwmpas,
> Danfoned imi fabi heb na dig nac anras.

[Send me an apple without a pip, send me a capon without feathers or bones, send me a ring without a circle or curve, send me a baby without anger or ungraciousness.]

Answering these puzzles called for instant ingenuity and a very agile mind. The answer to Richard Morris's riddle is as follows:

> Pan oedd yr afal yn ei flode nid oedd ynddo'r un dincodyn;
> Pan oedd yr iâr yn eiste nid oedd na phlu nac esgyrn;
> Pan oedd y fodrwy yn toddi nid oedd na thro na chwmpas;
> Pan oeddem ninne yn caru nid oedd na dig nac anras.

[When the apple was in blossom it did not have a pip; when the hen was sitting on her eggs to hatch them there were no feathers or bones; when the ring was melting there was no circle or curve; when we were lovers there was no anger or ungraciousness.]

From other carols it becomes obvious that the questions are asked by the wassailers and answered by the head of the household. One such carol is the work of Richard Parry, noted in the manuscript of John Owen of Dwyran in Anglesey. It is a mid-eighteenth-century carol and interrogates the household on the contents of the catechism. *Llawysgrif Richard Morris o Gerddi* (pp. 12–14) features a similar carol which examines the house-holders' knowledge of biblical characters and events. If the answers were not forthcoming then admittance was insisted upon.

> Dywedwch in pa hyd, yn hy,
> Cyn geni'r Iesu, o oesoedd
> Bu farw Moses, gynnes wedd,
> A phle mae'i fedd? Pwy a'i gwelodd?
>
> Dwy fil pedwar cant yn ddi-drist
> Cyn geni Iesu, neu ragor,
> Y claddwyd Moses gan Dduw mewn glyn
> Ar gyfer Glyn Bethpeor.
> Ni welodd neb erioed, drwy hedd,
> Ond Duw mo fedd hen Foesen.

[Tell us confidently low long it was before the birth of Christ, that Moses of the warm countenance died, and where is his grave? Who has seen it?

It was two thousand and four hundred, or more, with no sadness, before the birth of Christ that God buried Moses in a valley opposite the Vale of Bethpeor. Peace upon us, no one ever saw Moses' grave, apart from God.]

In time, such stanzas became confused with stanzas that were part of other genres and traditions. A song describing attempts at putting together the materials for brewing 'new beer' was sung at the Feast of the Virgin Mary, whereas it rightly belonged to the genre of songs listing impossible tasks. The singer tells of his intention to take two grains of barley and three grains of corn to be malted, an impossible task since the kiln was in Rhoscolyn, the mill in Llansilin, the miller in Newtown, the barrels were still branches and the carpenters yet to be born. None the less, if the wassailers happened to call while he was filtering, the drink would be ready for them.

Following the *pwnco*—the rhyming contest on either side of the door—the wassailers were admitted into the house, singing as they crossed the threshold a song which called for a chair to be placed in the centre of the room, and a virgin to be seated in it. To avoid misjudgements, a little girl took up the seat. This was followed by the 'chair carol'. In some areas of Caernarfonshire a six-week-old baby boy was put in the girl's lap so that they represented the Virgin and Child. A carol dated 1762 refers to Mary sitting in her golden chair in the temple when the wassail-bowl was passed to her. This explains the origin of the custom of seating the young girl, while the wassailers danced around her chair. With the assistance of strong liquor they commemorated her purification:

> Wel, bellach, mewn undod chwenychem gael gwirod
> O law y gŵr priod, dda fragod di-freg
> I blejio'r fun dyner sy yma yn ei chader . . .

[Well, henceforth, in unity we desire liquor from the hand of the married man, a good potent drink to pledge the tender maid here in her chair . . .]

Ben Jonson suggests that the one who 'pledges' with his eyes is merely mirroring an earlier activity:

> Drink to me only with thine eyes
> And I will pledge with mine . . .

This suggests that the girl drinks from the wassail-bowl, and that her action is repeated by the wassailers.

William Evans in 1762 suggests a slightly different order of play. He first commands the young girl to give the baby boy a drink, then to take some herself, and then to allow the revellers to take the wassail-bowl from her care. He allocates a stanza for the person who first takes the cup—possibly the householder or the wassailers' leader. The wassail-bowl is then passed from hand to hand until all have drunk from it. Toasting the virgin was intended to honour her as well as to promote her later fertility.

The craftsmanship of the wassail-bowl is referred to in many poems as being very fine. Those used in north Wales at the Feast of the Virgin Mary were very beautiful, with looped handles in which were placed lighted candles all the way round the bowl so that it was quite a feat to drink from the cup without burning. The baby and child would be in some danger if the detailed requirements of the custom were all followed:

> Gan rif y canhwylla nid yfaf fi yn deg
> Rhag llosgi yn ddifantes o gwmpas y geg;
> Fe riwniff yr aelia, mi dynga rwy'n dallt,
> A'r farf bod â blewyn, gwn gwedyn, a'r gwallt.

[Because of the number of candles I will not drink fairly in case I burn around my mouth to my disadvantage; it will ruin the eyebrows, I swear that I understand, and the beard every whisker, I know then, and the hair.]

After the feasting, the carol of thanksgiving and farewell was sung. Having kissed the virgin who had sat in Mary's chair, after which the young girl was asked to leave, the stumbling revellers would bless the house and all its inhabitants wishing them peace and prosperity, together with a happy old age under the patronage of their offspring.

This custom possibly has its origins in the Feast of Light, observed half way through the first six months of the year. Drinking and carousing at the end of the darkest three-month period would encourage the coming of spring, and the energy engendered by the feasting would assist the awakening of a new period of light. Drinking the health and fertility of the community would have its effect on the growth of new crops. To suppress the pagan elements of this spring feasting, all honour was handed over to the Virgin and Child, and the fact that Simeon had spoken of a Light to lighten the gentiles in the person of Jesus Christ paved the way for the Church to Christianize another pagan feast.

May Day marked the start of the second half of the Celtic year, and it bears an affinity with pagan spring festivals, which were also noted for their dances and festivities. Phillip Stubbes wrote of May customs in his *Anatomie of Abuses* (1583):

> But the chiefest jewel they bring . . . is their May-pole, which they bring home with great veneration . . . which is covered all over with flowers and herbs, bound round about with strings, from the top to the bottom, and sometime painted with variable colours; . . . and thus being reared up . . . then fall they to dance about it, like as the heathen people did at the dedication of the Idols . . .

Unrestrained love-making preceded the lopping of the tree and the birch remains to this day a phallic symbol.

Dancing is not specifically mentioned in the May carols, although all are sung to tunes which could easily accommodate dancing. However, external evidence points to the custom not only of dancing the round but also of morris dancing in Wales. This was a ritual dance observed by an experienced and much-practised group of dancers, dressed in the appropriate costumes and carrying staffs to awaken nature from its slumber and to frighten away infelicitous spirits. Nature was to discard her shyness and exult in her fecundity at this important juncture of the year.

Two characters who accompanied the morris dancers in north Wales were Bili Ffŵl and Cadi Ha. Cadi Ha was a man with a blackened face, dressed partly in women's clothing. He was the main character. William Roberts (Nefydd) describes a party of between twelve and twenty young people going May-dancing dressed in white clothes decorated with ribbons of all colours. They took with them a *cangen haf*, a summer branch, decorated with watches, teaspoons, silver dishes and various other gleaming objects. They were accompanied by a *crwth* or a harp, or both. The assembled dancers would set off on May Day morning, dancing on the village green and at each farmhouse visited. Cadi carried a ladle to receive monetary gifts and would thank all for their generosity with much bobbing and bowing.

But the main attraction of May Day was the maypole. The first reference to a maypole in Wales occurs in a poem by Gruffudd ab Adda (*fl.* 1340–70) which describes the uprooting of a birch tree and its transformation into a Llanidloes maypole. Maypoles were decked with ribbons and flowers. Twining or plaiting the ribbons did not feature in Wales until the nineteenth century, but dancing under the maypole was an old custom. William Thomas (1717–95), the diarist from St Fagans in Glamorgan, writes that it was customary for the inhabitants of one village to steal another village's maypole. No second maypole was allowed, and the locality would be bereft of its fertility symbol until the following May. This pagan festival was not superseded by a Christian festival but the carols sung were heavily Christianized.

It was customary to sing at the door of 'godly homes', the windows of which were usually decorated with rosemary, lilies and other garden produce. Having declared their presence the singers dwelt on the theme that the Lord God was responsible for bringing all scarcity to an end by sending fair weather for the propagation of crops. Rees Ellis, *c.* 1721, looks away from the wearisome winter to the pleasures of the coming months, encouraged by the fact that the chill has gone from the sky, and that the lately shivering birds are now singing an ode to summer. The poets rejoice that the animals that were half-starved during the cruel winter are now wasting their food, as there is such an abundance of it. The luxuriance and lushness of a spring teeming with produce has brought happiness to every living thing on earth.

Cupid's sting is particularly effective in spring and the warmth of the sun excites amorousness. Several carols encourage this optimism, but the carols which warn against imprudent spring entanglements are more numerous. Richard Davies in 1727 addresses every young woman, counselling them to abstain from sexual encounters as the safest way of avoiding unwanted pregnancies. His advice to the young men is that they should be very careful in choosing a partner; many fine-looking women have treacherous hearts.

Gratitude and thanksgiving rank highly in May carols. The carollers realize their indebtedness to God for all his blessings temporal and spiritual, although a slightly censorious note appears in a few carols to the effect that the birds are quicker to praise God's liberality than is mankind. Most May carols include a prayer for the monarchy. Dafydd Jones in 1733 asked God's blessing on George II and other members of the royal family:

> Bendithia, Frenin nefol,
> Ni dan dy was dewisol,
> Ail George a'i wraig briodol,
> Sef Caroline lwys;
> Ffredric a'r diwc ynta,
> Anne, Elizabeth ac Amelia,
> Mary lân a Louisa
> A phawb yn ddiau ddwys.

[Bless us, heavenly Father, under your chosen servant, George II and his wife, namely the beautiful Caroline; Frederick and the duke also, Anne, Elizabeth and Amelia, pure Mary and Louisa, and all in solemn sincerity.]

This was a conventional part of the May carol, whoever the monarch might be, and however adept he might or might not be in the art of governing the country. Tied in with the prayer for the monarchy was a prayer for the Church of England and the Protestant faith.

Often the carollers blessed the householder, his family, his stock, crops and garden produce, before taking their leave. Frequently, however, they did not mention such matters, although in earlier centuries that would have been the whole point of the exercise. In the eighteenth century, religious content often suffocated the pagan element. One carol of thirty stanzas with a refrain every four verses, dating from the first half of the eighteenth century and written by Dafydd Lewis, the vicar of Llangatwg in Glamorgan, urges its listeners to repent, rather than be cast away to the fires of hell. He cites many instances of early or unexpected deaths and exhorts the members of the community, as a well-wisher, to embrace the Christian faith before the opportunity escapes them, and to live profitable lives while they still have time.

Love-spoons still carry connotations of a typically Welsh love token. Not so the valentine, although examples of Welsh valentines date from the work of Huw Morys and Edward Morris in the seventeenth century. In the eighteenth century, the custom was to draw lots called valentines, *ei dynnu'n falendein* (to draw him as a valentine). Names were drawn and the couples looked upon the draw as a good marriage-omen. The valentine in these instances was therefore a person, although it could also be a gift, a message or a card, as became popular in the nineteenth century.

One feature of these valentine verses was that the initials of the loved one's name were woven into the opening lines. In the following anonymous stanza the letters LEWIS JONES feature:

> Hyd atoch, hafedd gannwyll Gwynedd,
> Gore ei fonedd o Gaer i Fôn,
> L E diledieth, W I diwenieth,
> Ac S eilweth mewn sylwedd sôn;
> I O diamhur, N E dan awyr,
> Ac S . . .

> [Unto you, summery light of Gwynedd,
> Of noblest lineage from Chester to Anglesey,
> L E pure of language, W I sincere,
> And S a second time speaks with substance;
> I O pure, N E beneath the sky,
> And S . . .]

Once a marriage partner had been chosen, there were many
customs to observe, for example *dyddio*, putting a date to the
ceremony; *rytydda* or *notydda*, visiting the bride's father to ask for
the bride's hand, together with a dowry; marriage banns; and
bidding. The duties of the bidder were often conducted in stanza
form. He would invite the friends of a couple about to be married
to their feast or wedding, reminding the invited guests that they
might wish to give the new couple a wedding present of a sum
of money, possibly in repayment of earlier debts of gifts or
kindnesses, so that all *pwython* (payments) due to the families of
the marriage couple could be repaid on a particular day.

Lewis Morris's song inviting guests to the wedding of Siôn
Siams of Llwyn Iorwerth and Catrin Wiliam of Hafodau in the
parish of Llanbadarn Fawr, in 1761, invited guests to bring with
them monetary gifts, butter, cheeses, in exchange for tobacco, beer
and sugared cakes. All gifts would be listed and looked upon as
debts, which would be repaid at the appropriate time:

> Ydd wyf yn adde eu bod hwynte yn addo
> Eu talu fel dyled pan ddelir i'w ceisio.

[I vow that they promise to repay your gifts as debts when someone
comes to collect them.]

On the wedding-day a party of young men called *gwŷr y
shigowts* (the men of the seek-outs) would race on horseback from
the groom's home to that of his fiancée to seek out the bride and
escort her to church. Many obstacles would have to be overcome
before they reached her home. On arrival, the bride's door would
be locked and bolted and the *shigowts* would have to win the
pwnco ritual in order to capture the bride. This would entail a long
question-and-answer debate at the bride's door which could last
several hours. A short run of stanzas was that sung prior to the
wedding of Dafydd Jones of Caeo, a country poet and later a
hymn-writer, *c.*1740:

> Pwy sydd yna'n aflonyddu
> Ar ein preswyl annwyl ni?
> Pwy sydd yna'n para i guro?
> Beth sydd eisie arnoch chwi?

Ai dyma Abercarfan,
Cartrefle'r eneth dlos
Sydd wedi addo dyfod
Yn wraig i Dafydd Jones?

Wel, ie, Abercarfan
Yw enw'r tyddyn braf,
Ond nid yw'r eneth gartref,
Aeth ffwrdd i'w gwyliau haf.

Rai tirion, peidiwch twyllo,
Nid deillion ydym ni;
Fe'i gwelsom ar y palmant,
Wrth groesi'r nant i'r tŷ.

Mae'r ferch yn edifaru
Rhoi gair i un mor bell,
Ac wedi dechrau caru
Â mab sydd lawer gwell.

Nis gallwn ni eich credu,
Rhaid cael Miss Jones ei hun,
Ei gair sydd wedi ei selio
Â chusan ar y fin.

Pa beth yw'r addewidion
Os daw yr eneth hardd
I'r eglwys i'w phriodi
Â Dafydd Jones y bardd?

Caiff orau'r mab amryddawn
A serch ei galon bur
Ac urddas Cwmgogerddan,
Siriolaf fan y sir.

[Who's there, disturbing our dear home? Who is still knocking? What do you want?
Is this Abercarfan, the home of the pretty girl who has promised to become Dafydd Jones's wife?
Well, yes, this pleasant smallholding is called Abercarfan, but the girl is not at home, she has gone away on her summer holiday.
Gentle ones, don't cheat, we're not blind; we saw her on the pavement as we crossed the stream to the house.

The girl regrets giving her word to one so remote and is seeing a much better young man.
We don't believe you, we must speak to Miss Jones herself, her word has been sealed with a kiss on the lips.
What are the promises if the beautiful girl comes to church to be married to the poet Dafydd Jones?
She will have the best of this versatile man and the love of his pure heart and the dignity of Cwmgogerddan, the most cheerful spot in the county.]

Having won the rhyming contest to gain access, the men would have to find the girl. She would be in hiding or in disguise but once tracked down she would be borne away to church on horseback by the seek-outs, with her own family chasing her to take her back home. Such a *priodas geffylau* (horse-wedding) was what every girl wanted, but poorer families had to make do with a *priodas dra'd* (foot-wedding) where they all walked to church.

Another form of *pwnco* is the question-and-answer stanzas, asked by the householder and answered by the groom's party:

> Beth wneir â'r wraig benchwiban?
> Beth wneir â hen gel truan?
> Beth wneir â thaflod heb ddim gwair?
> Beth wneir mewn ffair heb arian?

[What is to be done with the silly woman? What is to be done with a poor old horse? What is to be done with a granary/loft without hay? What is to be done at a fair without money?]

The seek-outs must answer:

> Ceir chwipio gwraig benchwiban
> A cheirchio hen gel truan;
> Ceir llosgi taflod heb ddim gwair,
> A gochel ffair heb arian.

[One may whip a silly woman and give a poor old horse some oats; one may burn a granary/loft without hay and avoid a fair without money.]

These, and others of a similar content, were sung to test the versatility of the men on either side. Once the contest was won and the marriage ceremony was over, divorce played no part in eighteenth-century life.

There is a form of poetry typical of the eighteenth century which we now classify as a ballad. Such poems were sung at markets and fairs and later published and sold by pedlars, for example Harri Owen, and Evan Ellis of Llanfihangel Glyn Myfyr, along with women such as Lowri Pari and Mary Fychan. Strictly speaking they were not free-metre compositions since *cynghanedd* was a prominent feature of most. They were embellished stanzas based on popular free-metres and consistently sung to popular tunes. Hundreds, if not thousands, of these poems were circulated during the eighteenth century. They served the purpose of today's popular press, providing satisfying sustenance to the populace which craved the exhilaration of news of murders and war crimes, the thrilling shock of unwelcome pregnancies and the heady content of the odd lascivious song. The following translation of a ballad title serves as an example of their content:

> Secondly, a compassionate poem, how a pregnant woman walked over a mountain in Radnorshire and on the way she became ill, and a blind Irishman led by a youth came up to her, and she gave the youth a shilling for going to fetch women to her aid, and the Irishman asked the youth how much he had received, and the youth went quickly on his way. And the Irishman pulled out his knife and killed the woman, and the servant of a gentleman came to the spot and took him and he was sent to Radnor gaol and was condemned, hanged and gibbeted in the year 1775 and his confession, that this was the sixth he had killed.

The author of this ballad, Huw Jones of Llangwm, a prolific ballad-writer, penned the lamentations of a man who had lost two geese from his shed just as effectively as he disparaged conceit and pride, 'and their evil from the beginning of the world until this hour'. The same men took it upon themselves to write on a vast number of topics to entertain their audience, each topic having its own market value.

Current affairs were always popular. Ballads on the effects of war against France, Spain and America were numerous; the sinking of the *Royal George* in its own harbour with a thousand people on board caused much grief at home, but also much joy abroad:

Roedd hen lawenydd calon i bob un o'i ddrwg elynion,
Roedd ei golledion i'w gwelláu
'Ran roedd y llong nodedig a'i hadmiral parchedig
Yn curo'r Ffrengig wŷr bob ffrae.

[Each one of his [George III's] evil enemies experienced much joy in
their hearts, his losses meant an improvement in their lot because that
notable ship and its revered admiral defeated the French at each fray.]

Ballads were written on the subject of counterfeit coins and on
the cries of those in abject poverty. Those on epidemics and
earthquakes, such as the one in Lisbon in 1755, always sold well,
as did ballads on fatal accidents:

Two new songs, firstly the terrible tale of what happened in the parish
of Llangian in Caernarvonshire, how a fire was kindled at the Plas at
Neigwl, and burned it to ashes together with six people who were in
their beds. Secondly, a conversation between a young man and a young
woman.

The first of these Welsh ballads was written by Ellis Roberts and
the second by Dafydd Thomas, but both themes, fatal accidents
and love, were Everyman's firm favourites.

The humours of love, the flutter of the heart in response to it
and the pains and resentment of unrequited love, are expounded
upon at length. Advice to young men and women in such contexts
abound. Conversations on this topic are many: between two girls
regarding marriage, between a mother and daughter, a bird and a
lover, or even the soliloquized sorrow of an unloved woman. One
anonymous poem details the conversation of the ghost of a soldier
killed in battle, one Rodric Llwyd, and his betrothed Sara. All are
variants on the same theme.

Religious poems were also extremely popular. Whether written
by religious men or otherwise, they were orthodox in doctrine, and
the moral lessons to be learned from them were acceptable to most
shades of religious thought. Ungodliness, sin and a poverty of soul
were frowned upon; most ballads encouraged godly living in
compliance with the Ten Commandments. Agnostics, free thinkers
and backsliders were urged to reconsider their ways. Two carols by
Ellis Roberts were published in 1787 with the (translated) titles:

Two Poems, firstly, A warning to every Man and Woman to consider the true God before leaving their houses in case they never return, like the poor souls who lost their lives returning from Bangor Fair, Monday 25 June 1787. Secondly: Taken from the evangelical sayings of the Lord of life, from John 6 where his blessed spiritual maxims are found.

Such sermons on scriptural texts were quite commonplace, as were sermons on moral faults such as avarice and drunkenness. The breaking of the sabbath day called for strong recrimination on the part of Huw Jones—and the topic was also a good seller.

Another popular theme was the new custom that was becoming popular at this time, tea-drinking. John Williams in 1796 published, in Welsh, 'A poem giving an account of a pack of women who got drunk on tea and brandy'. Other poems were quick to point out that tea-drinking caused women to gather together to eat bread and butter with their tea, causing their husbands many losses.

Each ballad was sung to a popular tune. There were many tunes from which the author might choose. Altogether, Thomas Edwards used over a hundred different tunes. Most were English tunes and even in eighteenth-century Anglesey, only one-fifth of the popular tunes had Welsh titles. The influx of English tunes continued throughout the century.

'Time runs on very fast and . . . we shall die like other men and be buried among the herd.' So said Lewis Morris. True enough, but the eighteenth century provided a palette of varied social diversions which has coloured our literary inheritance ever since.

BIBLIOGRAPHY

Rhiannon Ifans, *Sêrs a Rybana* (Llandysul, 1983).
E. G. Millward, *Blodeugerdd Barddas o Gerddi Rhydd y Ddeunawfed Ganrif* (Cyhoeddiadau Barddas, 1991).
Trefor M. Owen, *Welsh Folk Customs* (Caerdydd, 1959).
Thomas Parry, *Baledi'r Ddeunawfed Ganrif* (Caerdydd, 1986).
T. H. Parry-Williams, *Llawysgrif Richard Morris o Gerddi* (Caerdydd, 1931).
Enid Roberts, 'Hen Garolau Plygain', *Transactions of the Honourable Society of Cymmrodorion* (1952), 51–70.

CHAPTER 10

THE INTERLUDES

DAFYDD GLYN JONES

Key to interludes quoted

CaD   Ellis Roberts, *Cristion a Drygddyn* (Christian and Badman) (1788).

CD   Edward Thomas, *Cwymp Dyn* (The Fall of Man) (n.d.).

CO   Thomas Edwards, *Cybydd-dod ac Oferedd* (Avarice and Dissipation) (c. 1800).

CTh   Thomas Edwards, *Cyfoeth a Thlodi* (Wealth and Poverty) (1768).

GN   Ellis Roberts, Gras a Natur (Grace and Nature) (1769).

HCFf   Huw Jones, *Hanes y Capten Factor* (The Story of Captain Factor) (1762).

PCG   Thomas Edwards, *Pedair Colofn Gwladwriaeth* (The Four Pillars of the State) (1786).

PChF   Ellis Roberts, *Pedwar Chwarter y Flwyddyn* (The Four Quarters of the Year) (n.d.).

PG   Thomas Edwards, *Pleser a Gofid* (Pleasure and Affliction) (1787).

PN   Huw Jones, *Protestant a Neilltuwr* (Protestant and Dissenter) (1783).

TChB   Thomas Edwards, *Tri Chryfion Byd* (The Three Stalwarts of the World) (1789).

TChD   Thomas Edwards, *Tri Chydymaith Dyn* (The Three Companions of Man) (1762).

YDdG   Ellis Roberts, *Y Ddau Gyfamod* (The Two Covenants) (1777).

YBD   Huw Jones and Siôn Cadwaladr, *Y Brenin Dafydd* (King David) (n.d.).

YFF   Thomas Edwards, *Y Farddoneg Fabilonaidd* (The Poem of Babylon) (1768).

Seeing an Interlude

If I were a Welsh farm-hand living in the middle of the eighteenth century, with a couple of hours free and a few pennies to spend on a market- or fair-day, what could I find to amuse myself? I could spend the afternoon at an inn and get drunk. I could listen to the patter of the stallkeepers, and perhaps be persuaded to buy a fairing for my mother or my sweetheart, or something for my own use. I could stand listening to a wandering ballad-singer, and if I liked his telling of a murder, a disaster or an incredible event, I could buy the printed ballad for a penny. Over at the other end of the street there might be an unordained and unlicensed itinerant preacher, one of those called Methodists, striving to remind me of my fallen state and the offer of free grace; who knows but that I might come to scoff and stay to pray, as many apparently did. Or there might be a company performing an *anterliwt*.

Anterliwt is the commonest Welsh rendering of the word 'interlude'. *Enterlut, enterliwt* and *interliwd* are variants; *chwareuydd-iaeth* (play), *dangosiad* (illustration) and *cynhadledd ymresymeg* (reasoning debate) occur as alternatives or subtitles. Reduced to its essence, the interlude is a verse dialogue; other features occur with some regularity: a plot involving a Miser and a Fool; a sub-plot which can be a retelling of a biblical story, a folk-tale or an episode of history, real or imagined; an allegory of civic or moral life; theology and spiritual exhortation; social and political satire. But the *sine qua non* is that the presentation should be in dialogue form and in verse; there is no prose interlude.

Watching the play would cost me a penny, which would be collected at the end. Some of the audience might well make off without paying even that, but the author might warn them early on that he has his eye on them, as does Ellis Roberts (Elis y Cowper) in *Y Ddau Gyfamod*:

PROLOG:	Wel beth yw dy orchwyl, gwag 'i benglog?
FFŴL:	Chwarae *enterlut* am geiniog.
PROLOG:	Pwy rydd geiniog am dy glywed?
FFŴL:	Pawb a weli di, yn feibion a merched.
PROLOG:	Oni weli di rai yn mynd i lechu?
FFŴL:	Maen' nhw'n feilchion i beidio â thalu.
PROLOG:	Nid ŷm ni ond gwaelion yng ngolwg cwmpeini.

FFŴL:	Rheitia yn y byd rhoi ceiniog inni.
PROLOG:	'Rwy'n meddwl na thâl mo'r hanner ohonyn.
FFŴL:	Wyt ti'n meddwl fod pobl yn waeth nag undyn?
PROLOG:	Os rhôn' hwy dipyn diolchwn amdano.
FFŴL:	Nid oes dim ond rhegi y sawl a beidio.

[PROLOGUE: Empty-head, what are you doing? FOOL: Performing an interlude for a penny. P: Who'll give a penny to hear you? F: All those you see, men and women. P: Can't you see some of them going to hide? F: They're cheeky not to pay. P: We are but poor in the eyes of the company. F: All the more reason for giving us a penny. P: I don't think half of them will pay. F: Do you think people are the worst of the lot? P: If they give something we shall be grateful for it. F: We can only curse those that don't.]

A few pence more would secure me a copy of the printed interlude, which I could take home, to chortle over the rude bits and to ponder over the theology. An interlude was usually a combination of sermon and bawdy farce: the audience expected both and was not bothered by any inconsistency there might be between them. Perhaps there was no inconsistency.

The performance would be by the roadside, in the market square or in an inn yard. The stage would be a cart, a trestle-table or a door laid on two barrels. There would be no curtain to go up, no stage-lights to come on, and very little by way of a set. I would have to stand, unless I could climb to the top of a wall or the branch of a tree. When the players were satisfied that they had enough of a crowd, they would begin.

Let us say that we are in 1762 and that our interlude today is *Hanes y Capten Factor sef ei daith i Smyrna a Venis, a'r modd y dioddefodd lawer o adfyd ar fôr a thir* (The Tale of Captain Factor, being his voyage to Smyrna and Venice, and how he suffered much adversity on land and sea), by Huw Jones of Llangwm, also well known as a ballad-monger, editor and travelling bookseller. The author may well star in the play himself, and the mode of presentation is what later times will call ensemble, i.e. a small number of actors will take a wide range of parts. I may know all the actors; they are local lads, with men playing all the women's parts. There will be precious few props to suggest Smyrna, Venice or any of the other locations, but we will find ourselves transported with no difficulty through the power of the word.

Gwagsaw (Frivolous) comes on. His title in this interlude is *Y Diddanwr* (the Entertainer); more usually this character is called the Fool. He can't see very well:

> Gwaed y grog lân, fy eneidie,
> Mae yma niwl anaele.

[By the blood of the holy rood, my souls, there is a terrible mist here.]

But he has seen things in a dream from which he has just woken, a mixture of the impossible, the absurd and the obscene. Indeed he has come to believe he is something of a visionary, and he offers the audience a few of his prognostications: this coming year will be a hard one; girls' waists will swell; France will be in a dire condition, with the people dying in the fields; old Louis will be in a very bad mood; the misers will be well satisfied . . .

The *Traethydd* or Presenter comes in. True to fashion he challenges Gwagsaw and gives him a cue for a riposte:

> TRAETHYDD: Pwy sy yma'n geren a'i geg yn agored?
> GWAGSAW: Ond y fi'n pregethu i'r Methodistied;
>   Ond ni feddylies i erioed hyd yr amser hyn
>   Fod mo Harris cyn ddihired.

[T: Who is this here bleating, open mouthed? G: Why it's me, preaching to the Methodists; but up to now I never thought Harris could be such a rogue.]

Our first big laugh perhaps! Gwagsaw has mistaken the Presenter for the famous evangelist. After some verbal abuse, and then some knockabout, Gwagsaw is chased off, leaving the Presenter to give 'Mynegiad y Chwarae' (The Statement of the Act), the 'trailer' which names the main participants and gives an outline of the two plots, the amazing encounters of Captain Factor and the highly predictable tale of the Miser's come-uppance. Surprise is the one dramatic device that has no place at all in the interlude.

Gwagsaw then comes back, still complaining of the mist that blurs his vision, and delivers a speech denigrating himself and listing all his disreputable relatives. This features often in the interludes and was something the audiences had come to expect:

his father Bili Greulon (Cruel or Bloody Billy) who was once a burglar but later became a hangman, his mother Dowsi Aflan (Dirty Dowsi or Dorothy), his brother Sianco'r Perthi (Sianco of the Hedges) whom he has seen hanged, his aunt Gwen 'who used to go whoring with Owen Harri'. Poor Owen Harri! Would he be in the audience, we wonder. Gwagsaw has twelve sisters, with no two of them daughters of the same father, all notorious liars and drunks, some of them already transported for prostitution. Other relatives include Calsyth Afiach (Sickly Stiffcock), Auntie Ann who stole butter, Twm 'fu'n gyrru'r hoel/ I Gaenor foel o'r Felin' (who used to drive the nail into hairless Gaynor from the Mill), Ceillgrych Gwta (Short Shrunken-balls) and Beuno Frac (Beuno the Glib) 'fu'n neidio ar bac Rebecca' (who used to jump Rebecca) . . . and several more, all of them good for a horse-laugh. The speech concludes by calling on the fiddler to come up and accompany Gwagsaw while he dances. In the convention, references to the musician are disrespectful, and after he has done his best as an accompanist his music is compared to the braying of mules. Gwagsaw exits again, saying he wants a rest; but before he goes he makes a presentation:

> Dyma ichwi anrheg, gangen ffel;
> Derbyniwch hi, Nel, o 'nwylo.

[Here is gift for you, my pretty slip; take it, Nell, from my hands.]

The gift must be the wooden phallus which Gwagsaw has been brandishing from the beginning, and which has probably played some part in his dance. The audience had come to expect the moment when it would be offered as a present to one of the women, and we can imagine the whooping and squawking when the lucky one was chosen.

Those are the preliminaries, corresponding to what might today be called 'the warm-up', and they have taken some quarter of an hour. Now the story can begin. It is a borrowed tale, very popular in English chap-books. Captain Factor has lost all his estate, and with it his friends. Desperate for a livelihood, he agrees to captain the *Royal Mari* for two London merchants. He has barely mentioned the matter of raising a crew when up comes his first volunteer, Gwagsaw the Fool; no, he hasn't been on Mari before, he declares, but he's been on Dowsi behind a hayrick. They agree to sail together for Turkey. Captain Factor exits to make way for . . . yes it's Deifas (Dives) the Miser, the man they've all been waiting for!

The Miser, as expected, starts ranting against the audience: they are either a Methodist crowd or a bunch of fools watching an interlude, he says. Being dead against interludes is one of the Miser's traditional poses. Then he starts on another subject, even closer to his heart, namely all the losses he has suffered recently, what with the death of a mare and a cow, and the extravagance of his wife Gwerli:

> Mae gan i wraig ddiddaioni ddigon,
> Cerdded i'm digio hyd dai'r cymdogion,
> Ac eiste er ys dyddie ar ei stôl,
> A gosod ei phen ôl i'r gweision.

> Mi gymres yr hwch benchwiban
> Pan oedd hi'n ddeunaw oedran;
> Ni wnaeth hi erioed ond cadw lol,
> A bwrw yn ei bol lond bylan.

> Ni wnaeth hi erioed ar adeg
> Ond gweiddi a chwyno a bwyta chwaneg,
> A chario plant i lenwi'r fro,
> Mi fûm i'n bedyddio deuddeg.

> Fe fyddan o'm cwmpas ar ben bore,
> Yn waeth na gwybed ar geffyle,
> Rhai yn gweiddi am fwyd o'u co,
> A'r lleill wedi piso eu peisie.

[I have a wife who's completely useless, walking the neighbours' houses just to annoy me, and sitting on her stool for days on end, and letting out her backside to the serving-men. I took the flighty sow when she was eighteen; all she's ever done is talk nonsense and stash away a budgetful in her tummy. Never at any time has she done anything but shout, complain and eat even more, and bear children to fill up the countryside; I've been and baptized twelve. They'll be all around me first thing in the morning, worse than midges upon horses, some going mad and shouting for food, others having pissed in their petticoats.]

. . . and he names them all, ending with Dowsi, of whom we have heard before. Enter Gwerli, just catching the last part of her husband's tirade. With the Miser and his wife we are in a world very near to that of Punch and Judy. He accuses her of being a whore, detailing some cases in support. When she raises the matter of sending their children off to school in Chester, to have them educated as gentlefolk, Deifas reaches a new pitch of fury and reaches for his club in order to teach her a lesson. Gwerli's skin is saved by the return of Gwagsaw the Fool. Soon he gets the Miser talking about the new bills in parliament which will have the effect of raising the price of corn. This cheers the Miser up no end, and the audience will have a pretty good idea what happens next: the Miser will drop his guard and the Fool will lead him to the tavern where Pretty Nancy is ready to serve him with drink. Soon all his money is spent. Who should come in next but that ever popular figure the Taxman, with an enormous bill for the Miser. The ruined Deifas is hauled off to Ruthin jail.

We cut to Smyrna, where Captain Factor has come safely ashore. One day, walking in the city, he comes across a body lying unburied. Someone explains to him that the dead man was a Christian and that he could not pay for his funeral. The Captain pays fifty pounds for the corpse and takes it to receive a Christian burial. Soon comes another test of the Captain's charity in this land of the infidel. A young woman is being led to execution: she too is a Christian, who has been for three years the slave of a rich Turkish lady. After being beaten so often she has struck her mistress back, and is to be stoned. The Captain pays the Sultan a hundred pounds for her release, and offers to employ her as his housekeeper in London. The young lady, whose name is Prudensia, most gladly accepts.

Some individuals, however, are highly dispensable. The Captain has had enough of Gwagsaw the Fool, and has sold him as a slave to the Turks. Somehow he has escaped, and is now back on stage giving an account of his misfortune, again addressing the women. He was put to work as a haulier of wood, with a tether round his neck, and a blackamoor driving him with a rod. The food was terrible, a pie that seemed to be made of the meat of a scrawny old woman. There was no sleep at night, with all those black women climbing into his bed and never satisfied. One of them was particularly insistent and exceptionally ugly—and turned out to be a man. Gwagsaw is back in Wales just in time to witness the end of what he began, the utter humiliation of Deifas the Miser. Deifas, having done his stretch for tax evasion, is now a constable! But his term as an officer of the law comes to a sudden end when Pretty Nancy the barmaid arrives with her baby, which she says is the Miser's. Accusations and counter-accusations fly, and Gwerli the Miser's wife joins in the fray. A sergeant from the Bishop's Court at Bangor comes to summon Deifas to answer for adultery. Pretty Nancy also faces ruin: her old customers have all gone, leaving only their debts, and the brewer wants his money or all the beer barrels back. This is Nancy's punishment for the lie she told, for the baby does not belong to Deifas the Miser. For Nancy and her child, whoever the father may be, the only future lies in begging. With Nancy's warning to all innkeepers, that they should trade more honestly than she has, we cut to the Port of London.

Captain Factor, having made the very wise resolution never to go near the land of the Turks again, will now sail the *Royal Mari* to Italy. Before he leaves, his housekeeper Prudensia embroiders his waistcoat with a design 'suitable for the city of Venice'. She instructs him that, when he is summoned for an audience with the Prince of Venice, something which all visitors to the city can expect, he should open his coat and show the waistcoat. Back to Bangor, where an unrepentant Deifas is led before the Bishop by . . . Gwagsaw the Fool of course! The fiddler is called, and we have another dance, and then we are in Venice. Thus the two plots interweave, with the Fool stepping nimbly from one to the other. Nancy makes a public confession of her perjury and sings a song of warning and advice:

> Er na ddilynais mo'r ffordd dda,
> Rhof gyngor ara i erill.

[Though I did not follow the way of virtue, I shall give others considered advice.]

Deifas the Miser returns from the Bishop's Court to find chaos at home: the crockery is broken, the cattle are up to their noses in dung, the ashes from the fire reach the roof, the wheat is ruined, two shoes are found in the buttermilk, the mucking-spade is in a bowl of *llymru* (flummery), the children are starving, quarrelling and fighting, one has burnt himself and another has an axe embedded in his back. His son Twmi has got drunk in Chester and run enormous bills, and his daughter Dowsi has gone once more a-whoring, leaving bills for tea, sugar and snuff. Deifas is sustained by the one hope that wheat will go up again, and is cheered by the prospect that many beggars will starve to death. But alas, whatever the intelligence from the markets, Deifas will not be here to receive it. Death himself, another stock figure in the interludes, comes to summon the Miser. Deifas and Death wrestle together, leaving little doubt about the outcome. In a final cast, the Miser offers a thousand pounds to any doctor who can keep him alive till May Day, which should be a good time for selling the wheat. There are no takers, and Deifas dies, exhorting us all to pray that he may be forgiven. Often in the interludes the Fool comes to bury the Miser, but Deifas is less fortunate than the Christian whom Captain Factor saw lying on the road in Smyrna; Gwagsaw says he won't bother to bury him, but he will drag him to the top of a hill and leave him there to rot.

In the mean time, much has happened to Captain Factor. Stanislaus and Louisa, the Prince and Princess of Venice, have recognized the pattern on the waistcoat as the work of their daughter Prudensia. Explaining how he came to be wearing it, the Captain tells of her rescue from death in Turkey and how she became his housekeeper. The grateful parents will have nothing less than that the man who brings their daughter safely home have her for a wife, with a dowry worth £100,000 per annum.

On his voyage to collect his bride, Captain Factor is to be accompanied by Captain Convoy. But Convoy fancies the bride and the dowry, and remembers the promise that both will go to the man who brings Prudensia back to Venice. One night, he pushes Captain Factor overboard and sails on to Venice with the story that he has accidentally drowned. But Captain Factor swims for his life and reaches a small deserted island. After two days and two nights he is starving, but musters enough energy to sing a song of prayer for deliverance on 'The King's Farewell'. Sure as anything, through his spyglass he sees a small boat approaching 'towards the sunrise in rough waters', with one man on board. He waves his hat and is able to attract the Boatman's attention. Yes, the Boatman is willing enough to convey him to safety: the only condition is that he should have the Captain's son and heir when he is thirty months old. 'That will be the cause of bitter sorrow, but anything is preferable to death,' reasons the Captain, who has no son as yet. This is agreed upon. Captain Convoy reaches Venice with his lie about an accident. Prince Stanislaus is about to grant his request when Prudensia asks for the marriage to be postponed for forty days. Immediately afterwards, the Boatman brings Captain Factor ashore. We need not worry that Captain Convoy will get away with his crime; he has to answer for it as sure as anything, and the summoner will of course be—who else?—Gwagsaw the Fool. Convoy, as soon as he is indicted, plunges into the sea and is seen carried away on the waves. Gwagsaw, back in the service of Captain Factor and showing no apparent resentment for what happened last time, volunteers to be the Bishop who will tie the Captain and Prudensia in holy matrimony:

> Y fi ydi'r Esgob penna
> Sydd yn y deyrnas yma:
> Mi rof i'r Capten, gwych ei waed,
> Yn dinsyth rhwng traed Prudensia.

[I am the chiefest Bishop in this whole kingdom: I will put the Captain, noble fellow that he is, straight-arsed between Prudensia's feet.]

The marriage duly takes place.

Once we have been back in Wales to observe the end of the Miser, we return to Venice in time to see the Captain, Prudensia, their child and her parents about to take supper. Just before they sit at table, Prudensia asks her husband, 'Who is that ill-conditioned old man who's following you around?' 'Indeed, I do not recognize him,' the Captain replies, indicating at least that he knows he is there. It is the Boatman, coming to claim the child. Captain Factor tells his family for the first time of how the bargain was made. Stanislaus offers the boatman a shipload of gold and silver, but this is not accepted. The child is handed over to the Boatman who, satisfied that the agreement has been kept, immediately gives him back to his parents. He tells Captain Factor that this is in fact the third time they have met: he was, or is, the Christian man who was lying unburied in Smyrna. The ensuing few lines come dangerously close to what the interludes generally avoid—tenderness. The child's parents and his two grandparents sing a verse each of a song of gratitude, on 'Prince Rupert'. Gwagsaw comes forward to underline the moral of the tale, how the generous are rewarded and the hard-hearted called to account. He then sings the song which concludes the interlude, thanking the audience for its support, apologizing for any deficiencies there might have been, and praying that God will bless and prosper King George III. The audience will now disperse, not forgetting to pay the penny, let us hope. They have been told an amazing tale, they have had plenty to giggle and guffaw at, and they may well feel that they've had something to think about as well. All harmless entertainment, as Gwagsaw insists.

Only an Act

In naturalistic drama, it is only when they line up to take a bow that the actors announce that they were only actors after all: when mortal enemies become smiling fellow-players and tragic heroes return from the dead. In the interlude, the theme of 'I'm only an actor playing a part' is reiterated throughout. The player, coming on, greets the audience and announces his part:

> Yr howddgar dyrfa dirion,
> Rai gweddol, dethol, doethion,
> Mi ddois i'ch bro mewn modd di-brin
> Dan henw Brenin Hanon.   (YBD)

[Comely and kindly company, seemly, select and wise, I have come among you with no reservation under the name of King Hanon.]

> Mi ddois o'ch blaene'r cwmni mwynedd
> Dan enw pybyr Offeiriad Pabedd.   (YFF)

[I've come before you, gentle company, under the name of a staunch Popish priest.]

> Mi ddois o'ch blaenau'r cwmpni gweddus,
> Yn awr ar osteg, dan enw'r Ustus.   (PCG)

[I've now publicly come before you, seemly company, under the name of the Justice.]

In one instance, often quoted, the player draws a clear distinction between his persona in the play and himself in real life:

> Mi ddois o'ch blaene, y cwmni gwiwddoeth,
> Dan enw cofus Capten Cyfoeth,
> Er fy hunan na fedda' i heno
> Drwy ferw hynod fawr ohono.   (CTh)

[I've come before you, worthy and wise company, under the memorable name of Captain Wealth, although tonight, through some strange commotion, I myself own but little of it.]

The word *teip* (type) occurs with some regularity:

> Mi welsoch bawb o'r cwmni purffydd
> Mai fi oedd deip y brenin Dafydd.   (YBD)

[All of you, company of true believers, have seen that I was the type of King David.]

> Fe welsoch o'ch blaen y rwan
> Deip o'r proffwyd Nathan.   (YBD)

[You have just seen before you now a type of the prophet Nathan.]

> 'Rwyf innau'n deip o'r alwad honno,
> Dan enw'r Esgob mewn gwir osgo.   (PCG)

[And I am a type of that calling, under the name of the Bishop with true gesture.]

The actor is not tied to his part throughout the performance. His exits, for example, do not have to be dramatically motivated:

> Mi af inne draw i geisio cwrw i'r dre
> Yn nerth y carne corniog.   (YBD)

[And I'll pop over to town for some ale, as fast as my horny feet can carry me.]

Ffarwél i'r cwmni cryno,
Mi af i lawr i 'rffwyso;
I actio hyn o stori sâl,
Down yn ddiatal eto.   (HCF)

[Farewell to the assembled company, I'll go down and have a rest;
unimpeded we'll come again to act out this poor tale.]

Ond natur y byd yw cadw twrw;
Hir y cnoir y tamaid chwerw.
Mi redaf i draw ar hyn o dro
Mewn cariad i geisio cwrw.   (PCG)

[It is the nature of the world to complain; long is the bitter morsel
chewed. Right now I will run over with enthusiasm to look for some ale.]

Furthermore, there is an observable difference between *role* on the
one hand and *character* or *persona* on the other. The same
character is not obliged to play the same role throughout the
performance, and a character's role when interacting with other
characters can be different from his role when addressing the
audience directly. In confrontation with another character, the
miser, the idler, the loose woman will rebut all criticism and will
defend his or her way of life with absolute single-mindedness.
Immediately afterwards, in a soliloquy or in a song, the same
speaker will plead guilty to all the charges and will stand as a
warning to others. The Bishop in *Pedair Colofn Gwladwriaeth* has
reacted with disgust and disbelief when the Fool, Sir Rhys, called
the parish priests lazy and ignorant; but left alone facing the
audience, the Bishop sings a song listing all the failings of his
church, and departs with a warning against 'blindness of the
spirit'. In the same interlude the beggar-woman Gwenhwyfar
Ddiog (Lazy Gwenhwyfar) can turn round and say:

Cymerwch rybudd o'm trueni.
Ymhob ymddygiad, gwyliwch ddiogi.

[Take a warning from my misery. In all your conduct, guard against
idleness.]

This is in a soliloquy: seconds later, when the Fool comes and chides her, the old whining, self-pitying Gwenhwyfar is back again. One of the expected things is that the Miser should make a declaration of his repentance. But the repentance is always formal and symbolic, not psychological, and is often accompanied by a reference to the play as parable:

> Cymerwch fi'n siampl, y cwmni da,
> Nid yw'r helynt yma ond dameg. (CTh)

[Take me as an example, goodly company, this business is but a parable.]

> Am hynny'r cwmni, 'rwy'n eich cymell
> I gymryd rhybudd cyn mynd yn rhybell:
> Peth tost ydyw marw cyn ymorol esmwythdra;
> Gwybyddwch mai dameg yw'r holl siarad yma. (YFF)

[As a company I therefore urge you to accept a warning before you go too far: to die before seeking ease is a dire thing; know that all this talk is a parable.]

Thus *character* is not constant; at the same time a *role* is not easily abandoned. Captain Factor, disgusted at the behaviour of the Turks, cannot lay aside the role of the Christian among heathen. When buying Prudensia's freedom he dispenses with diplomatic language, and he would probably not be deflected by mention of Turkey's importance to NATO or the desirability of her becoming a member of the EC:

> Mi dalaf gan punt iddyn,
> Cei fod i mi'n ben morwyn.
> Sultan, Sarasin di-les,
> Dowch yma yn nes i'w derbyn.

[I'll pay them a hundred pounds, and you shall be my chief maid. Sultan, no-good Saracen, come up here to receive them.]

From beginning to end, the interlude comments on itself. It is both an act and an interpretation of the act. The word 'act' figures prominently, as does the name of the author, and sometimes other authors:

Mae gennyf act ar gynnydd
A freuddwydiodd Twm y Prydydd,
I adrodd ffyrdd naturieth ffôl
Y byd a'i ddynol ddeunydd.   (PG)

[I have an act in progress, dreamt up by Twm the Rhymer, to recount the ways of the world's foolish nature and its human material.]

Mae gennym fath ar chw'ryddieth,
Fel act, neu ddarn o gyff'lybieth,
A gwraidd ei sylwedd a'i hagwedd hi
Yw dameg y tri chydymeth.   (TChD)

[We have a sort of play, as it were an act or a piece of likeness, its substance and its attitude rooted in the parable of the three companions.]

The author has the choice of either praising his own act or apologizing for its deficiencies. Sometimes he will assure the audience that it will get better and that it is worth their staying till the end:

Y sawl sydd am brofi sylwedd,
Gwrandawed hyn i'r diwedd;
Os nad oes iddi ond dechrau bach,
Mae'n ffyrfach yn ei pherfedd.   (PCG)

[He who wants a taste of substance, let him listen this out to the end; though it has but a small beginning, it's stronger towards the middle.]

Huw Jones and Siôn Cadwaladr know that, as the play ends, the debate will start:

Wel! rwan bydd y dadal,
A'r Sesiwn Fawr a'r sisial,
Ar y chwryddion, a'r chwarae, a'r ddau fardd,
Os trwyiad y tardd y treial.   (YBD)

[Well! now begins the argument, and the Great Sessions and the whispering, concerning the players, and the play, and the two poets, if the trial gets off to a good start.]

Edward Thomas, anticipating that reactions will vary, counsels the listeners to make sure they know the rules of poetry before they judge:

A'r sawl sydd mewn dalltwrieth,
A deall riwl barddonieth,
Ni ddyfid mo'r llawer, oherwydd pam,
Lle gwelo gam brydyddieth.

A'r sawl sydd yn gwybod leia
Sydd yn at i feio fwya:
Ac felly maen' drwy barthau'r byd,
Yn hel rhyw chwdlyd chwedla.   (CD)

[And the one who has understanding and knows the rule of poetry will not say very much, and good reason why, where he sees a fault in the metre. And the one who knows least tends to censure the most: and that's how they are, all over the world, repeating some disgusting tales.]

Sometimes with Twm o'r Nant (Thomas Edwards), it is 'take it or leave it':

Pwy bynnag nad oedd yn ein leicio,
Na ddoed ddim atom eto;
Nid a' i ddawnsio ac i ledu 'ngheg
Ddim chwaneg. Nos dawch heno.   (TChD)

[Whoever didn't like us, let him not come to us again; I shan't be dancing or opening my mouth any more. Good night for now.]

At other times Twm can be quite disarming in his apology, as in this oft-quoted verse which provides an interesting sidelight on the mode of production:

A dyna ddarn dreiglad, egoriad o'r geirie;
I'w datgan yn gywren ni a wnawn yma'n gore;
Na ddigiwch, cyd-ddygwch, maddeuwch yn ddie,
Nid ydym ond egwan ddau ddynan ddiddonie.   (PG)

[And that's a part of its course, a key to the words; to perform it skilfully we shall do our best; do not be offended, but bear with us, and make sure to pardon, for we are but two little men of no talent.]

Some comments on the 'act' reflect on what is customary or expected in an interlude:

Wel 'rwyt yn traethu geirie,
Nid gweddus mae rhai'n eu godde,
Oblegid eu bod yn siarad syn
I ddal atyn mewn anterliwtie.   (TChB)

[Well you are declaiming words which some hold to be unsuitable, for they are a strange kind of talk to keep up in an interlude.]

Others suggest that the writing and performing of interludes was not universally approved of:

I'w danu mae'r gair rhwng dynion
Mai chware ydi a wnaed o ymryson,
O fod am y gore â Thwm o'r Nant,
I fwydo chwant ynfydion.   (GN)

[The word goes out among men that it is a play written in competition, contending with Twm o'r Nant in feeding the desire of fools.]

The 'act' nearly always begins with the Fool calling for silence and attention. He would probably have to shout:

Gostegwch, bawb, gostegwch,
Os ydych am wrando, rowndiwch;
Y fi ydyw'r crier ffraethber ffri
Ddaeth yma i gyhoeddi heddwch.   (PCG)

[Be quiet, all, be quiet, and if you are going to listen, gather round; I am the bold and eloquent crier who has come here to call silence.]

Mae gofyn i bawb sy am wrando
Roi pob ymddiddan heibio.
Ni ddichon neb ddeall unrhyw ddawn
Neu stori heb iawn ystyrio.   (TChB)

[All those who want to listen must cease from all conversation. No one can understand any gift or tale without proper consideration.]

The injunction to pay attention, to remember and to consider may be repeated at intervals; for, oftener than not, the 'act' will contain a message:

Mi gana ichwi bennill eto,
Os byddwch mor fwyn â gwrando,
A chymrwch ofal ar bob cam,
Yn gyfan am ei gofio. (PChF)

[I'll sing you another verse, if you'll be so kind as to listen, and take care every step of the way that you remember it whole.]

Here is a typical opening by Twm o'r Nant; Iemwnt Wamal, the Fool, speaks in *Cyfoeth a Thlodi*:

Wel, rhowch yma osteg, a gwnewch sefyll neu eiste,
Bawb yn gyflawn, yn hyn o gyfle;
Chwi gewch ddiddanwch bod yg un,
Os galla' i'n ddiddychryn ddechre.

'Rwy'n meddwl o ran eich moddion,
Eich bod yn gwmni heddychlon
Gobeithio'r ydwyf yn hyn o le
Y byddwch fel finne'n fwynion.

Y mae gennyf i chwaryddiaeth newydd,
A gefes gan Dwm y Prydydd,
Heb ddim ond dau ffŵl ar hyn o dro
I'w gweled yn ymgomio â'i gilydd . . .

[Well now, give us silence, and do stand or sit, all together while you have the chance; you'll have entertainment, each and every one, if I may confidently begin. I'm sure that by nature you are a peaceable company; and right here I do hope that you will be as kind as myself. I have here a new play which I received from Twm the Rhymer, with only two fools, for the time being, to be seen talking to each other . . .]

He says more or less what any compère would say when opening a show, only that it is in verse. Then, casting his eye over the audience, he spots some ladies whom he knows:

Edr'wch yma, mor lân eu boche
Y daeth fy chwiorydd i'm gweld yn chware.
Pwy ydi hon acw sy'n gostwng ei phen?
O, Neli, fy nghangen ole.

Corff barcutan! ond dacw fy chwaer Cati,
Siân a Gwenno, mewn syn gyni;
Mali, a'r snisin hyd ei thrwyn,
A'r bwtog fwyn gan Beti.

[Look you here, so fair of cheek, my sisters have come to see me play.
Who is that one there, lowering her head? Oh, it's Neli, my fair maiden.
Kite's carcase! but there's my sister Cati, Siân and Gwenno, in the most
amazing fix; Mali, with the snuff all over her nose, and little kindly Beti.]

The Fool could shout out Neli, Cati, Siân, Gwenno, Mali and Beti
with a fair degree of confidence that women in the audience would
answer to the names. A great many individuals are named in the
interludes, especially in the opening scenes; how many were real
people, we do not know; but there must have been a good few
topical and local references. Thus the 'act' starts in the midst of the
audience and backs away; it is something set apart from life for the
time being. At the end, players and audience will come together
once more, for the night is yet but young:

Dacw'r merched ar eu gore
Yn cerdded bawb tuag adre,
Ond rwi yn deud mai'r ddynes fwya'i chlod
A ddaw â chwrw ar ôl darfod chware.   (YBD)

[And there go the ladies, for all they are worth, starting off home, but I
say that the lady most worthy of praise will be the one who brings some
ale when we've finished the play.]

Ffarwél y glân gwmpeini,
Bendith Huw yn eich cwmni;
Dowch hefo fi i'r tŷ, oll, mawr a mân,
A dwsin o'r glân lodesi.   (CaD)

[Farewell to you, fair company, God's blessing be amongst you; come
with me to the house, all, great and small, and a dozen of the lovely
maidens.]

The 'act', we have suggested, can be about anything. But most
audiences would be disappointed if there were not a Miser and a

Fool. Their respective traits of character can be suggested by a selection of names. Here are a few Misers: Deifas (Dives), Rhinallt Ariannog (Rhinallt the Wealthy), Crintach Greulon (Cruel Skinflint), Caled Ddeddfol (Hard and Fussy), Madog Chwannog (Greedy Madog), Hywel Dordyn (Tight-bellied Hywel), Trachwant Bydol (Worldly Covetousness), Mr Blys y Cwbl (Mr Want It All), Arthur Drafferthus (Bothersome Arthur), Rondol Roundyn (Rondol the Roundhead), Siôn Llygad y Geiniog (Penny-pinching Siôn). And here are some Fools: Chwedleugar (Gossipy), Cecryn (Quibbler), Gwagsaw (Frivolous), Iemwnt Wamal (Iemwnt the Flippant), Mr Atgas (Mr Nasty), Mr Rhyfyg Natur (Mr Natural Rashness), Mr Pleser (Mr Pleasure), Mr Oferedd (Mr Dissipation), Ffowcyn Gnichlyd (Fornicating Foulk), Syr Rhys y Geiriau Duon (Sir Rhys the Sarcastic), Syr Caswir (Sir Unpalatable Truth), Syr Tom Tell Truth. The Misers' names, it will be seen, have a high degree of consistency. There is more variety in the Fools' names: the Fool can be rash, frivolous, immoral, irresponsible—but he can Tell the Truth. The contrast between Miser and Fool can be characterized in several ways, one of which is to say that they represent the principled and the unprincipled. The life of the Miser has been tied to a principle, the hoarding of money: with this go sobriety, censoriousness, self-righteousness and sometimes puritanism. But the day he meets the Fool, all is changed. For the audience, the moment to wait for is when the Miser lets down his guard and does something quite out of character:

> O Sionyn yr Heiddan, olew yr bregyn,
> Crasa cweryl, croeso i'm coryn;
> Troes cynildeb heddiw yn haelder,
> Mi gowswn godwm onibai'r gader.

> O ennaint annwyl, di am llygad-dynnaist,
> Fy holl feddylie i gyd a feddalaist;
> Fo wnaeth 'y nghalon oedd o ddur glowddu
> Fel menyn Mai ar ddrws y popty.   (GN)

[Oh John Barleycorn, oil of the malt, the thing I've quarrelled most with, welcome to my head; miserliness today has turned to generosity; I'd have fallen if it were not for the chair. Oh my favourite unction, you have beguiled me, you have softened all of my thoughts; it has made my heart, which was of shining black steel, like butter in May on the oven door.]

Before the night is out the Miser will be found lying drunk on the floor of the tavern, all his money spent; for good measure he may have got the barmaid with child. The Fool will perhaps have paid for the first pint. The Fool will sometimes steal the Miser's money and cuckold him, but not invariably; rogue and opportunist though he is, he does not always gain personally from his trickery. In the wider context, the Fool has been a means to the Miser's salvation, for this night on the tiles is the start of the Miser's progress from self-righteousness to repentance. So the familiar story contains some homely fun and the Christian message at the same time. The Fool is no fool, but he *acts* the fool. He is worldly-wise, mobile and not tied to any principle; he weaves between the two plots of the interlude, and it is he who makes it possible for us to accept two unconnected stories somehow as one. Time and distance do not constrain him: the Fool in *Y Ddau Gyfamod* arrives post-haste from America, where he has just killed his cousin in the War of Independence. The Second Book of Samuel omits to mention this, but according to Huw Jones and Siôn Cadwaladr in *Y Brenin Dafydd* it was Cecryn the Fool, for a guinea, who perpetrated the insult on the messengers of King David to King Hanun, by cutting short their beards and their skirts, thus bringing on the war between Israel and the sons of Ammon. The same Cecryn was later involved in summoning Bathsheba, the wife of Urias, to King David, in plotting her husband's death and in disposing of his body. He was also the first to call David and Bathsheba to account for their adultery. He still had time to spare for all his tricks on Madog Chwannog the Miser. From one interlude to the next the Fool fills many a vacancy—a land-surveyor, a lieutenant, a candidate for Parliament. He can always officiate at a burial or a marriage, because most parsons are only fools after all. In *Tri Chydymaith Dyn* the function of Rhyfyg Natur, the Fool, is to tell Lord Anima what he wants to hear and to oppose the pleadings of Conscience, but he warns his master that he cannot follow him everywhere: he cannot stand beside him in the Great Judgement—but of course he would be glad to come along with him to Chester or Shrewsbury, to an alehouse or a gentleman's mansion. When the Miser has driven his first wife to her death, as happens often, the Fool will gladly sing her elegy. In next to no time he will have found the Miser a new wife—a spendthrift of course. He marries them. In *Protestant a Neilltuwr* he gives the Miser, who is out of practice, a lesson in love-making.

Twm o'r Nant assigns to the Fool a somewhat more philosophical role. His scepticism is a foil to the dogmatism and obsessiveness of the Miser. The Miser sees the whole world as a conspiracy against himself; it falls to the Fool to generalize the issue, to observe that this is the way things are, and have always been. 'There's too much vanity,' says Arthur the Miser; 'all is vanity,' says Sir Rhys the Fool:

> Wel, oni chlywsoch chi draethu'n fanwl
> (Hen benbwl cebyst) mai gwagedd ydyw'r cwbwl?
> Gwagedd, O! wagedd, llygredd a llid
> Yw'n moddion i gyd, 'rwy'n meddwl.
>
> Nid oes ond y twyll a'r ddichell ddiffaith
> Ymhob rhyw alwedigaeth drwy'r gymdogaeth;
> 'Does odid un yn dilyn gwedd
> Gwirionedd yn ddiweniaith.   (PCG)

[Well, haven't you heard it explicitly stated (accursed old blockhead) that all is vanity? Vanity of vanities, and corruption rampant, that's all there is to it—or so I think. There is only guile and base deceit in every calling through the land; hardly a one follows the manner of truth without flattery.]

For Arthur, the measuring of land for enclosure is the end of the world; but Sir Rhys views it *sub specie aeternitatis*:

> Wel, mesura' hwy am y siwra'
> Eu tiroedd, mewn moddion taera';
> Daw dydd na roir fawr mwy o hon
> Na dwylath i'r dynion tala'.

[Well, let them measure their lands for all they're worth and as keenly as they like; a day will come when no more than two yards are allotted even to the tallest of men.]

Like all popular comedy, the interlude is full of the expected. As well as the stock characters (Fool, Miser, his two wives, his useless son, his Anglicized daughter, Doctor, Taxman, Beggar, Barmaid) there are also recurring situations which the audiences would not want to miss. They know how the callous Miser makes little of his first wife's illness, but there are always new levels of outrageousness to be reached:

CYNHWYFAR:	Mae ar y galon bach ryw ludded.
MADOG:	Ie, o fara gwyn, llaeth, neu ruel peillied;
	Hwnnw fu'n gwasgu arnoch yn rhol,
	Gwedi rhoi yn ych bol gryn beuled.
CYNHWYFAR:	Gelwch am ryw un i ddarllen gweddi.
MADOG:	Ni byddwch ronyn nes er hynny;
	Os gellwch gan ddiogi, streifiwch heb ffael
	Ychydig, i gael chwydu.
CYNHWYFAR:	Nid oes ynddw i ond gwynt, debygwn,
	Sy'n codi i fyny yn bylgrwn.
MADOG:	Rhowch chi'ch tin ar y garreg a rhechwch yn ffast.
	Dyna ichwi gast a'i gostwng.

[C: My poor heart is affected by weariness. M: Yes, of white bread, buttermilk or wheat flour gruel; that's what has been pressing on you all rolled up; why, you've put a whole sackful in your belly. C: Call someone to read a prayer. M: That won't help you one bit; if you're not too lazy, make a little effort right away to throw up. C: I suppose it's only wind in me, rising up all in a lump. M: Put your arse on the stone and give a strong fart. There's a trick that will bring it down for you.]

The first wife's elegy the audience will have heard many a time, but there are new depths of bad taste to be plumbed. Madog and Cecryn sing to the tune of 'Ffalantin Tw Tam Tiri':

Cân ffarwél yn hyn o bryd
I'r rhinclyd sychlyd sachlen;
Dyma yr hyllog foliog fawr,
Mewn gole ar lawr yn gelen;
Mi dorrwn dwll i'r faeden fwll,
Diame, ym mhwll y domen.

[Right now sing farewell to the boring, complaining old bag; here's the great big ugly fat-belly lying dead on the ground for all to see; we'll dig a hole for the sullen bitch, sure we will in the dung-heap.]

The audiences know there will be ructions when the Miser comes home and finds his wife holding a tea-party. He, the male chauvinist, cannot tolerate the idea that she should have a social life of her own. But what will he do? In *Cwymp Dyn*, he smashes the tea-things in his fury. In *Protestant a Neilltuwr*, he throws one of his clogs among the assembled guests, just as they are starting to read the tea-leaves. But the ladies were in an aggressive mood that day:

Nhw godason i gyd oddi yno,
Fel cacwn gan ddechrau cicio,
Rhai yn fy nhin â darn o bren,
A'r lleill â'm pen yn pwnio.

Fe lynodd rhyw faeden asw
Yn fy nghwd i a chorn fy ngwddw;
Fe'm gwasgodd honno fi'n ddigon siŵr
Oni chollais i 'nŵr yn arw.

Hwy fuant yn pwtio 'mherfedd,
Ac yn gwneud â mi amarch ffiedd;
Fe dynnodd un ei thin, myn caws,
Yn union ar draws fy nannedd.

[They all got up like wasps, and began kicking, some at my arse with a piece of wood, and others butting me in the head. One awkward bitch got hold of my balls and my throat, and she squeezed me really hard so that I lost a lot of water. They poked me in my tummy and abused me in a most disgusting way; and by my word [lit. by the cheese] one of them drew her arse right across my teeth.]

Just as well that the scene was described, not acted. Interlude-watchers know full well what will happen when the Miser's daughter goes to London or Chester and receives a lady's education. But her father's reaction is always worth waiting for:

Fe fu fy merch yn yr ysgol,
Tros ddau fis yn foesol;
Hi feder blygu ac ymystynnu, llamu yn ei lle,
Ac yn ei garre yn rhagorol.

Ni welsoch chi beth erioed 'run waneg,
Ond un o'r cesig rhedeg,

A phan elw i i ofyn rhyw beth i'r jâd,
Hi etyb 'i thad yn Saesneg. (YBD)

[My daughter went to school, being polite for over two months; she can bend and stretch and leap on the spot and curtsey most excellently. You never saw anything like it, except one of the racing-mares, and when I ask something of the jade she answers her father in English.]

There is an excellent scene in *Cwymp Dyn* between the Miser's wife Lowri and her daughter Bessi, just back from London and no longer able to understand her mother speaking. Several of the interlude-writers show an awareness of this chronic problem, still unresolved, the effect of education on a subject people; they have given us some very comic variations on a serious theme.

We have already mentioned the scene in which the Miser returns home from the market, from the law-courts or from his spree, to find a scene of chaos. Huw Jones, in *Protestant a Neilltuwr*, gives us a charming vignette of rural life:

Mi eis adre y bore wedi hanner ymrwystro,
'Roedd y plant hyd yr aelwyd yn dechrau riwlio,
Ac yn dechrau piso fesur y dau neu dri,
A Nedi a Doni yn dwyno.

Yr oedd un gwedi syrthio i'r lludw,
A llosgi ei din yn arw;
Mi welwn un arall yn dwad ata' i ffrit
Gwedi codi o'r mit llaeth cadw.

Gofyn am y forwyn firi,
Nid oedd hanes dim ohoni,
Gwedi carthu a rhoi bwyd i'r hwch,
A gweiddi 'Codwch, Cadi'.

Ni chlywn i leferydd undyn,
Ond mi eis i'r llofft yn sydyn;
Mi welwn yng nghanol y gwely glas
Ferrau'r gwas a'r forwyn.

Fe neidiodd y gwas i fyny ar fyrder,
Ac a gipiodd ei glos oddi ar y gader;

Os daw e ond hynny ger fy mron,
Mi a'i anafa, hangmon ofer.

Fe ddarfu imi ddechrau sgowlio,
A dweud, y gŵr mawr a'ch cotto:
Mi welwn y forwyn yn codi ar gais,
Ac yn gwisgo ei phais, a phiso.

Ac yn dweud, â'i llygad wantan,
'Beth sydd arnoch chi meistr druan,
Ysgowlio eich gwas o faes eich co'.
Nid oedd o yn ceisio ond cusan.'

[In the morning I went home in near-frustration, the children were beginning to take over the hearth and starting to piss in twos and threes, and Nedi and Donni soiling their pants. One had fallen among the ashes and burnt his arse badly; I could see another one darting towards me having just got out of the buttermilk tub. I called for the merry maidservant; when I had cleaned out the pigsty and fed the sow and shouted 'Cadi, get up', she was nowhere to be found. There was not a voice to be heard, but I quickly went up to the loft; in the middle of the pale bed I could see the legs of the manservant and the maid. The servant immediately leapt up and snatched his breeches off the chair; if ever again he comes before me, the useless hangman, I'll do him an injury. I began to scold, and said 'devil take you': I saw the maid get up straight away, then she put on her slip, and had a pee, and said with her wanton eye, 'Poor master, what's the matter with you, scolding your servant and going out of your mind? He only wanted a kiss.']

What a tragedy that these poets, in the last decade of the century, started writing odes on abstract subjects, in imitation of Goronwy Owen, and in competition for the prizes awarded by the London-Welsh societies. What they could have done if they had stuck to their own idiom and the world they knew!

Those are some of the features of the 'act'. Having gone to all the trouble of emphasizing that it is only an act, most of the authors, with no less a degree of conviction, will remind us at some stage that the act ultimately has to do with life. Thus Twm o'r Nant:

Felly ffarwél i chi gyd ar unwaith;
Chwi wyddoch nad yw hyn ond act a chwaryddiaeth,

Ond ni bydd gan angau ond chwarae prudd,
Chwi welwch ddydd marwolaeth. (PCG)

[Therefore farewell to you all at once; you know that this is but an act
and a play, but death will have but a grim jest, you will see when his
day comes.]

The act contains a message, which is reiterated and underlined at
several points. The message, simply put, is that all men stand in need
of redemption. It was for an audience which understood Christianity
and how it operated. A good many of the listeners would know what
'the Two Covenants' meant. For them there was no incongruity
between the stable-loft humour and either the theology or the
moralizing; the farce and the sermon in the interlude concerned the
same thing, nature unredeemed. After the usual tomfoolery, the
phallic object would be presented to a woman in the audience, often
with a pretty explicit injunction as to what to do with it—'stick it
under your navel' are usually the words. Then the Fool would
proceed to counsel the young women on the virtue of chastity, and
the dangers alike of an unwanted pregnancy and a hasty marriage. If
there is fertility ritual somewhere behind the interlude, as there may
well be, it has long ago been swallowed up in something else, whose
logic runs roughly like this: procreation is good and necessary, both
for the sake of rural Wales and the future of humankind; but as man
is a flawed creature, things tend to go wrong, in this as in every
human activity; hence the need for moral precept. But the Fool
knows that, due to the same fact of human folly, his advice will be
laughed at, and he will often end by saying 'it's no use':

Nid ydi cynghori merched na meibion
Ond fel mynd â'r gogr dellt i'r afon,
A hwnnw ni ddeil ef ddafn o ddŵr,
Fe'i cyll o'n siŵr yn union. (YFF)

[The counselling of women and lads is only like taking the leaky sieve to
the river; it won't hold a drop of water, it will certainly spill it straight
away.]

We have tried to say something of the content and spirit of the
'act'. Tenderness it has but little, and romance next to none,

although some plots do concern the coming together of lovers. It offers us ribaldry, theology, moralism, satire and political incorrectness, in varying degrees and combinations.

Some questions concerning the interlude are likely to remain unanswered. Why did it belong primarily to north-eastern Wales, the counties of Denbigh, Flint and northern Merioneth? Why do we not hear of it before the second half of the seventeenth century, and why did it have to die out so quickly in the first quarter of the nineteenth? Some interludes, it must be said, are abominably poor. Reading the two efforts of Thomas Williams of Tal-y-bont, Caernarfonshire, printed in his book *Mynegiad yr Hen Oesoedd* (1761), we can understand why the crowds preferred to stand in all weathers listening to the sermons of Howel Harris. The Welsh interlude is an archaic form, and why the contemporaries of Goldsmith and Sheridan took it up we do not know. Readers of Richard Southern's *Seven Ages of the Theatre* will recognize in it features recalling his 'second' and 'third' phases: the direct address to the audience, the naming of individuals, the self-introduction, the comment on the play itself. As the name suggests, it is in some ways a survival and an adaptation of the pre-Shakespearean interlude, a poor man's version of something which once belonged to courts and palaces.

All the dialogue is in four-line stanzas, sometimes broken up into couplets or individual lines to be spoken by different characters. Of the two predominant forms, the first is the *triban*, an iambic metre with the basic length-pattern 7 7 8 7 and the rhyme-pattern a a b a, with linking rhyme between lines 3 and 4. Several examples have already been quoted, but here is another one:

> Ni fynnwn ddim 'run faner
> Ag interliwtie'r Cowper,
> Bregethu duwioldeb yn ei chrys
> I rai fo â blys am bleser.   (PG)

[I would not wish, in the same manner as the interludes of the Cowper, to preach piety in shirt-sleeves to those that are eager for pleasure.]

Cynghanedd occurs often in the last line, and sometimes in the first, as in this instance. The second verse-form has eight- or nine-syllable iambic lines, rhyming a a b b:

Taw, taw â'th ynfyd chwedlau diflas;
'Rwy'n deip o frenin yr holl deyrnas;
Mi allwn alw milwyr gwaedlyd,
I wneud dy frad mewn llai na munud.   (PCG)

[Be quiet with your silly tiresome tales; I am a type of a king over the whole kingdom; I could summon bloody soldiers to do you to death in less than a minute.]

Less frequently used is a monorhyme stanza in twelve-syllable iambics, with full or partial *cynghanedd* in each line:

Mae'r prydydd, wŷr gwaredd, yn mwynedd ddymuno,
Cyd-ddygwch â'i 'madrodd, gwnaeth orau ag y medro;
Y gwanna o feirdd Gwynedd o anrhydedd sy'n rhodio,
Er hynny rhai dynion a gofiant amdano.   (PN)

[The poet, gentlemen, courteously requests that you bear with his phrasing, for he has done the best he can; of all the poets of Gwynedd walking abroad, he is the lowest in rank; none the less some will remember him.]

All the measures are roughly handled, with one or more syllables added here and skipped there. The effect is not impaired by this irregularity, but if anything enhanced. There is here vigorous spoken verse, with the linking rhyme, when employed, serving to drive home the message time and time again. The songs, punctuating the interlude at regular intervals, are written to the popular tunes of the day—'Blodau'r Gogledd' (Flowers of the North), 'Bryniau'r Werddon' (The Hills of Ireland), 'Glan Medd-dod Mwyn' (The Verge of Sweet Drunkenness), 'Miller's Key' (or 'Billiricay'), 'Crimson Velvet', 'Black-eyed Susan' and many, many more. In the songs, unlike the dialogue, the rules of measure are never broken, and their already intricate forms are further adorned with frequent touches of *cynghanedd*. They vary greatly in mood, and when sung to the original tunes they have the power to charm and sometimes to move the spirit. The interlude is a rough-and-ready play, but in one respect—its versification—it has a sophistication undreamt of by the authors either of the court interludes of the sixteenth century or of the masques of the seventeenth. Milton, thou shouldst have been living in the Vale of Clwyd.

Twm o'r Nant

Thomas Edwards (Twm o'r Nant; 1737–1810) was hailed in his day as 'our native Garrick' and 'the Cambrian Shakespeare'. Bobi Jones, writing in 1953, suggested that 'the Welsh Molière' might be a more apt characterization. Of all the interlude writers he is the only one whose work continued to be reprinted in the nineteenth and twentieth centuries; his *Tri Chryfion Byd* is the only interlude to be given an airing before modern audiences. There is one very obvious reason for this, namely that he is the least obscene. At the end of the day, Twm will probably maintain his position as king of the interlude writers, but reappraisal of some of the others is never out of place. For a story told vigorously and engagingly it is hard to beat Huw Jones. Ellis Roberts, Siôn Cadwaladr, Edward Thomas and others have plenty of lively scenes and passages. The best interludes need to be edited and published, and a little book of their scenes and songs would give hours of delight.

In a short autobiography published in 1805, Twm o'r Nant has given a selective account of his life as stonemason, carrier, innkeeper, tollgate-keeper and author. What he seems to be proudest of is his skill and inventiveness as a haulier of timber. His early escapades as a fighter are recalled with considerable regret; his legal tiffs with undying anger. The most memorable passages record his efforts as a lad, amid a great deal of discouragement, to learn reading and writing, and the precociousness he showed as poet, dramatist and actor. His acting career began when he was twelve, with a troupe of players taking him on to play women's parts. Already, before he was nine, he had 'written' (which may mean 'copied') 'two books of interludes' and a great many poems. When he was nearly fourteen his first complete interlude was acted; he had entrusted it to Huw Jones of Llangwm, who sold it to a company for ten shillings, keeping the money. But friendship apparently continued between Twm and his rogue literary agent, well-known for such tricks. The autobiography ends where most of the interludes also end:

Ac oblegid hynny, y mae achos mawr i mi ystyried fy ffyrdd, ac ymofyn am Waredwr, gan na allaf mo'm gwared fy hun, heb gael adnabyddiaeth o deilyngdod y Cyfryngwr; yn yr hwn, gobeithio, y bydd imi derfynu fy amser byr ar y ddaear, yn heddwch Duw i dragwyddoldeb. Amen.

[And for that reason, there is great cause for me to consider my ways, and seek a Redeemer, as I cannot redeem myself, without knowledge of the Intercessor's merit; in whom, that is my hope, I shall end my brief time on earth, in the peace of God for all eternity. Amen.]

There have survived, through being published, eight interludes under Twm's name. It seems that he wrote several more. Some 350 of his poems have been preserved in manuscript. A small selection of these, some three dozen, appeared under the title *Gardd o Gerddi* (A Garden of Poems) in 1790, and a further ten in nineteenth-century editions of the same book. Some forty-five of his poems had been printed during his own lifetime in leaflets or 'ballads'.

Twm, as a writer of interludes, phased out the obscenity, and proportionately increased both the allegory and the satire. Allegorical figures such as Cariad, Angau, Capten Tlodi, Cywir Gristion, Cyfaill Cnawdol, Rhagrith, Rhywun, Mrs Gwirionedd Cydwybod, Madam Duwioldeb Crefydd and Arglwyddes Chwantau Natur (Love, Death, Captain Poverty, True Christian, Worldly Companion, Hypocrisy, Somebody, Mrs Truth of Conscience, Madam Religious Piety and Lady Natural Desires) come to confront and interact with homely realistic characters such as Rhinallt the Miser and Lowri Lew his mother, Rondol Roundyn and Siân Ddefosiynol (Pious Siân) his wife, Arthur Drafferthus, Gwenhwyfar Ddiog (Lazy Gwenhwyfar), Zidi Drwsiadus (Well-dressed Zidi), Diogyn Trwstan (Clumsy Loafer) and many more. The strong allegorical element betrays an affinity with the morality play, which must be one of the antecedents of the interlude; but allegory had also been given a new lease of life from the 1670s through the influence of John Bunyan. Ellis Wynne, the 'Sleeping Bard', with his personifications of Pride, Pleasure and Profit, was another influence on Twm. As for the satire, we tend to think of it as belonging inherently to all interludes, but in fact the amount of satire in most interludes is minimal. On the most elementary level, it consists of a swipe at the taxman; Huw Jones and Ellis Roberts will occasionally complain about high prices, the extravagance of the rich, and the cost of maintaining the militia; the names of some politicians such as Pitt and Wilkes will be mentioned, but without much comment. Satire against Puritans and Methodists is a category in its own right. The authors, all Churchmen, do not observe any distinction between the two. Huw Jones opens an interlude by addressing the audience as 'y cablirs mwynion' (the merry cavaliers); to most eighteenth-century Anglican polemicists the Methodist, whether Wesleyan or Calvinist, was a return of the Roundhead. Quite soon after the Restoration, Huw Morys had written his interlude of the Civil War, a brisk dramatization of the conflict, Royalist to the last syllable, still with time to spare for the antics of the Fool. Over a century later, Huw Jones rehearses many of the same arguments in *Protestant a Neilltuwr*: the Miser changes his clothing to signify his repentance, and just about the same time the Dissenter announces his return to the Church of England. The Hogarthian *Ffrewyll y Methodistiaid* (The Scourge of the Methodists) by William Roberts of Llannor requires a class of its own. But when all is said, in the volume and the range of his social and moral satire, Twm o'r Nant stands apart.

A first impression might be that Twm shoots at anything that moves, making one exception alone in George III, that most satirized of English kings. The more we read of it, the more clearly we will see that his satire conforms to a pattern, and a very traditional one. Public enemy number one is the steward—who else?

> Dyma'r tiroedd, mae pawb yn taeru
> Y bydden' nhw i gyd yn codi,
> Ac ni wiw inni siarad a gwneud trwyn sur:
> Mae'r stiwardiaid yn wŷr stwrdi.
>
> Rhaid i ddyn ddysgu pratio,
> Tynnu het, a mynych fowio,
> Ac edrych pa sut yr egorir ceg,
> A dweud yn deg rhag eu digio.
>
> Ac ni chaniateir mynd i'w gwynebe
> I siarad, ond ar rai amsere,

A rhyfedd mor syth, oni leiciant chwi'n sôn,
Yn wŷr tonnog, y trônt hwy'u tine.

A rhaid yw eu tendio ar bob achlysur,
A mynd i'w cymhorthau, rhag ofn eu merthyr;
Os gwyddau, os cywion neu berchyll pêr,
Rhaid eu ceisio hwy i'r gêr digysur.

Ac os tyddyn fydd ar osodiad,
Daw yno i ymryson resiad;
Ni cheir na threfn na threial na thro
Heb iro dwylo'r diawliaid.

Mae'n rhaid i ystiward yn ei falchder
Gael llawer mwy o barch na'i feister,
On' 'te, ni chaiff dyn gwan ddim lle
Yn agos, os â fe'n eger.

Digiwch ŵr bonheddig, cewch bardwn ganddo;
Ond os digiwch ystiward, chwi gewch eich andwyo;
Mae hynny'n druenus ym marn pob dyn,
Fod rhyw helynt fel hyn yn riwlio.   (PCG)

[Then there's land, it will all go up, that's what they say, and it's no use us talking and making a face, the stewards are sturdy men. A man must learn to prate, to doff his hat and to bow often, and watch how he opens his mouth, and speak nicely so as not to offend them. Talking to them face to face is allowed only at certain times, and it's amazing how sharply, if they don't like the tone of your voice, they will turn their arses, capricious fellows that they are. One must attend on them on all occasions, and go to their assistance for fear of their reprisal; if it is geese or chickens or sweet piglets, they must be obtained for the cheerless rogues. And if a holding comes to be let, there will be a queue of people competing for it; there will be neither order nor trial nor chance unless the bastards' palms are greased. A steward in his pride demands much more respect than his master; if he doesn't get it, and if he turns nasty, a poor man had better stand clear. Offend a gentleman, you'll have his pardon; offend a steward, and you'll be ruined; it is pitiful in the opinion of all men that such a condition should rule us.]

Not far behind in the line of fire comes the gentleman himself. Twm, in his time, had sung paeans of praise in the *cywydd* form to Sir Watkin Williams Wynn and other Denbighshire landowners.

But he gives these lines to no less a person than Tom Tell Truth:

Heblaw'r hen felltith wreiddiol
Sy'n peri tlodi'n wladol,
Balchder gwŷr mawr yn gwasgu'r gwan,
Mae hynny'n rhan erwinol.

Balchder sy'n gyrru bon'ddigion segurllyd
Tua Ffrainc neu Loegr i rythu eu llygid,
I ddysgu ffasiwne a gwario yn fall
Ddau mwy mewn gwall nag ellid.

Mae ganddynt yn Llunden lawer llawendy
I droi'r gath yn yr haul i fon'ddigion Cymru,
Playhouses a *lotteries*, ffawdus ffull,
Ac amryw ddull i ddallu.

Ac yn y *play* y cân' hwy eu pluo,
Rhwng hwrs a licers bydd eu haur yn slacio;
Rhaid canlyn holl egni cwmpeini pur
'Ran crandrwydd gwŷr yn gwario. (TChB)

[In addition to the old original affliction which creates poverty in the land, there's the pride of the great oppressing the weak, and that is a dire fate. It's pride that drives the idle gentlefolk to France or England to goggle and stare, to learn fashions and to spend, wantonly and mistakenly, twice what they can afford. They have in London many a pleasure-house where the gentlemen of Wales can take their ease, playhouses and lotteries, with tricks of luck and many a means to make men blind. And in the play they will get fleeced, what with whores and liquors their gold will slacken; they must imitate all the exertions of the proper company with the ostentation of men throwing money away.]

Mention of lawyers will always get Twm going:

Wel chwi glywsoch fel cadd yr Aifftied
Ddiodde llawn gystudd rhwng llau a locustied;
Ond mae pla'r cyfreithwyr yn fwy o frad,
I wneud diben y wlad, 'rwy'n tybied. (PG)

[Well, you've heard it said how the Egyptians suffered every affliction, what with lice and locusts; but the plague of lawyers is a greater conspiracy to wreck the country, that's what I think.]

Cariad (Love) in *Tri Chryfion Byd* tries to instruct Rhinallt
Ariannog:

> O! rhyfedd y cariad sydd i'n cyrraedd,
> Hwyrfrydig i lid a mawr drugaredd;
> Fe all maddeuant fod ar gyfer
> Y gwŷr o gyfreth mwya'u trawster.

[Oh! wondrous is the love that is within our reach, slow to anger and great
of mercy; there may be forgiveness even for the most arrogant men of
law.]

Rhinallt is not impressed:

> Wel, os maddeuir i wŷr y gyfreth,
> Fe wneir ag y nhw lawer o ffafreth,
> 'Ran ni faddeuan' nhw i undyn mewn un man,
> Oni fydd yn rhy wan i 'medleth.

[Well, if the men of law are forgiven, they will be done a great favour,
for they will never, anywhere, forgive anyone unless he's too weak to
meddle.]

Rhinallt makes Cariad listen to his story of how he was double-
crossed by the lawyers of St Asaph when he went to court over his
mother's will. Cariad wants him to see the dispute in a wider
context:

> Dyma chwi'n rhoi'r bai ar gyfreithwyr trawsion,
> Heb ystyr na gweled beie'ch hen galon;
> Cariad a'i archwaethiad rhwng eich brawd a chwithe
> Allse, heb ddim dychryn, gytuno cyn dechre.

[There you go, putting the blame on oppressive lawyers, without
considering or seeing the faults of your old heart; love, just a whiff of it,
between your brother and yourself could confidently have brought
agreement from the start.]

No doubt Cariad is right. But some of Rhinallt's mud will stick.
Next after lawyers come excisemen, tax-collectors and supervisors

of all kinds. Rhys y Geiriau Duon lectures the King on what would today be called Parkinson's Law:

Wel, begio'ch pardwn chwi, Frenin tirion,
Pa beth y dewisech gymaint o weision?
Ni fu erioed yn y byd—ni wiw disgwyl bod—
Ddaioni lle bo gormod ddynion.

'Ran lle bo llawer o wein'dogion, bydd y diogi mwya';
'Cerdd di, cerdd dithau'—ni wyddir pa 'run anystwytha'.
A gyrru'r llanc lleia' wnânt hwy *stil*,
Trwy'r pwll i hôl y ceffyl pella'.

A'r rhai sy'n cael y cyflog penna',
Ym mhob lleoedd, sy'n gwneuthur lleia';
Maent hwy'n mynnu rhan, mi ddweda' i,
Dan fy nwylo, mai chwi sy'n ola'.

[Well, begging your pardon, kindly King, why do you want to appoint so many servants? There was never in the world—nor should it ever be expected—any good where there are too many men. Where there are many assistants, there will be the greatest idleness; 'You go, no you go'—you know not who's the most unwilling. And still they'll send the smallest lad through the puddle to fetch the farthest horse. And those who are paid the highest wages everywhere do the least; they will want their slice, and I'll say under my breath that you come last.]

If you are an official of any kind, you will be attacked, either for neglecting your duty or for performing it too assiduously, it does not matter which. This is the small man's perennial suspicion of anyone placed in authority over him. Twm, like all the interlude writers, belonged to the artisan class, and all his satire is class-based. Officials of all kinds, and members of the professions, were two categories sometimes feared, sometimes mocked and always held in suspicion. Lawyers, surveyors, excisemen, doctors, apothecaries—they had all acquired some sort of qualification: they had specialist knowledge with which they could bamboozle the rest of society.

As in the secular sphere, so in the spiritual, the man in the middle, the representative of authority, becomes the butt of satire. Rhys y Geiriau Duon tells the Bishop of his ambition to become a parish priest:

RHYS: Mae gen i ewyllys yn fy nghalon,
       Gael lle i fynd yn berson;
       'Rwy'n gweled y rheini mewn gwlad a thre
       Yn o glos yn eu cobe gleision.

ESGOB: Taw, lolyn ynfyd lledffol,
       A'th siarad ansynhwyrol.

RHYS: Wel, mi wnawn, os oes gen i rhy fach stad,
       Ficar neu gurad gwrol.

       Mi ddarllena Gymraeg ar redeg,
       A thipyn bach o Saesneg;
       A pheth, fy meistr, ellwch chwi ddweud,
       Neu chwennych imi wneud ychwaneg?

[RHYS: I have the desire in my heart to obtain a place as a parson; I see those, in country and town, cosy enough in their blue copes. BISHOP: Shut up you stupid half-witted driveller with your nonsensical talk. RH: Well, even though my estate is too small, I'd make a manly vicar or curate. I can read Welsh at a trot, and a little bit of English; and what, my master, can you say or require me to do beyond that?]

This is the parson's life, or at least this is how Rhys imagines it to be:

       Ffowlio a hela, a chware cardie,
       Ymladd ceiliogod, a thrin merchede,
       Darllen papur newydd, fel y byddan' nhw,
       Ac yfed cwrw am y gore.

[Fowling and hunting, and playing cards, and cock-fighting and handling women, and reading newspapers, as is their wont, and drinking ale for all they're worth.]

But what about the sects and the movements that had arisen either to challenge the Established Church or to reform it from the inside? When Rondol Roundyn becomes a Quaker, Mr Pleser the Fool is not convinced:

       Wel, Roundiad a Chwacers edr'wch acw,
       A droisoch yn barod yn eich trwst a'ch berw?

'Rwy'n ame y troir chwi cyn y Sul
Yn fastard mul am elw.   (PG)

[Well, Roundheads and Quakers, look over there, have you already
been converted amid your noise and fervour? I suspect that before the
week is out you'd be converted into mules if it brought you profit.]

And the latest sect to appear:

O, pobl dostion ydyw'r Methodistied,
Rhuo am eu crefydd y byddan nhw bob crafied,
Ceir clywed y carpie cas eu cuwch
Yn swnio'n uwch na'r personied.   (TChB)

[Oh, the Methodists are harsh people, roaring all the time about their
religion; they are to be heard, the nasty scowling rabble, shouting
louder than the parsons.]

The words are spoken by Rhinallt the Miser. Is the thought Twm's
own? In part, no doubt—but there is more to be said about this.
Here is the drover:

Ond o dafarn i dafarn 'roedd e'r hen borthmon diofal,
Heb fawr edrych at na thir na chatal,
Ond canu efo'r tanne ac ymlid puteinied,
A gwneud bargeinion a cholli, ni bu'r un cyn erchylled.   (PCG)

[But from tavern to tavern went the feckless old drover, with little care
for land or cattle, but singing to the harp and chasing after whores, and
striking bargains and losing, there was never a one so awful.]

Drovers are often satirized by the interlude writers, although
socially they were close to them. They represented coming and
going. In fact, Twm o'r Nant, Huw Jones and Siôn Cadwaladr
were more mobile than most Welshmen of their generation: the
first looking for work and avoiding the law, the second selling his
books, and the third transported for seven years to America; but
the interlude, when it comes to be written, reflects the countryman's suspicion of all mobility. Nearly all the categories satirized
by Twm represent movement and change; as always for the

countryman, new pursuits and fashions are to be denigrated: reading newspapers, playing cards, taking snuff, smoking, drinking tea—and going to the theatre, as opposed to standing in the open air watching an interlude. New taxes were to be decried, as in all societies; and also the new agricultural order based on land enclosure. New denominations and religious movements were alike suspect, and what better instance of coming and going than the itinerant Methodist preacher? Likewise open to attack was the countryman who of his own volition sought a different life-style. It is in such a context that we should see Twm's defence of the Welsh language, commendable though we may still find it. That, too, was part of something bigger, a suspicion of all those who seek to alter their circumstances. In *Tri Chryfion Byd* Lowri Lew, the tough, miserly peasant woman, was killed by the 'gentlemanly fare' put before her at her son Ifan's home:

> 'Roedd hi'n anghynefin â ffâr fon'ddigedd,
> Te, a rhyw gige, a bara gwyn gwagedd;
> Pe cawse hi uwd a llymru a bara llaeth,
> Ni fuase hi gwaeth gan mlynedd.
>
> Bwydydd breision sy'n gryfion eu *gravy*
> Wnaeth i'r hen wreigan druan ollwng drwyddi,
> A bod ymysg Saeson, mi gymraf fy llw,
> A'i chrugodd i farw i'w chrogi.

[She was unaccustomed to gentlemanly fare, tea, and various meats, and the white bread of vanity; if she'd had porridge and flummery and bread-and-buttermilk she would have been good for another hundred years. Rich foods with strong gravy gave the poor old woman the flux, and being among Englishmen, upon my oath, mortally afflicted her and that was her end.]

The story of Rhinallt, his brother Ifan and their mother Lowri is a microcosm. The mother brought up the two sons on the farm through penny-pinching and hard work. One of them stayed at home, a hard and sour miser. The other became a priest. He received a little education, learnt to speak English, and married an Englishwoman who cannot converse with her mother-in-law. His children have no Welsh. This was to be the choice for Welshmen over several generations. Going up in the world, even the least bit, meant becoming Anglicized. Not until the second half of the twentieth century were there any grounds for supposing that things might be different. Even today, the families who have remained natural Welsh-speakers for more than three generations after laying aside the pick and shovel are very few indeed. Eager to inherit her money, Ifan the Priest took his mother to live with him. He fed her on unfamiliar fare, which killed her. Has Twm given us a parable here?

Like most eighteenth-century satirists, Twm o'r Nant is a conservative, culturally and politically. Though some of his themes and his instances were later to become those of radical politics, he himself has very little by way of a programme to reform society. Sometimes we hear the voice of the leveller, as in the words of Iemwnt Wamal:

> Mae ambell grydd neu deiliwr ffrolig,
> A wnaethe reiol gŵr bonheddig;
> Ac ambell ŵr bonheddig hy
> Fuase reidiol iddo ddysgu redig.   (CTh)

[Occasionally a cobbler or a frolicking tailor would make a proper gentleman, and many a bold gentleman would be better occupied learning to plough.]

But it is surely significant that this equally famous stanza is put in the mouth of Gwirionedd (Truth):

> Duw ordeiniodd mewn modd enwog
> Rai yn dlawd a rhai'n gyfoethog,
> Rhai yn fedrus i wneud llywodraeth
> A rhai'n gysonaidd i bob gwasanaeth.

[It is God who has ordained, in a manner well-known, some to be poor and some to be rich, some with skill to govern and some consistently to all kinds of service.]

Twm's social satire, contemporary in its reference and sometimes giving the impression of having a radical slant, is ultimately seen to be rooted in an older tradition. *Pride* or *vanity* (*balchder*) is named often as being the cause of social and economic ills—'balchder

gwŷr mawr yn gwasgu'r gwan' (the pride of the great when they
oppress the weak), 'balchder rhai Cymry ffolion i ymestyn ar ôl y
Saeson' (the vanity of some silly Welshmen, striving to ape the
English). We have seen *jealousy*, such as that of the two brothers
Rhinallt and Ifan. There is no interlude without references to *lust*
or *fleshly desire* . . . Thus, by and by, the list of vices comes to bear
a close resemblance to the traditional catalogue of 'the Seven
Deadly Sins'. *Anger* is here, and what better example than
Rhinallt, in his disappointment at being left out of her will, cursing
his departed mother:

> O'r felltith greulon, trallodion llidiog!
> Be' wna' i o gynddaredd â fy mam gynddeiriog?
> Pe gwelwn i hi'r funud yma'n hyn o fan,
> Mi a'i curwn hi'n anhrugarog.   (TChB)

[Oh cruel curse and galling afflictions! What, in my fury, will I do with
mad mother? If I were to see her here right now, I'd beat her without
mercy.]

Gluttony comes into all interludes, and *avarice* is everywhere—in
landowners, in stewards, in lawyers, and in the Miser of course.
Idleness is well represented, and nowhere better than in the
testament of Diogyn Trwstan in *Cyfoeth a Thlodi*. The speech,
rather too long to quote, can be read on pp. 291–4 of the Foulkes
edition. The fellow's ability to excel himself in uselessness, from
one verse to the next, is quite breath-taking.

In the world of the interlude, all social, economic and political
ills have their root in the flawed nature of man. Twm's Fool will
not let us forget this:

> Mae dyn wrth naturiaeth wedi torri'n druenus,
> A'i feddylie'n anwadal, yn falch ac yn wawdus,
> Yn ymlid fel canghenne pren ar wynt
> Ryw helynt afreolus.   (TChB)

[Man has by nature broken down piteously, his thoughts inconstant,
vain and scornful, like twigs of a tree in the wind following some unruly
course.]

Yes, there is need for a great change:

> Mae'r diawl, fel melinydd, yn troi gelyniaeth
> Olwyn gocos chwant yn nhroell naturiaeth;
> Ni cheir fyth heddwch nac esmwythâd
> Heb ryw gyfnewidiad odiaeth.   (TChB)

[The devil, like a miller, turns the cog-wheel of desire in nature's whirl; there will never be peace or respite unless there is some remarkable alteration.]

Before it is anything else, it is a change in the heart. Some are capable of it, and others not. Why this should be so remains a mystery. When some of these things are touched upon, poetry breaks through, in this instance with a little help from the Apostle:

CARIAD: Y gwir gariad ewyllysgar
> Wna hir ymaros yn ddioddefgar;
> Nid yw yn cenfigennu un tro;
> Mewn osgo mae'n gymwynasgar.

> Y Cariad pur nid yw'n ymffrostio
> Mewn awch eiddig, nac yn ymchwyddo;
> 'Does feddwl drwg, na hunan-dra,
> Nac anweddeidd-dra ynddo.

> Nid yw lawen am anghyfiawnder,
> Ond cydlawenha â'r gwir bob amser;
> Y mae'n amyneddgar, ddoethgar, dda,
> Trwy lendid a ffyddlonder.

ALIS: Wel, ni fuasai waeth o ffyrlin
> Trwy lawnder iti siarad Latin,
> A sôn am dy Gariad, wastad wedd,
> Ni wn i am ei rinwedd ronyn.

> Y Cariad mwya' wn i amdano
> Ydyw ŷd ac enllyn i ymgynllwyn ag efo;
> Ceffylau a defaid a gwartheg iach,
> A chlywed llo bach yn beichio.

CARIAD: Mae'r rheini'n dda i'w lle a'u helynt;
           Ni wiw i neb roi'i galon ynddynt.
           Pethau'r byd i gyd sy'n darfod
           A thragwyddoldeb maith yn dyfod.   (CO)

[LOVE: The true and willing love will suffer long and patiently; it will
never once be envious, its inclination is kindly. Pure love does not
vaunt itself in jealous desire, and is not puffed-up; it thinks no evil,
there is no arrogance or unseemliness in it. It does not rejoice in
iniquity, but it always rejoices in the truth; it is patient, wise and good
through purity and faithfulness. ALIS: Well, for a farthing you might
as well talk entirely in Latin, and speaking of your love and its constant
aspect, I know not a whit of its virtue. The greatest love that I know of
is corn and victuals to concern myself with, horses and sheep and
healthy cows, and hearing a little calf lowing. L: Those are good in their
place and for their purpose; but no one should set his heart on them.
All the things of earth come to an end, and vast eternity draws near.]

Some will respond and some will not. Today we would probably
refer to 'genes', and most of Twm's contemporaries would refer to
'election'. Still the call goes out to all, as in the concluding words
of *Pedair Colofn Gwladwriaeth*:

           Gan hynny mae gair yn dywedyd,
           'Dewch bawb i'r dyfroedd hyfryd,'
           Mae'r bywyd yma ar ben;
           Er sôn am bob helyntion, adnabod ffyrdd ein calon,
           Sydd reitia' moddion i ni, Amen.

[Therefore it has been said, 'Come, all, to the pleasant waters,' this life
is at an end; whatever the matters we talk of, to know the ways of our
own hearts is the most needful remedy for us, Amen.]

Here, as elsewhere, Twm's message seems indistinguishable from
that of his contemporaries, the evangelical preachers called
Methodists. From time to time he had said—or at least allowed his
characters to say—some caustic things about them. But
increasingly as he grew older he felt drawn towards them and
defended them publicly against Anglican attacks. He must have
recognized their message as a traditional one which came close to
his own understanding of the Gospel. His last public appearance,
on 17 February 1810, was at the consecration of a new Methodist

chapel at Tremadog. It must have cost him the suppression of a considerable part of himself.

Twm o'r Nant is among the most quotable of Welsh authors, and some of his aphorisms became part of country wisdom. Like Bernard Shaw, he has to be the one who said it—even if we are not sure. Let us end with a few handy quotations from this master of the sound-bite. On Baptists:

> Wel ond y Dippers sy bron mynd yn dopie;
> Mae hwy braidd yr un egwyddor â'r hwyaid a'r gwydde
> Yn trochi ei gilydd tan ochr y geulan
> Fel y golchont hwy bechod mawr a bychan.   (PG)

[Well it's the Dippers nearly going mad; more or less on the same principle as the ducks and geese, they douse each other under the riverbank so as to wash away the sin of great and small.]

On the country-sports lobby:

> Wel, maen nhw i'w canmol draw ac yma,
> Am roi cynhaliaeth i'w cŵn hela;
> Maent yn llawnach o flawd, mi glywais sôn,
> Yn eu bolie na thylodion y Bala.   (TChB)

[Well, they are to be commended, here and there, for the sustenance they give their hunting-hounds; those, I have heard it said, have their bellies fuller of flour than the poor people of Bala.]

On the old universities:

ESGOB: Ni fuost ti erioed, un ffôl ei ledpen,
             O fewn Cambridge na Rhydychen.

SYR RHYS: Ni chadd y rhai fu yno fawr wellhad:
             Ni waeth i ni'n gwlad ein hunen.   (PCG)

[BISHOP: A dolt-head like you has never been inside Cambridge or Oxford. S.RH: Those who've been there aren't much better for it: we might as well stay at home.]

And the final verdict on sex education:

Chwi glywsoch lawer cyngor cryno,
Rhwng pob ffyliaid; ond mae'r cwbl yn ffaelio.
Po amla rhybudd, mewn llan a phlwy,
Yn ei herwydd mae mwy o hwrio.   (PCG)

[Many a tidy piece of advice you've heard, among all fools; but it's all in vain. The oftener the warning, in church and parish, all the more whoring as a result.]

BIBLIOGRAPHY

G. M. Ashton, *Anterliwtiau Twm o'r Nant: Pedair Colofn Gwladwriaeth a Cybydd-dod ac Oferedd* (Caerdydd, 1964).

Idem, *Hunangofiant a Llythyrau Twm o'r Nant* (Caerdydd, 1948).

G. G. Evans, *Elis y Cowper* (Caernarfon 1995).

Idem, 'Yr anterliwt Gymraeg', *Llên Cymru*, 1 (1950), 83-96, 224–31.

Idem, 'Er mwyniant i'r cwmpeini mwynion', *Taliesin*, 51 (Ebrill 1985), 31–43.

Idem, 'Henaint a thranc yr anterliwt', *Taliesin*, 54 (Nadolig 1985), 14–29.

Idem, 'Sut un oedd Twm o'r Nant?' *Taliesin*, 74 (Haf 1991), 76-81.

Isaac Foulkes (ed.), *Gwaith Thomas Edwards (Twm o'r Nant)* (Lerpwl, 1874).

Rhiannon Ifans, *Cân Di Bennill . . .? Themâu Anterliwtiau Twm o'r Nant* (Aberystwyth, 1997).

Idem, 'Celfyddyd y cantor o'r Nant', in J. E. Caerwyn Williams (ed.), *Ysgrifau Beirniadol XXI* (Dinbych, 1996), 120–46.

Norah Isaac (ed.), *Tri Chryfion Byd* (Llandysul, 1975).

A. Watkin Jones, 'The interludes of Wales in the eighteenth century', *Bulletin of the Board of Celtic Studies*, 4 (1928), 103–11.

Bobi Jones, 'Twm o'r Nant', *I'r Arch* (Llandybïe, 1959), 47–69.

Dafydd Glyn Jones, 'Thomas Williams yr anterliwtiwr', *Caernarvonshire Historical Society Transactions*, 57 (1996), 7-45.

Emyr Ll. Jones (ed.), *Tri Chryfion Byd* (Doc Penfro, 1962).

Emyr Wyn Jones (ed.), *Yr Anterliwt Goll* (Aberystwyth, 1984).

Idem, 'Rhai Methodistiaid a'r anterliwt', *Taliesin*, 57 (Hydref 1986), 8–19.

T. J. Rhys Jones, 'Yr anterliwtiau', in Dyfnallt Morgan (ed.), *Gwŷr Llên y Ddeunawfed Ganrif* (Llandybïe, 1966), 147–55.

A. Cynfael Lake, 'Cipdrem ar anterliwtiau Twm o'r Nant', *Llên Cymru*, 21 (1998), 50–73.

Saunders Lewis, 'Twm o'r Nant', in *Meistri'r Canrifoedd* (Caerdydd, 1973), 280–98.

Cecil Price, *The English Theatre in Wales in the Eighteenth and Early Nineteenth Centuries* (Cardiff, 1948), ch. IX.

Kate Roberts, 'Thomas Edwards (Twm o'r Nant)', in Dyfnallt Morgan (ed.), *Gwŷr Llên y Ddeunawfed Ganrif* (Llandybïe, 1966), 156–63.

D. D. Williams, *Twm o'r Nant* (Bangor, 1911).

Gareth Haulfryn Williams, 'Anterliwt Derwyn Fechan, 1654', *Caernarvonshire Historical Society Transactions*, 44 (1983), 53–8.

CHAPTER 11

WILLIAMS PANTYCELYN

KATHRYN JENKINS

Early in 1762 Britain declared war on Spain, Peter III ascended the throne of Russia, and Frederick II of Prussia signed a peace treaty with Sweden. At about the same time, rural Cardiganshire experienced a series of events which would define the ethos of the Welsh nation for some two centuries. The epicentre of these incidents was Llangeitho, a small village about fifteen miles south-east of Aberystwyth. It was there in 1762 that the preaching of a middle-aged Anglican clergyman produced dramatic results. The emotion engendered by his exhortations, enhanced and sustained by joyous hymn-singing, together with a number of startling and often mystifying effects consistent with a state of 'enthusiasm'—a collective emotional outpouring of experiences of the Holy Spirit—gave rise to the 'Great Awakening'. The influence of this revival spread throughout Wales and resulted in the eventual establishment of a new Nonconformist denomination, the Calvinistic Methodists, or the Presbyterian Church of Wales as it is called today. The preacher at Llangeitho was Daniel Rowland, ably assisted by William Williams, Pantycelyn, author of the intensely personal hymns which were possibly the chief catalyst of the awakening, and most certainly one of its main channels of success. The events at Llangeitho proved to be a turning-point in the history and development of the Methodist cause in Wales and in Williams's own literary career.

Williams's seminal religious experience had, however, occurred some twenty-five years before the Great Awakening at Llangeitho. The story is often recounted: a young student cherishes an ambition to be a physician and is studying at the Nonconformist Academy at Llwyn-llwyd, near Hay-on-Wye; one morning he stumbles on an open-air service in the nearby churchyard of Talgarth where another young man, 'full of bright fiery sparks', is preaching powerfully on the merits of the blood of Christ shed at the time of the Crucifixion; he experiences a dramatic conversion. The proclaimer of the gospel message on that fateful morning was Howel Harris, who, together with Williams and Rowland, formed the zealous and dynamic trinity of young leaders who are considered to be the founding fathers of Methodism in Wales. We are fortunate that, in his elegy to Harris in 1773, Williams has described his conversion and the content of the sermon which convinced him that he must become *homo regenitus*:

> Haeddiant IESU yw ei araeth,
> Cysur enaid a'i iachâd,
> Ac euogrwydd dua pechod
> Wedi ei ganu yn y gwaed.

[The merit of Jesus is in his words, which bring comfort and healing to the soul, and in that the blackest guilt of sin has been bleached in the blood.]

As a writer, Williams re-created this doctrine and emotion on countless occasions in verse and prose, in works which gained universal approbation within the Methodist movement and which represent a significant qualitative leap in Welsh literature and religious imagination.

There have been few more prolific writers in Wales than Williams Pantycelyn. More than ninety publications bearing his name appeared during his lifetime (1717–91). The scope and variety of these works are truly astonishing: more than a thousand hymns, approximately eight hundred of which are in Welsh; two epic poems running to thousands of lines; a collection of prose works; and more than thirty elegies. What emerges most clearly from his work, however, is that pragmatic and spiritual concerns about the condition of the Methodist cause were of far greater importance to Williams than the literary or aesthetic merit of his works. It is not that he was unaware of the development and importance of his literary career but that this was always seen in the context of his work's relevance to the spirituality of the Methodist movement and of his intrinsic concern for the salvation of his people's souls. It was because of these concerns that Williams consistently buckled under the pressure of what might be termed market forces, allowing his work to go to press before he could delete all errors and flaws. In this respect, the introductory remarks he used to preface many of his works provide invaluable information on his strategy as the anointed author of Welsh Methodism. In his preface to the first of his two epic poems in 1756 he makes this remarkably candid admission:

> Whosoever sets about studying this poetry in detail, I know that there is not one verse here without blemish. And this is what deterred me on many occasions from sending it to be printed. And the more I retain it, the more I am revising it. But I fear that to withhold it any longer would take away its relish. Therefore may it go as it is. (tr.)

Such creative constraints have obviously taken their toll on the artistic value of a considerable amount of Williams's work, and his Welsh output certainly suffered to a greater extent than his English works, whose diction and rhetoric predominantly correspond to the classical conventions of the age. The task of the critic, therefore, in presenting a balanced view of Williams's output is tantalizingly difficult and frustrating; yet in the finest of his work, it is not difficult to recognize his innate literary genius.

It is particularly significant that Williams was acknowledged as a spiritual and pragmatic leader of Welsh Methodism at the same time as he began to publish his literary works. Indeed, only some three months separate his recognition as a shining star among the Methodists and the publication of his first hymns. At a meeting of the Association (a gathering of leaders, exhorters and the faithful to organize the movement's work) at Trefeca on 27 June 1744, Williams was charged for the first time with the responsibility of acting as superintendent over various society meetings in north Cardiganshire. The term 'society' requires further explanation, for it was the most important and defining element of the Methodist movement. The *seiat*, to use the Welsh term, was an intense form of spiritual group therapy, an almost masochistic approach to the problems of sin and guilt in the Christian life or, as that observant character, Wil Bryan, in Daniel Owen's nineteenth-century novel *Rhys Lewis* described it: 'a lot of good people, fearing they are evil, and who meet every Tuesday night to place blame and denigrate one another'. Williams showed a prodigious talent for this kind of work, for in many ways he was far more personable than either Rowland or Harris. So it was that in June 1744 we see the

beginning of his official public career as one of Welsh Methodism's most competent leaders. The minutes of the Association at
Trefeca read thus:

> Agreed that Bro. Willm Williams shd visit the Societies in ye upper part
> of Cardiganshire on tryall till our next General Association.

The Association met again in Trefeca in October that year. In the
mean time, Williams and Rowland travelled to north Wales and
enjoyed a successful, unopposed visit. A considerable part of the
summer must have been spent in north Cardiganshire, visiting and
inspecting the society meetings at Llangwyryfon, Lledrod, Pen-y-
lan, Rhydfendigaid and Tan-yr-allt, which had a total of 128
members. It is clear from Williams's report, read at the Association on 27 October, that he was most diligent in his duties, for it
contains a timetable of all meetings held, together with the names
of those who were exhorting and reports on the quality of their
work. Of greatest significance, however, are Williams's comments
on the spirituality of the meetings and the condition of their
members. Although he was only twenty-seven, it is clear that he
already possessed a valuable understanding of spiritual experience
and the purpose and importance of the society meeting. This
sagacity would demonstrate itself on countless other occasions in
his later literary career. What is even more startling at this stage,
however, is the depth and complexity of spiritual experience that
he began to describe in his early hymns.

The small first volume of Williams's hymns, *Aleluia*, was
published towards the end of September 1744 by Samuel Lewis of
Carmarthen, one of the network of printers he regularly used, the
others being in Bristol, Brecon and Llandovery. This first part of
Aleluia contained just nine hymns and sold for a penny but,
however lowly it may appear, its significance cannot be overstated.
Harris and Rowland had both tried their hand at hymn-writing—
presumably out of sheer necessity and because of the weight of
demand—and had not displayed any great talent, although some
of Rowland's work is moderately acceptable. Methodism needed
to find a prolific poetic voice that could encapsulate in the verses
of a hymn the doctrine heard from the pulpits of Rowland and
Harris as well as the passionate emotions experienced by young
regenerate souls. Williams's early hymns are not totally inspiring:

he clearly has problems with even some of the basic prosodic skills
(perhaps an inevitable result of his English education at Llwyn-
llwyd), yet all the characteristics of his more mature work are
already present. In his verses it is always the individual believer
who is at the heart of the unfolding spiritual drama and trauma,
and the various aspects of the Christian life are frequently portrayed within the huge scheme of divine providence encountered in
the Scriptures:

> Pa'm 'r ofnaf mwy Elynjon Lû,
>   'Rw'i 'n llechu yn ei Go'l?
> Ac yn ei Glwyfau gwnes fy Nyth,
>   Pa'm deuaf byth yn ol?
> Wrth f'Ystlys, Deng-mil cwymp i'r Llawr,
>   Fy nghadw ma E rhag Briw a Brad
> Annwyl IESU dygaist fi,
>   I'r wledd sy *Nghanaan* wlad.

[Why fear further a legion of enemies? I am lurking in his bosom. And
in his wounds I made my nest, why should I ever backslide? By my side,
ten thousand fall, he keeps me from hurt and treachery, dear Jesus you
have brought me to the feast in the land of Canaan.]

Here there is allusion to the Book of Psalms and the Song of Songs
and to the plan of *heilsgeschichte* which underpins the Old Testament. It is also clearly an intentional part of the hymnist's
technique to entice the reader or singer into the complex psychological activity at the heart of the hymn, where the quality of
salvation is intimated.

What is emerging by the summer and autumn of 1744 is a picture
of a young man of considerable education and erudition, who has
enormous personal appeal and talent, and who, with great stamina
and zeal, is applying himself to promulgating the Methodist cause
in every way known to him. Henceforth, he alone would be the
author and entrepreneur *extraordinaire* of first-generation Methodism. The vicissitudes of that movement's development would,
however, both impede and inspire him in decades to come.

As Methodism gathered momentum and the need for close co-
operation between its leaders became essential, it also became
obvious that a clash of personalities existed between Harris on the
one hand, and Rowland and Williams on the other. Harris was

impatient, totally lacking a sense of humour and authoritarian, yet a superb organizer. Rowland, it is said, was the fickle, short-tempered but glorious master of the preaching theatre which he had created for himself at Llangeitho. Williams was, geographically and personally, stranded in the middle. By the end of the 1740s, Harris had become bombastic and dogmatic and was increasingly accused of the heresy of Patripassianism, a polemic concerned with whether or not God the Father suffered on the Cross. To further exacerbate the situation, Harris continually appeared in public with an indomitable married woman, Madam Sydney Griffith, who did nothing for his standing in the movement. Matters came to a head in May 1750, at an Association held at Llanidloes, and the Great Schism, as it has been called, occurred. Harris was not to be reconciled to his fellow leaders for another twelve years, during which time the movement suffered greatly from a lack of cohesion. What was Williams to do? He was by now a married man with a young and growing family; he was already recognized as Methodism's chief literary advocate, having published six parts of *Aleluia*, and with another work, *Hosanna i Fab Dafydd* (Hosanna to the Son of David; published in two parts, 1751 and 1754), already in preparation. He spent more and more of his time at home, studying and meditating on those subjects closest to his heart, and attempting to reconcile Harris and Rowland.

The crowning achievement of this enforced 'sabbatical'—though to suggest that Williams shied away from his previous duties would be quite wrong—was an epic poem, *Golwg ar Deyrnas Crist* (A View of Christ's Kingdom), first published in 1756. It has been strikingly described by Saunders Lewis as a failure, and in many ways he is right. With 1,367 verses it is insufferably long and monotonous, yet it was a pioneering work in eighteenth-century Wales. Its purpose was at least twofold, as explained by the author in his introduction. He focuses on what he considers to be the orthodox view of the person of Christ in a clear attempt to eradicate any misunderstandings which existed between Harris and Rowland, and possibly even to effect a reconciliation. But there was a further aim to this epic, which is also explained. Williams was reacting against the forces of science and deism that were already, in the mid-eighteenth century, contriving to undermine the tenets of revealed religion. Newton had published

his *Principia* in 1687 and his *Opticks* in 1704. Although Newton's
universe displayed law and order—'A mighty maze but not
without a plan!' (Pope)—it had no religious mystery. To Williams,
as both a Christian and a former science student, this was totally
unacceptable. He sided rather with theological scientists such as
William Derham and James Hervey, who saw scientific discovery
as merely proclaiming more loudly the glory of the Creator. Also,
between 1742 and 1746, Edward Young's *Night Thoughts* was
published and gained great acclaim as a Christian apologetic
confuting both atheism and deism. Williams's epic owes at least
something to all three works, for he sees science as validating
Scripture, and scientific facts being reconciled with faith. The
poem sets out to be an all-inclusive description of divine providence emanating from eternity and, through time and creation,
returning to eternity at the fulfilment of all things. The hero is
Christ himself as the chosen instrument of man's salvation:

> O IESU, mae'th ragluniaeth fath anferth led a hyd,
>   Mae'n dallu, mae'n terfysgu y doethaf yn y byd;
> Mae'n cyrhaedd at bob gweithred, y da a'r drwg yn un,
>   A neb 'd oes yn ei deall yn unig ond dy hun.

[O! Jesus, your providence is so huge in length and breadth! It blinds, it
troubles the wisest in the world; it reaches every act, the good and bad
as one, none can understand it but yourself.]

It has been suggested that *Golwg ar Deyrnas Crist* is more than the
sum of its parts. To a modern reader, the text can appear repetitive
and tedious in the extreme, yet its significance to the Methodist
cause, and indeed to the history of Wales, is of the utmost
importance because Williams created a groundswell of opinion
against the scientific revolution begun by Copernicus some 150
years earlier. This ensured that the popular enlightenment of the
eighteenth century did not affect Wales in general for quite some
time.

By the end of the 1750s, it had become clear that Methodism
might peter out. Williams was clearly discouraged. He had published a third edition of *Aleluia* in 1758; according to Thomas
Charles the preparation of his first epic, *Golwg ar Deyrnas Crist*,
had taken a toll on his health; and he had began to compose

elegies to early converts of the 1730s and 1740s who had died from tuberculosis or illnesses related to the poor quality of life in rural Wales at that time. By 1760–1 Williams had begun work on his third volume of hymns. His introductory remarks to this volume reveal the poet in sombre, introspective mood, not only regarding his own performance as the hymnist of his people, but also reflecting the condition of Methodism itself.

He states despondently that these hymns, *Caniadau y rhai sydd ar y Môr o Wydr* (The Songs of those on the Sea of Glass—a reference to the Book of Revelation), will be the last he will ever produce. Why he said this is unclear, though it was probably the condition of the Methodist movement which weighed particularly heavily upon him. There are a number of hymns which dwell on the poor condition of the Church in the wilderness, and the supplications for sustenance and consolation may be seen as a sincere reflection of his thoughts and experience. Yet he also states, in some introductory verses, that these hymns represent a considerable qualitative progression, experientially, spiritually and in terms of literary skill. He is absolutely correct. The hymns in this volume cover a wide spectrum of Christian experience and are not just the expression of *certitudo salutis* (the certainty of salvation) found so frequently in his earlier work. Now, also, his literary art is inextricably linked to the joys and anxieties he expresses:

> O am nerth i dreulio'm dyddiau
> > Yng nghynteddau tŷ fy Nhad;
> Byw yng nghanol y goleuni,
> > Twllwch obry dan fy nhra'd;
> Byw heb fachlud haul un amser,
> > Byw heb gwmwl, byw heb boen,
> Byw ar gariad anorchfygol
> > Pur y croeshoeliedig Oen.

[O for strength to spend my days in the vestibules of my Father's house; to live at the centre of the light, darkness below under my feet; to live without ever the sun setting, to live without a cloud, to live without pain, to live on the invincible, pure love of the crucified Lamb.]

Williams had become a master of repetition for cumulative effect; he had also gained sufficient confidence to use enjambment as a device to control the syntax's centre of gravity. As always, of course, his vision is thoroughly Christo-centric: the crucified Saviour whose death transforms the life of the sinner is always the object of his love and contemplation.

It is part of Welsh Methodism's mythology that, when Williams took this third volume of hymns to Llangeitho in 1762, the Great Awakening referred to earlier broke out and established Methodism once more as a force to be reckoned with on the religious scene. Such was the strength of this awakening that the influence of Methodism spread throughout the whole of Wales, even to areas outside the main activities of its leaders. The new-found success of the movement also meant that reconciliation was at last possible with Harris, who returned to the fold, as it were, in 1763, though by now he was a spent force. However, the most important consequence of the awakening for Williams is that it gave fresh impetus to his muse. Indeed, his literary career can be divided into two unequal parts: his gradual maturity from 1744 until 1762, including publishing *Golwg ar Deyrnas Crist*; and his development after the awakening at Llangeitho in 1762, which began a rush of creative activity which produced prose works, another epic poem, a substantial number of elegies, and at least two further major collections containing a total of about four hundred hymns. The prose works are probably the most interesting development in Williams's career at this time. They are his attempt to define and analyse the conversion experience which was gripping so many young men and women, and it is fair to claim that through them he offered an apologia for some of the outward signs of enthusiasm. In this respect, these works may be considered either as totally biased propaganda in favour of the Methodist movement, or as a brave attempt to offer a literary defence of phenomena which were totally new to Welsh life.

The first of Williams's prose works was published in 1762, the year of the Great Awakening. It is a short work in the form of a letter purporting to be an account of the thoughts of a young woman who has recently experienced conversion and who wishes to share some of the consequences with a spiritual counsellor. *Llythyr Martha Philopur* (Martha Philopur's Letter) is an interesting work in many ways, and it sheds light on much of Williams's prose output. The literary form of the work is, of course, totally conventional. The three most familiar prose forms at this time, which were inherited from Puritan literature, were the letter, the dialogue and the travel journal, and it is these which Williams used. They suited his objectives well: the theological and historical necessity of giving the impression of accuracy and fidelity in the account of religious experience could be sustained easily in the form of a letter, where the reader eavesdrops, as it were, on a living experience; and the dialogue form allows for the development of reasoned argument. It is also highly significant that the central character in Williams's first prose work is a young woman. This was often the case in the burgeoning novel of this period in English literature, though the portrayal of a woman's character was very much polarized between Daniel Defoe's *Moll Flanders* (1722) and Samuel Richardson's *Clarissa* (1747–9). In Welsh literature, however, there had been very little discussion of women's experiences and emotions, and it would be fair to claim that Williams is the first author to give women a central role in some of his works. Martha Philopur, an imaginary figure, here representing the hordes of young people who must have been clamouring for an explanation of their experiences, describes the psychological and emotional trauma of conversion:

> but when I saw my pitiful state (and I'll remember the place, the hour, the sermon and the preacher, while I breathe in the land of the living), I saw it so profoundly that I could never again be happy . . . the light dawned upon me. I felt in a moment that my sin had been forgiven . . . I have within me a new spirit that I never before possessed. (tr.)

The work concludes with a list and analysis of sixteen extracts from Scripture which are meant to validate the contents of the letter. It is clear that Williams was aware that he was dealing with a religion and an experience which had at least three dimensions: personal, congregational and scriptural.

Williams published the reply to Martha's letter a year later in 1763, *Atteb Philo-Evangelius* (Philo-Evangelius' Response). It is difficult not to conclude that he is here declaring his own stand-point on the phenomena of conversion and revival. The writing is vivacious, if somewhat presumptuous, and much of its power depends on the use of an almost subliminal leitmotiv, *'o'r Arglwydd y mae'r gwaith'* (it is the Lord's work). The language is prophetic, for this revival is the fulfilment of an age-old promise, and so we have echoes of famous Old Testament passages: the description of the valley of the dry bones in Ezekiel and the consolation of Isaiah chapter 40, among others. Ultimately, the awakening is portrayed as Wales's very own Pentecost:

> O heyday! it came, it came. Houses and chapels had been built to welcome it. Bibles filled the country when it began to direct the pilgrims homewards. Psalms, hymns and sacred songs were mature by the time the dawn broke . . . O Martha, sing! (tr.)

Philo-Evangelius does not mince his words, and he states quite categorically that the fact that this new religion is the subject of persecution is a mark of its validity and truth. Such writing must have had tremendous impact on its original readers, and it is noteworthy that, throughout this short yet potent work, Williams places much emphasis on the integral part that hymn-singing plays in the revival. Although much of the enthusiasm described here is alien to a modern-day reader, on a literary level alone Williams proves himself to be a succinct and cogent writer.

These first two prose works can only be appreciated in the context of occurrences at Llangeitho in 1762. The Great Awakening provided Williams with an eager new readership, and it soon became clear that the pastoral and civic needs of the new converts were legion. He therefore set about writing works that would address such issues as maintaining the fellowship of the church, civil duty and constancy in marriage. These works must be understood and appreciated primarily in the light of the needs of the expanding Methodist community for, if we begin to assess them purely as literary works, their shortcomings become obvious. Welsh prose at this time could so easily have developed in the same way as the novel in English literature, even though social circumstances in Wales were entirely different from those in England. The fact that it did not is due in no small part to Williams's own prose writing. He uses the storyline, characters and dialogue to fulfil his aims of moral inculcation: his is a didactic style befitting the needs of the Methodists' literary pedagogue. To him, the message is of far greater significance than the literary mode by which it is conveyed. In many of his prose works therefore, although there is obvious potential for the development of a sustained creative prose-style suitable for an early novel, Williams instead stifles the literary zest and momentum of his works in favour of ensuring the efficacy of his moral teaching.

His priorities can be seen quite clearly in two works which, nevertheless, have considerable credence and appeal. The first is *Hanes Bywyd a Marwolaeth Tri Wŷr o Sodom a'r Aipht* (The History of the Life and Death of Three Men of Sodom and Egypt). Published in 1768, it recounts the conduct and eternal fate of Afaritius, Prodigalus and Ffidelius, in much the same style as *The Life and Death of Mr Badman* by John Bunyan. They are archetypal characters with transparent names, exemplifying human traits which have been observed and portrayed on countless occasions throughout the ages. The piquancy of the writing is delicious as Afaritius and Prodigalus are condemned to eternal torture for their avarice and wayward life-style. However, the more solemn description of Ffidelius' integrity, which has both inward spiritual and outward altruistic manifestations, is twice as long as the preceding sections. As Williams states, his aim was to delineate an exemplary character 'in the noonday light', and at this level, of course, he succeeds. The other work which has the potential to be a novel is *Ductor Nuptiarum* or, in Welsh, *Cyfarwyddwr Priodas* (A Marriage Guide), published in 1777, in which the first three dialogues deal with the marital torments or triumphs of two young women, Mary and Martha. This work, similar to Martha Philopur's Letter, is unusual in the context of both English and Welsh literature, since it again places women to the fore, advocating faithfulness in marriage, and chastity as a foundation of personal morality. Williams's natural pastoral instinct realized that those who experienced dynamic and passionate spiritual emotions were also likely to seek physical satiation, and his eagerness to protect his people from possible transgressions is an all-important aspect of this work. Both Mary and Martha are eloquent and circumspect and are given considerable scope to portray their circumstances by the author. However, his didactic motive is far stronger than his artistic integrity and as a result the third dialogue, where Mary advises Martha to restore Christianity to the hearth, is a far lengthier treatment than that of the beleaguered Martha's description of her tribulations—a depiction that has great veracity and humour.

Many have argued that Williams's finest prose work is his analysis of the spirituality of the *seiat*. *Drws y Society Profiad* (The Door of the Experience Society) was published in 1777, and takes the form of a dialogue in seven parts between Theophilus and

Eusebius, who discuss the quality of religion and extol at length the
virtues of the *seiat*. The first part of this work is notable in that
it contains propaganda in favour of the Methodist movement in
much the same vein as Philo-Evangelius' Response. The remainder
consists of a systematic treatment of the aims, benefits and personae
of the *seiat*. This is an admirable exercise which succeeds to a great
extent, and on all levels. Williams's prose style complements well
the logical explanations he wishes to set before his readers. In
considering the content of the work it is impossible not to admire
the detailed analysis and the sagacious, pragmatic treatment which
is presented. His faith in the *seiat*'s inherent probity is unshakeable:

> to scold, to direct, to build and to support weak members who are
> ready to stray to one side, either to lust, pleasure, or the love of trinkets
> on the one hand, or to pride, impudence, self-importance or envy on
> the other, or otherwise be attracted by the wiles of men to deceit, to
> false and untrue doctrine, and to various other things which have done
> great harm to God's saints. (tr.)

Williams must surely be commended for such an able dissection of
man's tendency to transgress. His humanity is much in evidence in
this work, as is his balanced psychology: some thirty years of
counselling proved a firm foundation on which to construct such a
treatise.

The diversity and range of Williams's prose works are truly
remarkable, as is the quantity he produced, if his many other
activities as a central figure in the Methodist movement are also
considered. There is one work in particular which demonstrates how
versatile and conscientious an author he actually was. *Pantheologia*
is a history of world religions related as a travelogue, published in
seven parts between 1762 and 1779 at a total price of three shillings.
The travelogue was a common form of prose writing at this time,
with Defoe, Fielding, Sterne and Smollet each using it. Although the
form might therefore be considered somewhat conventional,
Williams uses it in a totally original way. In the case of the English
authors, their travelogues purport to recount their actual experiences when travelling to such countries as France and Italy, and it is
therefore their own egos which are at the centre of the work.
Pantheologia on the other hand reveals Williams as a pioneer in
adult education and the study of comparative religion: his are the

intentions of a continuing education tutor. His perspective is very different from that of popular writing because he sees the world in a different light, not as opening up possible locations for the travel of a refined gentleman, but rather as a dark and threatening mission field, where the light of the Gospel must be given ample opportunity to shine. However laudable his aims in this work, it must be said that *Pantheologia* was not well received. He includes a long apologia for his religious travelogue at the end of a translation he published in 1779, and his introduction to the work also contains some biting scorn about the ignorance of his would-be readers. As a writer he may well have felt that this was his *magnum opus* in the field of adult education; his readers, quite clearly, thought differently. What is significant, though, is that this work is without corollary in the whole of Welsh literature, and this might well explain the author's problems with his readership at the time, as well as the neglect of the work by critics since then.

Williams's prose writing is just one of the obvious consequences of the Great Awakening of 1762. In 1763, at the end of a volume of hymns, the publisher John Ross of Carmarthen placed an advertisement for other works that were then going to press: the second part of *Pantheologia*, a second edition of *Golwg ar Deyrnas Crist*, and a new epic poem, *Bywyd a Marwolaeth Theomemphus* (The Life and Death of Theomemphus), which was duly published in 1764. There has probably been more speculation about this work than about any other by Williams, much of it caused by the author's own laconic introductory remarks. As a literary enterprise, *Theomemphus* is on the same scale as Williams's first epic poem, some 6,000 lines in 1,500 verses, and could likewise be deemed to be insufferably long and monotonous. Some critics have considered it to be an embodiment of the doctrine of the Methodist movement at this time. Williams himself makes a number of quite startling claims in his introduction. He considers the work to be dramatic prosody (*prydyddiaeth ddramatig*) of a kind for which there is no precedent in English, Welsh or Latin. His ambition is that it should benefit others because of its description of a believer's trials and tribulations. He acknowledges that Bunyan has already trodden this path, but claims that his writing was incomplete since it did not sufficiently duplicate the biblical exemplar of the Christian life. Unlike the latter's ageless classic *Pilgrim's Progress*, Williams claims that *Theomemphus* is

not an allegory, but that the characters and heresies represented
during the hero's arduous pilgrimage are true figures. Clearly this
raises the question of whether Theomemphus is a portrayal of the
author himself: if so, nearly two and a half centuries of Methodist
apologetics would have difficulty in extricating Williams's reputation from such accusations as bestiality and homosexuality, not to
mention adultery and murder. The author states directly, however,
that neither he nor the faithful of the *seiadau*, whom he has
counselled over the years, are present in this work. This admission
is difficult to accept since it is incredible that he could write in such
a way about the Christian life without drawing on his own experience and those of others. It is likely, therefore, that Theomemphus
is a composite character whose experiences are drawn from the
joys and disappointments of countless Methodist converts—
including the author himself—with, of course, an added dose of
imagination contributing to the obvious hyperbole used in describing the hero's trespasses at the beginning of the poem.

Theomemphus is, as has been said, overlong, and various critics
have highlighted different aspects of the poem's structure and
content. The nucleus of the poem is a sermon that is recounted in
Chapter Five and is delivered by Efangelius, who is generally
believed to represent Daniel Rowland. This is the second sermon,
or the sixth presentation of the 'truth' to be heard by Theomemphus. The first, by Boanerges (possibly Howel Harris), on
justification by faith, had only a temporary impact on him. Having
received further representations from Orthocephalus and Schemat-
icus, among others—allegorical yet concrete portrayals of various
Christian sects and beliefs—Theomemphus needs to be convinced
further. Efangelius' sermon probably contains the clearest statement of Methodist interpretation of the Gospel to be found in the
whole of Williams's work:

> 'R Efengyl wy'n bregethu, nid yw hi ddim ond hyn,
> Mynegi'r weithred ryfedd wnawd ar Galfaria fryn;
> Cyhoeddi'r addewidion, cyhoeddi'r marwol glwy',
> A diwedd llygredigaeth i'r sawl a gredo mwy.

[The Gospel I preach is merely this, the proclamation of Calvary's
wondrous act; to announce the promises, to announce the mortal
wound, and an end of corruption henceforth for all who might believe.]

It is the crucified Christ who is the instrument of salvation, and those desiring eternal life must love and believe in Him. Theomemphus is duly converted, as his meditations in Chapter Six clearly show, but there are twenty chapters in this epic, and he has an extremely prolonged pilgrimage of sanctification to face. However, he is well assisted on his way by Dr Aletheius, his personal counsellor. He still has to wrestle with countless heresies, not to mention the temptations and tribulations he encounters in his relationships with members of the opposite sex—Philomela, Jezebel and Philomede, each of whom would, for varying reasons, drive any normal man to distraction. But this is an epic, and Theomemphus in so many ways, as both saint and sinner, is superhuman.

Reading *Theomemphus* is a strange and laborious experience for a modern reader, though it has been famously described by Saunders Lewis as the first great poem of the European Romantic movement. Much of Williams's literary output leaves us confounded: the content is disconcerting to the reader because of the intense focus on characterization and doctrine. His style is a meeting of ancient and modern, conventional and original: for example, such a stark and balanced prose-style as Williams possesses would be quite at home in a passage of Middle Welsh, and yet the intricacies that he uses to portray his character's psychological and spiritual complexities are virtually coterminous with modern poetry and prose. Whatever our difficulties might be with his works, however, we must never lose sight of their overall popularity at the time they were written. Although, as has been mentioned, not everyone wanted a copy of *Pantheologia*, Williams's works were the best-sellers of their day. It is difficult to imagine now, but in 1781, at the time of another revival at Llangeitho and when he was enjoying something of an Indian summer as a writer, he decided to republish *Theomemphus*—on condition that 1,000 subscribers pledged their support at short notice. This they certainly did, since a second edition of the epic was indeed published that year. As has already been suggested, market forces were a powerful influence on Williams's literary career, which was one of the most important in the whole of Welsh literature.

As he grew older, and particularly by the onset of middle age, Williams was faced with the prospect of losing some of his closest friends and allies. Life expectancy at this time was low, and diseases such as tuberculosis were rife. It became necessary, therefore, for him to write the poetic obituaries of the great and the good of the Methodist movement. His elegies are reliable historical documents containing depictions of sterling men and women, though the prosody is uninspiring. Williams's first elegy appeared in 1757, and his last—to Daniel Rowland—at the time of his own death early in 1791. He composed elegies in both English and Welsh, to the leaders of the movement and to the virtually anonymous adherents who were the otherwise unsung heroes of early Methodism. Some of these poems today raise a gentle smile because of the poet's use of the whimsical and baroque device of allowing the departed to speak from beyond the grave: how else could he imprint on Methodist minds that heaven was a glorious place filled with harmonious singing? Another aspect of the elegies relates to Williams's original ambition to become a doctor. For example, in his elegy to William Richard, who had acted as a superintendent of numerous *seiadau* since 1743 and who died in 1770, he describes in the most graphic detail the terminal symptoms of tuberculosis. It is also noteworthy that Williams draws attention to the role that a number of women had played in the early development of the Methodist movement, noting their conversions, their loyalty, the quality of their spiritual lives and their practical kindness in offering him hospitality on long preaching tours. Perhaps the most striking feature of the elegies, however, is that in his contemplation of the heavens and matters eschatological, Williams follows a theme similar to that of his first epic poem, and presents us with a thoroughly orthodox Christian view of the universe, one that is diametrically opposed to Newtonian and deist thought. For example, in his elegy to Lewis Lewis, a clergyman from Llanddeiniol near Aberystwyth who died on 9 June 1764, Williams uses the departed to express his own views on the value of the then modern scientific thinking:

> Nid yw doniau mawrion Newton
> O fawr gyfrif yn y nef;
> Mwy yw'r lleiaf wers o'r Bibl
> Na'i holl lyfrau enwog ef.

[The prodigious talents of Newton are of little import in heaven; greater is the smallest verse of the Bible than all his famous tomes.]

Unfortunately, the whole atmosphere of the poem is so ridiculously fantastical that one almost passes over these lines without properly addressing their significance.

There is very little personal grief expressed in Williams's elegies, for his interest lay elsewhere. His aim was to present exemplary spiritual lives and to extol the joys of heaven. The notable exception to this impersonal attitude is his elegy to his own daughter, the third of six, who died two weeks after her birth in 1758; yet even here the emotion is deflected in such a way that we concentrate on the mother's loss and the infant's escape from this temporal world of sin. Some of the elegies to the Methodist leaders are tinged with deep sadness, particularly those to Griffith Jones, Howel Harris and Daniel Rowland. His elegy to the last-named, as already mentioned, was Williams's last literary work, for Rowland died in October 1790, just three months before Williams. It was extremely popular, which is hardly surprising under the circumstances, and was reprinted within the year. The elegy is an all-encompassing account of the history of the Methodist movement and of the effect the great preaching at Llangeitho had on Rowland's converts, and it also contains some of Williams's thoughts on his own frailty: the humanity of this writer is one of his most appealing characteristics.

Despite the variety and obvious merits—and the occasional weakness—of all the writings discussed so far, few would argue that his hymns are Williams's crowning achievement, and in particular those hymns written during the decade immediately following the awakening at Llangeitho in 1762. He is the father of the modern Welsh congregational hymn: it has been calculated that his output accounts for some 30 per cent of all the hymns written in the fifty years between his first volume, *Aleluia*, and his death. His work transcends the solemn and often stifling verse of the metrical psalms and the doctrinal hymns of the early Nonconformists, so that it can be seen clearly that he had no substantial precursor. Because of his dramatic conversion and the revivalist experience, for the first time in Welsh literature a preoccupation with spiritual experience and personal salvation became the main topic of poetry. Williams had a new song to sing, and in the finest of his work he sings it incomparably well. He sings of the passionate and certain release of

regenerate man into the embrace of a wondrous Christo-centric
salvation. He presents us with a self-analytical expression of constantly fluctuating spiritual conditions:

> Cymer, IESU, fi fel ydwyf,
>   Fyth ni alla' i fod yn well;
> Dy allu di a'm gwna i yn agos,
>   Fy ewyllys i yw mynd ymhell.
> Yn dy glwyfau
> Bydda' i'n unig fyth yn iach.

[Take me Jesus as I am, I can never improve; you alone can draw me
near, my own will is to flee. Only in your wounds will I ever be whole.]

The quality of spiritual life intimated here had to be recognized,
analysed and adopted in the public domain. The singer or believer
takes upon himself the referential values of the hymn's experience.
Williams's hymns, therefore, portrayed and sustained religious
enthusiasm, forming an alternative liturgy for Nonconformist
worship, which is a combination of ultimacy and intimacy, and
providing a formative spirituality. His repertoire in these mature
hymns is truly stunning, as he delineates a composite picture of
Christian life, always presented with impeccable integrity.

The vast majority of Williams's hymns, as has already been
stated, deal with the Crucifixion and Christ's sacrifice to save
sinners. They recount a positive dependency: doubt, fear, failure
and guilt must be directed towards the cross, where the Saviour
will compensate for all insufficiency and sin. The crucified Christ
thus becomes the object of the believer's affections:

> Arnat, IESU, boed fy meddwl,
>   Am dy gariad boed fy nghân,
> Dyged sŵn dy ddioddefiadau
>   Fy serchiadau oll yn lân:
> Mae dy gariad
> Uwch y clywodd neb erioed.

[On Thee, Jesus, may I meditate, may my song be of Thy love; may the
mention of Thy sufferings steal all my affections completely; Thy love
surpasses any mentioned before.]

These 'love-songs' of Williams almost form a sub-genre of hymn writing with their own characteristic motifs as he encapsulates, within the relatively short compass of the hymn's verse form, his knowledge and wonderment at Christ's death. He frequently takes his imagery from the Song of Songs, and while the expression is sensuous, it is never sybaritic. His constant use of the second person imperative is the linguistic definition of the relationship—the I–Thou dialectic. We are aware that Williams is extending and, as it were, celebrating the creative possibilities of language in his attempt to express the inexpressible, namely the work of God's grace in the human soul. He wrestles with the language in order to mould the syntax to fit the metre, and is not always successful. Yet we are so accustomed to his style that his often elementary grammatical and lexical shortcomings are almost always excused.

There are a number of central themes in Williams's hymns, but he is perhaps most notably associated with that of spiritual pilgrimage. This picture particularly suited his view of the Christian life and it is, of course, both archetypal and scriptural. The hymnist's use of the Scriptures is the most striking feature of his work; he uses them to validate his depictions of the spiritual life. It is an omnipresent inter-text, representing an imaginative and spiritual universe shared by the hymnist and his congregations. He was able to do this because of the plurality of the image systems connected with the Bible's *heilsgeschichte*. Methodism was deeply rooted in the scriptural vision of the life of faith, and Williams's hymns often read like a stirring spiritual adventure: the perishing pilgrim leaves his sinful Egypt and passes through a wilderness of tribulation; in the wilderness, set upon by innumerable enemies and obstacles, he witnesses the spectacular miracles of an omnipotent God who is the author of sustenance and blessing; he imagines the fear of crossing the River Jordan (associated with the river of death because of its strategic and geographical place in the biblical narrative), and being brought to a feast in the Promised Land, the fulfilment of his eschatological longings for the joys of heaven. In this, the Scriptures are almost a highway code for the believer; geography and topography must be visualized and interpreted on a metaphorical and typological level. Williams's complete mastery of scriptural allusion is a mark of his spiritual and literary genius and, in particular, his use of typology is a meeting of providence and poetics, where the style bears the message of an ageless, universal salvation. In 1766, in his introductory remarks to a volume of hymns, Williams famously urged would-be hymnists to read:

> over and over, the Books of the Prophets and Psalms, the Lamentations, the Songs [of Solomon], Job, and the Revelation, those which are not only full of Poetic Flights, metaphors, variety, correct language and live similes, but also have Spirit which nurtures Fire, Zeal and Life in the Reader beyond (because they are God's Books) all Books in the World.

He certainly followed his own advice, for the lines of his hymns are enriched by an intricate texture of allusion which, while causing the modern reader to flounder and consult a concordance, would have proved no difficulty to the original congregations. The hymns are therefore witness to the socio-cultural context of the Methodist movement, in which thousands of ordinary men and women were inculcated with the interpretation of faith offered in the Scriptures:

> Arglwydd, arwain trwy'r anialwch
>   Fi, bererin gwael ei wedd,
> Nad oes ynof nerth na bywyd,
>   Fel yn gorwedd yn y bedd;
> Hollalluog
> Ydyw'r un a'm cwyd i'r lan.

[Lord, lead through the wilderness me, a wretched sinner; who has no strength or life as if lying in the grave; omnipotent is the one who restores me.]

In hymns and sermons the regenerate Methodist souls—like those of many religious communities before and after—travelled every inch of the journey from Egypt to Canaan, and other strategic places in the history of God's chosen people. Frequently, the hymnist uses archetypal contrasts to describe the transformative effect of God's grace: darkness/light, captivity/freedom, poverty/riches, death/life. His condition is directly related to the actions and attributes of God, as conveyed by the counterbalance of motifs to describe the sinner's condition and God's work in his soul.

The foregoing discussion is not a comprehensive treatment of Williams's literary works, for the scope and sum of his output defy the bounds of one article. Many aspects have not been mentioned: his numerous translations, his miscellaneous poems on both marriage and death, and his later hymns are but three examples. What our discussion has revealed, however, is the immense stamina and considerable genius of one of the most important figures in the history of Welsh religion and literature. His work is not without its problems for the modern reader, at a time when so much of the Nonconformist culture that he helped to create has been dismantled. Yet despite the dominant secular spirit of the age, his songs of praise still regularly resound throughout the land, reminding us of past glories and achievements which should be cherished forever.

BIBLIOGRAPHY

A. M. Allchin, *Praise Above All* (Cardiff, 1991).

J. H. Davies, 'The printed works of Williams Pantycelyn', *Cylchgrawn Cymdeithas Hanes y Methodistiaid Calfinaidd*, 3 (1918), 59–66.

Eifion Evans, 'William Williams of Pantycelyn', *The Evangelical Library Bulletin*, 42 (1969), 2–6.

H. A. Hodges, 'Flame in the mountains', *Religious Studies*, 3 (1967–9), 401–13.

Idem, 'Over the distant hills', *Brycheiniog*, 17 (1976–7), 6–16.

Idem, 'Williams Pantycelyn: father of the modern Welsh hymn', *The Hymn Society of Great Britain and Ireland Bulletin*, 8 (1976), 145–52.

Elsie Houghton, 'William Williams (Pantycelyn), 1717–1791', in *Christian Hymnwriters* (Bridgend, 1982), 113–19.

Glyn Tegai Hughes, *Williams Pantycelyn* (Cardiff, 1983).

Emyr Humphreys, 'The wind of heaven', in *The Taliesin Tradition* (London, 1983), 90–100.

Kathryn Jenkins, ' "Songs of praises": the literary and spiritual qualities of the hymns of Williams Pantycelyn and Ann Griffiths', *Hymn Society of Great Britain and Ireland Bulletin*, 214 (1998), 98–104.

Idem, 'Pantycelyn's women, fact and fiction: an assessment', *Journal of the Welsh Religious History Society*, 7 (1999), 77–94.

R. Brinley Jones, *Songs of Praises: English Hymns and Elegies of William Williams Pantycelyn 1717–1791* (Felinfach, 1991).

D. Martyn Lloyd-Jones, 'William Williams and Welsh Calvinistic Methodism', in *The Manifold Grace of God: papers read at the Puritan and Reformed Conference, 1968* (London, 1969), 76–95.

Alun Luff, 'William Williams Pantycelyn', in *Welsh Hymns and Their Tunes: Their Background and Place in Welsh History and Culture* (London, 1990), 93–103.

Derec Llwyd Morgan, 'More than a sweet singer: the achievement of Pantycelyn', *Planet*, 88 (1991), 56–63.

Idem, *The Great Awakening in Wales*, tr. Dyfnallt Morgan (Epworth, 1988).

W. Roberts, 'Saunders Lewis and William Williams: notes for a revaluation', *Anglo-Welsh Review*, 15 (1965), 18–25.

W. J. Roberts, 'The spiritual legacy of William Williams of Pantycelyn', *London Quarterly & Holborn Review*, 19 (1950), 330–4.

Stephen James Turner, 'Theological themes in the English works of Williams, Pantycelyn' (M.Th. thesis, University of Wales, 1982).

CHAPTER 12

THE LITERATURE OF THE
'GREAT AWAKENING'

BRYNLEY F. ROBERTS

On Palm Sunday 1735 a young schoolmaster, Howel Harris of Trefeca-fach, attended service at his local parish church in the small market-town of Talgarth, not far from the English border in south-eastern Brecknockshire. Then aged 21, he had been educated locally before embarking in 1732 on what he no doubt expected would be his career as a schoolmaster in nearby villages such as Llangors and Llangasty, where he was at the time. He had had an uneventful youth and had shared in the normal pursuits of boys of his day, neither excessively riotous nor unduly religious, however he may have viewed those years in later life. At the service that Palm Sunday he heard the vicar, the Reverend Pryce Davies, urge his congregation to be present at Holy Communion the following Sunday, warning them that if they sought to excuse themselves saying that they were not worthy to come to the Table, then nor were they fit to pray, to live, or to die. The words pierced Harris's heart and he left the service deeply moved, troubled enough to share the message and the concern which it had awoken in him with passing neighbours. On Easter Sunday, he took communion for the first time and he was to do so regularly over the following weeks. He spent his time reading some of the Anglican classics of devotion—*The Whole Duty of Man* (Richard Allestree), *The Practice of Piety* (Bayly), *Golden Grove* (Taylor)— and meditating on the sacrament of Holy Communion as a means of forgiveness for all who partook of it in faith. His uncertainties were resolved at communion in Talgarth on Whit Sunday, and he gave eloquent expression to his experience of acceptance and peace in his personal journal in June of that year, his heart 'melting as wax . . . from love for God my Saviour.'

Harris was a complex, passionate man, an enthusiast whose missionary zeal frequently became rashness and even opinionated arrogance, but in spite of a powerful, dominating personality he was able to attract many to his side, partly no doubt through his powers of eloquence, but more so through the strength of his character. Nor was he simply an itinerant evangelist, for it soon became apparent that his charisma was matched by equally effective organizational abilities. Harris was not able to restrain himself from sharing with others the newly found convictions which were to inspire him and govern his life henceforth. He began to discuss their spiritual condition with neighbours whom he visited to read to them, to exhort and to pray. His circle of visits expanded and soon he was travelling throughout Brecknockshire and into neighbouring counties, setting up small groups who met regularly with him to prepare for communion in their parish churches and to strive for 'a Strict Observation of our Duty', as he put it. In 1736 he visited Griffith Jones, vicar of Llanddowror, Carmarthenshire, who was then establishing a system of circulating schools to teach ordinary folk to read the Scriptures for themselves, and who was a familiar figure well known for his evangelical preaching, which was so much in tune with the new-found zeal of the young Harris. Jones was middle-aged and greatly experienced in educational endeavours as well as in religious instruction through the spoken and written word. He took Harris under his wing and encouraged him to seek ordination, but the young man was too restless to be confined to college or school-mastering, too enthusiastic to be accepted as a candiate for Holy Orders. He was unable to refrain from exhorting, at school or in private houses. Inevitably his exhorting and reading began to take on the character of preaching and his extempore prayers become ever more eloquent, developments which Pryce Davies could not countenance and which evoked his strong pastoral criticism. Nevertheless, Harris's work spread more widely afield and he began to attract the support of some clerics but more especially of lay people in the groups which he formed wherever he preached.

Unknown to Harris, the curate of Llangeitho in mid-Cardiganshire had undergone a similar spiritual experience to his own at about the same time. Daniel Rowland, son of a former vicar of Llangeitho, and himself influenced by Griffith Jones, had been 'converted' towards the end of 1736. He was a powerful preacher and he too appears to have set up small-group meetings for his converts in the parish. Harris and Rowland, neither of whom was aware of the work of the other, met by chance at Defynnog in Brecknockshire in 1737 and, though dissimilar in temperament and background, resolved to work together in the great awakening of the spirit which both had experienced and were now witnessing at work in others.

The small groups, 'private societies', set up to help converts prepare for the sacrament by self-examination of their spiritual condition, arose from the style of Harris's more informal exhorting around Talgarth, but he may subsequently have been influenced by Jacob Woodward's *Account of Religious Societies* (1697 and many times thereafter) or the *Abstracts of Dr Woodward's Book* (which the SPCK circulated) and by discussions with Griffith Jones. These societies (in Welsh 'society' became *seiat*, plural *seiadau*) soon developed into permanent gatherings, and as they grew in number and as Harris travelled more widely and for long periods, they began to form a network of regular meetings under the care of supervisors, both local and district—lay people, some clerics—who submitted reports first to Harris and then, by 1742, to the Society of Ministers and Exhorters, the Association of Societies (in Welsh, *Sasiwn*). By 1742 there were more than thirty societies in south Wales. They met regularly, usually monthly; some might be under the care of the same supervisor and some might at times meet together. They were not 'cells', nor were they Nonconformist, but groups whose members rejoiced in the shared experience which had led to their establishment and who were conscious of being part of the same working of the Spirit.

The paramount purpose of the societies was the nurturing of spiritual life, most particularly by means of the honest and searching examination of the continuing experience which had first brought these individuals into fellowship. The leader or supervisor of a *seiat* needed to question members acutely, he required counselling skills and spiritual sensitivities of a high order if the group was to grow in mutual trust and to mature spiritually. Conversation, question and response, expounding, were of the essence of the meeting, and members would have developed their own fluency in expressing their doubts, fears, questions and joys so that there is little doubt that the oral nature of the *seiadau* produced in many cases ordinary folk who were highly articulate, with a feel for language and effective forms of expression which were given a firm basis in extempore prayer, Bible reading and exhorting. Linguistic awareness and skills derive from listening and speaking and from consciously acquiring accepted stylistic patterns. The *seiadau* played a significant role in nurturing standards of orality and they created a class of people able to use language to voice deeply held emotions and to express them in imaginative, metaphorical styles, which have their origin in the Bible.

The spirituality of the *seiat* was by its very nature intensely personal, but it would be a mistake to regard it as individualistic, for the society, as the name suggests, was essentially a group meeting. Members shared their experiences, recognizing in others aspects of their own spiritual lives, be they of doubt or assurance, and deriving support and instruction from others. Though the *seiat* meeting was for edification and instruction, these were mediated in an atmosphere of worship, praise and thanksgiving, which have always been the subjects of song. The main medium for expressing these shared, communal experiences was the hymn, which became another element in the meetings, which were developing their own pattern. Harris had taught his pupils to sing psalms in his schools, and psalms, and later hymns, seem to have been an integral part of society meetings almost from their inception: certainly hymn-singing was a feature of the *seiadau* by 1737 when a colleague sent Harris some hymns 'since I hear reports that you sing the praise of the Lord in psalms, hymns and spiritual songs' (tr.). Though metrical psalms remained the only hymns used in the Anglican church and though opposition to non-scriptural hymns existed among some Nonconformists, hymns were not a new feature of religious services. Presbyterians and Independents had published a few small collections in the early years of the eighteenth century, some of which were used by Methodists, but by and large their uncompromising theological tone, lack of spontaneity and uncertain metrical forms did not ensure a warm reception. Adherents of the *seiadau* required more vibrant forms and they were forced to create their own hymnology. From about 1740, booklets and other collections of hymns in a markedly different style appear in significant numbers. The hymn was to be the typical literary form of the Great Awakening and the origins of Welsh hymnology, which has been such a potent force in Welsh literary history and popular culture, are to be traced to the place given to hymn-singing in the *seiat* meetings as an expression of grateful praise and of the work of the Spirit. Small wonder that heightened emotion characterizes so many of these hymns and that they have such a personal tone. Harris himself was moved to compose a hymn in 1739, to be followed by others throughout 1740–1 (though the only one which remains familiar is his translation of 'Praise God from whom all blessings flow'). When the first Methodist printed tracts begin to appear, they contain as appendices small collections of hymns. *Llwybr Hyffordd ir Cymru* (1740) contained four hymns by one Morgan [John] Lewis of Blaenau Gwent, and others, including one 'to be sung in the weekly meeting', by E. Rees, Griffith Jones, Daniel Rowland and others; in 1741, Lewis and Edmund Williams published *Hymnau Duwiol o Gasgliad Gwŷr Eglwysig;* and Williams also published two other collections, *Hymnau Duwiol . . . O Gasgliad Gŵr Eglwysig* (1741) and *Rhai Hymnau Duwiol* (1742). *Llyfr o Hymnau o waith Amryw Awdwyr* appeared about 1740. *Sail, Dibenion, a Rheolau'r Societies* (the Rules for Societies) was published in 1742 and this contained four hymns, a clear indication that by now hymn-singing was an integral part of the *seiat* meeting. Other collections, copied in the 1740s by some of Griffith Jones's schoolmasters and by *seiat* supervisors and members, were circulating and contained the work of the leaders of the movement. The use of hymns is made clear more formally in the title of a collection published in 1744, *Hymnau Duwiol Yw canu mewn cymdeithasau Crefyddol* (Godly Hymns to be sung in religious societies). This contained, 'for the most part', hymns by Daniel Rowland but included also were two hymns which were to be found in *Aleluia*, William Williams of Pantycelyn's first published collection of hymns, which appeared in 1744. Henceforth, composing and publishing collections of hymns were to be the major literary activity of the Welsh Methodists as hymns replaced psalms in their meetings.

Though the first collections stem from south-east Wales, most of this activity flourished in Carmarthenshire. This may have been due to a number of factors—the influence of Griffith Jones's schools and psalm-singing, the number of *seiadau* in a fairly small area, the availability of printers, especially in Carmarthen and Llandovery. The outstanding figure was William Williams, outstanding not only in the volume of his compositions and literary

work over a long period nor even in the new metrical forms which
he introduced in his writing, but more importantly in the breadth
and depth of the religious experience which he expressed and in the
power of his literary imagination. Granted that the selection of his
work which is contained in modern hymnals conceals the uneven
quality of his writing, nevertheless few were able to rival him in the
richness of his vision or the challenging vividness of his imagery. A
notable supervisor of *seiadau*, he was to become the voice of the
societies, the poet both of the community and of the individual
soul. He was not, however, unique in the nature of his vision or in
the character and style of his hymns, for a number of other hymn-
writers—like Pantycelyn both the product and the servant of the
seiadau—composed hymns in similar vein. Pantycelyn's work
arose from the same source and at the same time as that of these
other hymnists; at their mediocre levels there is little difference
between any of them and him; at their best the others write hymns
which Pantycelyn would have been happy to acknowledge as his
own. Their unassuming booklets are, perhaps, a better indicator of
the nature of *seiat* hymns and of the life of the societies, but the
hymns also serve to show how closely these writers interacted with
one another and with Pantycelyn himself.

Some of the hymns and verses are of dubious quality, verging on
the tasteless in their unsophisticated bluntness and earthy language:

> Un rhybudd byrr, wy'n awr yn roi
> I bawb o'r byd i ymbar'toi
> Pan bo'ch chwi'n handlo'r gaib a'r rhaw
> Im cuddio i, 'ch tro chwitheu ddaw.

[A brief warning I give now to all around to be prepared; when you're
handling the pick and shovel to hide me—your turn will come too.]

The author of this homely advice is Thomas Dafydd of Llanegwad,
who published some twenty pamphlets of hymns and elegies
between 1765 and 1792 and whose work is generally more polished
than this. He writes with great fluency and warmth and, though he
never attains the heights, his themes of longing for freedom from the
burden of sin, for union with Christ and the wonder of salvation in
God incarnate, and his use of scriptural exemplars and 'types', are
all characteristic of Methodist hymns, and must derive from the

nature of the discourse of the *seiat*. This untutored folk-poet was accepted as one of the hymnists of the *seiat* and he published one booklet of hymns with Morgan Rhys, one of the best and most theologically minded writers. Pantycelyn shared publication with lesser lights and the fifth and sixth parts of his *Aleluia* (1747) included a number of hymns by members of the *seiat* at Caeo— Dafydd Jones, John Dafydd (the exhorter at Llansawel *seiat*), his brother Morgan and John Jones (the overseer of *seiadau* in Neath); John Morgan of Caeo had been responsible for publishing the first part of *Alelujah*. *Seiadau* such as these were the nurturing ground of hymn-writers and it was to be expected that there would be a family resemblance of theme, style and imagery in the work of those who shared in the awakening and its culture. Their themes are joyful praise, the sinful state of humanity, the wonder of salvation and the hope of communion with Christ. Their favorite metaphor is of the journey of the soul through the wilderness to that Promised Land where Christ reigns, so that the Book of Exodus and the tribulations of the Chosen People, together with the influence of Bunyan's *Pilgrim's Progress*, became for these new Elect a pattern and a hope. The journey of the sinner through life and its dangers could be seen as a voyage through storms and tempests, but always towards holy Salem, that better city, the fair inheritance. Images of pilgrims, voyagers, crossing Jordan, or of prisoners abound, and hope resides in the Friend and Brother, Israel's shepherd, the Author of Salvation. Images such as these, and all those others of the home yonder, the Rock beneath one's feet, crushing the head of the serpent (Dragon), the Woman's seed, the second Adam, Jesus crossing heaven's account, the pardon in his hand, praising the Lamb—all from Scripture; and phrases like bidding farewell to the 'toys' of the world, the open path to heaven, the journey onwards, the unnumbered host, stand by my side—these have become so familiar as the commonplaces of Welsh hymnology that it is sometimes difficult to realize how frighteningly novel they were in the second half of the eighteenth century. This is the new language of a new experience, but the members of the societies would have recognized it as the language of shared experiences and as the language of Scripture which validated those communal experiences.

Exodus, the Prophets, Job, Psalms, the Gospels, Revelations— these were books which provided much of the imagery of these hymns, but they were not the only source for writers seeking to express their consuming love for Christ. Members of the *seiadau* were encouraged to turn their backs upon the delights and entertainments of the secular society of which they could not but be part, but the hymnists only partially forsook the tradition of folk-song with which they were familiar. Thomas Dafydd's fluency owes as much to his experience as a popular rhymester (*bardd gwlad*) as to *seiat* hymn-singing, and the metrics and style of folk-song influenced hymns. Jesus was the Loved One (*yr Anwylyd*) and love and desire for Him could be expressed in a curious combination of the Song of Songs and popular love-songs which modern congregations would baulk at singing, as in these three stanzas, out of eight, in the hymn by John Jones, Caeo:

> Mi fum dros Dro mewn Gaia'n drist,
> Yn wylo am GHRIST yn Geidwad,
> Ond Clôd fo i Dduw, fe ddaeth yr Hâf,
> 'Rwi 'nawr yn glâf o'i Gariad.

> O tyn Fi, tyn Fi, Arglwydd cu,
> Ar dy ôl Di 'rwi'n dwad:
> Dygaist fy Nghalon, f'anwyl Naf
> 'Rwi 'nawr yn glâf o'th Gariad.

> Yn llawen disgwyl f'Enaid llon,
> Mae'r Iesu bron a dwad,
> A'i Gwmp'ni gwych a'i Gerbyd brâf
> I hôl y clâf o'i Gariad

[I was sad for a time in winter weeping for Christ as a Saviour, but praise be to God, the summer has come, I'm now sick from love for him.
    O draw me, draw me, dear Lord, I'm coming, following you: you've stolen my heart, my beloved Lord, I'm now sick from love for you.
    In joy my happy soul awaits, Jesus is almost here, with his glorious company and his fine carriage, to fetch the one sick from his love.]

Even more striking is a song by Dafydd Jones, Caeo, 'The Soul slow to listen to the voice of her Love: he touches her heart till she is sick for his love. In the form of a dialogue'. The Beloved tries to awaken the Soul:

The dew drips from the skies, my hair is wet: the night is long and its touch is cold, my dove, open for me.

The Soul does not recognize the voice, she is in bed, why should she open the door?

Through a sea of difficulties I have come to save you from your troubles. For you I lost my fair life, open the door my Beloved.

The Soul recognizes 'gentle Jesus' and entreats him to enter:

Put your finger in the key-hole and I will come to open: and if the door does not quickly open, O break it in two, my Beloved . . . You are my Lord and dear King, and I am sick for love of you.

The motif of the lover without is taken from the Song of Songs, skilfully associated with the Christ of the Book of Revelation knocking at the door of the believer's heart so that He may enter and sup with him; but the hymn is set in a traditional form, perhaps a late example of the medieval *sérénade*, reminiscent of a *cywydd* by Dafydd ap Gwilym. Folk-song is translated by biblical imagery into a daring confession of faith.

Whether this song was ever sung is uncertain but John Jones's lyric is a hymn to be sung with fervour. *Seiat* singing must have been joyful and ardent. Many hymns have a line or a couplet as a refrain—'Ni alla'i lai na'th garu' (I can but love you), 'Mae arnaf chwant myn'd adre' (My desire is to go home), 'Ys truan, pwy a'm gwared?' (Woe is me, who will save me?). It requires little imagination to sense the effect of hymns such as these, or others of invocation ('O come dear Jesus, come closer') or those sung perhaps at the start of a service ('O gracious Lord, have mercy, look upon us sinners here: come into our midst, shed your dew, your blessing upon every soul'). Prayers for blessing, for growth in faith, for unceasing effort to gain Christ, are to be understood in the context of passionate worship and the communal aspect is clear in a number of dialogue hymns which assuage the doubtful and sustain the weaker brethren. Thomas Dafydd has put into verse the kind of probing and encouragement which was the task of the leader:

> Fy enaid gwan, mi weles ddydd,
> Y canit beth â'th draed yn rhydd,
> Dwed pam yr wyt ti 'nawr mor drist,
> Yn ffaelu canmol Iesu Grist?

O waith pechod cas 'rwy'n aros 'nol,
Euogrwydd llym ddaeth ar ei ol;
Am hyn 'rwy'n ffaelu d'od ymlaen,
I ganmol Iesu fel o'r blaen

O brysia dere atto'n glau,
Ei arfer ef yw trugarhâu;
Y mae e'n dirion addfwyn Oen
I'r enaid blin fo'n teimlo ei boen.

Gwynfyd na allwn gredu hyn,
Awn atto'n hu i Seion fryn;
Ond p'odd y gallai'n eon fyn'd,
Waith digio wnes fy anwyl Ffrynd?

Wel ar addewid hyfryd hwn
O tyr'd ymlaen er maint yw'th bwn,
Fe dderbyn e'r afradlon blant,
Ni fwr e' neb ddel atto bant.

Parch ac anrhydedd fytho i'r Tad,
A'r anwyl Oen am werth ei waed
Tragwyddol glod i'r Yspryd Glân
Y tri yn un, heb un ar wa'n.

[My weak soul I saw a day when you would sing unfettered, tell me why you are now so sad and unable to praise Jesus Christ?

Because of hateful sin I remain behind, bitter guilt came after it; this is why I can't come forward to praise Jesus as before.

O hurry, come to him quickly, he is accustomed to be merciful; he is a gentle kind Lamb to the troubled soul who feels its pain.

O that I could believe this, I'd go once more to Zion's hill; but how can I go confidently since I've angered my dear Friend?

Well, upon this beautiful promise, O come forward in spite of the weight of your burden; he accepts the prodigal children, he will not cast out any one who comes to him.

Reverence and honour be to the Father, and to the dear Lamb for the value of his blood, everlasting praise to the Holy Spirit, the three in one and indivisible.]

These *seiat* hymns frequently echo one another not only in style and imagery but in phrases and couplets, occasionally a whole stanza. In a more literary-minded environment, this would be condemned as plagiarism, or at best unacknowledged borrowing. But the culture of the *seiat* was predominantly oral; though many hymns were circulated in printed or manuscript copies, they were quickly learned by heart, and the process may have been in the opposite direction, from *seiat* to print. We should think, rather, in terms of the dissemination of folk-songs and folk-poetry and the influence of the community on both the composition and the 'ownership' of these hymns. Dafydd Jones, Caeo, ends a hymn, 'The Christian voyaging home', a sustained image of life's stormy spiritual passage, with this stanza:

> Ag yno gwyn fy Mŷd
> Tu draw i'r Byd a'r Bedd,
> Câf yno fyw o hyd
> Mewn Hawddfyd ag mewn Hedd,
> Yn canu'n bur i'r JESU mwyn,
> Am iddo'm dwyn i Salem dîr.

[And there I shall be in a blessed state, beyond the world and the grave; I shall be able to live there for ever, in ease and peace, singing pure praise to sweet Jesus for having brought me to Salem land.]

John Thomas of Rhaeadr has an almost identical stanza where the closing lines refer not to a safe passage but to singing the praise of Christ's sacrifice. It is futile to seek to condemn the one for borrowing from the other: rather, this is the *seiat* appropriating what it was responsible for creating in the first place. In the fellowship of *seiadau*, folk-poets could sometimes surprise even themselves when their mediocrity blossomed into something greater which has stood the test of time. John Dafydd, Caeo, has some laboured stanzas, 'Meditations on Eternity', but then suddenly, in the second part, overcome with joy as he contemplates Christ's victory and its fruits for the believer, he sings confidently:

> Newyddion brâf a ddaeth i'n Bro
> Nhwy haedden gael eu dwyn ar Go';
> Mae'r Jesu wedi carrio'r Dydd
> Caiff Carcharorion fyn'd yn rhydd.
>
> Wel, f'Enaid, weithian côd dy Ben,
> Mae'r Ffordd yn rhydd i'r Nefoedd wen;

Mae'r Llewod oll eu gyd ynawr
Mewn Cadwyn gan y Brenin mawr.

[Great news has come to this land, it deserves to be remembered; Jesus
has won the day, prisoners can go free.
   Well, my soul, raise your head, the way is clear to Heaven. The great
King has all the lions in chains now.]

Many other examples could be quoted of lesser-known poets
attaining the heights. John Jones, Caeo, his faith so weak, seeks
fellowship with Christ, but then, 'his Soul under a feeling of God's
love commits itself to love Him' and conscious only of God's
grace, describes his spiritual journey from condemnation to
acceptance and finally to praise: 'To Father, Son and Holy Ghost I
give praise in song unceasingly, The Three in One, the One in
Three that my Soul loves . . .'—'I can but love you' is his refrain.
   Methodism was experiential religion. It retained the 'warm
temper' (*twym ias*) which accompanied Howel Harris's conversion
and which characterized the worship of the *seiadau* certainly until
the beginning of the following century. The experience of
forgiveness following the struggle of repentance, of acceptance and
of love was such that its emotion could only be expressed in song.
But William Williams was not only the hymnist who gave *seiat*
members a voice to express and to enrich their experience; he was
also the writer of prose works in which he is the analyst and
guardian of the life of the *seiat*. The Methodists and others who
shared in their experience were not content to live on the emotion,
however exalted, of the awakening. Spiritual experience, deeply
felt and often traumatic, was the starting-point and then the
validation, but it could not be the substance of conviction unless it
became grounded in a deeper understanding of God's scheme of
salvation. If it was the Holy Spirit which had moved them and
revealed to them their condition and the riches of communion with
Christ, then the *seiat* leaders laid particular stress on co-operating
with the Spirit to search out the will of God and to understand His
ways. To feel the ardour of conversion, necessary though this was,
was not enough: it was to be built upon so that the believer might
grow in his understanding of the faith and of his path towards
sanctification. Instruction and edification, theological education,
were the framework within which the self-examination was to be

carried out. John Jones's hymn, 'Trwy râs 'rwi, Arglwydd, ger dy fron' (Through grace I am, Lord, before you), referred to above, reveals how systematically he had been able to analyse his journey to acceptance (and that of his fellow members), but he also reveals that this was no arid intellectual process, for its fruit was his even deeper love for Christ. Theology in the context of Methodist worship was intelligence revived, a source of greater joy and deeper wonder as believers contemplated the work of grace, the Person of Christ, the scheme of salvation, the mystery of Providence. Personal conviction and theology became fused in these hymns, many of them written by exhorters and teachers in Griffith Jones's circulating schools. But the way of salvation could not be described in two or three stanzas and these eighteenth-century hymns are significantly longer than the truncated versions which appear in modern hymn-books, where the hymns are often only a selection of stanzas from the original. Morgan Rhys (1716–79) has suffered more than most in this respect.

For most of his career Morgan Rhys was a successful teacher in Griffith Jones's schools and probably an Anglican in religion. His was an orderly mind, an astute and powerful intellect, and it is possible to see the schoolmaster at work in his hymns, which are educative as well as experiential. It has been claimed that at times one can follow both the order and words of the catechism in some of his hymns. More than any other hymnist of the Great Awakening, Rhys combines strength of mind and deep emotion, so that the personal conviction is expressed in objective theological terms and the warmth is kept in check from burning too fiercely. His honesty and self-searching have been regarded by some as a pessimistic attitude towards life (he is the author of 'Beth sydd imi yn y byd/ Ond gorthrymderau mawr o hyd?' (What does the world offer me/ But great oppressions all the time?)) but as others have seen, his true characteristic is his desire to transcend the earthly battles of the spirit and to be reborn into the joys of heaven. He said as much when he noted the theme of his collection of hymns *Golwg o ben Nebo* (A view from the summit of Nebo; 1775): 'Cwymp dyn yn yr Adda cyntaf a'i Gyfodiad yn yr Ail Adda' (Man's fall in the first Adam and his rising up in the second Adam). The realism of self-examination gives place to the joys of salvation, and this is to be traced in detail and in full in the song of the saints. His hymn 'Deuwch holl hiliogaeth Adda' (Come all the

race of Adam) follows the plan of salvation in Christ as laid out in
the Bible. Rhys invites his fellow Christians to meditate upon and
to praise the 'great Saviour' incarnate, 'the wonder of heaven and
earth . . . Alpha and Omega.' Though praised by angels in eternity
'his heart was with the unworthy dust of earth'; stars sang at his
birth, shepherds and wise men came to him. Isaiah prophesied his
coming, the Saviour, Healer, whose love is forgiveness. The hymn
ends, echoing the first stanza, with what this means for Adam's
children: 'He is the king of eternity, Ruler of heaven and earth,
Never will Adam's race see another Saviour but him, He is
sufficient, he is Everlasting Life.' The hymn in its nine stanzas
(modern hymn-books have only the third and eighth) is a song of
thanksgiving, but its restraint derives from its theological structure
and its firm scriptural basis.

Herein lay the strength of the life of the *seiadau*, that spiritual
experience was externalized in the light of Scripture so that the
individual believer could locate himself or herself in the greater
scheme. Rhys himself never loses sight of the ultimate truth of his
conviction. Many of his stanzas have a similar pattern—lines of
remorse and confession followed by lines of assurance and
forgiveness. The hymn quoted above, 'Beth sydd imi yn y Byd?', so
often sung as a melancholy hymn of resignation, develops into a
plea for purity and ends with a prayer that he might walk with
God, praising Him all his days. Rhys's great contribution to
Methodist hymnology was the firm theological anchor which he
provided, and his constant note of freedom following honest,
uncompromising confession. 'O open my eyes to see the mystery of
your providence and your word: . . . the soul he wounds he is sure
to heal.'

Dafydd Jones, Caeo (1711–77) was very different from Morgan
Rhys: different in occupation—a farmer and drover; in wordly
goods—Jones seems to have been moderately comfortable; but
most strikingly in personality. Rhys was intellectual in his
Methodism, meditative and serious-minded: Jones was a folk-poet
who never quite freed himself from the relaxed atmosphere of farm
and market. Before his conversion he was a typical witty
rhymester:

> Mae chwech peth a sych yn chwipyn—
> Carreg noeth a geiriau meddwyn,

> Cawod Ebrill, tap heb gwrw,
> Pwll yr Haf, a dagrau gwidw.

[Six things quickly dry up—a bare stone and the drunkard's lips, an April shower, a tap without ale, a pool in summer, and a widow's tears.]

After his conversion experience he continued to write songs of advice and warning to young Christians in popular ballad metres and style, to be sung on familiar tunes. These features spill over into his hymns too. He was the author of the love lyric already quoted, which owes much to folk-song tradition; another hymn, also based on the Song of Songs, finds him searching the streets of the town at night and enquiring after 'him whom my soul loves'. Another hymn, 'Invitation to the wedding of the King's son', though obviously based on the return of the prodigal son and on the parable of the unwilling wedding guests in Matt. 22, nevertheless is equally clearly written by one who knew something of the delights of feasts and parties. Jones was a happy spirit. He was a farmer and drover converted, it is said, when he happened to call at the meeting-house in Troedrhiwdalar on one of his return trips from England. He must have been a young man then, as he was twenty-six years of age when one of his first hymns was published in part five of Williams's *Aleluia* in 1747. Jones became a member of the Dissenting church at Crug-y-bar and worshipped there until his death in 1777. Dissenters were not noted for the freedom of their worship (they were called *sentars sychion,* 'dry dissenters', in Welsh) and Jones became known for his fervour, both spiritual and physical. He may have felt the need to defend himself from criticism:

> Mae Plant y byd yn holi
>   Ac yn rhyfeddu'n syn
> Pan fwy'n moliannu f'Arglwydd
>   'Beth yw'r ynfydrwydd hyn?'
> Rhyddhawyd fi o'm caethiwed,
>   Ni thawaf ddim â sôn
> Mi gana'n wyneb gwawdwyr
>   Am Rinwedd Gwaed yr O'N.

[The children of the world ask and stand in wonder when I'm praising my Lord, 'What's this nonsense?' I've been freed from my captivity, I will not be silent, I'll sing in the face of those who mock of the power of the blood of the Lamb.]

Jones's warmth in worship is commented upon in an elegy by John Thomas—'I saw him many times here laughing tears beneath the Word'—and he was probably an example of that change in affective worship which the Methodists experienced after the 1762 Revival at Llangeitho: 'and what if I were to jump as long as I did so in reverence', he asked in his hymn, following the advice of Williams to believers in his *Llythyr Martha Philopur* (Martha Philopur's Letter) and *Atteb Philo-Evangelius* (Philo-Evangelius' Response).

Dafydd Jones had learned English, probably in the course of his business as a drover, and he was urged by some ministers to translate Isaac Watts's versions of the psalms, presumably for Dissenters, like those at Crug-y-bar, who still distrusted non-scriptural hymns and who saw these as a half-way house. Jones's versions of Watts appeared in three collections, *Salmau Dafydd* (1753), *Caniadau Dwyfol i blant* (1771), *Hymnau a Chaniadau* (1775). His striving after close translations make many of his versions rather laborious, and he failed to catch the simplicity of Watts's hymns for children. Nevertheless, Jones's experience as a fluent and competent versifier saved him many times, and a number of these 'Christian psalms' have gained a place in the canon of Welsh hymnody. He may have had much in common with Watts, who has been described as one who 'though a strict Calvinist, was a cheerful, singing soul, a severe person but with something of a twinkle'. There is no mistaking Jones's seriousness of purpose: he is as 'severe' as any of his contemporaries in his view of sin, judgement and Hell:

> Poeth, Poeth
> Fydd Uffern i eneidiau noeth
> O eisiau gwisgo'n dduwiol ddoeth.

[Hot, hot will Hell be for souls naked for want of wise and godly garments.]

'Righteousness is satisfied, the Law fulfilled, God and we, old enemies, made at peace by both': 'strict Calvinist' indeed. But to a greater degree than almost any other hymnist, Jones's reaction to forgiveness and salvation is happiness and praise: 'No one has greater cause to sing even in deep grief than the children of the King', 'Why should I be sad? No one has greater reason than I to be cheerful for I am the Lord's.' His own collection of hymns, published in three parts between 1763 and 1770, suggests something of Jones's attitudes in its title *Difyrrwch i'r Pererinion* (A Pleasure for Pilgrims). His assurance is joyful but humble; it is a condition to be shared. It is remarkable how many of his hymns and stanzas open with 'Dewch' (Come) and the evangelical appeal to others to enjoy the blessings which he has experienced is, perhaps, the hallmark of Jones's work.

The 'Great Awakening' was, of course, not confined to Carmarthenshire. By 1742, following tours to north and mid-Wales by Harris and his helpers, and the preaching of Rowland, the Revival had spread throughout Wales, though not without opposition, vocal, physical and literary, in some areas. Societies had been set up throughout the country, most especially in south Wales. The characteristic features of *seiat* meetings were transferred with the societies and it was not uncommon for leaders and overseers of well-established societies to be sent to assist new ones. Across the Carmarthenshire border in west Glamorgan, Dafydd William of Llanedi (1720–94), an exhorter and one of Griffith Jones's schoolmasters, settled in Llandeilo-fach, Pontarddulais, though he subsequently, in 1777, became a member of the Baptist church. Between 1762 and 1793 he published over thirty booklets of hymns similar in tone and style to those already described. Like Morgan Rhys, he structures many of his hymns around the progression from despair at his sinful state to the joy of salvation, but he seems to have been assailed by doubts, as many *seiat* members were, both of the possibility of forgiveness and of the basis of their assurance, and to have been ready to express them, though he never allows them to become rooted. One of his most famous hymns opens 'Anghrediniaeth, gad fi'n llonydd' (Unbelief, leave me be), but progresses to 'Ychydig ffydd, ble 'rwyt ti'n llechu?' (Little faith, where are you hiding?), and then to conviction: 'Anghrediniaeth, er dy waetha, Mae tŷ Dafydd yn cryfhau' (Unbelief, in spite of all, David's house grows stronger) and to a vision of Christ the Archpriest. Other hymns have as their subject 'Faith casting out fear', 'Confident Faith'. The tone is as positive as that of any of his contemporaries, but the battle may have been more prolonged and the skirmishes more frequent. For this reason, perhaps, his hymns to the Holy Spirit, the 'wind of heaven', his 'inspiration', have a greater intensity of feeling and directness than many of those of other writers. The struggle for faith and the thought underlying his hymns give William's work greater stability than many of the outpourings of *seiat* meetings and in this, too, he resembles Morgan Rhys, though he is not as systematic as he.

Dafydd William shared in the use which Rhys made of the Bible to provide both the guidelines for thought and his imagery, as he makes clear in his listing of scriptural references before his hymns and in a title such as 'Christ the true substance excels all the images' (*cysgodau*, 'shadows', more technically 'types'). This allegorical, 'typical' use of the Bible underlies much Methodist writing (as Pantycelyn himself explains), but William seems to have been particularly affected by it and he has been criticized for 'mixing metaphors' in the abundance of his images. In a single hymn he hears the proclamation that the fountain of healing is opened and urges his soul to pass through the open door: a ladder whose rungs are promises lies before him and the sun of righteousness has risen: he sees the altar and hears the song on the golden harps. The effect, however, is not of a muddled mind but rather of one well-versed in Scripture overwhelmed by his vision of God's grace in Christ. A favourite image is that of crossing the waters, of sinking in the flood, of landing safely. The most familiar example is:

> Yn y dyfroedd mawr a'r tonnau
> Nid oes neb a ddeil fy mhen
> Ond fy annwyl Briod Iesu
> A fu farw ar y pren.

[In the mighty waters and waves there is no one who holds up my head but my dear spouse Jesus who died upon the tree.]

Dafydd William's verses have movement and energy. 'Hosanna, Haleliwia, Fe anwyd brawd i ni . . .' (Hosanna, Hallelujah, a brother has been born to us . . .) sings its message of joy in every line and phrase of its confident metre. This is a reflection of the assurance of William's convictions, but these features also derive from his experience in song-writing in popular metres and, one suspects, from familiarity with the conventions of folk-song and poetry. One of his most common traits is his repetition of phrases throughout a stanza or a hymn. 'Brawd' and 'Hosanna' ring through the hymn referred to and in others he repeats, for instance, 'Dyma gariad' (This is love), 'Dacw' (Behold), 'Dy Ysbryd' (Thy Spirit), 'Derfydd' ([It] ends/dies), in the manner of popular verse, while his address to 'Anghrediniaeth' (Unbelief) brings to mind verses of address in the folk tradition to 'hiraeth' (longing) or 'angau' (death). William may well have been reflecting upon his own experience when he sang, 'Let the children of the world sing their songs to their false gods, while I have breath I'll sing to the Lamb who died on the tree.'

Many of the Methodist hymn-writers had learned their versifying as popular poets. Reference has already been made to Dafydd Jones: another of a similar cultural background but with a different temperament was John Williams (1728–1806) of Llandyfaelog, Carmarthenshire, who settled at St Athan, Glamorgan. A Methodist exhorter, he left the movement in 1791 following the expulsion of Peter Williams for heresy (he was moved to write a long poem in response to that event) and joined the Dissenters. His secular verses, in traditional Glamorgan *triban* form, show how typical a folk-poet he was in style, metre and theme, but the few hymns he composed have an intensity of phrase and he reveals a strong visual imagination as 'he allows his muse to range over precious words' in Isaiah 63, as he was requested to do by the Reverend David Jones of Llan-gan. The hymn 'Pwy welaf o Edom yn dod?' (Whom do I see coming from Edom?) is inspired by the passage in Isaiah but the scene has been made vivid as Williams allows his imagination to dwell upon it. David Jones's request and John Williams's response serve to show that the Bible was not only a source of language and imagery but that hymns could arise from sustained meditation on particular passages (or combinations of passages) as the writers read all parts of the Old Testament in the light of Christ's person and work. Here, therefore, the victorious, blood-stained conqueror is Christ, who has won the day 'through his blood.' Williams cannot be compared to Ann Griffiths but her hymns are the ultimate examples of the imaginative Christ-centred reading which is so clear in this hymn and with which David Jones was obviously familiar.

Poets such as Jones, Williams and Dafydd William used their songs or ballads for didactic purposes (and it is striking that, working within established forms, their poems are more literary in style and conventions than their hymns), but the genre which the Methodists popularized was the elegy. Early Methodism was neither a denomination nor a church but it was, nevertheless, very aware of its corporate fellowship. The journeys and visits of the leaders and the movements of overseers and exhorters had brought them into contact with many *seiadau* whose members would have been familiar with names and people outside their own narrow circle. There was an exchange of news at a deeper level than mere anecdote, for it was important that all should share in knowledge of the working of God's grace among His people, as testimony and as mutual support. Elegies to the leaders but also to 'ordinary' *seiat* members by Williams Pantycelyn and a number of other hymn-writers did much to promote the corporate awareness of Methodism, and as the century drew to its close and the first generation passed on, the elegies became a means of preserving and transmitting the common memory of the nature of that golden age. Methodism was to become the most historically minded of all the Welsh denominations, developing its own mythology of its early years. The seeds were being sown in those years themselves in the elegies, which are more important for what they say than for their literary quality. Cast in free verse (often in the metres of the hymns) they are prosaic in content and style. There are stereotyped elements but frequently there is a sense of encountering real people and real circumstances; this, surely, is what was intended and what gave them value.

Literacy went hand-in-hand with Methodism—and by Methodism we must understand not only the *seiadau* and the structure set up by Harris but a style of worship and religious conviction which had permeated other churches by the second half of the eighteenth century. The oral nature of the *seiat* instruction was supported by literary means in the preparation and publication of prose works, many of them translations from English—sermons, catechisms, works of spiritual edification and apologetics.

Prose was not, however, a preferred medium for eighteenth-century Methodist writers and apart from the body of publications by Williams Pantycelyn after 1762, little original prose was produced which examined the nature of the religious experience and which guided the converts. But though few in number, these works are significant in the way they extended the boundaries of Methodist writing in both its content and in its audience. By its nature, prose was more restrained and the writing could become more generalized: the religious experience could be more fully described and analysed at greater length, greater depth. Unlike the hymns, prose tracts were not intended for the group or congregation so much as for the private reader wherever he or she might be found, and publication ensured that they reached a wider audience. Many were frequently reprinted in the nineteenth century, suggesting that they were used as devotional or edifying reading by Nonconformists of all denominations as the suspicion of book religion waned.

Spiritual autobiography and biography was a well-established Puritan genre which could, like the elegy, be used by Methodists to portray and evidence the work of grace and providence in the individual soul. Howel Harris's *Cennadwri a Thystiolaeth* and *The Last Message and Dying Testimony of Howell Harris* were published in 1774. It was almost inevitable that a selection from his journals and letters (edited by Benjamin La Trobe), *A Brief Account of the Life of Howell Harris* (1791), *Hanes Ferr o Fywyd Howell Harris* (1792), should appear after his death as the first biography of one regarded by so many as their father in the faith. The memoir by David Jones, Llan-gan, of the young Methodist cleric Christopher Basset was published in the form of a letter to John Williams, St Athan, in 1784. It is biography in that it offers an account of his life, but in effect it is a prose tribute akin to the elegies already referred to and it was appropriate that the published letter should also have contained a poem in memory of Basset by Williams.

The first full-length spiritual autobiography which Welsh Methodism produced was *Rhad Ras* (Free Grace) by John Thomas, born in Myddfai, Carmarthenshire, in 1730. He 'came to religion' after hearing Harris preach but his early years were a protracted effort to gain the freedom and assurance which he saw in others. He joined Griffith Jones's household as a servant when he was about fifteen years of age, but Jones was not prepared to allow the boy, probably still largely uneducated, somewhat naive and intense, to follow his burning desire to preach. Harris, however, invited him to attend his school at Trefeca a few years later and within a year, in 1749, he had been accepted as a teacher at Jones's circulating schools in Brecknockshire. He was to spend the following years teaching, exhorting, preaching and establishing societies throughout south Wales and gaining a name for himself as a preacher. He attended the Dissenters' Academy in Abergavenny in 1761 though he feared he would be infected by their 'dryness' and lose 'the fire of Llangeitho'. He was ordained to the charge of churches around Rhaeadr, Radnorshire, in 1767, but returned to Carmarthenshire in 1794. He spent his last years at Carmarthen where he died, probably about 1805. During his long ministry he translated tracts by Bunyan and Romaine, wrote some short works of his own to encourage the saints, and composed elegies and some 170 hymns between 1758 and 1788, only a handful of which rise above mediocrity. His autobiography, however, has energy and sincerity, and is an uncomplicated, straightforward account of one whose whole life was spent in the atmosphere of early Methodism, so that *Rhad Ras* is probably the best, because it is the most open, description of the life of the *seiat*, its anguish and its joy.

The book was in preparation in 1788 but the narrative comes to an end in 1803–4: it was not published until 1810. It was written, therefore, over a long period in the closing years of a life spent in constant awareness of the working of the Spirit and of God's Providence. Thomas had respect for the externals of his autobiography: he is meticulous in recording dates, places, names, persons. His narrative is strictly chronological until his movements as an itinerant schoolteacher, preacher and *seiat*-planter after 1749 made it difficult to follow such a scheme in detail, though the framework for his ancedotes remains firmly sequential. But it is clear that, important as the chronological narrative is as the objective verification of his account, this is not of the essence, for his life, its setbacks, disappointments and achievements are all to be interpreted in the light of the divine will. Thomas's recollection of events and conversations is vivid and real, but though there is little reflection in any depth, the fervent apostrophes, appeals and occasional hymns which are interspersed within the narrative remind the reader that these are not merely the reminiscences of a middle-aged man but rather his attempt to re-experience his spiritual progress and to discern God's hand in his mortal life. No doubt Thomas was aware that he was writing in a familiar genre and this would have influenced his narration of events and periods; presumably too not a few episodes had been frequently rehearsed at meetings; but what runs through the book is its genuinely personal and honest tone. Thomas writes with an intensity and conviction which reflect the nature of his exhorting and preaching, which seem to have had as their main themes judgement and the fate of his listeners in eternity. He notes regularly the effect which his preaching had, and though he experienced the joy and peace of the love of Christ—he too is 'claf o gariad' (sick with love)—these periods appear to have been a lull amidst 'the storm clouds and unbelief' and even to have been occasioned by the repentant groans of his congregations. The life of the believer was a war, a constant struggle against doubt and despair, against the correction of conscience and the Law, and Thomas seems never fully to have gained release from the fears of his early years. *Rhad Ras* is as much a book for the author as for his reader.

The autobiography is an intimate portrayal of the nature of *seiat* life, not only in its extended self-examination but in its descriptions of preaching and its effects (Thomas notes these not from personal pride, though he was sensitive and unsure of himself, but rather as signs of the validity of his calling), in the attitudes that it displays towards book religion—catechisms, service-books, devotional reading—as contrasted with the freedom of the Spirit in extempore prayer and preaching; in its attitude to the more cerebral Dissenter worship, and the hints that it gives of theological divisions. The descriptions of attacks by 'mobs' on open-air services remind us that opposition was not merely vocal. Thomas is not an unself-conscious writer. He had always been a regular reader of books both in Welsh and English; he was not uneducated. He uses the phraseology of the Bible and tracts as well as that of the *seiat*, but the power and fluency of his narrative derive from his seriousness of purpose and his sense of urgency. His style is based on his command of spoken Welsh, seen most clearly in the conversations which he reports and especially in his two letters to his mother, which reflect the passionate extempore appeal which probably characterized his exhorting. However conscious he may have been of composing in an established form for an external audience, this has not over-influenced his writing, for what shines through this 'minor classic' is the sincerity and faithfulness of an essentially honest and dedicated man.

Robert Jones of Rhos-lan (1745–1829), schoolmaster and exhorter, belongs to the second generation of Methodists and he was to contribute crucially to the historiography of the movement in his *Drych yr Amseroedd* (A Mirror of the Times; 1820) and to its hymnology through his anthology of hymns, *Grawnsyppiau Canaan* (The Grapes of Canaan; 1795, 1805). His earlier work *Lleferydd yr Asyn*, 1770 (The Words of the Ass, i.e. Balaam's ass, Num. 22, who corrected his master), is couched in the form of a letter 'to a gentleman who sent his servant to disrupt religious worship on the Lord's Day'. It is written in a more classical style than Thomas's autobiography and Jones has clearly taken care over his polished, balanced manner of writing, which is somewhat removed from the immediacy of appeal which characterized *Rhad Ras*. It is, however, vivid and unpretentious and Jones writes with an attractive air of feigned, injured innocence, a light touch of sarcasm and humour. But the letter soon becomes a defence of Methodist meetings in unconsecrated buildings or in the open, and is a robust apologia for the evangelical call to repentance. It evokes the contentious atmosphere of Methodism but in a more restrained way than Thomas's descriptions, and in a style more suitable for its recipient. Methodism was the religion not only of *y werin* (the lower sorts) and Jones's work is a reminder that it could call upon a more finished style than the spontaneity of '*seiat* literature' when it needed to.

A third work published towards the end of the eighteenth century is quite unlike any other Methodist prose-writing in Welsh. Hugh Jones of Maesglasau, Merioneth (1749–1825), better educated than many of his day, was a schoolmaster, a prolific 'professional' translator and musician who published two volumes of verse, songs and hymns in 1776 and 1797. During a period in London in 1772–4 he published his first and most innovative book. *Cydymaith i'r Hwsmon* (The Husbandman's Companion) is a collection of allegorical meditations on the seasons of the year and the farmer's round of tasks—ploughing, sowing, harrowing, threshing, winnowing—and on other aspects of his work such as care for animals, lost animals, the dog's love for his master, rent-day, rams fighting. The short meditations contain verses in popular song metres and in traditional strict metres. Some of his ideas, says Jones, were borrowed from English authors but it is not difficult to sense here the thoughts of a young, deeply religious countryman exiled in a strange city. His unaffected simple style allows his warmth of feeling to be easily transmitted so that these generally unlaboured allegories are still a delight to read.

The second generation of Methodists, working in the quieter aftermath of the Great Awakening, built upon the foundations laid by the fathers. They turned towards exegesis, education and systematic theology, and to history and biography, in the work of Thomas Charles, Thomas Jones and Robert Jones. These changes are reflected in the more conceptual and theological hymns of Edward Jones, David Charles senior and David Charles junior. Benjamin Francis, a Baptist who spent his ministerial life in England, expresses more clearly a doctrine of the Church. Methodism became a separate denomination in 1811 and the boundaries between Nonconformist denominations and the Anglican Church became more marked. The extempore and enthusiastic character of much of the earlier Methodist writing was lost, as was its association with the modes of folk-literature and its verse. Henceforth, religion would acquire its own distinctive style.

BIBLIOGRAPHY

Evan Isaac, *Prif Emynwyr Cymru* (Lerpwl, 1925).

Hugh Jones (ed. Henry Lewis), *Cydymaith i'r Hwsmon* (Caerdydd, 1949).

Robert Jones, ' "Lleferydd yr asyn", Gwaith Robert Jones Rhos Lan', *Y Llenor*, XV (1898), 120–41.

Bobi Jones, *Pedwar Emynydd* (Llandybïe, 1970).

E. G. Millward, *Blodeugerdd Barddas o Gerddi Rhydd y Ddeunawfed Ganrif* (Llandybïe, 1991).

Derec Llwyd Morgan, 'John Thomas, awdur *Rhad Ras*', *Pobl Pantycelyn* (Llandysul, 1986), 20–7.

Idem, *The Great Awakening in Wales* (London, 1988).

Idem, 'Llenyddiaeth y Methodistiaid (1763–1814)', in Gomer M. Roberts (ed.), *Hanes Methodistiaeth Galfinaidd Cymru*, vol. 2 (1978), chap. 9.

Gomer M. Roberts (ed.), *Hanes Methodistiaeth Galfinaidd Cymru*, vol. 1 (Caernarfon, 1973).

Idem, 'Llenydda a chyhoeddi 1737–1762', in ibid., chap. 12.

Idem, *Hanes Methodistiaeth Galfinaidd Cymru*, vol. 2 (Caernarfon, 1978).

Idem, *Morgan Rhys, Llanfynydd* (Caernarfon, 1951).
Idem, *Dafydd William, Llandeilo Fach* (Llandysul, 1954).
Idem, *Dafydd Jones o Gaeo* (Aberystwyth, 1948).
Idem, *Emynwyr Bethesda'r Fro*, (Llandysul, 1967).
John Thomas (ed. J. Dyfnallt Owen), *Rhad Ras* (Caerdydd, 1949).

CHAPTER 13

ANN GRIFFITHS AND THE NORM

R. M. JONES

Ann Griffiths (1776–1805) seems to be lauded rather immoderately. Her poetic output scarcely amounted to more than some seventy stanzas. The scope of her thought, even from a theological or experiential point of view, was not diverse in character, and coincided with the Calvinism accepted by all the Protestant denominations in Wales at the time. Her religious experience followed the evangelical norm. She died young and never had much opportunity to write: indeed, we know of only one stanza that she herself recorded on paper. She was primarily a contributor to oral literature. Her hymns were wasted on the rural air, preserved providentially by the memory of an illiterate maid-servant, Ruth Evans, who had heard the 'mistress' singing them around the farm. Her intellectual training too was, though profound, basically aural and quite narrow in compass: her knowledge of politics, history and geography and the sciences was probably painfully limited, as she had never had a formal education as that is generally defined.

Yet, her emotional training and her knowledge of people were substantial, and certainly her thought about matters of the spirit profound and perhaps unsurpassed in depth in the history of our country. From a literary point of view she had presumably been immersed in a complex and intricate culture from her early days and her immediate environment was intellectually vital and stimulating.

This statement may seem strange as she was born in what many would account a remote hamlet in the European context. Perhaps as a result of that supposition, Ann Griffiths may sometimes be depicted by critics as a lonely figure, hidden away in a secluded backwater. Exceptional she certainly was, as will be everyone gifted as she was. But she was neither alone in an area where the intellectual and emotional stimulus she enjoyed within a live and warm social background was considerable, nor a pelican in the desert of Welsh hymnology. Nationally, she was just one single bud, perhaps the most beautiful, in a verse-flourishing of great vitality and highly developed finesse. The post-Pantycelyn hymn movement of which she was a part included Edward Jones (1761–1836), Thomas William (1761–1844), David Charles senior (1762–1834), Robert ap Gwilym Ddu (1766–1850), John Elias (1774–1841), John Hughes (1775–1854) and Pedr Fardd (1775–1845). There had been a significant shift from south to north and mid-north in the flood of hymns being produced, particularly with Hugh Jones (1749–1825), Siôn Singer (c.1750– 1807), Gwilym ab Ellis (1752–1810), Thomas Jones (1756–1820) and J. R. Jones (1765–1822). In her own area, where just before her time this great movement was getting under way, one finds the epicentre of the carol-composing and singing that evidently influenced her considerably; and of course, Montgomery-shire remains still the area where unique *carol plygain* singing continues unabated.

Internationally, due to Wales's political anonymity, Ann Griffiths may be considered slightly less than a nobody. Born in 1776 to an unknown peasant family, her parents being John Evan Thomas and Jane Theodore, in the unknown parish of Llanfihangel-yng-Ngwynfa in north Montgomeryshire, and having received little schooling, she lived her brief life till August 1805. During that seemingly inconspicuous life-span she published nothing: she hardly left her parish apart from occasional visits to nearby villages and forays to Bala. She married an ordinary unknown small farmer from her neighbourhood in 1804, and died during the subsequent year, unknown to all but a favoured few, a month after giving birth, and shortly after the child herself died.

Yet, as her work was composed during the first years of the nineteenth century, one could make a good case for considering her the most talented writer of Welsh in that century, and (much perhaps to the embarrassment of some) the most gifted ever of our women writers. Just as the immense intellect of George Eliot marked the apex of the novel-form in England in that century, and just as the equally unknown genius of Emily Dickinson marked the apex of American verse in that same century, so too the modern presence of the female gender in Welsh, succoured by the same burgeoning of evangelical Nonconformity—of all things—during that same remarkable century, brought forth this singularly talented hymnist.

Our knowledge of Ann Griffiths's life is comparatively sparse, and as a result one may be tempted to romanticize her as an entirely untutored highland lass in a remote hill parish leading a sheltered existence far from civilization. But amongst her acquaintances was one of the best theological minds in Europe at the time—as his *Geiriadur Ysgrythyrol* testifies—namely Thomas Charles. She had furthermore been trained in one of the most intricate and highly developed metrical systems in the world, as her knowledge of *cynghanedd* exemplifies, and she knew the dramatic work of Twm o'r Nant and was surrounded by practitioners such as Eos Gwynfa (Thomas Williams), Evan Williams and Harri Parri, as well as by her father John Evan Thomas. Just as she was immersed in the hymns of Pantycelyn she was also cognisant of the preaching of John Elias, who was generally agreed to be one of the finest preachers at the turn of the century. She was closely acquainted too with substantial intellectuals such as John Davies (Tahiti) and John Hughes (Pontrobert), and well versed in some of the most able devotional works of the period, such as *Gwisg Wen Ddisglair* (Shining White Raiment) by Timothy Thomas, and *Athrawiaeth y Drindod* (The Doctrine of the Trinity) written by the person who had been the medium of her conversion, Benjamin Jones, as well as works in translation such as *Tragwyddol Orffwysfa'r Saint* (*The Saints' Everlasting Rest*) by Richard Baxter.

*   *   *

I suspect that Ann's compositions were carried out orally, not, by far, a rare occurrence in Welsh literature. The majority of the poems composed for a thousand years, from the sixth to the sixteenth centuries, were put together in that way, even in the aristocratic tradition. But this seeming disadvantage, from the point of view of careful reconsideration of individual lines and of structuring the relation between one part of a poem and another, did not deter her from thinking of her hymns as complete wholes, nor from the consideration of internal detail.

Take her hymn to the 'Way'. This is a particularly important poem as it touches on a topic frequently discussed by critics who refer to mysticism and see such as a development over three stages. Dr R. Tudur Jones has dealt specifically with the seemingly rather academic and theoretically narrow steps outlined for mysticism in one particular tradition, namely from Purification through Enlightenment to Union. He points out that in the biblical tradition, Union exists already from Christian rebirth through the immediate occurrence of conversion. And this comes through in Ann Griffiths's poem:

> Ffordd heb ddechrau, eto'n newydd, . . .
> Ffordd yn Briod, Ffordd yn Ben.

[A Way without beginning, yet new; a Way that is a married partner, a Way that is a Head/a Way that has already come to the end.]

Ann begins with a stanza that was not unlikely to have Bunyan in mind, as he was a major influence on Welsh hymnists. She sees herself as contemplating this Way on which she has been unexpectedly placed, realizing that, compared with her usual environment and its regularities and irregularities, this way by its nature was quite contrary to natural values.

She refers modestly first of all to her own way as a 'path', 'in', not 'through', the world. Having set her position and course in the first four lines as being under the—existentially 'your'—face of Christ, she immediately must refer to the strangeness of this path, now endowed with the term 'Way'. And she does so typically in paradoxes, three in a row: the first recognizing the cross as a crown, the next recalling immediately and referentially all the context of Romans 5, and thirdly one of the important realizations of the mature Christian that this way, although so mysteriously complicated, is terribly simple (echoing Psalm 107.7):

> Er mai cwbwl groes i natur
> Yw fy llwybyr yn y byd,
> Ei deithio a wnaf, a hynny'n dawel
> Yng ngwerthfawr wedd dy wyneb pryd;
> Wrth godi'r groes ei chyfri'n goron,
> Mewn gorthrymderau llawen fyw,
> Ffordd yn uniawn, er mor ddyrys,
> I ddinas gyfaneddol yw.

[Though entirely against nature
Is the pathway that I pace;

Yet I'll tread it, in all meekness,
By precious vision of thy face;
Lift the cross, a crown regard it,
In oppression live serene;
A Way straight, though so entangled,
To a City, my demesne.]

It is inevitable that the second stanza therefore should commence with one of her most characteristic epithets: 'Wonderful'. That leads her to the biblical statement that this 'Way' was a person, Christ himself, one of the basic themes of the poem. She is already in Christ. The way that she now celebrates leads her then to use the old Welsh technique of 'dyfalu', the cascading of metaphor after metaphor. These metaphors, however, reflect the organic co-relationship of various aspects of the Way.

At first she sees the Way in its relationship to time, full of years and yet impervious. Then she takes Hebrews 7.3 in a new direction by seeing it with Hebrews 10.20; very simply, the Way is there but is not there, it is strangely new although it has been there even before the beginning, and it possesses the peculiarity of giving life to the dead. This leads her to consider the direction of the Way (Math. 7.14), proceeding as it does towards Life, and also life-giving to its travellers, she says; and this odd gift is something she insists upon in one of her letters: 'I am thankful for the legality of the way, and for the fact that it glorifies its author, more than because it requites its travellers' (tr.), a principle that is central to her tenets—the Christian lives primarily for the exaltation of God rather than simply for the salvation of man. The Way is a bride (or husband) but has headship (and is already an end); and then we return to Hebrews 10 (the salient biblical reference for this hymn), as I suspect that this Way has not only been consecrated but has been turned into a Way through the veil into the consecration of the Holy of Holies:

Ffordd a'i henw yn 'Rhyfeddol',
Hen, a heb heneiddio, yw;
Ffordd heb ddechrau, eto'n newydd,
Ffordd yn gwneud y meirw'n fyw;
Ffordd i ennill ei thrafaelwyr,
Ffordd yn Briod, Ffordd yn Ben,
Ffordd gysegrwyd, af ar hyd-ddi
I orffwys ynddi draw i'r llen.

[Way whose name is simply 'Wondrous'
Old and yet for ever new,
No beginning and no ageing,
Where the dead their life renew;
Way that wins lives of travellers,
Way that's Head, a Way that's Bride,
A Way made holy that I'll follow
Beyond the veil and there reside.]

The first four lines of the third stanza leave this shower of diverse descriptions to concentrate on one central attribute, the 'invisibility' of the Way.

The 'vulture' of the English Job 28.7 is 'barcut' in Welsh, a cultural translation; possessing an eye to penetrate, though failing here even at full light (possibly thinking of Proverbs 4.18). Now she explains that this unseeable Way can be perceived by some, returning via Psalm 107.4 to Hebrews 11. These particular seers have no virtue in themselves (Romans 4.5), and she now parallels one of the lines in her stanza too: the Way raises the dead to life, at the same time returning to parallel the letter I quoted in discussing stanza two, concluding with a line resting again with Romans (5.1) and Luke 1.30.

Ffordd na chenfydd llygad barcut,
Er ei bod fel hanner dydd,
Ffordd ddisathar anweledig
I bawb ond perchenogion ffydd;
Ffordd i gyfiawnhau'r annuwiol,
Ffordd i godi'r meirw'n fyw,
Ffordd gyfreithlon i droseddwyr
I hedd a ffafor gyda Duw.

[Way by eye of kite unnoticed
Though it be bright light of day;
Save for those by faith accounted,
An unseen and untrodden Way;
A Way to justify the godless,
A Way to bring the dead to life,
A just Way for sinners into
God's accordance, without strife.]

The word 'way' is still echoed in the final stanza, where she returns to the theme of stanza two—time. The birth of this Way has been planned before the world began (2 Timothy 1.9), the promise having been made in Eden (Genesis 3.15). Note the rhyme in this stanza of 'rhaid' with 'wraig': this is known as generic rhyme, here a voiced plosive with a voiced plosive, not uncommon in early Welsh as in Irish verse, and often used in folk poetry. We now return to the legality of the Way, referred to in her letter: the Way is the basis of the second covenant (Hebrews 8.6–7)—note, the terms are technical—and that this covenant was the conclusion of the Council of the Trinity (1 John 5.7). It provides therefore joy for celebration, although in using the word 'wine', the stuff of revelry, we realize that this revelry is in blood, it makes the heart glad (Psalms 104.15; John 2.1–11) but is represented in the sacrament, which is the end of the Way.

The whole poem is substantiated in the intellect, but the 'Way' rings throughout, time after time nailing our attention to the central image and object. She leads further and further along it, deepening our contemplation as we stride on. It is as if the way is already in her as she herself moves in the Way.

*   *   *

The topic that has attracted most interest in Ann Griffiths's work has been her mysticism. But there is a problem here. Conventional liberal thinking has concluded that by rights she should never have turned out a mystic. Mysticism—so this accepted wisdom persuades us—is vaguely emotional, subjective, delightfully nebulous (on principle) about doctrine, slack and ecumenic, prone to ecstatic imagining. Hardly good form for a convinced Calvinist like Ann.

It is therefore appropriate to examine the alleged contradiction between Calvinism and mysticism, as this would provide a method for defining the quality of Ann Griffiths's mysticism precisely. Neither her Calvinism nor her mysticism has been questioned separately: the stumbling-block has always been the fact that such a theology should co-exist in a person possessing such an intense personal experience. This should hardly cause surprise in Welsh, where it is a central characteristic of the Protestant tradition of mysticism from Morgan Llwyd, through Williams of Pantycelyn and numerous other Welsh hymn-writers, diarists and letter-writers such as Ann Griffiths, on to Islwyn.

Mysticism comes in all shapes and sizes and takes on variegated garments. It can come in drugs and swoons, fancies and foibles. It is usually interpreted at the secular level as predominantly subjective, often self-propelled, and certainly 'romantic' in nature. In order to comprehend the distinctive and objective nature of Welsh reformed mysticism, one can hardly do better than start with Calvin. Particularly by liberals who have not read him, Calvin is perceived as beyond the pale from the mystic point of view, too objective, over-disciplined by Scripture, too involved in a belief that should dominate political, social, economic, artistic and all other spheres of life, too rational and doctrinal.

Calvin in his ninth Sermon on the Passion describes the union Ann Griffiths experienced:

> Let us know the unity that we have with our Lord Jesus Christ; to wit, that he wills to have a common life with us, and that what he has should be ours: nay, that he even wishes to dwell in us, not in imagination, but in effect; not in earthly fashion but spiritually; and that whatever may befall, he so labours by the virtues of his Holy Spirit that we are united with him more closely than are the limbs with the body.

Some of these phrases might have been Ann's, and particularly the precision that negates, 'not this but this'. This was a felt knowledge. Calvin's description can often be as exhilarating as Ann Griffiths's, as in his Commentary on 1 Corinthians 6.15:

> The spiritual union that we have with Christ belongs not only to the soul, but also to the body, so much so that we are flesh of his flesh and bone of his bone (Ephesians 5.30). Otherwise the hope of the resurrection would be faint indeed, were not our union what it is; namely, complete and entire.

No Christian mystic can be more intense than this.

What is this 'mystic' knowledge of union with Christ as expressed by Ann Griffiths?

> O am bara i lynu wrtho,
> Fy enaid, byth yn ddiwahân . . . (I)*

*These figures refer to the poem number in Bobi Jones, *Pedwar Emynydd* (Llandybïe, 1970).

[O! to continue clinging to him
Ever my soul with no divorce . . .]

Dŵr i'w nofio heb fynd trwyddo,
Dyn yn Dduw, a Duw yn ddyn. (III)

[Water to swim through, without crossing,
A man who's God, and God who's man.]

The image here is important in that the Christian is in Christ, but is not dissolved. When we speak of mystic union, we are dealing—to generalize—with at least two concepts. On the one hand, in some Eastern religions, we have confused union, where identity dissolves and the distinction between the Godhead and manhood is ambiguous and obscured. This is frequently related to depersonalizing. On the other hand, we have a union that has been described with some precision by Calvin, which maintains man's identity, but nevertheless is a genuine concord.

Am fod arna i'n sgrifenedig
Ddelw gwrthrych llawer mwy . . .
Sêl yn tanio'n erbyn pechod,
Caru delw santeiddhad . . .
Addurna'm henaid ar dy ddelw. (V)

[Because there's written on me the stamp
Of one who's an object greater by far . . .
A seal (or zeal) being enkindled against sin,
As I make love to the imprint of sanctification . . .
Adorn my soul upon your imprint.]

The image we have here is of the human being conformed or being moulded under the impression of the divine form.

Rhyfedda fyth, briodas-ferch,
I bwy yr wyt yn wrthrych serch. (XII)

[Be ever amazed, O bride,
To whom you are made an object of affection.]

O am dreiddio i'r adnabyddiaeth
O'r unig wir a'r bywiol Dduw,
I'r fath raddau a fo'n lladdfa
I ddychmygion o bob rhyw. (XVIII)

[O to penetrate in personal knowledge
Of the only true and living God
So far that imaginings of all kinds
Are simply killed outright.]

Marriage is Ann Griffiths's usual image for this union; and Joseph Clancy translates:

Heb ddychymyg, llen, na gorchudd,
A'm henaid ar ei ddelw'n llawn;
Yng nghymdeithas y dirgelwch
Datguddiedig yn ei glwy,
Cusanu'r mab i dragwyddoldeb,
Heb im gefnu arno mwy. (XX)

[Without fancy – veil – or cover –
My soul – his image – to the full –
As fellow – in the mystery –
Opened to us – in his Wound –
Kiss the Son – for everlasting –
Turn my back on him – no more.]

J. R. Jones argued that the Calvinist could not properly use the biblical metaphor of marriage in describing the union of the Infinite and the finite, as marriage presupposed two equals. J. R. Jones (like W. J. Gruffydd), however, had not studied Calvin himself on this, nor had he chosen to interpret the supernatural as understood in historic Christianity. Here we have Calvin in his *Institutes* III, 1, 3:

Now we know that he is of no avail save only to those to whom he is a head and the first-born among the brethren, to those, in fine, who are clothed with him. To this union alone it is owing that, in regard to us, the Saviour has not come in vain. To this is to be referred that sacred marriage, by which we become bone of his bone, and flesh of his flesh, and so one with him (Eph. 5.30), for it is by the Spirit alone that he unites himself to us. By the same grace and energy of the Spirit we become his members, so that he keeps us under him, and we in our turn possess him.

Marriage as a trope maintains the distinction between two beings. The finite does not become omnipotent, omniscient nor omnipresent, and yet the union is none the less genuine, and even requisite. It has been conveyed by Calvin once again in the *Institutes* where he speaks of the Son's absolute essential union with every Christian. He even claims that without such a union there is no Christian: 'To communicate to us the blessings which he received from the Father, he must become ours and dwell in us.'

This is Calvinism. It is also a type of what is termed mysticism. W. J. Gruffydd, Thomas Parry and J. R. Jones, besides others, all claimed that Calvinism should properly militate against any sort of union between the believer and God; and J. R. Jones argued that there were two factors that established an insurmountable division—man's eternal creatureliness and the abyss of sin that man himself had embraced. J. R. Jones's difficulties, however, simply arose out of his anti-supernatural presuppositions.

In her second letter to John Hughes, Ann Griffiths puts it like this: 'It came to my mind that I was prepared to give all I have, my good and my bad, for the Son, in matrimonial union.' And writing to Elizabeth Evans, she says:

> Dear sister, I see more need than ever to spend the portion that is left in giving myself daily and continually, body and soul, into the care of Him who is able to keep what is presented to him until that day. Not just giving myself once, but living to give myself, until and whilst putting this tabernacle aside.

How does one locate Ann Griffiths within the context of the Christian mystical tradition? There are three characteristics that mark her out as being within the biblical and Calvinist strand. First of all, there is no dark night of the soul. The only darkness she encounters is that of sin and unbelief. Everything in Christ is light. The image of God as a black night, that one encounters in St John of the Cross (and the Pseudo-Dionysius, *The Cloud of Unknowing*, Meister Eckhart and the Rhineland mystics, the strand that proved so potent for Saunders Lewis and R. S. Thomas) is foreign to Ann, as it was to the Gospel of John, Pantycelyn and Augustine, Gregory and Bernard. In the Augustinian biblical stream that passed through the Puritans and continued in Wales up to the twenty-first century, darkness is always related to sin and death. The experienced negation is towards negation itself, not towards the fullness and richness of content in Christ (*Pedwar Emynydd* (*PE*) XX, i, iii; XXI, iii).

Secondly, there is no evidence of a mechanical progression through various precise stages towards eventual Christian union with Jesus. There is growth, of course (*PE* IV). But from the precise point of her conversion, there is immediate union: she is in Christ and Christ is in her. Henceforth there should certainly be greater surrender to the spirit of Christ, a more faithful walk with God, a warmer devotion; but union itself is irrevocable once Christ is born in the heart of the believer, and the believer's spirit belongs to Him (*PE* XXXVI).

Thirdly—and this may seem strange from a Calvinist like Ann, but it was true of Calvin too—there is a 'mystical' experience but no attempt to intellectualize that experience itself systematically. There was order in providence, an order in Christ's saving work (*PE* II, ii; VI, i; VII, ii), an order in the truth, but no scholastic presentation that analysed a uniform pattern of mystical contemplation. There is no schematization or theorizing of the soul's relationship.

Mysticism in itself—like 'believing'—has nothing essentially to do with the truth. It can, of course, be an experience related to the genuine: it can also be embroiled in the ego or the fake. There are gods and gods. In the Protestant theological tradition to which Ann Griffiths belonged, a normal mystic experience would be monitored by the objective, historical materials of scriptural revelation. Mysticism as a general phenomenon can be subjectively irresponsible and lacking in meaningful substance. It can be delusionary and superficial, romantic and self-centred. A Calvinistic mystic like Ann, on the other hand, is a mystic whose experience is disciplined within the context of doctrinal content, just as in every person's daily existence action and freedom have also to be disciplined by natural law (e.g. gravity). The feelings are secondary to the meaning: they are checkable and objective, as well as being mysterious and subjective. They are historically and transcendentally diffused and linked to the conscious intellect as faith is to action.

This aspect of Ann Griffiths's work was bolstered rather than undermined by her intellectual understanding of the faith. In this she was not departing from the thirty-nine Articles and the beliefs of the Nonconformists on the one hand and the Methodists on the other. The only practical distinction (apart from organization) was that not only did the evangelicals believe seriously and earnestly the doctrines that the others claimed, without seeking ambiguity, but that these beliefs were of eternal consequence and enrapturing inspiration to them.

Ann Griffiths, like her critics, would not have taken her Calvin neat. But she, unlike her critics, would have had, as well as an acquaintance with Puritan literature, direct contact with one of the most knowledgeable and vital Calvinists Wales has known, namely Thomas Charles. And on that great biblical comparison of marriage as an image of union with Christ, his comments in his *Geiriadur Ysgrythyrol* (Scriptural Dictionary; 1805–11, pp. 743–4) are most relevant. Having passed through her conversion revelation, Ann Griffiths would then share with Thomas Charles, as with Calvin, the excitement of knowing the biblical comparison as a reality in her own spirit. It should constantly be remembered: comments by others on her Calvinism inevitably reflect a crushing ignorance of Calvin himself. I have somewhat laboured this particular point as the Ann Griffiths discussion throughout the twentieth century was dogged by a cartoon of Calvin's ghost.

The crux of the controversy surrounding Ann and the main Welsh mystic stream is that doctrinal truth, clear and precise, should hardly co-exist with experiential ecstasy. Yet, says Calvin: 'Jesus Christ dwells in us, not only adhering to us by an indissoluble bond, but, by a wonderful union that surpasses our understanding, he daily unites himself with us more and more in one same substance' (*Institutes* III, 2, 24). He speaks of an *unio mystica*. In commentary on Ephesians 5.29 Calvin again elucidates this:

> As Eve was formed of the substance of Adam her husband, so that she was like unto a part of him, so in order to be true members of Christ we communicate in his substance, and by that communication are assembled into one and the same body.

There is no need for the moment to dwell on the opposing tendency or on the safeguards that Calvin formulated, particularly in his controversy with André Osiander.

*   *   *

A brief essay such as this does not afford space to deal adequately
with Ann Griffiths's mind: either with her doctrinal understanding, or with her ideas about life. These have unfortunately
been fiercely misunderstood and consequently misrepresented in
the twentieth century, basically because of ignorance or at least
animosity regarding her theology, and because of dogmatic
presuppositions that are anti-Methodistical. Perhaps, by taking
this particular bull partly by the horns, that is to say by dealing
specifically with one such discussion, aspects of her position may
be illustrated in the process.

In discussing her imagery, in the volume *Y Ferch o Ddolwar
Fach* edited by Dyfnallt Morgan in 1977, Euros Bowen raises a
number of relevant questions. The first is relevant in considering
almost all Welsh literature during the period between the
Protestant Reformation (and even before that) and the beginning
of the twentieth century: pietism. It caused believers and others to
deny the relevance of their faith to the practicalities of life and to
be over-wary of the significance of the physical, a tendency in
monasticism as well as in Puritanism and Methodism. It may be
defined as a betrayal of God's sovereignty and negligence of a
healthy attitude towards creation. Pietism emphasizes direct
worship and tends to narrow Christian duties to maintenance of
good ethics, prayer and devotion, whilst ignoring the duty to be a
steward and bring forth fruit, responsible within the whole of life.
Euros Bowen argues that Ann Griffiths lacked a proper realization
of herself as being in the image of God—a matter that has
significance within the doctrine of creation, and he claimed that
she shared this deficiency with Luther and Calvin.

What Euros Bowen has in view here is the fact that Ann
Griffiths's central concern was with God's glory in salvation and
with the restoration towards God in Christ, rather than with
creation. He discusses her use of the word 'delw' (image, imprint)
and claims that God's image does not depend on God's action on
the cross, but simply continues in man despite the Fall. Therefore
the emphasis on salvation to the detriment of creation was
unsatisfactory.

There are two points to be noted; firstly, the nature of man's
corruption and his ability or otherwise to reach God under his

own steam, and secondly the question of God's image remaining in man. Calvin and Ann Griffiths shared with all the Protestant denominations in Wales up to the first decade of the nineteenth century an agreement that every aspect of man's nature was corrupted by sin/death through the Fall. Yet, according to the doctrine of Common Grace, God gives earthly blessings 'indiscriminately' and via the conscience withholds man from destroying himself completely. Then, according to the parallel doctrine of Particular or Saving Grace there are some who through spiritual revelation gain sight of God having been humbled to Him through the propitiatory and sovereign work of Christ. They become His children. These are matters not referred to by Euros Bowen.

In Ann Griffiths's work the use of the word 'delw' is important. It is the key word in Hymn V (*PE*), beginning 'Mae'r dydd yn dod' (The day is coming). Admittedly, it refers to Christ placing his image on the needy sinner; but the inability of that person to gain eternal life through his/her own actions is obvious: all is through grace. Ann Griffiths admits that her former passions are now banished solely because God has inscribed the image of sanctification in her; she wishes to have her soul 'adorned' with His image. Again in Hymn IX (*PE*), 'Am fy mod i mor llygredig' (Since I am so corrupted), she speaks of fully enjoying his 'image', which seems to suggest that her use of the word is a matter of concretizing, even sensualizing: 'with my soul completely on his image'. God thus simply does not depend on any remnants of the creative image of Himself in fallen man to restore such a helpless wretch to His family; and Ann Griffiths would never have dreamt of placing such conditions on Him. The specific creation image certainly never attracted Ann Griffiths's brief attention; but Calvin inevitably deals with it (*Institutes* I, 15, 3–5; III, 7, 6) and sees it as the basis of man's dignity and uniqueness. For Ann Griffiths, the mystery of the Propitiation itself was central and obsessional.

At one point, Euros Bowen contrasts the standpoint held by Ann Griffiths's closest Christian guide, John Hughes of Pontrobert (together with Calvin) on the one hand, emphasizing God's sovereignty and honour, with Ann Griffiths on the other, who underlined his Love. This may seem sweet. But to ignore or minimize the love portrayed in the sermons of both Hughes and Calvin— or more relevantly on this matter the absolute sovereignty of

Christ as seen in Ann Griffiths—is simply seeking desperately for a
debating point and finding a fancy. Ann speaks of 'grym y
rhoddion' (the force of the gifts), 'Teyrnwialen aur sydd yn ei law'
(In his hand a golden sceptre). She speaks of having 'direct
admittance to his throne', 'Ffordd yn Ben' (A Way that is
sovereign), 'Ymostwng i'w ewyllys' (bending to His will), 'Mae'n
Dduw i gario'r orsedd/ Ar ddiafol, cnawd a byd' (He is God to
carry the throne/ Over devil, flesh and world). She longs to 'come
to the King's table': 'Oh to be able to honour Him'. Through a
word from the Lord the dead will arise. Certainly, God's
beauteous and ecstatic love is very present to her, but not more so
than his honour and sovereignty.

As Dr Bowen attempted to contrast Ann Griffiths with Calvin,
he coupled Calvin with Anselm, denying to them both the fullness
of realization of the grace of God issuing from His love:

> For Anselm the atonement is external to man . . . In Anselm's doctrine
> there is no faith relationship to permit the sinner to partake in what
> Christ did for him. This particular faith relationship, however, is
> essential from Ann Griffiths's point of view . . . the realisation that
> salvation has its source in the depths of God's love, without venturing
> so far in Ann Griffiths's comprehension as John Calvin transforming
> such a realisation into a dogmatic system of sovereign election that
> destroys the nature of this salvation.

There is, however, absolutely no doubt in Ann Griffiths's mind
that the salvation obtainable in Christ was external, historical,
objective, and entirely applied through grace. One of her great
words, repeated continually was 'gwrthrych' (an object). And even
the act of salvation itself was not simply subjective, but objective,
not relying on the psychological vagaries of 'realization'. This was
equally true of Calvin. To argue that Ann Griffiths was somehow
superior in that she withheld from analysing that situation in a
systematic theology is just nonsense, as too is the suggestion or
myth that Calvin's intellect, which enabled him to produce a
biblically oriented description of what Protestant doctrine was all
about, somehow dampened any possible passion that he possessed
for his Saviour. This is just wishful thinking.

Dr Bowen argues that:

> there is a difference between the meaning of Christ's death according to

Anselm, on the one hand, which, according to the principle of the perfect law of justice, satisfies God's honour and the Protestant doctrine, on the other hand, which conceives of the Atonement, according to the principle of just punishment, as suffering the punishment of God's anger towards man's sin. If the first doctrine is correct, there is no need of the second; if the second, there is no need of the first. The two doctrines are woven together in Ann Griffiths's hymns.

Actually, they are woven together simply because both are acceptable Protestant doctrines, and the need for both is apparent. Perhaps the difficulty arises from not realizing that one may understand the Atonement as towards God and man simultaneously.

In the peroration closing his essay he states:

The great wonder of her life was Jesus Christ. Ultimately she does not think in terms of Calvinism nor of mysticism nor of these two plaited together, but rather in terms of the salvation through Jesus Christ, son of God. For Ann Griffiths the great dowry was Christianity witnessed in the deliverance of the Church and personal salvation.

A most worthy sentiment, but loaded. Actually, there is just no necessity to make these violent contrasts between Ann Griffiths and orthodox doctrine, between mysticism and Calvinism: many of the distinctions are blurred in realizing and admitting that they are all about different aspects of the identical task. Although Calvin uses different forms, his sermons, letters and volumes of Christian theology on occasion orientate to the same topics as Ann Griffiths, although admittedly the vast volume of his writings allows him to deal with many other aspects as well.

*　　*　　*

I want to quote, in Joseph P. Clancy's translation, one complete hymn by Ann Griffiths as an unbroken whole, as it is arguably one of the profoundest lyrics in the Welsh language between Wiliam Llŷn in the sixteenth century and Waldo Williams in the twentieth. It is a hymn of utter praise to Christ, the God-man. Between the sixteenth and the twentieth centuries no Welsh writer—with the notable exception of Pantycelyn—had the wide knowledge of

language combined with the splendour of intellect that could
permit such an explosion of ordered feeling.

> Wondrous – wondrous to the angels –
> Great wonder – in the sight of faith –
> To see the giver of being – sustainer –
> And governor – of all that is –
> In swaddling clothing – in the manger –
> With no place to lay his head –
> And yet the shining host of glory –
> Worships him – as their great God –
>
> When the smoke – is shrouding – Sinai –
> At the trumpet's loudest sound –
> I will go – across the boundary –
> To feast in Christ the Word – unslain –
> There – fulfilment – has its dwelling –
> Full – the void man's loss once made –
> The breach – between divine and human –
> His self-sacrifice – reconciled –
>
> He – the Atonement – between the robbers –
> He – endured the swoon of death –
> He – empowered his executioners'
> Arms – to nail him on the cross –
> Paying the debt – of brands for burning –
> And honouring – his Father's – law –
> Justice – it shines forth – in fervour –
> Forgiving – freely reconciled –
>
> See – my soul – where he was lying –
> Lord of kings – author of peace –
> The creation – in him – moving –
> And he – dead – within the grave –
> Song – and life – of all the lost ones –
> Greatest wonder – of heaven's host –
> God – in flesh – they see and worship –
> The choir cries – 'To him be praise –'
>
> Thanks ever – thanks a hundred thousand –
> Thanks – while there is breath in me –
> Because an object's there – to worship –
> And an endless text – for song –

Who was – in my nature – tempted –
Like the worst of human kind –
Tiny infant feeble – strengthless –
Infinite truth – and living God –

Rid of this body of corruption –
To pierce – with the fervent choir on high –
Deep – into the boundless wonders –
Of salvation – on Calvary –
To live – to see – the unseen One who
Died – and who is now alive –
Eternal – undivided – union –
And communion – with my God –

There – I will exalt the name that
Is the Atonement – God – has willed –
Without fancy – veil – or cover –
My soul – his image – to the full –
As fellow – in the mystery –
Opened to us – in his wound –
Kiss the Son – for everlasting –
Turn my back on him – no more –

The motivation for composing these stanzas she mentions firmly at the outset. It is simply wonder, beginning at the Incarnation. Like many mystics, Ann conveys her response to that amazing event in paradox: 'the governor of being . . . in swaddling clothes'. And this can but remind us of two striking lines in Hymn I (*PE*):

Rhoi awdur bywyd i farwolaeth,
A chladdu'r atgyfodiad mawr.

Putting the author of life to death,
And burying the great resurrection.

The emphasis is now on seeing: '*See* – my soul – where he was lying –'. And what does she see? No less than 'the creation – in him – moving –/ And he – dead – within the grave.' She returns later in the same stanza: 'God – in flesh – they *see* and worship', which climaxes again finally in the paradox 'To live – to *see* – the unseen One'. Her relationship with Christ is direct: 'Without fancy – veil – or cover'; and the contact is close: 'Kiss the Son – for everlasting'. The relationship of the final stanza is complete. To quote Calvin:

Such is the union between us and Christ, who in some sorts makes us partakers of his substance. We are bone of his bone and flesh of his flesh, Gen.2: 23, not because like ourselves he has a human nature, but because, by the power of his Spirit, he makes us a part of his body, so that from him we derive our life. (Commentary, Eph. 5.31)

The continual looking, surveying, leads Ann Griffiths on to union. As Calvin again put it: 'Faith does not look at Christ merely from afar, but embraces him, that he may become ours and dwell in us. It causes us to be united in his body' (Comm. John 6.35).

It is strange to imagine Ann throwing away these marvellous phrases with no thought of publication and forging such a splendid expression of her vision of Christ. But no doubt the stimulus was simple and expressed by Calvin, 'I am overwhelmed by the depth of his mystery' (Comm. Ephes. 5.32).

This hymn was composed in her favourite 8:7 measure, although it is not strictly accurate to speak of syllabic verse when referring to Ann Griffiths (nor to Welsh traditional prosody in general). That must be merely shorthand. Ann Griffiths the unsophisticate has been accused of being narrow and limited in her metrical scope. Certainly the predominance of this eight-line stanza following the blurred 8:7 syllabic pattern is very obvious. Eighteen of her thirty poems conform to that same pattern. Critics noting the predominance of that metre have used the fact to disclaim her authorship of one of her most popular hymns, namely 'Gwna fi fel pren planedig' (Make me as a planted tree). Euros Bowen added that this is a missionary hymn and exceptional to her usual topics. He also considered the reference to Hottentots rather incongruous. But the hymn comes from the same textual stable as the others. Her undoubted personal interest in the missionary John Davies (her neighbour) and her direct acquaintance with Thomas Charles, who referred in his pamphlet published in 1804 (the year when the hymn was probably composed) both to the Hottentots and Koranians, here mentioned, lead one to conclude—even apart from manuscript evidence—that she would certainly be the most likely candidate in Wales to compose such a hymn. Thomas Charles was her hero, and she communed with him regularly every month, and he visited her in Dolwar-fach. John Davies sailed in May 1800. His missionary cause would be a subject of regular prayer in Llanfihangel.

The monotony of this particular metre does not set Ann apart from most poets, her contemporaries, who often tend to gravitate to this or that particular form, as witness Emily Dickinson. Though she often plumped for this stanza pattern, there are no fewer than nine different patterns in the restricted compass of her recorded hymns: 9:8 (8 lines):I; 8:7 (8 lines): II, III, IV, V, VII, IX, X, XIV, XVII, XVIII, XIX, XX, XXI, XXIV, XXV, XXVI, XXVII, XXVIII; 7:6 (8 lines): VI, XXIII, XXX; 8:7:8:7:6:7 (6 lines): XI; 8:8:8:8 (4 lines): XII; 8:7:8:7:4:7 (6 lines): XIII, XVI; 8:4 (8 lines): XV; 10:10 (4 lines): XXII; 8:8:8 (6 lines): XXIX. If such is the diversity, one would be bold to claim that a divergence from her favourite pattern proved anything.

*   *   *

In a Calvinistic civilization like Wales, unfortunately at the same time pietistic, the finest intellects of the period as well as the most artistic abilities were channelled into the dominant literary genres, the hymn, the sermon and biographies of divines. This is not to deny the dynamic presence of the traditional *englyn*, *cywydd* and *awdl*, nor of romantic nature-poetry and beginnings of the novel, nor that there always existed an 'underground' secular culture of minor talents. But the thrust of creative energy was taken over by these other—comparatively newly—dominant genres. These 'modern' means of literary expression were the channel for the greatest passion of the time, the sharpest intelligence and the most energetic aesthetic and imaginative celebration. There was obviously a certain amount of anti-Methodistic work being written, and historians rightly draw our attention to this. We can easily be hoodwinked into thinking, because the standard of Christian writing was so much higher and deserves more considered literary attention, that the presence of non-believers and indifference galore were less than they actually were. Paganism and anti-Christian feeling were certainly historically significant. But, from a purely literary point of view, Talhaiarn (1810–70) was the only representative of some distinction of that particular standpoint during the rest of the nineteenth century.

I suspect many, if not all, of Ann Griffiths's hymns were composed as responses to sermons. Sermons, together with prayer-meetings, were no doubt the pinnacles of her week, and occasions of great jubilation. The sermon, to a modern superficial observer, may seem simply a means of moralizing, which it rarely was, or at best a medium of persuasion, which it often approached when dealing with the grandeur of doctrine. But the mind was never to be divorced from the affections. Unless truths were applied to the heart, their seriousness was suspect.

So, it seems likely (as Dr E. Wyn James has suggested) that John Parry's sermon on 14 December 1802 on the Song of Solomon V.10 was the stimulus behind her hymn on the Person of Christ (*PE* XIII), just as Benjamin Jones's sermon on 28(?) March 1796 in Llanfyllin on Revelation 3.8 had been the stimulus behind her Conversion Hymn (*PE* I). The sermon was not by nature too far unrelated to the hymn. It was—despite all appearances to the contrary—directed principally to worship. It may seem paradoxical, but in a strange way the congregation was almost incidental, in so far as the object of adoration and praise was other than the people themselves. To explain and exegete was to direct the personality with meaningful content towards another Being.

What was amazing was that such sermons met in the orthodox Calvinist mind and the evangelical norm of Ann Griffiths's affections a formidable intellect, an imaginative sensitivity to diction, and an experience of profound consequence that left for subsequent generations a handful of hymns and letters unsurpassed in our literature.

BIBLIOGRAPHY *of English Items about Ann Griffiths*

A. M. Allchin, *Ann Griffiths* (Cardiff, 1976); revised as *Ann Griffiths, the Furnace and the Fountain* (1987).

Idem, 'Ann Griffiths—mystic and theologian', in *The Kingdom of Love and Knowledge* (London, 1979), 54–70.

Idem, 'The place of Ann Griffiths', and 'The mystery of the Incarnation: the *plygain* carols and the work of Ann Griffiths', in *Praise Above All* (Cardiff, 1991).

Joseph P. Clancy, 'Ann Griffiths and Emily Dickinson: contexts and convergences', *Literature & Theology* 7 (1993), 149–70.

H. A. Hodges, *Homage to Ann Griffiths* (Church in Wales Publications, 1976).

R. M. Jones, 'Ann Griffiths (1776–1805): scriptural mystic', *Evangelical Magazine of Wales*, 24 (1985), 14–16.

Idem, 'Another Celtic spirituality—the Calvinistic mysticism of Ann Griffiths (1776–1805)', *Foundations*, 38 (1997), 39–44, and 39 (1997), 31–6.

Evan Richards, *A Short Memoir of Ann Griffiths* (1916).

John Ryan, *The Hymns of Ann Griffiths* (Tŷ ar y Graig, 1980).

M. Wynn Thomas, 'Ann Griffiths and Morgan Llwyd—a comparative study of two Welsh mystics', *Studies in Mystical Literature*, 3 (1983), 23–39.

R. R. Williams, *The Hymns of Ann Griffiths* (Hugh Evans, 1947).

Index

Parry, Harri, 307
Parry, John 326
Parry, Richard, 197–8
Parry, Siân, 82
Parry, Sir Thomas, 139, 315
Parry, William, 90
Paston letters, the, 65
Patripassianism, 15, 261
Peace Library, the, The Hague, 140
Pedair Colofn Gwladwriaeth, 220,
   221, 222, 224, 226, 231, 236,
   238, 242, 247, 252, 253–4
Pedwar Chwarter y Flwyddyn, 227
Pedwar Emynydd, 316, 319, 323, 326
Pedr Fardd, *see* Jones, Peter
Pembrokeshire, 5, 7, 131, 192
penillion telyn, 5, 73
Pennant, Thomas, 34, 36, 37
Penywenallt, 54
Percy, Thomas, 121, 187
Peterhouse, Cambridge, 118
Pezron, Paul-Yves, 28, 178–9
Philipps, Sir John, 13
Pietas Hallensis, 14
Pietism, 14, 16
Pilgrim's Progess, 269, 285
Pitt, William, 4, 241
Pleser a Gofid, 224, 225, 237, 243,
   247, 253
Plot, Robert, 152
plygain, 187–9, 306
Poems, Lyric and Pastoral, 136, 153
Pontarddulais, 295
Pope, Alexander, 107, 108, 119, 262
Port Dinorwic, 7
Powel, David, 28, 34, 56, 116
Powell, Vavasor, 40, 41
Powys, 131
Presbyterianism, 10, 29, 282
Price, Richard, 17
Prichard, Morris, 65, 78
Prichard, Rhys, 191
Priestley, Joseph, 133

Prif Addysc y Cristion, 46
Principia, 262
Protestant a Neilltuwr, 231, 233,
   234–5, 238, 241
Protestantism, 3, 9–10, 38–9, 56
Prys, Sir John, 56, 116, 170
Pryse, Robert John (Gweirydd ap
   Rhys), 177
Pugh, David, 42
Pugh, Evan, 170
Pughe, William Owen, *see* Owen
   Pughe, William
Punter, David, 111
Puritanism, 39, 41, 318
Pwyll Pendefig Dyfed, 184

Quakerism, 10, 40, 247
Quevedo Villegas, Don Francisco
   Gomez de, 47

Radnorshire, 29, 300
Red Book of Hergest, 117
Rees, E., 283
Religion des Anciens Gaulois, 116
Rhad Ras, 299, 300–2
Rhaeadr, 300
Rhai Hymnau Duwiol, 283
Rheol Buchedd Sanctaidd, 45, 46
Rheolau a Threfniadau, 134
Rhodri Mawr, 67, 68
Rhydfendigaid, 259
Rhoscolyn, 198
Rhys Brydydd, 152
Rhys Cain, 141
Rhys Fardd, 47–8
Rhys Goch ap Rhicert ab Einion ap
   Collwyn, 140, 143–4
Rhŷs, Sir John, 141, 178
Rhys, Morgan, 285, 291–2, 295, 296
Rhys, Morgan John, 17
Rhys, Siôn Dafydd, 116, 119, 180
Richard, Edward, 66, 67, 113–14,
   117